Praise for *Rigby's Encyclopaedia of the Herring*

'All there is to know of the herring, the fortunes of the silver darlings, great and small. Bravo Mr Rigby.'
Jeremy Lee, Chef/Proprietor, Quo Vadis, author of *Cooking: Simply and Well, for One or Many*

'It is not inverse snobbery that causes me to prefer herring to salmon. It is, quite simply, a matter of taste. Which is just one of this creature's manifold properties: for the rest, get reading.'
Jonathan Meades, journalist, essayist, film-maker and author of *Empty Wigs*

'I was raised on fried herring on slices of brown bread—to me, that is the very definition of luxury. I have a love for young herring, especially the way it's savoured in Holland: delicate, with a touch of chopped onion and frozen gin. It's food that speaks to the soul and this book is nothing short of a delight.'
Richard Corrigan, Chef/Patron of The Corrigan Collection

'An incredible insight into hidden histories surrounding the herring trade. Graeme Rigby reminds us why this little silver darling is so important to understanding the past, the present and learning for the future. Absolutely lush!'
Joanne Coates, award-winning working-class photographer and artist, and curator of the Red Herring exhibition, Helmsdale

'Graeme Rigby has done for the herring what Pliny the Elder did for everything else. Erudite, eccentric and unexpectedly moving, this encyclopaedia rescues the herring from obscurity and repositions it—gleaming, iridescent and gloriously pungent—at the very centre of history. A shimmering feast of facts and fables, with a glint in its eye and a whiff of brine in its wake.'
Christopher Beckman, author of *A Twist in the Tail: How the Humble Anchovy Flavoured Western Cuisine*

'Rigby's is a treasure trove of all things herring—brimming with dazzling facts, deep history, and irresistible oddities. Dive in and prepare to fall head over heels for the silver stars of the sea.'

   Poul Holm, Trinity Centre for Environmental Humanities, Trinity College Dublin

'An original, poignant excavation of one of history's most misunderstood fish. Layering deep scholarship with mischievous wit, Rigby builds a kaleidoscopic monument to the herring's place in science, culture, war, art and memory. This is not just a book about a fish—it's a brilliant meditation on curiosity, storytelling, and the shimmering drift of history itself.'

   David Willer, Department of Zoology, University of Cambridge

'Just like the small but power-packed herring, these encyclopaedic pages are stuffed with a dream-like fishy sufficiency to satisfy the neediest herring aficionado's appetite; "only nibbling at the edge of the shoal", doubtful, I'd say! From now on, my world of herrin'ology will never be the same again.'

Mike Smylie, aka 'The Kipperman', author of *Herring: A History of the Silver Darlings*

RIGBY'S ENCYCLOPAEDIA OF THE Herring

First published in the United Kingdom in 2025 by

C. Hurst & Co. (Publishers) Ltd.,

New Wing, Somerset House,

Strand, London, WC2R 1LA

© Graeme Rigby, 2025

All rights reserved.

Printed in Scotland by Bell and Bain.

Typesetting and Design: Gavin Morris

The right of Graeme Rigby to be identified as the Author of this publication is assertedby him in accordance with the Copyright, Designs and Patents Act, 1988.

A Cataloguing-in-Publication data record for this book is available from the British Library.

ISBN:

9781805264163

www.hurstpublishers.com

Printed and bound in Great Britain

by Bell & Bain Ltd, Glasgow

RIGBY'S ENCYCLOPAEDIA OF THE Herring

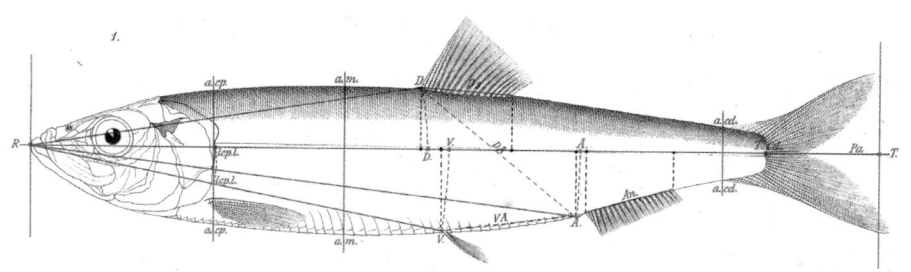

Adventures with
the King of Fishes

GRAEME RIGBY

Y IS FOR WHY?

'So, what do you do?' people ask. 'I'm a writer... but just about the herring, these days... I'm working on an Encyclopaedia...' There's a pause, then maybe, 'The heron?' I shake my head, 'No. Herring. The fish.' Another pause, then, 'Why?'

There is more beautiful information about herrings than any other fish. Fact. Zoologically, taxonomically, its fisheries, in literature, art and song, in histories of trade, European wars fought, associated general human folly: even before we get to cures and recipes (but in them too) it's a fish with stories.

In the late 1990s, I was commissioned to make a BBC Radio 4 documentary on Bombay duck, which you couldn't get in the UK at the time. I returned from India with my tapes. 'Can you do a series?' Possibly a little too quickly, I said, 'Yes. Yes, of course... It'll be about preserved fish. Bombay duck, then the Arbroath smokie, stockfish, lamprey pies and... the red herring. It can be called, *Rigby's Red Herrings*...'

I'd bring back samples to the kitchen of my friend, the late, great chef Alastair Little and we'd have a jokey conversation while he did something simple and wonderful with them. For the Bombay duck episode, I tried drying herrings on a rotary washing line as an alternative. 'They're a bit pokey,' Alastair said. I explained their provenance. 'You've just given me botulism!' he cried. It was a good radio moment.

For the red herring episode, I brought prime smoked products from H.S. Fish of Great Yarmouth, but it was the least satisfying programme. I'd simply found too much material: there was no end to the stories. After more than twenty-five years I still haven't found one. After the series, I looked at all my herring material again. 'I'll write an encyclopaedia,' I said, but halfway through the first draft, it was actually just a rehash of the enthusiastic histories of the late nineteenth and early twentieth centuries. My agent at the time asked, 'Have you thought of making it a proper encyclopaedia?' I balked at the implications: everything separated into its own alphabetical entry; no excuses for blurring over the zoology or the riggings of different sailing drifters. I fought against it, but the logic grew.

It was in the days before the proliferation of online digitised downloads. Based on a sole mention in one herring history, I ordered a photocopy from the British Library of Paul Neucrantz's *De harengo* (1654), a defence in fifteen chapters of a fish fallen from grace. For me, Latin had stopped at thirteen, but my sister had a friend who'd retired from teaching Classics. Seventeenth-century, German, academic Latin was another matter altogether, but my sister's friend struggled heroically to produce a literal translation. At first it was as impenetrable as the original. The more I learned about herrings, the more I understood what Neucrantz was saying. Later, Wikipedia, online translators and the digitisation of many of his sources were a great help. It took eighteen years, but in 2020 I finally completed a version of *On Herring* for the blogging website I'd started in retirement.

In 1999 I joined a documentary collective. I continued to work on the herrings, even though films, photographic exhibitions and funding applications became major distractions from much more than research. The herrings, meanwhile, brought their own distractions. I was drawn to website development and how to deliver meaningful access to a documentary collection and its interconnected narratives. 'An online encyclopaedia,' I thought. 'You'd never have to finish it!'

It was 2010. I was visiting Stavanger's Norwegian Canning Museum—Norwegian sardines are juvenile herrings and sprats. I stood in front of an informative display about North East England grocery entrepreneur Angus Watson and his role in the early days of Norway's sardine industry. No! Had I not, only a couple of months earlier, put my signed copy of Angus Watson's *My Life* in the box for Oxfam?

Fellow teetotallers in the same Methodist congregation, Watson had given it to my grandfather. After my father had been expelled from school, I now realise it was Watson who'd found him a berth in the Merchant Navy (just in time to be on the second ship sunk in World War II). When my grandfather gave me the book, I suspected him of proffering some kind of teetotal role model. In forty years, I'd never read it. Standing there in the Canning Museum I felt sick to the stomach. It was two years before I discovered that although I'd put *My Life* in the Oxfam box, I must have had a change of heart. It was a moment of redemption. It was destiny gathering dust in a pile of books hidden behind another pile of books.

Mark Kurlansky's *Cod: A Biography of the Fish that Changed the World* was first published in the United Kingdom in 1998. I was working on the Radio 4 series, already aware that, even if I looked only at red herrings, I'd never be able to fit them in so neat a barrel. More than any other literary form, the biography presupposes a narrative arc, so Kurlansky can be forgiven. The more I studied herrings, the more I realised they just don't swim in neat arcs: an orca comes along and they shoot off in a hundred different directions. After Kurlansky, the short book proliferated: so many neat arcs conveniently changing the world. Everything changes everything. The question is, how to do justice to a fish, flashing with a thousand silver narratives, each with its own tragi-comic hero? This became an evolving logic.

The Encyclopaedia brings its own vivid dreams. There's something in the organisation of memory and information which seems to trigger them, correspondences perhaps or maybe the mind is troubled by alphabets. I was working on Dumas' *Grand Dictionnaire de Cuisine*. In my dream I was constructing four large letters, a bit like the monolith in the 1980s AIDS advert except, instead of chisels and a tombstone, I was using a scalpel and precisely folded black paper. The first letter was an N and it signified something to do with memory.

The suggestion of me doing anything with precision was sheer fantasy, but it did not take much analysis to realise the N had been for my brother, who'd been diagnosed with Alzheimer's and who now lives in a home. My sister Janet died in 2023 after fifteen or so years with it. Practical skills may elude me, but I've always had a good memory. I'm able to connect almost any casual conversation to some beautiful herring fact swimming about in my head, a trick which isn't always appreciated as much as you might think.

So much of this Encyclopaedia has been rooted in improvisations with chance and memory. It's what makes it mine. There's room for a hundred others, but this one's dedicated to the memories of my brother Nigel and my sister Janet, both of whom once also delighted in beautiful information.

Graeme Rigby, *Victoria Garesfield, 2025*

RIGBY'S ENCYCLOPAEDIA OF THE HERRING

HERRING ADVENTURES: A is for A Beginning; Atlantic Herring: A Natural History; Baltic Herring; Farting; Grand Migration; Otoliths & Scales; Pacific Herring; Racial Theory; Sardine Litigation; Sensitivity; Svetovidov the Systematist; Taxonomy; Zuiderzee.

FISHERY ADVENTURES: Appearances & Signs; Baskets; British Fisheries; Cooperage; Danish Fisheries; Dutch Fisheries; French Fisheries; Ganseys & Guernseys; German Fisheries; Herring Boats; Herring Lasses; Icelandic Fisheries; Irish, Manx & Welsh Fisheries; Klondyking; Measuring the Herring; Nets & Weirs; North American Fisheries; Norwegian Fisheries; Quotas; Reduction Plants; Ring Net Struggle; Russian Fisheries; Swedish Fisheries.

OTHER HISTORICAL ADVENTURES: Aquinas, St Thomas; Archaeology; Battle of the Herrings; Beuckel, Willem; Fasting; German Spies; Herring Industry Board; Måløy Raid; Medicine & Health; Olivier, Laurence; Pamphleteers; Processions & Celebrations; Prophecy; Smith, Adam: The Wealth of Nations; Sovereignty of the Seas; Ullapool & The British Fisheries Society; Witches; X Formerly Known as the Difficult Letter; Yarmouth's Greatness.

FOOD ADVENTURES: Bloater; Buckling; Canning; Caribbean & West African Food; Dried Herring; Dumas, Alexandre; Filleting & Stuffing; Fish Fingers; Hareng Saur; Jewish Food; Kipper; Mediterranean Food; Oatmeal; Objects of Desire; Past(r)y; Potatoes; Red Herring; Roe; Salt & Salting; Shuba & Sour Cream; Smokehouse Tale; Surströmming; Vinegar.

CULTURAL ADVENTURES: Britten, Benjamin; Caller Herrin'; Documentary; Dutch & Flemish Art; Etymologies, Euphemisms, Names; Eyvindr 'Skáldaspillir'

Finnsson; Hareng Saur Monologues; Herringism; Herrin's Heid; Iddis; King of Fishes; Life of St Herring; Luck; Miller's Letters; Monkey Business; N is for Nashe & Neucrantz; Neckam. Alexander; Pickelhering; Proverbs & Sayings; Red Herring Joke; Two Contemporary Artists; When Herrings Lived on Dry Land; Z is for Zeno's Paradox.

TRANSLATIONS

The translations of French poems draw on the invaluable help and collaboration of Isis Olivier. All extracts from Neucrantz's *De harengo* draw on the initial literal translation by Ingrid O'Mahoney. Eyvind 'Skáldaspillir' Finnsson's old Norse poems were translated using the literal versions on the *Skaldic Project* website. The rest have relied on online translation tools and dictionaries.

A IS FOR A BEGINNING

My family Bible (*Brown's Self-Interpreting*, 1878) is categorical: the beginning began in 4004 BCE. Assuming a New Year start, fish came along on January 5th. Before we get into fish/egg which-came-firsts, it's worth saying an attentive God would have noticed the spectacular herring spawning in the clear waters of the North American Pacific North West at least 5,000 years earlier. Even without His vantage point, recent archaeology suggests indigenous peoples already had.

Alternative beginnings may, of course, apply. In one of them, Earth was formed 4,600 million years ago out of planetesimals, accretions of cosmic dust and gas in our solar system, which, colliding, stuck together. As an accretion grew, it gained gravitational strength and attracted others. Before you knew it, there was a planet. A mere 800 million years later, Earth acquired oceans. Herrings took a bit longer.

The sea-girt landmasses moved on Earth's tectonic plates, eventually coming together 1,100 million years ago, to create Rodinia, which was once billed as the first supercontinent. These days people aren't so sure. Posited predecessors include Ur (3,000 million years ago or mya), Kenorland (2,500 mya) and Nuna or Columbia (1,800 mya). Some even fit in a Pannotia, between Rodinia's break-up and the formation, 375 mya, of the last one, Pangaea. The problem with tectonic plates is they swallow up most of the evidence.

With or without intervening supercontinents, the key thing is that, at some point between Rodinia and Pangaea, the first fish appeared in the world ocean, Panthalassa. And a bit later still, centred on the Equator when Pangaea had coalesced, there was an inner ocean: the Sea of Tethys. Well, all right, no one even knew about this first Sea of Tethys until the 1980s. Most of its traces were obliterated by the second Sea of Tethys, which was identified all the way back in 1893. Starting as a small ocean in the southern hemisphere, just over 250 mya, Tethys II expanded northwards, swallowing its predecessor into the Tethyan Trench.

Not content with that, the Tethyan Trench extended its line, opening up a continental rift, creating the Central Atlantic and the separated landmasses of Laurasia (North America, Europe and Asia) and Gondwanaland (South America, Africa, India, Australia and Antarctica). In the warm, equatorial waters of the still opening Sea of Tethys, the first herrings evolved roughly 100 mya. I have a fossil, found in Morocco: a very small herring, maybe a juvenile— Cretaceous whitebait, possibly. Most things will never be known.

ATLANTIC HERRING

The world's herrings, shads, sprats, sardines and/or pilchards come together in an adaptable family known as the *Clupeidae*. Between its different species, sub-species and varieties, it has colonised most of the world's oceans.

Predominantly, the Clupeidae are fish of the continental shelves— the opening Sea of Tethys formed many of the world's coastlines. As Tethys had been a warm sea, most of them are found in similar waters today. Some developed to accommodate low saline, even freshwater conditions; some, such as the boreal herring, colonised the far North. When the world's climate cooled in the Miocene (23 to 5 million years ago), these boreals moved south and became the **Atlantic herring**, *Clupea harengus*, **King of Fishes**, hero of this encyclopaedia. Still a cold water fish, so far it has continued to cold-shoulder the High Arctic. The smaller number of these cold-water clupeids created the ecological space for huge populations, which, together with their innate tastiness, generated a huge economic importance.

A herring shoal can stretch for miles. Even in the fisherman's earliest engagements with the sea, more could be caught than a community on its own could ever eat. It's an oily fish: it will go off faster than cod or ling or haddock. Herring fishing communities had to develop curing techniques and trade. With those in place, the scale of catches delivered cheap nutrition and sometimes wealth.

In Western Europe, Catholicism did its bit, demanding **Fasting** during nearly half the eating week, along with Lent. The application of logic wouldn't necessarily help in understanding why it was acceptable to eat fish on a fast day, but it created the kind of market monopolists can only dream of. A ubiquitously cheap and conveniently meal-sized fish, herring often came to be resented by even the most religiously devoted. Fresh and badly cured herring smells and so, like the fart, it was funny. A joke universally recognised and shared, its economic importance fused with its cultural significance. This is why there's more beautiful information about the Atlantic herring than any other fish.

DISTRIBUTION & DIVERSITY

The Atlantic herring is found from North Carolina's Cape Hatteras to Canada's Davis Straits; on Greenland's western and eastern shores. Those found off Iceland belong to the European continental shelf, which also plays host to different populations from Russian waters to the Bay of Biscay. It reaches its highest latitudes on the west coast of Spitzbergen, but also takes in Novaya Zemlaya, the White Sea, the Kara Sea and the Barents Sea. When it originally moved down from the North Pole, a land bridge across the Bering Straits blocked access to the Pacific. Fish moving between the North Atlantic and the Pacific have generally used the North West Passage: Siberia's rivers create too great a freshening effect for most saltwater species. In a post-glacial period around two million years ago, however, Atlantic herrings made their way East. Against the advice of **Svetovidov the Systematist, Taxonomy** has granted these travellers (but not most of the Atlantic's variants) separate species status as the Pacific herring (*Clupea pallasii*). Some Pacific herrings swam part way back and became White Sea and Chosa herrings, now identified as Pacific herring subspecies.

Herrings adapt genetically to variations in salinity and temperature. Astute readers may ask, 'But aren't sea temperatures rising all over the world, even as we speak?' Yes. Some populations may move in pursuit of colder waters, or they might get smaller. The food they eat may drift on altered currents and they'll follow. Herrings have never offered constancy in their relationships with mankind. They don't even recognise the species-separating taxonomic binomials we've given them: marine geneticists have identified evidence of miscegenation.

Like all great subjects, herrings resist categories and definitions; they represent both more and less than they are; they accept derision and devotion with equanimity. An encyclopaedia will not hold them.

APPEARANCES & SIGNS

Before the days of echo location technology and its convenient picturing of a complete shoal in the waters around and beneath them, herring fishermen would identify the position of their prey by means of *appearances* or *signs*. Like a *tell* to an archaeologist, they suggested a shoal. Jim Muir, interviewed in 2005 in the Coigach, north of Ullapool, explained the role played by gannets, known in those parts as solan geese (see Will Maclean's *Gannet Fishing* in first image section):

> You'd just see birds, solan geese diving, birds sitting in the water and a certain oiliness in the water: signs of herring as they called them. When the solan goose dived at a 45° angle into the water, they'd reckon that was mackerel it was diving on. And when the solan goose went straight down, they reckoned that was herring.

> With the boat, you'd see a gannet sitting in the water, or maybe one or two gannets sitting and you would chase one. Of course the gannets, they would vomit prior to taking off, because they couldn't take off, because they were so heavy, so full. So you'd got him. You chased him with the boat and the gannet would vomit and then you'd see whether it was herring or mackerel he vomited. That was another method.

APPEARANCES & SIGNS

Will Maclean documented the ring-net herring fishery of the West Coast in the 1970s (see **Two Contemporary Artists**). In his exhibition, *The Ring Net*, he devoted a whole section to the Appearances and provided a more comprehensive list. As well as the solan goose, there were the whales: 'The fishermen knew when a whale was working a shoal of herring by the infrequency of his blowing— when he did blow the stench was said to be foul.'

The presence of a basking shark did not necessarily indicate herrings, but it fed on the same zooplankton as they did. In warm summer weather, the fishermen would also see the copepod *Calanus*, on which herring fed, drifting close to the surface. 'Small bubbles, "like lemonade" rising to the surface. Caused by the herring swimming, the fizz has been heard through the hull.' (See **Farting**.) The fishermen watched the porpoises (*buckers* or *stinkers*) because they would herd the shoals and feed on the herring at their edges. Individual herrings would leap out of the water and could be recognised by the sound of the *plout* as they fell back. There was what was known in Gaelic as *feith is sabh* (wait and see)—'a glossing on the surface of the sea caused by a slick of fish oil. A fishy odour may accompany it.'

Both Jim Muir and Will Maclean talked of *fire in the water*, a phosphorous glow given off by the shoal. As Muir described it, 'In the September, the back end of the summer, in the sea lochs, you'd go along with your chap up for'ard with a chain. He'd give the chain a rattle and you'd see the shoal would move. They'd rattle the chain to make a noise: it has to make a noise. And you got this, what they called, fire in the water. It was phosphorous, as the herring darted about or rose. It depended on the movement in the water for the phosphorous breaking. You could see a glow in the water with a big shoal of herring.'

Drift net fishermen used some of these signs, but it's a passive form of fishing. Drift nets were shot when the herring shoals were gathered on the seabed, or at least lower in the water. They were aimed at where it was thought they might rise in their nightly approach to the surface. It was the ring netters who developed reading the waters to a fine art, because they actively hunted the rising or risen herrings, surrounding them with the net. One of the ring net crew would be employed to hold a weighted piano wire, feeling from its vibrations as it was struck by the fish, the size and position of the shoal.

These skills mostly died out once a shoal's size and direction were so plainly visible on a screen, but in its early days on the West Coast, echo location technology, beyond the wallets of most, also became a kind of sign. As Jim Muir described it, 'If one bought the echo sounder, you had a tail of another half the fleet following it. This chap would have invested heavily in the echo sounder and everybody would be following him. If he set his herring nets, there'd be a hundred others setting their nets as well.'

Muir and Maclean both talk of the Scottish West Coast, but appearances were noted and used to greater and lesser extents by all herring fishers, many of whom adopted ring netting and pelagic trawling far earlier than the British East Coast fleets. Meanwhile, for a little East Anglian wisdom, it's worth quoting A.M. Samuel in *The Herring: Its Effect on the History of Britain* (1918, see **Herringism**):

> In Norfolk, according to Notes and Queries, October 7th, 1865, a queer legend existed that fleas and herrings came together. As an old Cromer fisherman said, "Times is as you may look in my shirt, and scarce see a flea, and then there won't be but few herring. But when you see my shirt alive with fleas, then there is certain to be a good tidy lot of fish."

AQUINAS, ST THOMAS

Notwithstanding *The Miracle of the Fresh Herrings*, there were those who did not go along with the canonisation of Thomas Aquinas. I know what you're thinking:

'Franciscans! Averroists!' But jokes have been made, at least since the fifteenth century (see **Life of St Herring**). The world has never been short of herring doubters. There were, however, two Papal inquiries into the heavenly candidacy of Thomas Aquinas and the herrings played a key role in his elevation. There are records.

Tommaso d'Aquino was born in Sicily in 1225 CE. He became a Dominican friar and is best known for his *Summa Theologica*, which underpinned what became known as *Thomism*, a cornerstone of Western medieval thinking. In this and other works Aquinas attempted to square God with Aristotle, thus opening up the new possibilities for Christian philosophy which were to flower in the Renaissance. He never finished the *Summa*, telling a Brother Reginald, 'I cannot, because all that I have written seems to me like straw compared with what has now been revealed to me.' We don't know what the revelation was and whether it might have changed history even more than Aristotle, but most writers are familiar with the 'straw' thing.

Having worked on the text since 1265, he reached the straw point in 1273. Between 1268 and 1272 he'd been doing a third stint at the University of Paris, arguing with the radical Aristotelians or Averroists as well as with the Franciscans who, while they might not have thrown Aristotle out altogether, could best be described as inhabiting the comfort zone of Augustinian-Platonism. Aquinas' intellectual and spiritual struggles had been wearing and, having done his bit, he moved to Naples to set up a *studium generale*.

In 1273, while in Naples, Domenic of Caserta came across him levitating in front of an icon of the crucifixion. Jesus clearly did not hold with either the radical Aristotelians or the Franciscans and from his cross said to him something to the effect of, 'Thomas, you've done a top job writing all this stuff. Name your reward.' Thomas answered right back, '*Non nisi te, Domini*,' (Lord, nothing but you).

It was in the following year that the Miracle of the Fresh Herrings took place. Pope Gregory X had convened the Second Council of Lyon and wanted Aquinas to talk to everyone on the subject of the *Greek errors* being propagated by the Averroistas. He hadn't been well, but maybe he was feeling a little bit better, he thought. He set off for Lyon on a donkey and got as far as Monte Cassino, about 65 miles, where he was struck on the head by a 'fallen branch'.

The account says fallen, not falling. Maybe he had fallen asleep, then fallen off the donkey as it negotiated the branch, which he then hit on his way down. Some aspects of the story remain mysterious. Anyway, as a result of the blow to his head, Aquinas suffered a relapse and was taken to the nearby Castle of Maenza: it was there the miracle took place.

Aquinas has been described by some as corpulent. In one or two of the paintings he fills out his habit, seems a little jowly, but no more than would be described as comfortable. He liked his food, apparently, but at Maenza couldn't be persuaded to eat at all. 'Can we tempt you with anything?' he was asked.

'I might be persuaded by some fresh herring,' he said.

In 1274, fresh herring was unknown in Italy. Salted or white, red, gold or silver herring might all have been possible, but fresh, pretty much restricted to the coastal areas where it was caught, was never going to be on the cards. There were rapid, fresh fish transports to Paris, at least by the early fourteenth century and Aquinas might possibly have eaten it when he was at the University, but he might equally have tasted it on a visit to one of the herring ports on Normandy's Alabaster Coast.

The Dominicans will have had their own houses there, but the Benedictines were reasonably open to the Church-sanctioned works of Aristotle and in 1220 they'd completed an abbey with its own scriptorium at Fécamp. They'd been active campaigners for the Herring Fair established there by Duke Robert II in 1088. This engagement with the fish is celebrated today in jars of Fécamp smoked herring & Bénédictine *rillettes*.

But back to the Castle of Maenza. It just so happened a travelling fish merchant, Bordonario, arrived there more-or-less at the same time as Aquinas had put in his request. Bordonario thought all he had was salted pilchards (sardines), but, when they were examined, it turned out one of his baskets was filled with fresh herrings. Peter of Montesangiovanni, who was at the castle at the time, had seen salted herring at the Papal court in Viterbo, so was later able to vouch for the miracle.

The castle kitchens prepared the herrings, boiling some and frying others, but neither tempted the future saint, who despite the miracle of their appearance, resolutely ate nothing at all. Some accounts say he ate them and pronounced them delicious, but they don't have the ring of truth. Understandably, some have questioned Aquinas' rejection of the herrings, criticising, even mocking him for it. But was he being tested? And did he perhaps recognise this? He was on record with his *non nisi te, Domini*. If he'd eaten them, the virtues of their flesh might have saved his life (see **Medicine & Health**), but at what cost?

God was demonstrating the extent of His love for Aquinas and, by extension, His considered will on radical Aristotelianism and the comforts of Platonism. At the same time, he was saying, 'I made the herring on the Fifth Day and I was pleased. In that basket, I have placed the finest examples of the finest fish that ever swam in the waters, but, Thomas, they are as nothing compared to those you will eat by My side in Heaven.' The uneaten herrings can be compared to the unfinished *Summa Theologica*.

Realising their patient was close to death, it was deemed prudent to get Aquinas to a religious establishment as soon as possible. He was taken to the Cistercian abbey at Fossanova, where he died a month or so later, on March 7th 1274. Writers on the canonisation of Thomas Aquinas sometimes give the Miracle of the Fresh Herrings pride of place, but then again some ignore it altogether, along with the *Miracle of the Tooth Which Was Giving Him Trouble and Then Fell Out*. The levitation thing likewise doesn't always get a mention.

Miracles exist to test our faith. Technically, at least two have to happen after death, proving active intercession. Fortunately, alongside the herrings and the dental extraction, the Papal enquiries took evidence of a Sicilian soldier who had regained the use of his limbs after visiting Aquinas' tomb and of a woman who'd prayed to him while she was hearing the bells of Fossanova Abbey and who was cured of a tumour in the throat.

Nevertheless, he hadn't been martyred and he'd never been one for mortifying the flesh. The Dominicans were active canonisation promoters from the start, along with the Cistercians who still held the body. The Papal inquiries took place in the early fourteenth century and over a hundred witnesses were interviewed. One cardinal objected on the basis that Aquinas himself had performed no copper-bottomed miracles. The Postulator, making the case for a canonisation, came back with, *Quot articuli, tot miracula* (as many articles, so many miracles): every one of the approximately 3,000 articles of the *Summa Theologica* should be considered a miracle.

The Franciscans predictably remained in the No lobby. Their top thinker, 'the subtle doctor', John Duns Scotus agreed with Aquinas on several points, but not enough for sainthood. One Franciscan friar was quoted as saying he'd prefer to die before seeing the day when Thomas was canonised. Sometimes it may seem that God is just playing with us: he waited until the day after sainthood status was granted before he obliged.

For 646 years, the Feast Day of St Thomas Aquinas was held on March 7th, commemorating the day he died. This often conflicted with Lent, which, while it was great for herring, wasn't so good for a feast. In 1969 the Catholic Church rescheduled his day to January 28th, when, in 1369, the fifty relic bones of his body had been *translated* to the Church of the Jacobins (aka the Dominicans) in Toulouse. The Dominican Order in France was disbanded following the French Revolution. Toulouse's Church of the Jacobins was deconsecrated and handed over to the city in 1804. Aquinas' bones were moved to the nearby Basilica of Saint-Sernin, but were returned in 1974, after the church's restoration as a museum.

ARCHAEOLOGY

Across Europe, 1848 was the Year of Revolutions, a *Springtime of the Peoples*. In that year, playing their part to the full, Danish archaeologists began to look beyond the tombs of the great, beyond their halls and monuments. Inspired by the excitement of the age, they pioneered the excavation of kitchen middens, the great piles of the people's leftovers. Elsewhere in Denmark a constitutional monarchy was being negotiated, but there are many roads in the democratisation of culture.

Early Neolithic Danes weren't the first people on earth found to have eaten herring, but they were the earliest in Europe to have left surviving, incontrovertible evidence. At coastal sites in Jutland, archaeologists found shells (mussels, in particular) and fishbones, the commonest being herring, cod, flounder and eel. Across Europe, the people's archaeologists went mad for kitchen middens, but herring-eating records did not keep pace: the delicate bones don't survive as well as those of some other fish, particularly in acidic, peaty soils.

Hooks of various designs were discovered, but although no boats or nets had survived (see **Herring Boats** and **Nets & Weirs**), the abundance of herring bones, along with other deep-sea fishbones, pointed to them not having been caught exclusively from the shore or with hooks. Some form of seine net has been suggested as the probable technology.

The Southern Scandinavian fish-eaters associated with these Jutland middens are known as the Ertebølle Culture (EBK), after the village where the bones and shells were first discovered. This places the earliest recorded European herring fishery somewhere between 5,000 and 3,000 BCE. EBK began to replace Kongemose Culture around 5,300 BCE. After an expansion which took them as far as Rügen, at a point not long after 4,100 BCE the EBKs were in turn replaced by Funnelbeaker Culture (TBK). They probably all ate it, but the smart money is still on the EBKs as Europe's earliest recorded herring fishers.

HÖGLUND

Herring archaeology took a major step forward in the 1950s, when Swedish marine biologist Hans Höglund dug up several waste pits used during the Bohuslän herring boom of 1752 to 1810 (see **Swedish Fisheries** and **Reduction Plants**). He wanted to settle the question of which herrings were responsible for the booms. The assumption had been Norwegian spring spawners temporarily moving south, but Höglund established that it was mixed southern North Sea populations moving east. His research was published in the 1970s. His herring bones were at most a couple of hundred years old and he could easily count the number of vertebrae and examine the **Otoliths & Scales** which identified the waste pit fish.

DNA

Zooarchaeology is now transforming our understanding of herring cultures. With no mention of herring in Pliny's *Natural History*, did the Romans eat it? Analysis of fermented fish sauce amphorae in Belgium has said, 'Yes they did!' Recent Spanish research into a fish sauce shop in Pompeii suggests the presence of what must have been salted herring. From Belgium? from Gaul? from Britain?—who knows? Meanwhile, did the Dutch develop new gutting techniques in the fourteenth century? Maybe not. The cut marks on herring bones from the Scania fishery reveal much the same techniques had been used in the twelfth and thirteenth centuries.

Fish weirs have been discovered in straits, inlets and bays still frequented by herring. With finer and finer archaeological sieves, herring remains have been found in more kitchen middens throughout Northern Europe and the Atlantic and Pacific coasts of North America, DNA traces enabling the identification of smaller and smaller fragments. Discoveries in the Pacific North West make it clear that there were herring fishing indigenous peoples, there, 11,000 years ago (and contrary to previous assumptions, it seems they ate it five times as much as salmon). Today's First Nation activists are using this reclaimed knowledge in their struggles for sustainable fishery rights. We are talking Pacific rather than Atlantic herring, but what is a Pacific herring? (see **Svetovidov the Systematist** and **Taxonomy**). Either way, the EBK may have been Johnny-Come-Latelies.

ATLANTIC HERRING: A NATURAL HISTORY

"...A scientific man said herrin' came on cycles –"

"He's a liar, anyway," said the Captain, with conviction. "They were in Loch Fyne afore the cycle was invented. Are you sure, Macphail, it's no' the cod he means?"

"He said the herrin' fishin' aye missed some years noo and then in a' the herrin' places in Europe as weel's in Loch Fyne, and the Gulf Stream had something to dae wi't."

"That's the worst o' science," said the Captain piously; "it takes aal the credit away from the Creator. Don't you pay attention to an unfidel like that; when the herrin' was in Loch Fyne they stayed there aal the time, and only maybe took a daunder oot noo and then the length o' Ballantrae."

"If it's no the Gulf Stream, then ye'll maybe tell us whit it is?" said the engineer, with some annoyance.

"I'll soon do that," said Para Handy; "if you want to ken, it's what I said—the herrin' iss a mystery, chust a mystery!"

The Herring: A Gossip, Neil Munro (1911)

Long before the arrival of *Homo sapiens* or the Neanderthals, the Atlantic herring's sperm a-spawning was visible from space. In 2023, the milky spectacle, several kilometers long, was seen again off the coast of Wester Ross in Scotland. Even after so much overfishing, so many population collapses, the herring's close-packed shoals bring together one of the most abundant vertebrates on earth. We have the word of Chungang Feng *et al.* for it ('Moderate nucleotide diversity in the Atlantic herring is associated with a low mutation rate', 2017). Across its distribution areas the population is estimated at a trillion individuals. The bristlemouth may be even more abundant (and it puts on lightshows) but who eats bristlemouths?

DESCRIBING THE ATLANTIC HERRING

The Atlantic herring is a pelagic marine teleost: a sea fish with a skeleton which lives in the water between seabed and surface. If it were to stay on the seabed it would be a demersal marine teleost.

Scales: It has cycloid scales, which means they are smooth, flat and rounded on their overlapping edges.

Fins: It has a single dorsal fin (i.e. on its back), a single anal fin (immediately behind the anus), two pectoral fins positioned, one on each side, at the bottom of and just behind the gill openings and two small pelvic fins, roughly in line with the middle of its dorsal fin and either side of the line of bluntish scales which form its keel. The tail fin is strongly forked, almost resembling the flights of an arrow.

Teeth: It has teeth, but they're nothing to worry about.

Colouring: Its back is a blueish green, although on the fishmonger's slab this becomes more of a blueish grey. The herring's belly is white. Accentuated by its scales, it has a bright sheen which is responsible for the name, 'Silver Darling'.

Size: Adults can vary in size between 15 cm (6") and 45 cm (18"), but mostly they come in at between 25 and 30 cm (10–12"). The size range can be broadly accounted for by whether they are inshore (smaller) or offshore (larger) varieties; from warmer (smaller) or colder (larger) waters; low (smaller) or high (larger) saline seas. The largest variety is found in the Norwegian and Barents Seas, where cold waters combine with around 35% salinity.

GENETICS

The variation in the size of different populations has been achieved, partly, because herrings are euryhaline (able to tolerate a wide salinity range). The small **Baltic Herring** is adapted to low salinity and is recognised as a subspecies. There are small freshwater populations in Finland's Turku Archipelago and in Sweden, to the north of the Virboa River estuary. Like the Lake District's char, these were originally separated from the sea during the last Ice Age.

In one of Earth's warm periods, roughly 2 mya, some swam over the top of what became Russia, precisely because they could tolerate the volume of fresh water pushed north by Siberia's rivers. The descendants of those that remained became what is regarded as the separate species, *Clupea pallasii*, the **Pacific Herring**. See **A is for A Beginning** and **Taxonomy** for the partial returnees, but some came all the way back, creating a hybrid population, stable for thousands of generations, in Balsfjord, near Tromsø. There has also been some interbreeding between Atlantics and the White Sea herring (a Pacific herring subspecies).

It is specifically the salinity and water temperature at spawning and just after that determine a population's small genetic changes. These include the number of vertebrae, which delivers the variability in length. Early thinking as to why this is the case suggested the need for northern deepwater herrings, involved in much longer migrations, to be stronger and therefore larger. Shallow water fish with small migrations do not need the burden of concomitantly greater food consumption. Without negating any of that logic, papers on herring genetics have been growing like topsy of late. Whole genome studies have been carried out, identifying the small spikes of variability. They seem to coincide with the genes associated with the herring's immune system. The suggestion is that there is also a natural disposition towards variability as a defence against disease, which might otherwise have plagued such large, closely-packed and frequently intermingling populations.

The herring's ready adaptability enables abundance, but it also delivers variation in oil levels, which in turn affects taste. In more herring-appreciative nations than England, this is often noted: gourmets delight in diversity. Genetically-concerned marine scientists are also now arguing for far greater sophistication in establishing fishing **Quotas**, with a view to conserving the herring's taxonomically unrecognised diversity from whole-shoal-scooping trawl capacities. For a detailed, pre-genetics, zoological description, it's worth reading *Clupeidae* by A.N. **Svetovidov** (1952).

SPAWNING

On the spawning grounds (and while on their sides) females lay between 10,000 and 70,000 eggs each. An average female in the Downs stock (East Anglia and the eastern English Channel) lays 42,000, whereas the Buchan stock (North East Scotland) lays 67,000. The most ever recorded is 95,000 (from the Schley estuary).

Either way, that's a lot of eggs and they're laid in ribbons, effectively carpeting suitable areas of the seabed.

Egg size varies in line with that of the spawner but is commonly around 1 mm in diameter. 60% of the egg is taken up with an oil globule yolk. Precise pairing isn't involved, but the male, swimming above the female, releases its milt or sperm (see **Roe**). Given the sheer numbers in the shoals, large areas of seabed are involved, requiring lots of sperm just to make it all worthwhile. Where the grounds are in shallow enough water, the amounts of sperm turn the sea milky, allowing the events (let's face it, humbling our own mere couplings) to be captured by standard-focus satellite cameras in space (see first image section).

Movement within the water can take the milt away from the eggs, disrupting fertilisation, and if this happens over a broad area it can have severe effects on the size of a particular year group. Cod and haddock have a taste for herring eggs, but it's clearly an effective strategy for reproduction, which can see remarkable levels of stock recovery after bad years and persistent overfishing. The volumes both encourage and cope with high levels of predation.

LIFE CYCLE

Depending on temperature, eggs hatch at up to three weeks. Larvae, between 6 and 8 mm, at first depend on the yolk reserves. In water under 19°C the larvae mature faster the warmer it is, but if the water is over 19°C they simply don't mature at all. With regard to predicted end of the century sea temperature and CO_2 levels they would seem to be reasonably tolerant, but much will depend on their zooplankton diet, which evidence—including the Historical Plankton Index (see **X, Formerly Known As**)—suggests can be more sensitive.

At varying points between one and three weeks the larvae develop mouths and swim to the surface. Until they reach 45 mm (around 3 months) they have a thin, eel-like appearance and are not strong enough to swim against the predominating current. Like the zooplankton they feed on, they drift considerable distances to their nursery grounds. Murman herring larvae are carried from the Lofoten Islands to the Barents Sea; Downs larvae to the German Bight; Buchan drift to the Norwegian or Danish coasts and to the Skagerrak. Where the currents are more localised, as with many of the small coastal populations, the drifting journeys are much shorter. The effect of water temperature on the number of vertebrae can also be noticeable between year groups in the same population.

Scales appear as they change from larvae to juveniles (between 3 and 5 cm). At 5 cm, able to swim more strongly, they begin to form shoals and move inshore, mixing with young sprats and, together with them, they are fished as whitebait, once thought of as the separate species *Clupea alba*. At the end of the first year (up to 8 cm), they move offshore. By the end of the second year they reach between 13 and 18 cm. Maturing timescales again vary, fattening at between three and five years and becoming sexually mature between five and eight years (colder water means longer growth periods). Maturing virgins leave the juvenile shoals and join adult ones.

The Eight Ages of the Herring

Norwegian marine science pioneer Johan Hjort (1869–1948) came up with a Shakespearean *Seven (St)ages of Herring*, but, in 1962, a Herring Committee Working Group of ICES (the International Council for the Exploration of the Sea) recommended the eight stage Bergen Scale. It's largely based on the classifications of different maturities proposed by Friedrich Heincke and A.C. Johansen (see **Racial Theory**):

1. Virgin herring which are very small with thread-like gonads 2–3 mm across (wine red ovaries; whitish to grey brown testes);

2. Virgin herring with small sexual organs: ovaries (bright red) and testes (reddish-grey) 3–8 mm in height, eggs visible with a magnifying glass;

3. Filling herring with gonads occupying about half the ventral cavity, sexual organs 1–2 cm across, eggs small but visible to naked eye; orange ovaries and reddish-grey or greyish testes;

4. Filling herring with gonads almost as long as the body cavity, opaque eggs larger but varying in size; orange or pale yellow ovaries and whitish testes;

5. Full herring, the gonads of which fill the body cavity, large round eggs (some transparent); yellowish ovaries and milk white testes, eggs and sperm do not flow, but sperm (milt) can be extruded through the application of pressure;

6. Spawning herring with transparent eggs or white testes, free-flowing eggs and sperm;

7. Spent herring with baggy, bloodshot gonads, empty ovaries and testes (or containing only residual eggs/the remains of sperm);

8. Recovering spents with wine-red gonads, firmer and larger than Stage 2 with striated walls and prominent blood vessels, eggs not visible to naked eye.

Stage 8 passes into Stage 3 again and so it continues. If a herring manages to avoid nets, whales, gannets and other predators, it can repeat the annual cycle several times: 1.5% of the year class from a very successful 1904 Norwegian spawning were still being found in 1927. Modern fishing techniques have generally reduced the survival rate of herrings, much as they have those of other species.

FEEDING

Herrings are not vegetarian and avoid areas with high levels of phytoplankton. They instead follow the zooplankton. Shifts in where they can be caught were, historically, perceived as the wrath of God at the behaviour of communities/predominating fishermen nearest to the original site. This needn't be discounted, but God's herring-related anger was generally assuaged through the quantity and drift of copepods. One of herring's favourites is *Calanus finmarchicus*, which, at 2–4 mm long, looks a bit like a very small shrimp. High in polyunsaturated omega 3, it is a main source for the herring's taste and for its noted benefits (see **Medicine & Health**). It prefers colder waters and although it tolerates a range of temperatures, climate change is thought to have been responsible for some location shifts and reduced abundance. In the 1960s it represented 70% of the zooplankton biomass in the northern North Sea; by the late 1990s this had declined to 50%. The adult herring's palate also runs to *Temora longicornis*, various *Pseudocalanus*, *Oikopleura*, the small sand eels known as *Ammodytes* and, cannibalistically, its own larvae.

Wherever they are, herring make daily vertical migrations, feeding on or near the seabed during the day and approaching the surface at night. Echo-sounding of the shoals, first carried out in 1960 in Passamaquoddy Bay, New Brunswick, presented a slightly more complex picture of this nighttime feeding, with a rise to the surface at sunset, a midnight sinking to intermediate depths, another rise to the surface at dawn, followed by a return to the bottom. This pattern correlated with the one recorded in *Der Rhythmus der Nahrungsaufnahme beim Hering* (The Rhythm of Herring Food Intake) a 1931 study by S. Muzinic of herring on the Fladen Ground (halfway between John o' Groats and Bergen) and at Bruceys Garden (off Hartlepool). This showed that most food is taken between 3 and 6am and between 5 and 9pm.

Herring larvae feed on diatoms, copepod eggs, flagellates, metazoan and copepod larvae, as well as small copepods. They start off on the smaller planktonic items and work their way up. As a general rule, warm, sunny summers produce rich plankton and consequently deliver the healthiest, best tasting herrings. On the other hand, rising sea temperatures reduce plankton abundance. There is a discernible, but not exclusively reliable, correlation with good vintages in European wine. Herrings don't feed during spawning and, as spents, take a few months to recover their body weight.

MIGRATION & MOVEMENT

The general diagrammatic principle of fish migration is an initial triangle: a denatant larval drift with the current from the spawning ground (A) to the nursery ground (B), followed by recruitment from B to the adult feeding ground (C). At this point it then becomes a straight back and forth: contranatant return to A, followed by denatant journey back to C. This then continues until the grim reaper intervenes. Herring can swim at roughly three times their length per second (1.5 knots for a 25 cm specimen).

The largest herring will always be at the front of a shoal, which may explain the East Anglian folk belief that shoals were led by a 'demon herring' or even a shad. The migratory journey of the Norwegian spring herring stands at 1,800 miles. Although elsewhere its journeys are shorter, Atlantic herrings make the longest migrations among the *Clupeidae*.

The dorsal fin allows the fish to move in a straight line and to stabilize itself in body turns. The anal fin enables it to raise and lower its head and to move the tail end in the opposite direction to the front. The removal of the anal fin apparently leaves herrings unable to lower their heads at all. The distance between dorsal and anal fins is significant in sustaining the possibility of longer migrations and is consequently greatest in the Norwegian spring spawning and Murman herrings. For what it's worth, body pigmentation is also apparently strongest in the more extensively migrant.

The basic journeys can be complicated by immature and mature herring preferring different feeding grounds. Migration is an adaptation towards abundance and takes account of supply levels. Stock abundance in absolute terms (if over-fishing is removed from the equation) is determined both by migratory range and duration: Norwegian and Murman populations are particularly large.

In his investigation of migratory navigations, Svetovidov numbers the herring among those fish with a finely developed network of cutaneous nerve endings. They appear to respond to the natural electrical currents that occur in the sea. In experiments conducted by the Russians in the 1940s, the Atlantic herring reacted very sensitively to artificially introduced electrical impulses, orienting themselves in the direction of the anode and moving toward it when a direct current field was set up. In this way, Svetivodov noted, shoals of fish may be held in one place or moved at will. The practical applications of this technology were not explored but may be inconsistent with a sustainable fishery.

SHOALING

The complete-meal dimensions of an individual Atlantic herring resulted from evolutionary adaptation to the colder latitudes of the North. This handy size combines in shoals of extraordinary dimension and it is this which determined the huge economic, historical and cultural role the fish has played in the history of Northern Europe: the scale of shoals made it hard, when you found one, to catch herring in anything other than ridiculous numbers, which in turn determined the need for effective preservative cures (and trade).

Writing in 1918, but drawing on Thomas Huxley's figures from the 1880s, A.M. Samuel (*The Herring; its effect on the history of Britain*) wrote, 'A shoal usually covers half a dozen square miles though it may be very much larger; it is often eight or nine miles in length, three or four miles in breadth, and of unknown depth, the fish being closely packed like sheep in a flock moving along a country lane.' In 1973, D.V. Radakov (*Schooling in the Ecology of Fish*) estimated shoals of up to 4.8 cubic km at a density of 0.5 to 1 fish per cubic m. Measurement may be more accurate these days; shoals may have been larger; either way it's a lot of fish. (See first image section.)

The strategy of the shoal is based on losing quite a few to predators. In the face of attack, herrings increase its density, coming close together, presenting the sense of a single, shining monster of the seas. Even if predators aren't convinced by this, they can become temporarily confused as to what their line of attack should be. Orcas have a neat trick of flicking their tails with sudden force against the water, sending shockwaves against the shoal, disorienting and dislodging sufficient individuals to satisfy their needs, but once a pod of orcas, whales or other predators have had their fill, the shoal forms again. Everybody's happy. The approach has worked successfully for the Atlantic herring. It was even known to work with fishermen: there are several records of fishing boats, capsized and lost beneath the sheer weight of herring catches. As recently as 1920, the *Mary Ann*, a drifter out of Penzance was lost in this way, only one survivor left to tell the tale. The shoal as a defence mechanism did not take account of the modern pelagic trawler, its capacious nets guided by sonar technology, its vacuum pumps sucking out the catch.

BALTIC HERRING

The Baltic Sea becomes progressively less saline the further East and North you travel. In the Gulf of Bothnia it is almost brackish. Just as genetics deliver the largest herrings in the colder, salty Norwegian and Bering Seas, so they determine that those of the eastern and northern Baltic are the smallest (see **Atlantic Herring: A Natural History**). The Baltic herring is the only recognised subspecies of the Atlantic herring. Geneticists may propose more candidates for the status than you could shake a stick at, but the problems of mixed populations and commercial fisheries' love of simplicity have, by and large, left that stick unshaken (see **North American Fisheries**, **Racial Theory** and **Taxonomy**).

With an average length of only 15 cm (around 6"), subspecies status was a good call. Taxonomy's Mr Big himself, Carl Linnaeus came up with the trinomial, *Clupea harengus n membras*, only a few years after his 1758 classification of the Atlantic herring: anyone could see the similarities, but that's one short-arse herring.

Strömling in German, *strömming* in Swedish, there are Autumn and Spring spawning varieties and, just to confuse matters, you can get giant strömling in both, which grow up to 30 cm. I've not seen one, but to the untutored eye, they're probably indistinguishable from the main species. We also now know there are greater genetic differences between Autumn and Spring spawners, whether Atlantic or Baltic, than between Atlantic and Baltic herrings as such. The world seems content in allowing such anomalies to ride.

Most Baltic herrings may be small, but they punch above their weight with fat content which, in turn delivers flavour and sweetness. Whether they should be used in Jansson's Temptation is an open question (see **Potatoes**), but it is the essential herring of **Surrströmming**. The Estonians, meanwhile, eat it with sliced strawberries, horseradish, red onions and chives in *seto kala ja maasikasalat*, a summer salad. It's also pan-fried, pickled, smoked and stewed.

BASKETS

Arthur Beech's basket making tools are laid out on the table (see first image section). At the front there's a one-sided shave, a two-sided shave (which strip the willow to an exact thickness) and two cleaves (which split a willow into three). Behind that there's a commander (which bends thick willow), three rapping irons (for knocking down the weave and bending), a knife (for slyping short points, scalloming longer points and other sharpening cuts which enable willow to be pushed through a weave), a whetstone, eleven bodkins (opening the weave to push the willow through), three shell bodkins (easing willow through awkward spaces, including pushing uprights into a base) and two braille rulers. In the third row there are four pliers, a leather-headed hammer, a pair of loppers, two pairs of shears (for cutting willow), a grease horn with tallow (for greasing bodkins). Behind that there's a screw block (for clamping the uprights rigid in square work).

I met Arthur Beech on several occasions. He was great. A plain food man, he once sat smoking his pipe on the steps outside our kitchen. 'I'm not going to eat that muck,' he said. Blinded by an accident at the age of thirteen, he'd been trained as a basket maker at Henshaw's College and then employed in its workshop mostly making big rectangular baskets for the railways and for laundries. The pay was poor and conditions weren't great. When he met his future wife Audrey she told him he could do better. They moved to Liverpool and he got a job at Lockheed. He kept all his tools but never made another basket.

Many years later, in his final days, he started telling his daughter Liz, in detail, how you made the base for a basket, his hands demonstrating on his chest the complete process. She came back the next day with a tape recorder, but he could no longer speak and a couple of days later he died. By common agreement with her sisters, she was the only one who would ever do anything with them, so she inherited all the tools and, a few years later, over a bad winter, cleaned them up. She joined a basketry group, learned and taught herself to use them. She now coppices a willow patch at the bottom of the garden. I'd clocked herring baskets as an entry I'd have to write at some point but hadn't really thought much about them until she set about making a quarter cran basket and asked if I wanted to go to Seahouses to see one, reportedly hanging from the ceiling of the Olde Ship Inn. The person behind the bar lacked the authority to allow us to take it down, which was probably wise.

Basketry is a world of its own. Countless books have been written on the subject. Liz's quarter cran looked fine to me, but she wasn't overly pleased. An intuitive experiment, it was maybe something to come back to, but she advised looking online at the baskets of John Cowan, who has a workshop in Lanark. On his website, in a section of *Special Traditional* Baskets, there's one for potatoes (all your tatties 'n' herrin' needs), a Herring Washing Maund (which, see **Measuring the Herring**, may have originated as a Cornish pilchard basket, but was also used for cleaning herrings split to make **Kippers**), an Eighth Cran and a Quarter Cran Basket. Of the Quarter Cran, Cowan says, 'it took many years of hard work to learn how to make this basket.'

The quarter cran was ubiquitous in Britain's herring industry: circular, two handles and a raised-centre base from which the uprights open up to a wider top. A cran became the standard for a barrel: too many herrings for practical carrying. There are half cran baskets, but, full, they too would be heavy and awkward: a two-person job. An eighth cran was generally used to display the quality of a catch. Fishermen would put a sample on the quay, beside their boat, and the buyers would walk up and down buying or not. If, from the sample, they chose to buy your catch, they'd expect it to be thrown in on top. Displaying a quarter cran would have been a tad over-generous. For lifting and winching the catch out of the hold, for general carrying, the quarter cran was just right (or it was with the biceps you got on a herring drifter or on the quay).

The cran was standardised at 37.5 imperial gallons; the quarter, thus, would, if it wasn't a basket, hold 9.375. The dimensions had to be specific. There are discrepancies across different accounts of the quarter cran, but these are probably down to exactly where (to and from) you're measuring—external, internal, top of handles or rim, etc—but Cowan gives them as height: 39 cm, width: 57 cm (the base is narrower). Mostly woven from willow, every sixth, seventh or eighth upright was generally hazel, offering greater rigidity. A branded oak slat replaced some willow uprights to indicate that it adhered to the specifications. Rattan was also sometimes used around the top and/or for the handles.

It is worth noting another basket specific to Yarmouth, where the network of very narrow streets called The Rows required something which went round the body. There are examples at the town's Time and Tide museum.

On their *The Quarter Cran—a little bit of history* web page, St Andrew's University Woven Communities research project notes: 'A contemporary common misconception has been that all quarter crans were made in Great Yarmouth and imported to Scotland from there. This is perhaps because … the last known workshop making quarter crans was in Great Yarmouth … But a little research reveals that at the height of the herring industry, these baskets were made in several basket works across Scotland, including in the Royal Institute for the Blind Workshop in Dundee in the 1920s.'

BATTLE OF THE HERRINGS

Technically, Joan of Arc did not prophesy France's defeat at the Battle of the Herrings: her voices were providing her with a live commentary. On February 12th 1429 she was 240 miles away in Vaucouleurs, doing her best to persuade Robert Baudricourt, Captain of the Garrison, that he should immediately escort her to the Dauphin. For four years, already, her voices had been talking to her about the need to expel the English from French soil, but they were becoming more insistent. Saints Margaret, Catherine and Michael watched as events unfolded and informed her of what was going on. 'Even now,' she told Baudricourt, 'a great misfortune has befallen the forces of the Dauphin, somewhere near Orléans.'

The voices did not specify Rouvray, which is a shame, because, if they'd taken just a little more trouble, it could have cleared up the argument as to whether the battle took place at Rouvray-Sainte-Croix or Rouvray-Saint-Denis, both some twenty miles from Orléans (opinion has shifted towards Sainte-Croix). There was no dispute when official news of the battle arrived in Vaucouleurs: Baudricourt was convinced.

Shakespeare omits mention of the Battle of the Herrings from *Henry VI Part 1*, but one of his major historical sources, Raphael Holinshed's *Chronicles*, gives a detailed account. Written 150 years after the event, he gets some things wrong.

> In the Lent season vittles and artillery began to wax scant in the English camp, wherefore the Earle of Suffolk appointed Sir John Fastolfe, Sir Thomas Rampston, and Sir Philip Hall, with their retinues, to ride to Paris, to the Lord Regent, to inform him of their lack, who incontinently upon that information

provided vittles, artillery, and munitions necessary, and loaded therewith many chariots, carts, and horses: and for the sure conveying of the same, he appointed Sir Simon Morhier, Provost of Paris, with the guard of the city, and diverse of his own household servants to accompany sir John Fastolfe and his complices, to the army lying at the Siege of Orleans. They were in all to the number of fifteen hundred men, of the which there were not past five or six hundred Englishmen.

Vittles in Lent meant herring and included in the manifest for the 300 or so wagons and carts were many barrels of herring, and they will have been both red and white. In the picture of the battle included in Martial d'Auvergne's *Les Vigiles de Charles VII* notwithstanding their colour, the herrings in the baskets would have been reds: they were also packed in barrels, but, unlike white or salted herring, they did not have to be.

The English had been besieging Orléans for four months. Charles of Bourbon, leading the French army, may have been more concerned about the munitions in the wagon train than the herrings. He had around 5,000 men, together with a contingent of Scottish troops under the command of Sir John Stewart, Constable of the Scottish Army in France (the Scots saw the Hundred Years War as another opportunity to fight England). Charles of Bourbon's plan was perfectly sound: his artillery would pound the hell out of the English before going in and mopping up. John Fastolf organised his wagons, fixed sharpened stakes to deal with cavalry and installed bowmen behind the stakes. The bombardment kicked off and from a French perspective everything was looking fine.

The Scots, meanwhile, had been told to hang back (apparently more than once) but Sir John Stewart seems to have become a tad overexcited and sent in his 400 infantry early. Not wanting to kill their allies, the French paused their bombardment. The Scots did not go in much for armour and were picked off by Fastolf's archers fairly easily. Charles hesitated and the English saw an opportunity for counterattack. Holinshed puts French and Scottish casualties at 2,500 along with 1,100 prisoners although he admits the French estimates were lower. The main French source, *Journal du siège d'Orléans*, was written only thirty-eight years after the event and suggests something closer to 400 casualties. Sir John Stewart and his brother were both killed.

The herrings, along with the munitions, were saved. It was a great victory and Fastolf was made a Knight of the Garter for conspicuous gallantry. Four months later, the Garter was removed when he was accused of leaving the field early during Joan of Arc's victory at the Battle of Patay. Shakespeare includes this but omits the bit where he gets it back because the rest of the English cavalry had galloped away before he had. Notwithstanding the fact that the Battle of the Herrings took place fourteen years after Agincourt, as well as being a disgraced Fastolf in *Henry VI Part 1*, Fastolf also became Sir John Falstaff, who makes his first appearance in *Henry IV Part 1*, but that is another story (see **Red Herring Joke**).

Naturally enough, Fastolf/Falstaff's wagon train defence was originally called the Battle of Rouvray. The French first called it the Battle of the Herrings, in mockery of the English victory, but, a bit like football supporters, the English decided to own the joke.

BEUCKEL, WILLEM

In 1556, at the town of Biervliet in the Dutch province of Zeeland, Charles V & I (retiring Holy Roman Emperor and King of Spain) knelt at the tomb of Willem Beuckel, who may have died 150 to 200 years earlier. It wasn't his actual tomb, the original Biervliet having been destroyed by floods some years before and the entire town rebuilt on higher ground.

There is some confusion as to the forename, which can be given as Willem, Wilhelm or George, but that's as nothing compared to the surname, which can be Beuckel, Beukels, Beukelz, Beuckels, Beuckelsz, Benkel, Beukelszoon, Beukelzon, Beukelsen,

Lithograph of Willem Beuckel by H.J. Backer (1821) copied from a stained glass window in a church in Biervliet.

Beuckelsen, Benkelen. Alexandre **Dumas** calls him Bruckalz. Never mind. The Emperor gave public thanks to God for Beuckel's transformative contribution to the Dutch (and therefore at the time, the Holy Roman Empire's) herring industry. Exactly what that was is similarly confusing.

According to Dutch-Australian enthusiast W. Preger (*The Humble Dutch Herring*, 1944), Willem Beukelszoon 'discovered that herrings could be preserved in salt.' The ancient Egyptians and the Romans salted fish. The monastery at Evesham levied herring taxes on the East Anglian fisheries in the seventh and eighth centuries and even the strictest vow of obedience is unlikely to have persuaded a monk to eat an unsalted herring after a 200 mile journey by cart.

In Dumas' *Grand Dictionnaire de Cuisine* (1871), Bruckalz 'invented the art of smoking herrings.' The origins of smoked fish are shrouded in mystery. The first literary mentions of red herring and *hareng saur* don't come until the fifteenth century, so, having variously died in 1347, 1397 and 1401, Beuckel could have come up with this one, but the Dutch overwhelmingly put their wealth down to salt herring and it is hard to imagine their Emperor kneeling before the inventor of reds.

Anthony Beaujon in *The History of Dutch Sea Fisheries* (1884) says Beuckelsz was a *stuyrman* or skipper, who came from a wealthy family, but obviously created his own coat-of-arms, which 'is said to have consisted of two crossed "*kaeckmeskens*," or knives used in curing herrings after the manner invented by him and to which his name will be for ever attached.' He is referring to a Dutch gutting technique, leaving in the pancreas, which improves the flavour. Recent analysis of herring skeleton cut marks from the Scania fishery suggests they might have used similar methods in the twelfth and thirteenth centuries.

Modern histories of the Netherlands often remove Beuckel from the narrative, but, as a myth, he has significance. He may have improved salting: the Dutch constantly innovated, even if they did not invent the basics. If he had been a *stuyrman*, he could have been involved in the development of the herring buss (see **Herring Boats**), the great factory ships which allowed them to salt at sea. His key role, however, was as an origin story, differentiating Dutch herrings from those of rivals. The English tried something similar with a Peter Chevalier, who appears in various accounts with the claim he invented salt herring 200 years before Beuckel. Sadly, England always let itself down with its quality control in salting and the Chevalier story never really took off.

The Dutch were good at quality control and at hoopla. Whether Beuckel existed or not, he was great hoopla and Charles V was happy to play his part in promoting the Holy Roman Empire's man.

BLOATER

Postcard, Great Yarmouth, early twentieth century

A.M. Samuel (*The Herring; Its Effect on the History of Britain*, 1918, see **Herringism**), looking back on the pre-war herring boom idyll of 1913, calculated that, in that year he'd eaten 161 herrings, 'but, being a Norwich man, principally as bloaters.' He describes the smoked delicacy with love:

> The Yarmouth bloater is an ungutted, unsplit herring, one-third fresh, one third slightly salt, and one third lightly smoked, and to my taste, is of the right delicacy and quality only in or near Great Yarmouth; bloaters procured anywhere else than in that town or in its near neighbourhood, lacking to my mind, the peculiar excellence of the fish as eaten there. Since, however, the fish begins to deteriorate rapidly in condition and flavour within five days of being taken from the sea, it is obvious that the bloater is not the most economical, though in perfection it is the most delicious, method of preparing the herring.

The 'Yarmouth', as well as its place of origin, denotes *modern*, distinguishing the object of Samuel's praise from the old-style bloater, which is heavily brined, heavily smoked and pretty much indistinguishable from the **Red Herring**, for which Yarmouth was also traditionally famous. The only thing to add to Samuel's description is that it is cold smoked, like the kipper (the only traditional hot smoked fish in the United Kingdom is the Arbroath smokie).

Most smokers would offer it a shelf life of more than five days, but as with all light cures, fresh from the smokehouse will always be best. Sadly, there are no working smokehouses left in Great Yarmouth—try Orford, Lowestoft, Sheringham or Cley Next the Sea. The nation's remaining smokehouses often experiment with wider product ranges these days, but the bloater remains, principally, an East Anglian delicacy.

THE MODERN BLOATER

Like the **Kipper**, today's bloater was very much a product of the railway age: lighter cures would only have been locally viable before the development of rapid transport. Its creation in 1835 and in Great Yarmouth is attributed to a man called Bishop. Whoever he was, he must have been a visionary as the railway did not reach Great Yarmouth for another nine years. Interestingly, 130 miles away, Alexander Thorn's Oil and Italian Warehouse of 223 High Holborn was already offering *Thorn's Potted Yarmouth Bloaters* in 1835, which seems like quick work. By 1840 it was being advertised as:

> Now in high perfection. The increasing demand for this delicious preparation proves beyond all doubt it is far superior to anything of the kind ever yet offered to the public, for sandwiches, toasts, biscuits, &c., and as an excellent relish for wine. In pots 1s. and 2s. each, warranted in all climates.

Thorn makes clear that the bloaters he uses are free from the 'rancid, oily, salt flavour, so generally complained of,' although they will have required some salt and the latest bottling techniques for him to warranty his pots 'in all climates'. People talk of contemporary bloaters being brined for anything between a few hours and a few days (particularly for export), dried, then smoked from a few hours up to two days.

Will Buckenham in Lowestoft (see **Smokehouse Tale**) would brine his bloaters for four to five hours, *speat them up* (put them on spits) and hang them for four or five hours to dry before lighting the fires. He would smoke them from 4.30 in the afternoon to 7 in the morning: 14½ hours. The result was delicious, but salting and smoking times are individual choices within a generous continuum. The 'modern bloater' may or may not have been *invented* in 1835, but contemporary smokers, all of them using refrigeration, many using vacuum packs, have tended to reduce salt and smoke levels. Bishop's invention is best seen as a staging post on a journey.

WORDS & MEANINGS

In the aftermath of a gunpowder-sparked fire on the spice island of Ternate, in Act II of John Fletcher's *The Island Princess* (1619) the playwright has an unnamed firefighting citizen complain, 'I have more smoke in my mouth, than would / Blote a hundred Herrings.' Prince Charles (later Charles I) led the principal masquers in the court première of Ben Jonson's *The Masque of Augurs* (1622), at the beginning of which the Groom of the Revels addresses a low-life band of anti-masquers, 'Who you? You a masque? Why you stink like so many bloaters newly taken out of the chimney! In the name of ignorance whence came you? or what are you? you have been hanged in the smoke sufficiently, that is smelt out already.'

Jonson may have been playfully referencing his, Shakespeare's and Thomas **Nashe**'s earlier form with the **Red Herring Joke**. Nashe makes such extensive verbal play with red herring in 1599's *Lenten Stuffe*, it is close to inconceivable he would have ignored the bloater, if it had been current. The *Oxford English Dictionary* identifies the earliest surviving usage of *bloat* as a curing process to 1611, but says it is one 'which leaves them soft and only half-dried. (*Bloated* herrings are opposed to *dried* or *red* herrings).' The term red herring covered a range of curing options already, however.

Both bloaters and reds are salted and smoked whole (ungutted). *Bloater* comes from bloat herring, the term deriving directly from the Swedish *blöt* (wet or soaked/steeped —as in brine). Bloaters aren't bloated as in swollen, the earliest usage of bloat with this meaning appearing in 1664. Between 1556 and 1589, however, there was a Bohuslän herring period (see **Swedish Fisheries**). The records are patchy, but, certainly in later ones, these vast gluts led to innovation and cheap exports. It is possible early red herring relied on dry salting rather than brining and imported Swedish reds were seen as different from home production. The time lag between the 1580s and 1611 for the penetration of both a new technique and a word is plausible.

Things worth noting at this point include:

i) red herring production has involved brining for a long, long time;

ii) Caribbean usage of the word bloater seems interchangeable with *red herring*; it was introduced through the provisioning of slave plantations, where there would have been little use for milder cures;

iii) a mildly brined, 'soft and only half-dried' Yarmouth bloater arrived in the 1830s.

It seems more likely that any initial distinction between bloaters and red herring rapidly disappeared in practice. In the seventeenth century, English and Scottish curing salt was often, anyway, an unappetizing sludge, which may have helped to blur any differences. When English and Scottish curers eventually began to tighten the rules for their barrelled salt herring, red herring and bloater production continued to be unregulated, delivering the same level of diversity we associate with kippers. Meanwhile, the French bloater, *un bouffi*, draws on the transliteration of the later English meaning, swollen. With the coming of the railways, bloater, especially if qualified by Yarmouth, was deemed available to denote one of the new lighter cures. Kippers differentiated themselves by being split and gutted; red herring carried on as red herring, but with a declining market in the British Isles.

EATING BLOATERS

As with the red herring, leaving the fish ungutted gives bloaters a pleasantly gamey taste. Will Buckenham thought the best were made with the smaller herrings, full with roe, which appear off East Anglia in November, although most bloaters and kippers are these days made with the larger herrings from Scotland's offshore shoals, from Norway or Iceland. Several smokehouses do excellent mail order deliveries.

The secret is not to overcook them. In Anne Bramley's 'Tracking the Elusive Bloater', Glen Weston of Cley Smokehouse quotes the traditional advice, 'Wrap 'em in newspaper, chuck 'em on the back of the fire and by the time you've buttered your bread they'll be done.' He's also clear they should be served unfilleted. If you have a problem with the bones, try the potted bloaters recipe of Charles Elmé Francatelli, Queen Victoria's one-time cook:

> Cut off the heads and tails from six fresh-cured Yarmouth-bloaters; immerse them in scalding water, to remove the skins; take out the backbones, and put them in a stewpan with six ounces of clarified butter, a bit of mace, a teaspoonful of anchovy, and a pinch of cayenne; simmer all together over a slow fire for ten minutes; pound in a mortar, rub through a coarse hair sieve, and use this preparation to fill small pots, which must be covered in with clarified butter, and kept in a cool place for use.

BRITISH FISHERIES

In his *Histoire Naturelle des Poissons* (1798) the Comte de Lacépède writes, 'The herring is one of those products, the use of which decides the destiny of empires.'

He was certainly thinking about the rise and fall of Scania (see **Danish Fisheries**) and of the **Dutch Fisheries**. He might also have been reading the herringbone runes for a British fishery only beginning to sort itself out—or wondering at how, from its overwhelming natural advantage, it had taken over 400 years of incompetence to oust the Dutch as top herring nation.

EARLY ENGLISH FISHERIES

> The Romans, we are told, looked upon the herring as a dainty dish, and their knowledge of it is believed to have been obtained from their soldiers on the Eastern Coast at a mural encampment called Garianonum, that is 'the mouth of the Yare.'
>
> *The Herring and the Herring Fishery*, J.W. de Caux (1881)

De Caux (see **Herringism**) does not reveal where he found this pre-zooarchaeological titbit, but like most of England's traditional herring industry historians, he came from East Anglia and happily located it on home turf. Garianonum may have been at Caister on Sea, north of Yarmouth or at Burgh Castle, a little to the west. The mouth of the River Yare has changed hugely since Roman times, when the sandbank, on which **Yarmouth's Greatness** was eventually built, was only beginning to emerge. Without De Caux's sources, it took DNA analysis of Roman fish sauce amphorae to substantiate his claim.

Taxation in the form of cured herrings, levied by various monasteries and abbeys, suggests a healthy Anglo-Saxon herring fishery from the seventh century. The fly in the ointment comes with the recently postulated *Fish Event Horizon*. Proper historians (as opposed to the enthusiasts of **Herringism**) have come late to the fish, but they bring their challenges. In 'The Early Documentary Evidence for the Commercialisation of the Sea Fisheries in Medieval Britain' (2016) Maryanne Kowaleski points to 'analysis of stable carbon and nitrogen isotope ratios in human bones,' showing that, 'even coastal residents ate little marine protein until the late ninth to eleventh centuries.'

HERRING-BOATS IN WICK HARBOUR, LARGEST FISHING STATION IN THE WORLD.

(Author's collection).

The word *weir*, as in riverine or marine fish trap, derives from the Anglo-Saxon *wer* and there were plenty of them on Anglo-Saxon coasts, quite apart from fishing boats, herring taxes and strangers (fishermen from other parts). It is hard to square this with Kowaleski's analysis, but you can't argue with the bones.

Anglo-Saxon herrings may initially have sustained the more strictly observant fasting of an elite (always juggling divine approval with the freedom to kill each other) and of religious institutions (channeling that approval). Around 1000 CE, however, there was a shift towards marine fishing (and eating) throughout Northern Europe, coinciding with the beginnings of the *Medieval Warm Period*. Warmer waters reduce the availability of the zooplankton on which herrings feed and therefore shoal sizes (see **X Formerly Known**), but in a still-developing market this may not have created difficulties.

As the Church's cultural hold increased, there was a demand-side aspect to the marine fish revolution. The *Domesday Book* records salt pans at Gorleston, five miles from Yarmouth, which speaks of herring curing. The first written evidence of the peat excavations which formed the Norfolk Broads comes from the twelfth century and herring salting will have played its part in the demand.

There is no record of when Yarmouth Herring Fair began officially, but the fishery on which it was based was pursued by both locals and strangers long before the Conquest (see **Yarmouth's Greatness**). The Barons of the Cinque Ports later claimed their authority over it preceded the Conquest, but their charter dates only from 1135. Their relationship with the town was not a happy one and King John began transferring rights back to the town, in return for naval service. Edward III's 1357 *Statute of the Herrings* is the first attempt at organising the English fishery and, to Lowestoft's annoyance, it officially concentrated the herring market at Yarmouth.

The statute confirmed a free right of fishermen and traders to buy or sell, to and from anyone they chose, while fixing a maximum price. Edward codified what had long been England's *laissez-faire* policy towards the fishing industry. Back in 1295 Edward I had commanded his subjects to be nice to the fishermen from Holland, Zealand and Friesland, *who are our friends*. This meant they had paid him for a licence.

EARLY SCOTTISH FISHERIES

Herring will have been fished for on the coasts of Scotland from early times too, but the first mention is from 1138, when King David I granted fishing rights to the Abbey of Holyrood. The early Scottish herring fisheries were concentrated in the firths of the Forth and the Clyde. James R. Coull, in *The Sea Fisheries of Scotland* (1996), sees the Scottish feudal system as acting against their development. Fishermen had no property rights and therefore no access to capital. Lairds were responsible for investment in any required new boats and nets. Willingness to invest depended on how much spare cash they felt they had. Fishermen were lucky if they got one of the small open boats suited to the firths.

Scottish kings, on the other hand, became resentful observers of the hugely successful Dutch herring fleet which had appeared off their coast in the early fifteenth century. By the 1470s James III was encouraging the building of Dutch-style factory ships: herring busses. Coull identifies the Dutch fleet's advantages as technique, capital, organisation and market control: everything but the fish. Meanwhile, the House of Stuart became herring-obsessed. To understand this and the way it played out in the seventeenth century it is necessary to look, with the Stuart kings, across the water at the rapid growth of Dutch sea power, wealth and empire. The Dutch saw God using the herring shoals at his disposal to reward their Protestant virtue (see **Grand Migration**) but the Stuarts, noting this divine providence was heavily reliant on Scottish waters, wanted more than just a piece of the action.

TOWARDS UNION & THE BLOCK

Bo Poulsen in his book *Dutch Herring* (2008), while comparing different fisheries from 1600 onwards, points to the disappointing lack of records for English catches and exports. Such figures as there are point to England being a relatively small player in both the salt herring market and the history of fish-based bureaucracy. The Reformation had a devastating effect on English fisheries. Without the enforcement of fasting, the home market never recovered. In 1563, against considerable Protestant opposition, Elizabeth I felt the need to introduce Wednesday as a secular fish day.

On Elizabeth's death, James VI of Scotland became James I of England & Ireland. His unfulfilled vision of a United Kingdom was in part shaped by his Stuart sense of the herring riches his combined coastlines were still delivering to others. The international dimension this took on and the role it played in the fortunes of James and his son Charles I are explored in **Sovereignty of the Seas**. Knowing James' concern, England's **Pamphleteers** went into overdrive pointing to the riches a herring buss fishery would bring the nation and in 1607 William Camden updated his national epic *Britannia* to acknowledge 'the goodness of God towards us in the herring fisheries off the British coast.' In the face of James' diplomatic offensive, the Dutch resolutely pursued a policy of procrastination.

In domestic policy, to encourage the demand side James took up the idea of fish days and extended them to forbid the eating of flesh during Lent too. At its heart, Protestant England equated fish eating with Popery. On the supply side James tried to establish a fishery on the Isle of Lewis, granting patents to merchant adventurer fishermen. The Earl of Seaforth, who owned Lewis, was developing a deal with the Dutch and, at his suggestion, his people set about dissuading the adventurers… in some cases terminally.

With Charles I on the throne, Seaforth was ordered to kick out the Dutch and a grand plan for an Association for the Fishing was announced: a joint stock company with rights in English, Scottish and Irish waters. There would be 200 busses of between 30 and 40 tons following the herring around the British coast from June to the end of January. The Scottish parliament was as keen to keep out English 'strangers' as Dutch ones, but after much haggling and rank-pulling an agreement was reached in

1632, giving Charles what he wanted. If buss building enthusiasm was limited in his kingdoms, it declined even further as Dutch men-of-war and privateers from Dunkirk took the limited number of busses the Association had managed to accrue.

Charles could do little about this with the weak navy he had. Nor could he rebuild his navy without expanding his Ship Money tax base. The lavish expense of the flagship he commissioned (see Sovereignty of the Seas), together with his naval humiliations (including those in pursuit of Dutch herring licence payments) all contributed to Ship Money resentment, one of the major causes of the English Civil War. It is not known to what extent, as he later laid his head on the block, Charles reflected on the herring and its role in his misfortunes.

Oliver Cromwell may not have been a herring man, but the dynamics James and Charles had engendered continued regardless. Under Admiral Blake, the Commonwealth's fleet fought the first Anglo-Dutch War (1652–4), England winning the battles of the Kentish Knock, Portland, the Gabbard and Schevingen, the Dutch the Battle of Dungeness and the struggle to lift the blockade of their ports. It is a universal law that wars are bad for herring fishing. By the end of 1652, the people of Yarmouth were already complaining to Cromwell's General Monck that they'd lost £200,000 and, 'Not three boats are now preparing to go forth fishing, where 150 sail used to be making ready at this season.' In addition to the Dutch and the Dunkirk privateers, English fishermen were also having to put up with Prince Rupert's small Royalist navy—effectively another bunch of privateers. The conclusion of the war, which had devastated both British and Dutch herring fleets, left matters unresolved.

TOWARDS MORE OF THE SAME

If Cromwell's Protectorate had offered little protection to its fishermen, it had offered even less encouragement to the observation of religious fasts, but with the Restoration, Charles II issued a proclamation encouraging the observation of Lent and, throughout the year, Wednesdays, Fridays and Saturdays were to be fish days. While Elizabeth I and James VI & I both had impeccable Protestant credentials, Charles I, Charles II and James II were all suspect.

To Charles II, Catholicism and a strong herring fishery were complementary virtues. He was a man on a mission, announcing an intention to give £200 to anyone who built a herring buss. It took him nearly three years, but in March 1664 he established both English and Scottish Corporations for the Royal Fishery. He made his brother James Governor of the English one. Samuel Pepys, a member of the English corporation's council, described it in his diary as made up of 'Several other very great persons, to the number of thirty-two.' By July, however, he was finding 'the company generally so ill-fitted for so serious a worke that I do much fear it will come to little.' By September his diary records:

> After dinner to Whitehall, to the Fishing Committee, but not above four of us went, which could do nothing, and a sad thing it is to see so great a work so ill followed, for at this pass, it can come to nothing but disgrace to us all.

To the charge of incompetence, Pepys was soon adding the suggestion of corruption, but fortunately for all concerned, the Corporation's records were destroyed in the Great Fire.

The Second and Third Anglo-Dutch Wars (1665–7 and 1672–4), together with the five years of hostilities in between, finally did for the Corporations. Conflict discourages investment and James' conversion to Catholicism, which had become public in 1673, did not help the herring cause. Charles II, the great herring promoter, was in cahoots with Louis XIV and, against the French offer of money, had secretly promised his own public conversion and more. Meanwhile, the Third Anglo-Dutch War went even worse than the Second. Parliament insisted on peace without any benefits to the herring industry at all. The Corporation reorganised and tried to raise more capital, but it gave up when Charles died in 1685. The parallel corporation in Scotland had already abandoned any pretence at developing a fishing industry, although it continued collecting taxes until someone noticed in 1690.

James became king on his brother's death but did not last long enough to do anything of importance for the herring fisheries. The Glorious Revolution of 1688 brought in William and Mary. Stadtholder of the United Provinces of the Netherlands as well as King of England, Ireland and Scotland, William can be forgiven for his lack of commitment to the Stuart herring cause. When Queen Anne came in (1702), she usefully reorganised herring laws, introducing regulations on the quality of curing salt and bounties to encourage exports. That was about it. The Stuarts' huge herring ambitions had come to naught, but the struggle they launched broke the back of the Dutch fishery. They can be credited with clearing the way for the eventual rise of the Scottish and English herring fleets, even though it took until the nineteenth century to get there.

TOWARDS NEW MARKETS

Bo Poulsen shows the Scottish herring fishery as beginning its journey towards dominance from the mid seventeenth century. Others date its rise from the following century. It may have been helped by its distance from the main Anglo-Dutch War fields of action, but it also coincided with British colonisation of the Caribbean, where the slave plantations became a major market for Scottish salt and red herring. In the seventeenth century the reputation of Scottish curing was even worse than that of the English, but this did not bother the plantation trade. Slave provisioning ships sailed out of the Shannon—the shortest route—and this particularly benefitted the Scottish fisheries.

Early in the reign of George I, 1718 saw *An Act for recovering the credit of the British fishery in foreign parts*. The Dutch may have been weakened but their reputation for curing was still high; the English and the Scots may have had to deal with less competition on the fishing grounds, but when exporting they were still selling to the cheap end of the market. Dutch success had also encouraged the rest of Northern

Europe's herring fishing nations to build busses and set sail for British waters. The reputational problems of British salt herring came from inferior quality salt and salting, a relaxed attitude to when the herring was salted and frequent use of thumbs rather than gutting knives. The quality of barrels was suspect, and the packing was bad too.

Income from the plantation market may have helped Scottish curers begin to address these issues, but, either way, they did so earlier and more consistently than the English. From 1710 onwards, the Scots began to break into the important Hamburg market and the weakened Dutch found it difficult to maintain the monopolies they had negotiated in better times.

George II raised the question of the herring industry at the opening of Parliament in 1749. The Society of the Free British Fishery was established with Frederick, Prince of Wales, as its Governor. Its Secretary John Lockman became known as The Herring Poet and was an avid pamphleteer. As with the Royal Fishery Corporations of the seventeenth century, there were suggestions of corruption, but Lockman was able, at least, to answer them in verse. The Society lasted until 1772. A series of fishing acts in 1750, 1753 and 1755 developed a system of bounties on the building and fitting out of herring busses. On the back of subsidy, the acts enforced improved curing.

Adam **Smith** attacked herring buss subsidies in *The Wealth of Nations*, but his analysis and statistics were dodgy. In *The Herring and the Herring Fisheries* (1927) James Travis Jenkins shows that between 1762 and 1796 there was a doubling of the tonnage involved in the Scottish herring fishery and more than a tripling of the catch. The bounty system was open to fraud—fishermen have always tried to keep an eye open for opportunity—and factory ships weren't absolutely necessary when you were fishing close to your own shores. However most herring writers have seen the encouragement of larger vessels as having provided one of the keys to the eventual establishment of Great Britain as top herring nation.

PATHS OF GLORY

In 1809 a Fishery Board was created. The curing of salt herring was subject to regular inspection and a *Crown Brand* gave the assurance of quality. The Scots had already been promoting the Scotch Cure, which differed little from the Dutch one. Even as Adam Smith had been arguing against the busses and their bounties, fishermen were moving towards the French-style lugger, which combined catch capacity with the speed to bring the herring to shore-based curers. With the size of catches increasing, the need for subsidy declined and the bounties were phased out completely by 1829.

Within a few years a rapidly growing railway network had opened many more inland markets for fresh fish. The herring resentments of the sixteenth and seventeenth centuries still ran deep in the English psyche and the home market for the fresh version was never as enthusiastic as that for cod, haddock and other white species. It was cheap, however. At the same time, rail enabled the development of the milder smoked **Kipper** and **Bloater**.

Tatties and herring (made with fresh or salted) contributed to an almost folkloric sense of Scotland's identity as it became the dominant force in UK herring exports. Over the nineteenth century, as the boats got bigger, English drift netters voyaged north as much as the Scots came south, but the Scots curers also headed south, using the railways to transport their own skilled teams of **Herring Lasses**. In the herring ports they maintained an infrastructure that was used in the few weeks the shoals would be there.

By the end of the nineteenth century, the Scottish fleet on its own was catching more herring than the Dutch had ever barrelled, and the English fleet almost matched it. Such were the successes, the 1880s brought a glut, temporarily depressing prices, but in the peak years before World War I the United Kingdom was selling 1,400,000,000 cured herrings to the Germans per year and only slightly fewer to the Russians. Scotland had roughly 60% of this trade.

BRITISH FISHERIES

Published in August 1883, this Yarmouth feature coincided with the International Fisheries Exhibition in London (author's collection).

DECLINE

Before the war, sailing drifters had been giving way to steam and the increased capacity it brought, while herring populations offered no limits to the advance of the Scotch Cure. After the war, it was a different story. The disruptions were compounded in its main markets by economic blockades of the Soviet Union and the effects of the Treaty of Versailles on the German economy.

British herring curers lost substantial sums to the catastrophic devaluations of the mark and some went out of business. Germany, which had begun building its herring fleet before the war, was encouraged in a movement towards self-reliance by its lack of foreign currency. The relatively high cost of exported, barrelled herring encouraged **Klondyking**, shipping fresh herrings direct by steamer to picklers in Hamburg. This generated some excitement, but it only masked an underlying decline. When trade was possible with the Soviets, the curers found they drove far harder bargains than their Tsarist predecessors ever had.

On Scotland's West Coast, working in pairs, the ring netters had pioneered trawling techniques which were adopted by other national fleets, but in the North Sea, by and large the British stuck to drifting. Drift nets were better at targeting only adult fish and delivered a better quality product. Purse seine trawling was developed by the Americans, but was taken up enthusiastically by the Scandinavians, the Icelanders and others. However bad it might have been for the herring populations, the catches undercut Britain's drift netters.

The **Herring Industry Board** was set up in 1935 to arrest the decline. It regulated the industry, offered loans, encouraged the building of fishmeal plants and tried hard, with adverts and recipe books, to encourage a home market for the refrigeration-enabled fresh trade. The British public, however, particularly the English, resisted their encouragement. On top of this, even before World War II, herring populations were beginning to show signs of overfishing.

There were investigations into the potential impacts of beam trawling, but not enough was known about herrings to recognise the importance of the maerl beds that were being damaged. Meanwhile, the purse seiners were taking the juvenile herrings along with the adults. The outlets provided by fishmeal and fish oil factories meant that the natural disincentives produced by market gluts disappeared. The introduction of diesel engines contributed to ever-greater catch capacities.

World War II gave the herring some respite, not least because, as in World War I, the Royal Navy commandeered much of the fishing fleet. After the war things rapidly deteriorated. The British North Sea fishery began to move towards pelagic trawling in the 1950s, which just compounded the problem. With Britain outside the Common Market, the import duty on its herring gave Dutch and Danish producers the advantage in the important German trade. Just before Britain's accession to the EC, Europe pulled a fast one, rushing through legislation granting all member nations access to each others' waters—the main reason Norway did not join—and this increased pressure on stocks. Meanwhile, the tipping of fly ash from power stations was covering more of the spawning grounds.

The United Kingdom's few fishmeal plants were closing, but encouraged by the Herring Industry Board, pet food plants were taking higher and higher proportions of the catch. Icelandic herring stocks dramatically collapsed in the 1960s, but instead of noting this, the Board encouraged fishermen to buy the redundant Icelandic purse seiners. North Sea and West Coast herring populations then collapsed in the 1970s, leading, in 1977, to the British government initiating a total ban on all directed herring fisheries in its Exclusive Economic Zone. A couple of Dutch boats were arrested by the Royal Navy, but the potential for a fifth Anglo-Dutch War was averted by scientists, who persuaded other herring fishing nations to join in with the ban, which lasted until 1983.

WHOSE FISH? (AGAIN)

Costly increases in catch capacity have concentrated ownership of the increasingly large vessels. The European Community and then the EU introduced quotas to address overfishing and, in the United Kingdom they were mostly allocated to large scale owners. Globalism and Adam Smith-inspired free market convictions, both in governments and among the handful of very rich quota owners have created the situation in which, according to Greenpeace, 'around half of England's quota is ultimately owned by Dutch, Icelandic or Spanish interests.' The overwhelming proportion of England's herring quota was sold to a single Dutch company (and a single trawler, the *Cornelis Vrolijk*). The herring is landed in IJmuiden, which is why it has become such a rarity on English fishmongers' slabs.

Scottish fishing quotas have remained in Scottish hands. The £63m 'black fish' scam, between 2002 and 2005, saw processing plants in Peterhead and Shetland secretly using underground pipes and covert weighing machines to land 170,000 tonnes of over-quota herring and mackerel, but at least Scotland still eats herring. There are herring lovers in England, and even a few top chefs champion it, but its continuing cheapness only contributes to its image problem (even in fish-eating Norway, cheapness has recently begun to count against its popularity). There have been marketing initiatives, but these days, whilst torched mackerel has almost become a culinary cliché, the most imaginatively satisfying of all the world's tasty fish hardly gets a look in. Even the burgeoning market for gastro cat food prefers salmon and tuna. It is possible to despair at the folly of a nation.

See also **Irish, Welsh & Manx Fisheries** and **Ring Net Struggle**

BRITTEN, BENJAMIN

Benjamin Britten (1913–1976) only wrote two herring-connected operas and some might question the fish's significance in the second of these. Even one is more than can be found in the output of most composers. Britten grew up in Aldeburgh and went to prep school in Lowestoft. When he wrote *Peter Grimes* and *Albert Herring* at Snape in Suffolk, it was still herring country.

PETER GRIMES (1945)

With a libretto by Montague Slater, Britten's *Peter Grimes* is loosely based on a tale from George Crabbe's *The Borough* (1810), set in a fictionalised Aldeburgh. Was Crabbe's Grimes a herring fisherman? With one boy in his employment already having died at sea, the Borough villagers begin to get suspicious when the replacement dies too:

> … One night it chanced he fell
> From the boat's mast and perish'd in her well,
> Where fish were living kept, and where the boy
> (So reasoned men) could not himself destroy.

Live fish wells enabled genuinely fresh supplies to the market. Regardless of whether Grimes was guilty, conventional wisdom had it that herrings died immediately on being lifted out of the sea: they were never kept in wells. Crabbe's father was a collector of salt duties, so he will have known his fish.

Banned by the Mayor of the Borough from further employment of young boys, Grimes is pictured 'Cursing the shoals that glided by the spot, / And gulls that caught them when his arts could not.' The species concerned are never specified. Britten and Slater may be ambiguous about Grimes' guilt, but they're never in doubt about what is in his nets. The herring shoals resonate throughout the opera.

ALBERT HERRING (1947)

This time with a libretto by Eric Crozier and based on *Le Rosier de Madame Husson* by Guy de Maupassant, Britten's comic opera *Albert Herring* is the story of a timid and virginal shop assistant. In the fictional Suffolk town of Loxford, he is elected King of

May by his fellow citizens. After an evening of drinking, Albert summons the courage to break free from his mother's apron strings and enjoy a night of sexual adventure.

The name was apparently drawn from a real Suffolk grocery, but it is also clearly used for its humorous effect. Fish often take on phallic significance and herrings, because they are also comic, have excited ribald associations more than most. Call a virginal boy Herring and have him deflowered down at the wrong end of Loxford, the resonances aren't too far away from the imagined momentary caress of the herring gutters.

On a literal level, unlike *Peter Grimes*, the opera has nothing to do with herrings at all, but Humphrey Carpenter's biography notes that, in season, Britten's mother ran a canteen for the herring lasses and that he and his sister would go down with her, fascinated by the different world presented by the quayside. There is a sexual frisson in *Albert Herring*, which is enriched by innuendo. Some productions of the opera don't quite take this aspect in hand.

BUCKLING

Hot smoked herring, buckling has become more common in Britain with the development of specialist, delicatessen fish smokers. It seems to have originated in the Baltic. In the 1960s Polish archaeologist Professor Z. Rajewski discovered thirty-four pear-shaped holes and sixteen hearths, together with the bones of pike, bass, roach, bream and catfish, in Biskupin, to the south of Gdansk. The site indicated hot smoked fish production thriving between the eighth and tenth centuries. Apart from the Arbroath Smokie, which only dates from the nineteenth century, hot-smoking is not a UK tradition, whereas around the Baltic they'll hot smoke any fish at the drop of a hat.

The method involves cooking the fish in the smoke of a hot wood fire. Hardwoods are preferred—from oak and beech to alder. The additional use of aromatic branches, such as juniper, is common. Different temperatures are achieved for different parts of the process, but can reach between 212°F (100°C) and 248°F (120°C) in the cooking period.

It is impossible to date the earliest experiments with *bücklinge*, but it may have been one of the forms of 'dried' herring in use before the German Hanse levered a takeover of the Vikings' trading empire through the salt they brought to the Scania herring boom. *Strohbücklinge*, hard-smoked and packed with straw, would keep for two to three weeks. It is possible some harder-smoked varieties lasted longer.

The undisputed buckling heartland is the Danish island of Bornholm. Production here is in brick kilns, roughly three metres square and narrowing towards the top like a decapitated pyramid. Fires, preferably made of alder, are raked backwards and forwards across the floor, or moved about on trolleys, to give an even distribution of heat. The herrings are usually gutted, then salted for half an hour before being dried, toughening the head and skin so the herrings don't fall off their sticks in the cooking. Sometimes they are smoked unsalted but sprinkled with salt when packed. They are cooked in a thick smoke for between 1 ½ and 2 hours, the heat raised gradually from around 60° to roughly 100° C.

The great buckling dish is *Sol over Gudhjem* (Sun over Gudhjem), in which it is served, whole or filleted, with a raw egg yolk (usually held in place with an onion ring) and a range of trimmings, from chives to radishes. It looks beautiful and as you break the membrane holding the sunshine together, you realise just how perfect a dressing a simple raw yolk can be. Go to Bornholm. Visit the small fishing town of Gudhjem and have a *Sol over Gudhjem* lunch down by the harbour, preferably on a good day, the warmth of the sun on your head as you gaze east across the Baltic Sea, imagining the shoals beneath its surface. Look down on your plate and feel the contentment of a well-chosen metaphor. After lunch you could visit the Oluf Høst Museet and see his paintings of herring smoking kilns.

You could take yourself on a Baltic island buckling art tour by also visiting Rügen, where, along the harbour wall at the former GDR holiday resort of Sassnitz, you'll find a line of old fishing boats which have been turned into smokehouses. If it swims in the sea, they'll smoke it, but get yourself a buckling *brötchen* (bread roll) and walk out of town, into the woods, until you come to some remarkably beautiful chalk sea cliffs: *I know this!* you might think. Eat your brötchen and imagine the German Romantic painter Caspar David Friedrich eating one beside you.

CALLER HERRIN'

It's Edinburgh, late eighteenth century: the cries of its Newhaven fisherwomen, 'Wha'll buy my caller herrin'' (who will buy my fresh herring) ring out against the pealing of its church bells...

CALLER HERRIN'

Wha'll buy my caller herrin'?
They're bonnie fish and halesome farin';
Wha'll buy my caller herrin',
New drawn frae the Forth?

When ye were sleepin' on your pillows,
Dream'd ye aught o' our puir fellows,
Darkling as they fac'd the billows,
A' to fill the woven willows?
Buy my caller herrin',
New drawn frae the Forth.
Chorus

Wha'll buy my caller herrin'?
They're no brought here without brave darin';
Buy my caller herrin',
Haul'd through wind and rain.
Buy my caller herrin',
New drawn frae the Forth.
   Chorus

Wha'll buy my caller herrin'?
Oh, ye may ca' them vulgar farin'
Wives and mithers, maist despairin',
Ca' them lives o' men.
Buy my caller herrin',
New drawn frae the Forth.
   Chorus

When the creel o' herrin' passes,
Ladies clad in silks and laces,
Gather in their braw pelisses,
Cast their heads and screw their faces.
Buy my caller herrin',
New drawn frae the Forth.
   Chorus

Caller herrin's no got lightlie:
Ye can trip the spring fu' tightlie;
Spite o' tauntin', flauntin', flingin',
Gow had set you a' a-singing.
Buy my caller herrin',
New drawn frae the Forth.
   Chorus

Neebour wives, now tent my tellin';

When the bonnie fish ye're sellin',

At ae word be in yere dealin' —

Truth will stand when a' thin's failin'.

Buy my caller herrin',

New drawn frae the Forth.

Chorus

NATHANIEL GOW & MRS BOGAN OF BOGAN

The tune *Caller Herrin'* was written by Scottish composer Nathaniel Gow around 1798, evoking the fisherwomen's cries and the pealing bells. Son of the great fiddle player and composer Niel Gow, Nathaniel wrote the tune for harpsichord. Sara Stevenson's *Hill and Adamson's Fishermen and Women of the Firth of Forth* (1992, see **Documentary**) notes that Gow's song, 'preserved the tones of the fisherwomen, with the music of whose cries, as they hawked their wares, he was so struck, that he had often followed them for hours on the streets of Edinburgh.'

Fisherwomen were both a formidable musical and a conflicted aesthetic presence. From the eighteenth century to the twentieth, it was not uncommon for men of an artistic sensibility to be drawn to the younger fisher lasses. Strangely, they seem to have found the older fish wives intimidating. (See **Herring Lasses**)

Gow did not write the words, however. Carolina Oliphant, Lady Nairne, heard the tune being played at country house balls around her own family seat at Gask in Perthshire. She may also have drawn inspiration from the bleak poem Jonathan Swift includes in his *Verses for Women who cry Apples etc* (1746).

HERRINGS

Be not sparing,

Leave off swearing.

> Buy my herring
> Fresh from Malahide,
> Better never was tried.
> Come, eat them with pure fresh butter and mustard,
> Their bellies are soft, and as white as a custard.
> Come, sixpence a dozen, to get me some bread,
> Or, like my own herrings, I soon shall be dead.

From a Jacobite family which had been exiled after the '45 Rebellion and had only returned two years before her birth in 1766, Lady Nairne was the Scarlet Pimpernel of Scottish lyricists. As well as *Caller Herrin'* she wrote *Charlie is my Darling, Will Ye No' Come Back Again* and many others, but did not admit to any of them. At the time of writing *Caller Herrin'* she used the pseudonym Mrs Bogan of Bogan. Later Mrs Bogan became BB, SM (for Scottish Minstrel) or just Unknown. Having written the lyrics in a disguised or 'borrowed hand', she gave them to a confidante, who passed them on to Gow.

THE FILM: CALLER HERRIN' (1947)

The Gow/Bogan popular song later provided the title of a short film, funded by the Central Office of Information for the Scottish Home Department. At 18 mins long, directed by Alan Harper, *Caller Herrin'*, like John Grierson's *Drifters* (1929), is a documentary the purpose of which was to encourage the home market for herring (see **British Fisheries** and **Herring Industry Board**). Many of the steam drifters and their crews had been drawn into military service during World War II. The film balances its highlighting of the herring industry's modernisation—diesel, science, freezers, mechanisation and canning—with a celebration of traditional values in food production. Needless to say, the home market for herring continued its decline.

CANNING

Unexpected visitors? Supper Snacks are no problem if you've got some canned herrings...

Out of the ten 4-page *Have Herrings* leaflets, issued by the **Herring Industry Board** in the 1940s/50s, nine devote whole pages to the delicious treats that can be made with canned herring. It went out of fashion. To be fair, canned herrings were only ever fashionable when people thought they weren't eating it (see **Sardine Litigation**). In *Fish Saving* (1955) C. L. Cutting explains the initial military imperative which gave us canned food:

> Marlborough's army at Blenheim in 1704 numbered only 54,000 men, who could almost live off the land. Napoleon invaded Russia in 1811 with over a million, and a highly organized food commissariat was required.

In 1795, a prize of 12,000 francs was offered by the French Directory for a means of preserving not just food, but even a significant proportion of the original taste and texture. Nicholas Appert won the award in 1809 for a bottling process. *The Book for All Households, or the Art of Preserving Animal and Vegetable Substances for Many Years*, which he published in 1810, was translated into English the following year. By 1814, Appert was supplying the French government and the product lines included fish.

The Dutch were already selling salted, juniper-smoked potted salmon in tinned-iron boxes and in 1810, the British merchant Peter Durand, working to specifications supplied by the French inventor Pierre de Girard, patented a tin-plate container, which could be adapted for Appert's new technique. When he applied for an American patent in 1818, Durand coined the term *tin canister*. The derivation is from the Greek *kánastrou*, Latin *canistrum*, originally meaning a basket of reeds, but already in English usage meaning a case or a box. From 1819 Thomas Kensett and Ezra Dagget began preserving seafood

John Ellis, 83 and still working on North Shields Fish Quay, handed me a large envelope of the worn, once-stapled pages of a 1950s Picture Post-style advertorial for Shields-based canning factory Tyne Brand. The photographer, Hans Bauman, worked under the pseudonym Felix H. Man.

in New York, later extending the business to Baltimore. They patented an improvement to the canning process in 1825. Meanwhile, from the early 1820s William Underwood was preserving salmon, lobster and other products in Boston.

Each machine, operated by two girls, deals with 6,000 fish an hour: the laborious hand process is superseded.

From Tyne Brand Herrings

One story has it that Underwood's canisters became cans in 1839, an abbreviation introduced by his bookkeepers, as they tracked his sales. The OED expresses uncertainty

From Tyne Brand Herrings, printed across the fold it is captioned, 'FULL SPEED AHEAD: The Tyne Brand Cannery in full production. Everyone knows his job. Machinery is harnessed for human benefit.'

on this. *Kánastrou* derived from *kanne* or reed (from which we get *cane*), but there's also an Old English *canne* from the Proto-Germanic for cup, mug or tankard (from which we probably get *canned*, as in drunk). This was still in currency and Underwood's bookkeepers could have chosen to use what they assumed was just the shorter, less highfalutin' word. *Tin* just comes from the tinplating of the cans.

The first pressure steam steriliser was invented in 1876 and this transformed the can's usefulness by significantly extending shelf life. This was also the year the Maine or Brunswick Sardine was first successfully canned by Julius Wolff and Herman Ressing in Eastport. The **North American Fisheries** breakthrough, using juvenile herrings, led to a rapid expansion of canneries along the coasts of Maine, New Brunswick and Nova Scotia.

A cannery established in 1903, Tyne Brand was bought by Spillers in 1967 and briefly converted to producing pet food before the factory was closed in 1976.

In 1900, Joseph Sutton Clark invented a can, easily opened with a key. Early can openers, with heavy-duty blades, weren't ideal for the small sardine cans. The Norwegians were quick to adopt the new technology and early cans of King Oscar Sardines (sprats or herrings) pictured the king inside a conceptual key-opened can which looks a bit like a guillotine (see **Iddis**). The French were much slower at modernising their canning processes. In the great **Sardine Litigation** before World War I, Skippers sardine magnate Angus Watson ran newspaper adverts comparing his key-opened, solderless cans to 'the heavy, soldered French tin with which you ran the risk of mangling the fish—and your fingers.'

It wasn't until 1932, in Blacks Harbour, New Brunswick, that Henry T. Austin developed the iconic sardine tin with its own detachable key. Ring-pulls have now mostly superseded this wonder of twentieth-century technology, but Blacks Harbour is home to Connors Bros, the largest sardine cannery in the world (see **North American Fisheries**).

CARIBBEAN & WEST AFRICAN FOOD

The Atlantic herring does not swim on the coasts of Africa and neither does it swim in the Caribbean, but then, most of the West Indies' ancestors did not get to the Caribbean from West Africa under their own steam. There are involuntary connections involved here.

Around 1999 or 2000, the late fiddle player, clog dancer and comedian Joe Scurfield came to see me with a bag of cassettes. He had recently returned from Grenada and the nearby, small island of Carriacou where he'd recorded a unique and extraordinary fiddle tradition. Mostly the tunes were quadrilles. *Tune* is a misnomer: the fiddles supplied rhythm without any reference whatsoever to melody or tuning. It is a dance music which grew out of the cultural interaction between African slaves and Scottish indentured labour. Along with a large bottle of Grenadian rum Joe had also brought me a **Red Herring**.

As part of red herring researches for the radio series which set this encyclopaedia on its way I had visited H.S. Fishing Company of Great Yarmouth, who exported red herring to the Caribbean. The sample Joe brought was nothing like theirs. For a start it had been gutted; second, it looked like it might have been a *spent*: thin and wasted after spawning. At the heavy end of both the salt and smoke spectrums, it was dry and a deep, deep red. Joe had no idea where it had been smoked. The Caribbean, together with its British diaspora, had provided one of the last markets for H.S. Fishing's reds. Their output came in a range of strengths but all were produced from fish in prime condition.

From the earliest days of Britain's colonial involvement in slavery both red and white (salt) herring became a major export, provisioning the slave plantations. It was a cheap source of protein, mostly produced on Scotland's North East and West Coasts, as well as in Ireland. When the **Swedish Fisheries** were dealing with their late eighteenth/early nineteenth century Bohuslän gluts, they got in on the act too. English smokers held a poor opinion of Scottish red herring, but quality was not so much of a concern as price or proximity to the provisioning ships of the River Shannon.

Meanwhile, one of the other markets to which H.S. Fishing sold its red herring was Ghana. It may originally have been exported to West Africa on the first leg of the slave trade triangle. Ghana is a country of many languages, but herring tends to be called *amane* or *eban*, which can also refer to smoked bonga shad, another clupeid of a similar size. Hot and cold smoked herring, bonga shad and other fish are common throughout West Africa. English is also one of the major languages spoken and it seems as though (smoked or unsmoked) imported herring, bonga shad and possibly other fish can all be called 'herring'.

Early reds may have been sold or exchanged by slavers in a market where it was simply recognised as interchangeable with locally-produced smoked fish. Equally, imported reds may have inspired or influenced home-grown West African smoking traditions. Plantation owners looking for the cheapest protein to keep slaves alive and labouring may have been responsible for the Caribbean culinary tradition. Alternatively transported slaves may have carried with them the taste for hard smoked clupeids. There are many Caribbean salt cod recipes, but fewer salt herring ones, even though it was also sold to the plantations. This may support a pre-existent taste for smoked fish.

One of the classics of Jamaican cookery is salt fish and ackee, which tends to use the cheapest cuts of salt cod, but recipes for red herring and ackee are quite common. In the culinary traditions of the Caribbean, Reds are also called **Bloaters**, smoked or smoke herring. One recipe I found called for rubber gloves on the grounds that reds were 'smelly'. Scotch bonnet levels on your fingers might raise greater concern.

The saltiness of red herring is a virtue in Caribbean cooking, but even so most recipes suggest some soaking: boil it for 5 to 10 minutes; pour over boiling water and let it stand for 15 minutes; soak in cold water for half an hour; combinations of any of the above. The recommendation is to taste the reds at the beginning and as you go along. You should not lose all the salt or the smoke. Dishes are often referred to as *pick up red herring*, because, having desalinated, you pick the flesh from the bones or at least most of the bones—but it's usually broken or cut into small pieces, reducing to insignificance what the Welsh call the herring's *hairs*.

STEWS AND GRAVIES

The standard dish can vary from island to island and family to family. Generally called stew or gravy, at their core there's usually half a pound or 200 gms of soaked and picked up red herring added to a sauce made of fried onion, garlic, sweet pepper, chilli (often Scotch bonnet) and tomatoes. Additions include fresh thyme, fresh coriander, lemon juice, black pepper, allspice, Caribbean seasoning (including mixes bound with vinegar), tomato ketchup, tomato paste and bottled hot sauces. Instead of coriander, some recipes suggest the Caribbean herb chadon beni, a kind of coriander on steroids. Scotch bonnet isn't just advocated for its fierceness—it has a fruitiness. You can reduce the heat by de-seeding the chilli and only using small amounts. Some recipes just specify a fruity hot sauce. Some involve cooking only a short while, others suggest until the red herring has softened.

The resulting stew or gravy can be served with Caribbean water crackers, fried green plantains, boiled bananas, yams, dumplings, johnny cakes (a thick cornmeal pancake), cou cou (a cornmeal and okra dumpling) and salads. Dumplings can be boiled or fried or boiled then fried. There's a Trinidadian recipe for red herring stir fry-stuffed dumplings, boiled and then added to a vegetable stir fry (see first image section). Highly recommended, there are recipes online.

Alternatively, if you're in more of a West African mood, you could go for a deeply warming red herring jollof rice.

COOPERAGE

James Watt, interviewed for David Butcher's *Following the Fishing* (1987), recalled the year of 1912, when his employers, W. Slater & Sons, cured 100,000 barrels of herring. Each will have been branded, specifying and guaranteeing its contents, as well as ensuring it would not be reused (although the lack of a home market for salted herring will also have helped in this regard). A skilled cooper could turn out around seventy a week: curing companies employed many coopers. (See first image section.)

Barrels were standardised at 32 gallons, to hold a cran of herring (notionally 1,200 or a long thousand of fish, but dependent on size—see **Measuring the Herring**). The herrings were allowed to settle in the pickle before the barrel was topped up to make the required number. In the nineteenth and twentieth centuries they were generally made of imported Scandinavian spruce, although larch and birch were both also used traditionally. The barrel's staves, which had to be ½" thick and closely fitted, were cut and planed to size, moistened, heated and shaped. The hoops which bound the barrels had originally been made of a flexible wood, but over the nineteenth century this was replaced by steel—initially just for the top and the bottom ones, but eventually for all of them.

Pliny the Elder suggests barrels were developed by the Alpine Gauls and the Celtic tribes in that area, who were using them around 350 BCE, although the Egyptians were drawing on the same construction principle to make tubs over 2,000 years earlier, leaving plenty of time for the completed article to have been imagined.

Sealing salted herring from exposure to the air is an essential part of the preservation process and, as the range and ambition of the trade grew, the barrel became a signifier of its contents. The difficulty with all air-tight containers is that they can also mask giveaway smells. Both at Scania (see **Danish Fisheries**) and in the **Dutch Fisheries**, they developed quality control regulations to ensure their products were consistent, their branding enabling direct attribution of responsibility for the contents and a system of compensation across extensive trade areas. The barrel also enabled the factory ship processing of the long voyage Dutch herring buss. Red herring did not require barrelling to extend its shelf life, but it was still usually transported in barrels—a practice extended for kippers well into the twentieth century (see **Monkey Business**).

Smaller barrels and casks were used in the grocery trade, where customers wanted to store their herring at home and these developed an iconic quality in Jewish culture. Less aesthetically pleasing but nevertheless functional, the plastic tubs holding whole salt herrings in Eastern European grocers are the descendants of these small barrels.

A dual-use herring barrel was developed in the early years of the Soviet Union. If you are ever in Vardø, a small Norwegian fishing town not far from the Russian border, I'd strongly recommend a visit to Pomor Museum, which celebrates the relationship of the coastal peoples of both countries. In the socialist enthusiasm following the Russian Revolution, Vardø's postmaster led the town's own revolutionary cell with the support of a tall, blond political organiser sent by Lenin himself. To hasten the coming of the Socialist Republic of Finnmark the Soviets sent propaganda leaflets to Vardø in the bottoms of herring barrels. The postmaster's cell was less keen on Stalin and eventually dropped the plans for revolution, but the museum proudly celebrates its barrels.

DANISH FISHERIES

With North Sea and Baltic coastlines, the Skagerrak, the Kattegat and the Sound, Denmark was made for herring glory. There have been ups and downs and it's still a major herring nation, but it'd be hard for any nation to compete for significance with what is generally known as the Scania Fishery.

Danish peoples and the herring go back together over 5,000 years (see **Archaeology**) although the details of the relationship over most of this era remain vague. Christianity only joined them in the tenth century and soon after this herring numbers declined —God testing his people with the reduced plankton levels of a two-century long Medieval Warm Period (see **Atlantic Herring**/Feeding and **X Formerly Known**). He was widely credited, anyway, for the Scanian explosion of herring numbers in the late twelfth century, thought to be a miracle of the age. 'There are so many fish in the Sound that the ships can hardly use their rudders and one can catch them with the hand alone, without the use of instrument,' wrote Danish historian Saxo Grammaticus (c 1160–c 1220). God subsequently also took credit for the perceived decline in the fifteenth and sixteenth centuries.

The phenomenon Saxo described wasn't merely a glut, but a vast number of herrings magnified in the confined waters of the Sound. The account, with its miraculous aura, may or may not have heralded the herrings' return (there have been debates amongst later historians) but for **Herringism** it enabled a neatly structured episode in their books, Scania: the beginning, middle and end of the world's first great industrial-scale herring fishery.

Woodcut from *History of the Northern People*, by Olaus Magnus, 1555. The halberd demonstrates the sheer mass of the shoal supporting it—and how co-operative they are being in remaining so still. (Alamy.)

SCANIA

The Scania herring fair ran from August 15th to October 9th. The county of Skåne forms the southern tip of Sweden, a region which was then part of Denmark. The salt herring produced was initially traded by the Vikings on the extensive trade routes, which were later largely taken over by the German Hanse. The Hanse was only beginning to come together in the twelfth century, but, from early on, it controlled the supply of salt from Lüneberg. In the presence of so many herrings, this gave it leverage. A network or federation of cities, as it grew, the Hanse's inland membership also helped deliver overland trade routes to Southern Europe. Scania was Denmark's fishery, however. The Danes collected the taxes and wrote the *Motbok*, which set out the fishery's constantly-proliferating rules and which was read out in its entirety before each season was allowed to begin.

There was herring fishing in and around the Sound before Scania and Danish fishermen had their own curing sites, but twenty-six Hanseatic cities, from modern day Germany, The Netherlands, Poland, Russia and Switzerland, had *vitten* or gutting and curing lots on the Skåne coast. The *Motbok* insisted on all catches being sold to licensed processors. At some point in the eleventh century, Denmark's kings had lost their lordship over Danish seas and fishing itself couldn't be taxed. Landing was another matter.

DEMAND SIDE FACTORS

The Scania fishery coincided with rising demand for marine fish in Northern Europe. While it may be explained by other reasons, it was significantly driven by the idiosyncrasy of Roman Catholic **Fasting**, which allowed, encouraged and then almost insisted upon the eating of fish on fast days. A cynic could suggest ecclesiastical taxes might have played some part in this. Demand had begun to increase from the ninth century, but around the year 1000, with what recent historians have called the Fish Horizon Event, things really took off. Herring population levels may have been depressed, but European population levels were also low. Caught in such large numbers, the cheapness of preserved herring enabled the Catholic church to base its mortification of the flesh on something tastier than turnips.

You can dry oily fish, especially if you have cold, dry winds, but salt helps to make the product less pungent. The manufacture of sea salt is made easier by warm, dry and windy coastlines but in the twelfth century there was salt production on the Danish island of Laesø, based on saline groundwater, which is more concentrated than sea water. These days, Laesø salt serves a gourmet market, but it may not have been quite as fancy then. There are no salt deposits in Sweden. The shift in production scale, however, necessitated huge quantities of the stuff. The salt processed at Lüneberg may not have been perfect, but at the time it was better than most and there was plenty of it.

HANSEATIC FACTORS

The Hanse did not bring only salt to the table. The Vikings were great traders too and recent evidence shows they had already been trading herring for over 400 years. The Hanse, however, was run by merchants and it maintained an admirable focus on their interests. Its network was largely in the Holy Roman Empire, subject to the Emperor and a host of kings, princes and dukes, but the money it generated allowed it to develop as an alternative model to the simultaneously emerging nation state. Growing out of German merchant settlements in the Wendish lands of the Baltic, the Hanse protected its own, challenged arbitrary power, bribed or threatened princes, insisted on favourable trade conditions, imposed and maintained monopolies. If necessary, it would go to war. Members dropped in and out as some balked at the rules, responded to pressure from their princes or negotiated trade deals of their own, but at one time or another around two hundred towns and cities were part of it. London's Steelyard was one of its settlements.

Lübeck, itself only founded in the mid-twelfth century, stood at its heart as the network began to emerge a century later, a kind of administrative capital among equals. Along with neighbouring Rostock, Stralsund and Stettin to the East, it was involved in the Rügen or Greifswald Bay fishery, a major herring spawning ground with salt spring proximity. It was Lübeck, in partnership with Hamburg to the West, which controlled the trade routes from Lüneberg.

Denmark identified the Lübeck problem early on and captured a *Who's Who* of its merchants when they were visiting the Scania herring fair in 1201. The Danes went on to conquer and control Lübeck, but in 1226 the Holy Roman Emperor declared it a Free Imperial City. Money may have changed hands. In the shifting and uneasy balance of power the parties gradually came to an acccommodation. A second Danish-

Hanseatic War was concluded in 1370 with the Treaty of Stralsund: if it favoured the members of the Hanse, this was because they had won.

Herringists have promoted a picture of a Danish crown controlling the fishery and taking the taxes, whilst Lübeck and the Hanse controlled curing and trade, but this is a misrepresentation. In *The Medieval Herring Fishery in the Western Baltic* (2008) Carsten Jahnke argues forcefully that while the Germans also fished, the Danes also traded. Historical revision has been hampered, because during World War II, the Nazis, who were keen on German Hanseatic history, decided to put its records down a salt mine in what became East German Saxony-Anhalt. Some key records are still in Siberia.

THE SCANIAN FISHERY

The relative importance of the Rügen fishery declined in the face of Scanian numbers. Based on current analysis of the relevant herring stock, the Scania fishery was a mixed population and its major component was the population which spawns near Rügen. There, the herring shoals will have been in peak condition, whereas the Sound and the Western Baltic provided feeding grounds for their post-spawning recovery. There were local spawning populations too, but, in any quality consideration spawning herrings trump feeding ones. In compensation, herring spend longer at their feeding grounds than they do spawning.

Together with the local spawners, the herring presented critical mass and it was an early example of mass production prioritised over taste. At the same time, Scania grew on the organisational model provided by Rügen's experience. Fishermen's camps or *fiskelejer* spread out along the foreshore and, behind them, the curing station pitches for the Hanseatic cities were parcelled out. There were a number of herring fairs, where fish and other goods were traded, but the main one was at Skanör, on the small peninsula facing the Danish mainland. In the fifteenth century, with the fishery beginning to decline, it transferred to nearby Falsterbo.

In 1375, along with Rome, Venice, Pisa and Florence, Lübeck was named by Emperor Charles IV as one of the five glories of the Holy Roman Empire. Its pitch at Skanör was less glorious, but, as well as fish processing, it had space for a church, a cemetery and its own executioner. The *vitten* were effectively small colonies for their home towns, each of which was run according to home town laws. It is worth noting that ten of the twenty-six towns were in the Netherlands. The Dutch loved herring even then, but the scale of their involvement in Scania was to play a significant role in their later rise as a herring power.

The fishing was usually conducted from undecked boats, which could hold up to two herring lasts. Depending on their size, you got roughly 12,000 herrings to the last. The boats were crewed by between three and six men, who used drift nets. Beyond the fishermen, thousands came to work at Skanör in the season. As became standard with onshore curing, women did the gutting, salting and packing. As well as those of the Danes and the Hanse, boats were drawn from Norway, England, Scotland, Wales and elsewhere, but these fishermen were *vitten*-less.

Unsurprisingly there were attempts to evade the insistence on selling catches to the licensed processors—foreigners at the Yarmouth Herring Fairs enjoyed more freedom. Specifically the Scots, English and Welsh were forbidden from salting the herring they'd caught and in 1470 English involvement in the fishery was prohibited altogether. In the fourteenth century, at least 10,000 boats were involved; by 1400 there were around 900 herring merchants in Lübeck alone. The town imported in the region of 65,000 registered barrels annually, while overall production in Scania reached close to 300,000 barrels a year.

Danish taxes and privileges were significant: for one day a week the catches could only be bought by the Danish crown; fishermen were taxed for use of the foreshore (in 1520, it was 10% of the catch plus a boatload at the start of the season). There was an additional tax of ten pfennigs per last for foreigners and five for Danes. As the fishery grew, Lübeck opened up salt mines at Oldesloe and took control of the salt springs on the Pomeranian coast, but by the late fourteenth century they were importing Bay salt from Bourgneuf on the French Atlantic Coast. The quality advantages of sun and wind-dried production were increasingly recognised and if you were trading further and further south anyway, it made sense.

Salt and salting procedures were strictly controlled, as was barrel size. Barrel branding acted as a quality guarantee (see **Cooperage**) and Jahnke talks of how this gave Scanian herring preferred purchase status across the Hanseatic network.

DECLINE

Herring fairs in the Middle Ages were viewed as modern equivalents to Sodom and Gomorrah. God was seen as acting with good cause. In *De harengo* (1654), written in Lübeck, Paul **Neucrantz** writes, 'as stated in the Annals of that time, numbers had seriously declined on the Scania shore, which was God's judgement on its licentious Herring Fair.'

Edgar March, in *Sailing Drifters* (1952), dates the disappearance of the Scanian shoals very specifically to 1425. Jahnke, who has gone through the records, notes there were bad catches that year and in several others during the fifteenth century. He identifies a decline from a peak in the 1370s, but he also points to the herring fairs continuing right up until Sweden occupied Scania in 1658. Neucrantz talks of the infrastructure of Lübeck's little Scanian colony having been neglected for many years, but Jahnke puts paid to the herringist narrative. For him the main cause of the decline was 'the policies of the Wendish Hanseatic cities around Lübeck which attempted to keep their competitors from the North Sea and the Baltic away from the fairs, which caused the fairs to lose their significance as an international clearing house.' He points out that, after 1425, there were still plenty of herrings being caught in the Western Baltic— and that there were also plenty there before things took off in the twelfth century.

'Centuries of data demonstrate that herring stocks in the Sound were at a stable level as a general rule; this level sufficed for the demands of the merchants serving the European markets.' In the twentieth century the narrative of departing shoals saw a range of scientific explanations, but Jahnke argues 'the rise and fall of the fairs of Scania had no biological basis': the complex of economic and political explanations for what was a much slower decline would be more than enough. To a certain extent it depends on what you consider *biological*, but Jahnke challenges the way in which, for Scania, the herring's legendary fickleness was being uniquely projected over a timespan of centuries.

Scanian fishermen would not have seen their herring catches as coming from different populations (see **Grand Migration**). In a developing market, any problems with one population might have been compensated within the wider resource. Fishermen and fish curers do not welcome gluts because they depress markets. Individual boats may celebrate when they catch more than others, but in the end (in the absence of **Reduction Plants**) they will work to the available market. Medieval data will reveal particularly bad years but may be less effective in picturing individual population fluctuations.

BIOLOGICAL FACTORS: A WIDER CONTEXT

The phenomenon Saxo describes has enough form to have been captured on camera. It has a name: *stimenbildung*. Concentrated herring shoals can appear as a kind of boiling of the water. The shape of the Sound would have naturally concentrated a glut and made it miraculous. Helped by Saxo's great history of the Danes, *Gesta Danorum*, word will have spread.

Jahnke links the Scania, Rügen and Bohuslän fisheries in an interactive relationship. At least from the sixteenth century Bohuslän experienced thirty to sixty year 'herring periods' in which the mixed herring populations of the Southern North Sea are drawn into the Skaggerak and Kattegat and also come down into the Sound.

The Medieval Warm Period might have depressed herring numbers. 'Linking individual physiological indicators to the productivity of fish populations: A case study of Atlantic herring' (Moyano, Illing *et al.*, 2020) looks specifically at the Rügen spring spawners. Both in the laboratory and in Greifswald Bay itself the larvae reacted badly to warmer water, which induces heart arrhythmia. The authors picture recent climate change as depressing numbers in this way. Proportions may have changed, but 'Distribution, Density and Abundance of the Western Baltic herring in the Sound' (2000) by Rasmus Nielsen and others identifies these as providing 75% of current populations in the Sound between August and March: having spawned, they migrate there for feeding.

There are also factors associated with marine water coming into the Baltic from the North Sea. Temperature, wind and nutrient load can deplete oxygen levels in the Sound, particularly from August to October. In 'The effects of periodic marine inflow into the Baltic Sea on the migration patterns of Western Baltic spring-spawning herring' (2014), Tanja Miethe *et al.* suggest low oxygen levels may trigger early autumn migrations away from the Sound and into the Arkona Sea (between Scania and Rügen). This was in the fishery's range, but the time and effort involved in locating and bringing catches to shore from more distant and wider waters will have affected the economics.

The dates of the Skanör herring fair, presumably constructed around maximum convenient average catches, would mean much of the haul would have been recovering spents. At the beginning of the Scania season this proportion would not have recovered all that much. However well salted and quality controlled, they are not as desirable as spawners. From the early fifteenth century the Dutch were catching the large spawning population off the Shetlands, capturing the market nearly two months earlier with fatter fish. Neucrantz, who was familiar with the delights of both Dutch and Rügen spawners, is clear on the value of spents: 'Weak and dry, these herrings are only suitable for the lower orders.'

DUTCH FACTORS

There were regular struggles within the Hanse. In the 1390s the Dutch were prevented from Hanseatic participation by Duke Albert of Bavaria. Both Dutch-Hanseatic and Dano-Hanseatic wars were fought in the 1420s and 30s over Dutch access to the Eastern Baltic trade. In the end, the merchants of Lübeck found that they were as happy to make their profits on Dutch herring as Denmark was to tax it as it came into the Baltic.

The **Dutch Fisheries** were working North Sea stocks made accessible through their own factory ships. Their season now lasted six to eight months—three to four times as long as Scania's—and they had no need to pay the taxes of other nations. Barring the Dutch from Scanian access will have encouraged their pursuit of alternative herring sources, but only alongside other persuasive logics. Having learned much of what they needed from Hanseatic participation, the Dutch also turned out to be in a class of their own as marketeers (see **Beuckel** and **Dutch Fisheries**).

Political, economic and biological factors are hopelessly entangled. The Scanian fishery did not come to a halt in 1425, but in 'Catches & Manpower in the Danish Fisheries c 1200–1995' (1996) Poul Holm notes, 'Catches seem to have been decreasing throughout the fifteenth century.' Later, he writes:

> In the 1560s, fishermen from the town of Helsingør (Elsinore) gathered at the traditional time of the Sound autumn fisheries and set sail for Norway instead. Along with them came fishermen from practically all other towns on East Denmark. Quite possibly, the Sound fisheries by this time were so poor that the fishermen sought new grounds.

The Norwegian herring fishery, at the time, was focused on Bohuslän (then part of Norway, which was in a union with Denmark). Between the influxes of North Sea and Bohuslän herring, regardless of how far Scanian populations might have declined, the importance of the Scanian fishery declined further.

AFTER SCANIA

In 'Danish Fisheries, c 1450–1800' (2001) Poul Holm and Maibritt Bager write, 'There is no single explanation for the contraction of Danish fisheries in the late sixteenth and early seventeenth centuries.' They offer a complex of economic and environmental possibilities: falling fish prices, reduced investment, post-Reformation reduced fish-eating, Dutch competition, Bohuslän *periodicity*, the decline of herring stocks in the Sound, shifts in preferred spawning grounds taking shoals beyond the reach of a small boat fishery and the temporary collapse of the Limfjord's brackish-water herring population (a storm, which breached the barrier with the North Sea, led to the influx of higher salinity seawater).

Strangely, Holm and Bager don't mention the wrath of God, notwithstanding the apparent **Prophecy**, written in what seemed like Gothic script on the sides of two herrings caught in 1587. If it was, as some thought, a warning of Danish herring fishery decline, it proved broadly correct. There were rallies and collapses but, in general, things just bumped along. Bohuslän glut periods returned, notably in the second half of the eighteenth century, but by then Bohuslän was Swedish. The herring Denmark exported mostly went to Lübeck and Gothenburg. 1825 saw another great storm affecting the Limfjord herring population, compounded by fishermen using trawling methods which damaged the spawning grounds.

With its history of experimentation with seine net technologies and with the investment that came after the Second World War, the purse seine and echo locator were widely adopted in Denmark's pelagic fishing. Together with Norway, Iceland and several other North Sea fishing nations, Denmark contributed significantly to the spectacular collapses of North Sea and Atlantic herring populations in the 1960s and 70s. When stock management approaches had improved (and when the herring populations had largely recovered) Denmark and Norway led the way in renewed exploitation with their new generation pelagic trawlers.

Where has God been in all of this? It is a good question. Damage to herring scales by trawl-based fishing may well have left any number of Gothic script prophecies unread, but, with Denmark's modern pelagic fleet, more than 100,000 tons are annually landed in Skagen, justifying its claims to be Northern Europe's most important herring port.

DOCUMENTARY

Given the long-standing national decline of British herring eating, the impact the fish has had in the history of British documentary is remarkable. Herring fishing itself was once considered remarkable and documentary-makers are drawn ineluctably to the imperatives of decline and disappearance. That the herring's role is rarely remarked upon by historians of documentary is because they each tend to restrict themselves to the single medium of their academic competence. Knowing even less about herring than they do about other academic disciplines probably also helps.

PHOTOGRAPHY
Fishermen & Women of the Firth of Forth, Hill and Adamson.

David Octavius Hill and Robert Adamson announced their intention to publish photographs of the fishing community of Newhaven in 1844: fewer than ten years after the invention of photography and eighty years before documentary photography became a thing. Hill was a painter; Adamson had been taught the process of creating calotypes by his brother. Fox Talbot himself had only introduced the new method to the market in 1841. Fascinated by the chemistry of it, Adamson had set himself up as a photographer in 1843.

This was the year of *The Disruption*, when the Free Church of Scotland broke away from the Auld Kirk. Hill had been commissioned to paint its First General Assembly: a group portrait of the 450 dissenting ministers as they signed the Act of Separation and Deed of Demission. Each one needed to be recognisable: he approached Adamson.

Excited by the possibilities, the two became partners. Calotypes worked best with outside light and they collaborated on images covering a range of subjects, including architecture, distinguished Scotchmen, Highland characters and costumes. Hill was drawn to the distinctive dresses of the Newhaven fishing community, although it might not have been entirely to do with the light and dark stripes of the fisherwomen's skirts.

Selling from their baskets, the fisherwomen were part of the sights and sounds of Edinburgh and had already given rise to the popular song, **Caller Herrin'**. Their menfolk caught fish all year round. They were fishwives and fisher lasses not the **Herring Lasses**, who were a slightly later phenomenon. They were strongly associated with the herring, and among them there were noted beauties, who were often still called lasses after they were married.

To be fair to Hill and Adamson, they were as diligent in their portraits of the menfolk. Fishing communities were tight-knit, well used to dealing with any misunderstandings around the necessary independence of their womenfolk. Picturesque images of the working classes became one of the key early tropes of photography, but *The Fishermen and Women of the Firth of Forth* goes further than much which came after. It portrayed a culture. Calotypes were produced from paper negatives; exposure times required poses. Following the fishermen to sea wasn't an option, but the body of work shows a functioning community, secure in its own identity. It is now recognised as the first social documentary project.

Adamson was the cameraman; Hill brought his painterly eye to composition, posing the subjects with a view to structure, light and imagery. Documentary has never excluded posed pictures and often reflected complexity of vision. Jeannie Wilson was already a fisherman's wife and one of the community's noted beauties. The photograph of her with her friend Annie Linton seems to inhabit a slightly different artistic world from the others (see first image section). The traditionally suggestive oyster shells, scattered at their feet, look deliberate—they do not appear prominently in the other photographs. The way Jeannie gently prods one of the four fat fishes, which lie temptingly on the lid of the basket; the way Annie looks on... The aesthetically pleasing indistinctness of calotypes makes it hard to say with confidence whether Jeannie is prodding herrings or small haddocks—I'd say haddocks, but, as far as I'm aware, historians of photography have never even raised the question. The photograph later acquired the name, *They Were Twa Bonnie Lasses*.

Nothwithstanding all the pictures Adamson had taken for him, it took Hill until 1866 to complete *The First General Assembly of the Free Church of Scotland*. It is possible his artistic eye was easily distracted. Adamson, who had never enjoyed good health, sadly died in 1848 at the age of twenty-six.

FILM
Drifters, John Grierson.

Scottish film director and producer John Grierson coined the term documentary to describe the nature and value of film in capturing observed behaviour in the *real world*. He was writing a review of Robert Flaherty's Samoa-set *Moana* (1926), which, like its predecessor *Nanook of the North*, used 'real people', even though this was in staged recreations of cultural rituals which, for the most part, had disappeared. People often assume documentary claims an objectivity in its presentation of reality, but the vision of filmmaking which began to formulate in Grierson's mind, rather than this, had been one of film narrative constructed out of captured actuality and focused on contemporary working lives.

Grierson was working in the United States. He was inspired by Flaherty, but he'd been even more inspired by Sergei Eisenstein, particularly *Battleship Potemkin* (1925). Filled with his vision of documentary, he came back to a Britain where Eisenstein's work had been banned as communist propaganda. Grierson was of the Left, although he was imagining a more 'British', slightly less heroic style than Eisenstein's. He did, however, want one which derived its rhythms from the modernist energy of the Soviet filmmaker's montage techniques. This vision delivered *Drifters* (1929), a story about the North Sea herring fishing, the first film to be called a documentary and the spark for what was to become the British Documentary Movement. It is the only feature documentary for which Grierson takes full directorial credit, but it would be hard to overstate its importance in the development of British film.

Drifters projects a romantic heroism in the herring fisherman (it is far less concerned with curing or the market), but compared to Flaherty and Eisenstein, it exudes diffidence. Driven by the tension between tradition and the machine age, the film focuses mostly on the boats, the crew, nets and catch. It sets the details of passing on traditions through the avuncular relationship between the men and a young apprentice, juxtaposing this with montage sequences of the steamer's engine, the herring shoal and its other predators. Grierson shot the shoal in a research tank and the herrings look vaguely bemused. Technically, underwater camerawork was possible at this time, but he was working to a tight budget.

Herrings may not have been at the front of Grierson's mind when he'd taken his vision to the Empire Marketing Board's Stephen Tallents. Amongst its other activities, the EMB supported film production as *background publicity*—soft marketing. It promoted the work of government agencies and products which the government wanted people to buy. Sadly, more-or-less the entire budget for that year had been given to Rudyard Kipling to produce *One Family* (1930, Walter Creighton) in which a boy, in a dream, gathers the ingredients of the King's Christmas pudding from all corners of that happy family of nations, the British Empire.

If Tallents couldn't fund Grierson's vision, he knew somebody who just might. The Financial Secretary to the Treasury, Arthur M. Samuel (see **Herringism**) was the author of *The Herring; Its Effect on the History of Britain* (1918). Patriotically engaged, Samuel's loosely-connected compendium of beautiful herring information was itself prime EMB territory. You can almost hear Tallents asking, 'Can it be a

DOCUMENTARY

Still from *Drifters*, John Grierson, 1929. (Alamy)

film about herrings?' and Grierson's reply, 'I've been waiting all my life to make a film about herrings!'

Samuel had published his book at a time of herring optimism, an imagined return to the glories of the pre-war fishery. Undercut in the key markets for British salt herring, moves were already underway to set up the **Herring Industry Board**. Grierson, the Empire Marketing Board and Arthur Samuel were a *ménage à trois* made in Heaven and Grierson got £3,000 to make his film.

Drifters was premiered at The Tivoli on November 10th 1929 in a double bill with *Battleship Potemkin*, which British audiences were at last being allowed to watch. Ralph Bond, a filmmaker who joined Grierson's celebrated GPO Film Unit in the mid 1930s, recalled the impact:

Everybody thought Potemkin, of course, would get all the headlines and that Drifters would be regarded as something that was shown, but not much talked about. Well, the contrary happened. Actually, all the critics who were there, the press people and so forth, were absolutely astounded when they saw Drifters. They realised that this was a new type of filmmaking, a new type of themes for filmmaking and there was tremendous excitement and Drifters was an instantaneous success. And it was because of that success that the government department decided that they would develop the GPO Film Unit—or the EMB Film Unit as it then was. And that's how the thing developed very rapidly—on the success of Drifters.

(*The ACTT Interviews*, AmberSide Collection)

RADIO

Singing the Fishing, Ewan MacColl, Charles Parker, Peggy Seeger.

By the 1950s documentary was an established creative option. *Singing the Fishing* wasn't the first radio documentary. Nor was it even the first in the series of eight *Radio Ballads* developed for the BBC Home Service between 1958 and 1964. It was the third and it was broadcast on August 16th 1960. For a full account of the *Radio Ballads*, it is well worth reading Peter Cox's *Set Into Song* (2008). *Singing the Fishing* is the best and not just because it celebrates the herring (although that helps). The innovation and insistent energy of the *Radio Ballads* resulted from several factors and they first came together in this one.

In the 1930s the American folklorist Alan Lomax had heroically carried huge pieces of kit up hill and down dale to record traditional singers and musicians. In the early 40s he'd developed the folk-music-and-stories radio series *Back Where I Came From* with Nicholas Ray—who went on to make such great films as *Johnny Guitar*, *Rebel Without a Cause* and *The True Story of Jesse James*. The 1940s saw the introduction of the portable tape recorder in US radio, but it was the following decade which saw its more widespread use, opening up the creative possibilities of radio 'actuality'.

In 1950 Lomax had moved to the UK, partly to escape the attentions of Senator McCarthy's House Un-American Activities Committee, but there were already early BBC documentary experimentalists such as the frequent collaborators Philip Donnellan and Charles Parker, both engaged with traditional music and both exploring the richness of unmediated working class voices. Ewan MacColl had come out of Salford, the 1930s theatre activism of the socialist Clarion Cycling Club and its work with the unemployed. He set up the Theatre Workshop with Joan Littlewood in 1946 and, particularly inspired by Lomax, he moved increasingly towards traditional music, becoming a leading figure in Britain's post-war folk revival.

The young American folk singer Peggy Seeger, daughter of Charles, sister to Pete and Mike, had grown up at the heart of the American folk movement and came to the United Kingdom to transcribe music for Lomax. In 1956 she met MacColl and they fell in love. Traditional song, which has always performed a documentary function, was suddenly central to an experimentation in how you could collect and tell British working people's stories in the new age of mass communication.

MacColl had first heard Norfolk traditional singer and ex-fisherman Sam Larner on radio programmes made by Donnellan. When you listen to *Singing the Fishing* it's hard not to feel the degree to which the participating, recorded 'speakers' join the production as equals: it is their narrative as much as it is that of the documentary makers. Larner (the first singing voice you hear) was one of the great singers upon whom the post-war folk revival drew. Already in his 80s, he had gone to the fishing as a boy in the early 1890s.

Another speaker, Ronnie Balls, was a Yarmouth ex-fisherman, who'd served on World War I Royal Navy minesweepers and is credited with being one of the first to have seen the potential of echo-locators in the fishing industry. The voices in *Singing the Fishing* span British herring history from sail to steam and through to the transformations of modern technology; from East Anglia to the Moray Firth;

from the pre-World War I glory days to the symptoms of contemporary herring population collapse.

MacColl, who together with Parker recorded the fishing community voices, wrote the programme's songs out of their stories, phrases and rhythms, shaping most around the narrative of Larner's life. Parker and MacColl had gone back to their interviewees and, in new recordings, pushed them further, to get the performative energy they wanted. As documentary relationships develop, sources can sometimes offer their stories gift-wrapped. There are moments in *Singing the Fishing* when Larner is dramatising his own memories for the tape recorder.

In *Singing the Fishing* the weaving of MacColl's songs with the testimony of the fishermen and women, with the actuality recordings of the fishing and of the auctioneer, is all seamlessly edited. One of the remarkable aspects of the studio recording process was that each section was done live, the singers responding to the voices played into the studio floor: record, repeat, record, repeat until it was right.

In 1972 Donellan made a film version, blending the radio programme with film from *Drifters*, *North Sea* (Cavalcanti, 1938) and **Caller Herrin'**. He used montages of photographs and other still imagery, used some of his own earlier footage and added new footage and interviews. Updating it more fully to encompass the over-exploitation of the herring populations, he also wanted to home in on the exploitation of the fishermen. It is great—he was a great documentary filmmaker—but it loses some of the energy and structural integrity of the radio ballad as it drifts away from a celebration of fishermen and women's lives as they themselves saw things.

DRIED HERRING

There are references to dried herring in some older herring books, usually in relation to the Vikings. Some commentators suggest this may refer to an early smoked cure—not least because its oil content makes the herring hard to dry. In *The Scots Kitchen* (1929), however, F. Marian McNeill quotes Martin Martin (Màrtainn MacGille Mhàrtainn) in *A Description of the Western Islands* (1703):

> The Natives preserve and dry their Herring without Salt, for the space of eight months, provided they be taken after the tenth of September; they use no other art in it, but take out their Guts, and then, tying a rush about their Necks, hang them by pairs upon a rope made of Heath, cross a House, and they eat well, and free from Putrefaction.

The timing is important, because after spawning the oil content goes down considerably. For the main herring fishing in Scottish waters spawning has been completed by September 10th (see **X Formerly Known as**). The taste for dried herring continued in the Scottish Highlands and Islands mostly in fishing families. On the boats, sun-dried on the deck, it seems to have provided a snack alternative to boiled herriing (see **Ring Net Struggle**).

Meanwhile, hung on wooden frames, dried herring continues to be produced in the curing traditions of Alaska's and British Columbia's indigenous communities such as the Tlingit and the Haida. A half-dried herring, *gwamegi* or *billfish*, is produced in South Korea. Most are sold filleted, but they also do a whole, ungutted version, *tongmari*, which sells to local aficionados. The Japanese never miss out on anything to do with fish and they do lots of things with dried herring. West Coast indigenous peoples, South Koreans, Japanese and Filipinos are all eating dried **Pacific Herring** (*Clupea pallasii*, see **Atlantic Herring**, **Svetovidov** and **Taxonomy**).

Special mention should be made of the Filipino dish *Champorado*. The word itself started life as a Mexican cornmeal and chocolate drink, but the Spaniards took it to the Philippines, where there was no tradition of growing corn. They began to mix their chocolate (*tablea*—roasted and ground cacao made into tablets) with sticky rice instead, creating a kind of porridge which today they sweeten with evaporated milk. However tempting that may sound, just as it is, one day a Filipino genius came up with the idea of adding fried, dried, salty herring: *Champorado* with *tuyo*. Tuyo can be a range of fried, dried, salty fish, but herring is considered the best.

You boil your sticky rice, melt the *tablea* into it (cocoa or unsweetened dark chocolate can be substituted), ladle it in the bowl and add a swirl of evaporated milk. Fry your *tuyo* until it's crisp and lay up to three whole ones on top or break the fish over it like Bombay duck over a curry. You can buy *tuyo* and *tablea* online. Apparently, it is the Filipino breakfast of choice.

DUMAS, ALEXANDRE

A friend sent scans of the Herring entry from Alexandre Dumas' *Dictionary of Cuisine*, as translated and abridged by Louis Colman (1964). Growing up, I'd read all the *Musketeer* novels, then *The Count of Monte Cristo* and *The Black Tulip*. I knew nothing of his encyclopaedic dictionary. Online I tracked down the digitised French original.

Dumas was a generous man. In the slightly straightened circumstances of his final years, he'd given us *Le Grand Dictionnaire de Cuisine* (having reduced it to 288 pages, Colman also abridged the title). Complete with introductions, letters, menus and appendices, the original comes in at 1,208 pages. In 1978 the great Alan Davidson (who wrote the fish Bible *North Atlantic Seafood*), together with his wife Jane, gave us their selections in *Dumas on Food* (327 pages). Since the first edition, which appeared posthumously in 1873, even in French no one had ever republished it in full. An original would set you back £1,500 or so, but digitisation has now made it available in all the glory of online and print on-demand editions.

His full name was Alexandre Dumas Davy de la Pailleterie, although there's debate as to whether he was permitted to use all of it. In Saint-Domingue, which in 1804 became Haiti, his father had been born to the enslaved Marie-Cessette Dumas and a French aristocrat. Alexandre had to deal with racism. His contemporary, the English playwright Watts Phillips said he was 'the most generous, large-hearted being in the world.'

> He was also the most delightfully amusing and egotistical creature on the face of the earth. His tongue was like a windmill—once set in motion, you never knew when he would stop, especially if the theme was himself.

Throughout *Le Grand Dictionnaire*, Phillips' description rings true. It's not always accurate. He borrows freely from others (at times verbatim and uncredited). He strangely misses out Mustard, but then, before publication and, apparently in response to an anonymous correspondent, he gives us a Study on Mustard as an appendix. Addressed at the top to *Maison Alexandre Bornibus, 60, Boulevard de La Villette, à Paris*, at 9 pages, it is witty, well-researched, eloquent and filled with joyous anecdotes. Only on page 9 does he confess he had never been that bothered about mustards until he'd tried those of M Bornibus, both the ones for men and those for ladies. A big-hearted advertorial is such a rare thing, you can't help smiling.

The Herring entry is heavily abridged by both Colman and the Davidsons, but the complete text of it gives a sense of Dumas' heroic intentions at their best.

DUMAS ON HERRING

Everyone knows the herring. I would even say there are few who dislike it. In life, it is green-backed, its sides and belly white; dead, the green turns blue. It is a child of The Pole. From its place of birth to the forty-fifth latitude, it can be found in every sea, from June 25th making what the Dutch call *the herring lightning*, shoals several leagues in length and breadth, so thick in the shallows they stifle each other in their thousands. Sometimes the nets they fill, not strong enough to lift the weight of them, tear and release the catch only half taken. Like the pillar of fire and smoke of the Hebrews, their migration may be followed day and night —at night by the phosphorescent glow they cast, in the day by the flocks of gulls which follow them, plunging every now and then and rising with a flash of silver in the beak. Whales, sharks, porpoises, tuna and sea bream follow them, all catching fish from the shoal and consuming them in enormous quantities.

According to Victor Meunier, Bloch has stated, from a single Swedish port more than seven million are taken annually; but the fecundity of this fish compensates for all the destruction of its progeny. Sixty-six thousand, six hundred and six eggs have been counted in a single female. On top of that, there are seven females for every two males.

While the cod fisheries have declined, the herring fisheries have become the most important of all. Le Havre, which once sent out up to forty cod fishing boats, this year sent only one. Eight hundred thousand people make their living in this industry; in Europe it's said to be worth close to four million francs.

It was a man called Bruckalz who invented the art of smoking herrings.

The finest of the fresh herring to be had in Paris comes from the Normandy coast; we describe below the ways in which they can be prepared.

Freshly salted herring should always come from Rotterdam or Enkhuizen, in Holland. It is cut into slices and eaten raw, with no more preparation than that of a salad. The finest smoked herring, the largest, fleshiest, most golden and best juniper-smoked are those of the Germuth smokehouses in Ireland.

Salt herring almost never appears on the tables of the rich, but in the lands where it abounds, it is of the utmost utility to workers and the poor. In some parts a very pleasant and appetizing fricassee is made of herring cut into small pieces and, without desalting, fried in lard with plenty of chopped, raw leeks, mixed with potatoes of a large and floury variety, previously boiled, along with a few sprigs of rosemary, in well-salted water.

Fresh herring is an excellent fish, which people would make considerably more fuss about if it were rare and expensive. Look for ones with red gills, shiny scales and well-rounded bellies: these are full. Herring is rarely eaten at its best, however, until the end of August or mid-September.

A bizarre custom involving the canons of Reims Cathedral survived until the sixteenth century. On Holy Wednesday, after Tenebrae, they would process to the Church of St Remy in twos, each dragging a herring on a string. Each canon would try to step on the herring of the one in front of him, while saving his own from the one behind. It was only possible to put an end to this extravagant custom by banning the procession.

As everyone knows, the herring fisheries are, financially, one of England's most productive industries. Vast quantities are exported to Italy for Holy Week. When Rome fell to the revolutionary French army and Pope Pius VI was obliged to leave, in London a member of the parliamentary committee responsible for the herring industry observed that, with the Pope chased out of Rome, Italy would presumably turn Protestant. "May God preserve us!" cried another. "Why? Would it upset you to see the number of good Protestants increase?" asked the first. "Not at all," came the reply, "but if there were no more Catholics, what would we do with our herring?"

There's this Gascon. He says, "If I were governor of a besieged town, I'd hold out against even the cruellest pangs of hunger." "I believe you, Sir," says his valet, "Look at how long you spend with nothing more on your plate than a smoked herring."

Fresh Herring with Mustard Sauce

Take 12 herrings. Remove the guts through the gills, scale, wipe and place in an earthenware dish, marinating them in oil with salt and sprigs of parsley. A quarter of an hour before serving, grill on both sides. Once they're cooked, place them on your dish and serve with a white butter sauce into which you have blended 1 tablespoon of fresh mustard. Other *sauces grasses* can be used. Served cold, you may use any oil-based dressing you consider appropriate.

Fresh Herring with Fennel

Split your herring down the back and brush with melted butter and salt. Wrap in fennel and grill and serve with a roux-based sauce into which you have blended finely chopped fennel leaves and stalks blanched in white wine.

Soft Herring Roes in the Pan

Take the milt or soft roes from around thirty herrings, blanch and drain them; place a knob of butter in a saucepan, with mushrooms, parsley, shallots and scallions, all finely chopped; salt, pepper and Spice Parisienne; simmer gently, then add the soft roes, letting them cook briefly in the mixture; you will have prepared a round or a square pan with a gratin at the bottom—fat or lean—about the width of half a finger deep, drizzle with oil and put it in the oven until the gratin is cooked; just before serving, add the soft roe mixture, degrease, dress with a reduced espagnole sauce, into which you have squeezed the juice of one lemon, and serve.

Fresh Herring Matelot

Put your herring in a saucepan with butter, parsley, mushrooms, scallions, a clove of garlic, 2 good glasses of Burgundy or Bordeaux, salt and pepper. Cook on a high flame, serve with its own sauce and garnish with fried croutons.

Salt Herring Hors d'Oeuvres

Clean a dozen herrings, remove their heads, tails and fins, skin them and place them on the stove in a pan of milk and water. When they're just cooked, drain and plate with slices of raw onion and Reinette apples. Serve with a marinade or a well-beaten vinaigrette and watercress.

Red Herring

Take five or six of these herrings and wipe them. Remove heads and tails. Cut them, head to tail along the backbone and open their backs. Place them on an earthenware dish, sprinkle with oil and let them marinate for a moment before grilling for five minutes, turning once. Plate and serve.

Red Herring à la Sainte-Menehould

Desalt in cream. Cook for 20 minutes in a Sainte-Menehould you have prepared as follows. In a saucepan mix an ounce of butter with flour and milk, parsley, scallions, garlic, thyme, bay leaf, basil, a little pepper. Add your herrings and cook. Remove and dip them in melted butter, then cook in a country oven until they take on a good colour. Serve on an olive oil remoulade.

Preparation of Red Herring for Good Use Later

Desalt in milk and then grill good Irish herrings; let them cool and remove the fillets to use later in sandwiches or served on toast with fresh butter; to serve as an hors d'oeuvre, dressed with fine oil and the juice of bitter oranges; to place on a bed of buttered noodles or lasagne, or of mashed potatoes, chestnuts, sweet potatoes or creamed white beans; to make a hash for an omelette or to serve in scrambled eggs, adding chopped picholine olives, semi-salted cream cheese, and a little walnut cordial; it makes for tasty and distinctive starters.

NOTES

i) See **Beuckel** for the fact that neither he nor *Bruckalz* invented herring smoking.

ii) The Davidsons suggest *Germouth* is Yarmouth, which, of course, isn't in Ireland but was famous for its red herring.

iii) The passage on the canons of Reims Cathedral and their **Processions** is lifted word for word from *Mme Clement's History of Civil and Religious Festivals, Ancient and Modern Customs of Flanders and a large number of French Towns* (1845). He omits the next paragraph in which she erroneously suggests its origin as a mockery of England's victory at the **Battle of the Herrings**. I like to think it was because he was saving it for an unwritten prequel in which D'Artagnan's ancestor saves Joan of Arc from being burned at the stake and takes her back to Gascony. The belly bump-off between Falstaff and Porthos' ancestor is one of world literature's great lost comic scenes.

iv) A good friend of Dumas and a collaborator on the book, Denis-Joseph Vuillemot, had been trained as a chef by Antonin Carême; his grandfather had been a British MP and may have been the original source of the story about the parliamentary committee of the late eighteenth century.

v) Neither Colman nor the Davidsons include the Gascon joke, even though D'Artagnan came from Gascony and shared the hot-headed boastfulness for which Gascons are stereotyped in French joke tradition.

DUMAS & HIS COOKERY BOOK

The Davidsons question how much Dumas cooked himself, although there are stories. There's a nice one of how he managed to make a magnificent meal out of the various random items his guests had brought. He loved playing host and the anecdotes, historical snippets and jokes of his *Grand Dictionnaire* provide an almost endless supply of material with which to entertain at any imaginable meal.

He's supposed to have thought of it as his magnum opus, the crowning glory to a career in which he claimed to have written around 500 works. This may have been just the kind of thing you say to encourage readers or your publisher and some might choose to stick with *The Count of Monte Cristo*, but he invested considerable time and planning into the project.

Dumas was in his late 60s and already ill when, in 1869, he took his books, his correspondence with Vuillemot and his research, decamping to Roscoff in Brittany to write his epic tome. You don't get to 500 works writing with the editorial care and precision of Flaubert. He'd had a cavalier attitude to facts in most of them and he was never going to hang about when he finally came to write this one. He sent the bulging manuscript to his publisher in early 1870. Sadly, the Franco-Prussian War and the events of the Paris Commune intervened. He died that December, never seeing the great work in print.

DUTCH FISHERIES

On the opening page of his *Short Description of the Herring Fishery in Holland* (1639) Mynert Semeyns states that the first Dutchman to have caught and eaten a herring did so in 1163 CE. Once upon a time, there was a healthy and distinct, inshore herring population in the **Zuiderzee**, so this should be taken with a pinch—even a barrelful—of salt. Marcus Zuerius van Boxhorn's *Town Atlas of Holland* (1634) has Dutch fishermen participating in the Danish herring fairs in Scania before the end of the twelfth century and they seem to have been at the Yarmouth Herring Fair long before that.

Through their *Groote Visserye* or Grand Fishery, the Dutch became top herring nation before—having gained independence from the Holy Roman Empire—they became a nation. In English, for many years, the great source of information on this was Anthony Beaujon's *The History of Dutch Sea Fisheries: Their Progress, Decline and Revival, Especially in Connection with the Legislation in Earlier and Later Times* (1884).

Written for London's Great International Fisheries Exhibition the previous year, it tells the story of a great industry, built on quality control and strangled by regulation. Bo Poulsen's *Dutch Herring, an environmental history, c 1600–1860* (2008) contains fewer stories but brings a remarkable analysis of the statistics: the great advantage of being strangled by regulation is the paper trail it leaves.

INNOVATION

Amsterdam, Den Briel, Dordrecht, Elburg, Hardervijk, 's-Hertogenbosch, Kampen, Stavoren, Zierikzee, Zutphen and Zwolle had all been part of the Holy Roman Empire, as well as signed-up members of the Hanse with their own curing sites at the Scania fishery. They all fell within the borders of what would become the Dutch Republic. For over 200 years, they'd learned everything there was there to learn from the Scania experience. The complex of reasons for their disengagement are discussed in **Danish Fisheries**, but having discovered the extent of the herring resource off Shetland and Scotland—in addition to the herring fisheries they already knew off Eastern England—they brought to the opportunity a deep understanding of the Hanse's organisational methods, its curing techniques and its markets.

The first large herring net was made at Hoorn in 1416. The Dutch had developed the factory ship from which it could be deployed: the aforementioned and celebrated herring buss (see first image section). Hand in hand with their mythologising of Willem **Beuckel** as the new fishery's founding father, they wove a mystification of its curing techniques, projecting them as a national secret. Starting with a higher proportion of top grade herring and salting them straight from the nets, they ruthlessly ensured the quality of the curing process and then did everything in their power to suggest their branding guaranteed herring beyond comparison with the products of their rivals.

The closer you look at their operation, the more remarkably modern they appear. What, undeniably, was an innovation was the gutting, salting and barrelling of herring at sea: take the fish at their freshest and keep them at their best. The Scania fishery was taxed through an insistence on land-based curing at licensed sites. The Dutch may have naively hoped, curing at sea, they would avoid altogether the taxmen of other nations. One way or another, they got away with quite a lot for quite a while. Concerning themselves with the best ways of packing the herring, the best kinds and proportions of salt, the dates between which herring in prime condition was caught and much more, they built on all they'd learned at Scania with great focus and diligence.

THE GRAND FISHERY

The Dutch herring busses would gather around Midsummer at Bressay Sound in the Shetlands and off Fair Isle. Fishing would begin on St John's Day (June 24th), around which the spawning shoals arrived. The high proportions of *maatjes* herrings, the sweet, small, virgin spawners provided the spearhead for their marketing drive.

Fast yachts or *ventjagers* (sale-hunters), would race from the Shetland grounds with the new catches, each aiming to be first to reach its home port with the prized barrels. These were auctioned off at vastly inflated prices, which contributed to the hoopla. Herring lover Nicolaes Tulp, the great Amsterdam doctor whose anatomy lesson was painted by Rembrandt, corresponded on the subject with Paul Neucrantz (see **N is for**). In *De harengo* (1654) Neucrantz reports his description of how, in some inland markets, the brined herring was adorned with green garlands and brought to the crossroads where it was displayed and ceremonially eaten. It's possible no other nation has ever honoured herrings as much.

Each buss made up to three voyages during the season, which ran through to January. An average sized buss could hold upwards of 400,000 barrelled herrings, the level of catches determining the length and number of voyages. In *A Representation of the Wholesome Political Grounds and Maxims of the Republic of Holland and West Friesland* (1669), Johan de Witt claimed that in 1560 the Dutch had 1,000 boats involved in the fishery and that by 1620 it was 2,000, yielding 2,000,000 guilders and supporting the employment of 450,000 people.

Among his sources for this, he included Sir Walter Raleigh whose *Observations touching trade and commerce with the Hollander and other nations* (see **Pamphleteers**) had been written in prison in 1605. Attempting to curry favour with King James after his involvement in the Main Plot (see **Red Herring Joke**), he could be forgiven for exaggeration. Emulating Dutch success, other nations were also sending their own busses to the same fishing grounds by the seventeenth century. Bo Poulsen suggests there were around 800 actual Dutch busses in 1600 with numbers occasionally peaking around 1,000 or close to it in the three decades which followed.

The fishery, running North to South, followed the appearances of the Buchan, Dogger Bank and Downs herring populations, the first of which offered the highest proportions of full, spawning and therefore most economically desirable fish. The mixed populations further south, by way of compensation, offered even larger catches. The standard pattern of the fishery, tabulated in Poulsen's research, saw the fleet, from Shetland in June/July, move down to the Scottish East Coast in July/August, to North East England and Yorkshire in September, the Dogger Bank and East Anglia in October/November and the Channel in December and January.

They fished on the West Coast of Scotland and off Ireland too, but the East Coast provided the main progression pictured by the Dutch as the providential source of all their miraculous wealth. From the 1750s, with the Dutch fishery in decline, December and January were gradually dropped from the season.

REGULATION

Quality control was regulated from the early days of the Grand Fishery. In 1424 John III Duke of Bavaria and Count of Holland, aka John the Pitiless, issued edicts on the fabrication and marking of barrels and on the curing of the fish. He was poisoned the following year, but this is most likely just to have been a comment on his pitilessness. His brother-in-law, John the Fearless, had a son, Philip the Good, and he took up the cause in 1439, issuing an edict on Last Money—a tax on each last of herrings (12 barrels—see **Measuring**). This theoretically funded the cost of naval convoying for the herring fleet. Other edicts prohibited selling herring in foreign ports or salting the re-barrelled herring at home ports before St Bartholomew's Day (August 24th). Philip also specified the kinds of **Salt** that could be used.

The top Holy Roman herring man, however, was Emperor Charles V, who inaugurated a systematic approach to fishery legislation in 1519. He made obligatory the branding of barrels to establish their quality. Each barrel would bear the marks of both the cooper who'd made it and the shipmaster who'd filled it. New barrels were to be used each time and cure masters were appointed in every fishing town and village to certify them. Only refined salt or moor salt could be used. Quality certificates were required and proportions were specified.

Charles legislated on the precise way herrings should be packed in the barrel; that different qualities should be packed in different barrels; that barrels filled with the prime herring caught before St James' Day (July 25th) should be branded with the scallop shell. Dealers were required to make a declaration of the quality of herring contained in a barrel. At sea, the salted herring was to be moistened with seawater every fortnight. Inshore herring, caught in the estuary of the River Y was not to be salted for export, but only used for home consumption and **Buckling**. In decline, this odd restriction was abandoned.

In his abdication tour, Charles V famously visited **Beuckel**'s supposed tomb in Biervliet, giving one last PR boost to his belovèd income generator. In Spanish retirement, he became an anchovy man.

WARS, PIRACY AND REVOLT

Regularly at war with the French, Dutch busses were vulnerable to the Dunkirk privateers. The nearby Normandy Coast had its own herring fishery, but Dunkirk more than played its part in the story that the golden age of piracy saw more fish stolen on the high seas than gold or silver. As pioneers in on-board salting and barreling, the Dutch presented a ready-packed commodity.

The Last Money, which Philip the Good had established to deal with the privateers, was increasingly used for other imperial needs and the naval convoys were becoming old and ill-equipped. The privateers were happy to offer safe conducts for a fee, but the ship owners understandably then resented paying Last Money, which the Emperor's taxmen continued to collect along with additional, new taxes. Dutch unhappiness seems to have found a natural home in the pool of general Protestant resentment.

William the Silent, Prince of Orange, was appointed Stadtholder of Holland, Zealand and Utrecht in 1559 and was strategically lenient in the collection of herring taxes. Ferdinand Alvarez de Toledo, Duke of Alva, on the other hand, was not. He was sent to the Netherlands to put an end to all the Reformation nonsense. He increased the taxes, enforced loans from the ship owners, conducted mass executions and, if engravings are to be believed, ate babies. William may not have said much, but he was more popular and he it was who led the Revolt, which eventually brought about the Dutch Republic.

DUTCH REPUBLIC

There seems to have been a Dutch herring committee even in Charles V's day, but in the 1560s the Republic established a *College van de Grote Visserij*, giving it monopolistic control of every aspect of the salt herring industry. Responding to renewed leniency in taxation as well as generous loans to the ship owners, by 1575 the industry was agreeing to levy the Last Money itself and the convergence of interest between state and fishing industry saw the further growth of the herring trade.

Increased legislation and codification came with the territory. The herring trade was recognised as 'the chief industry of the country and principal gold-mine to its inhabitants' (*Resolutions of the States of Holland*, 1581). It was granted immunity from the excise duty on salt, although, possibly to counter abuse, this was converted into an annual payment of 6,000 florins. On top of this, an extraordinary subsidy of 20,000 florins was made to the industry, out of which they were expected to fund their own men-of-war.

Calvinism, the Republic and the herring industry worked together seamlessly and it paid off. As Meynert Seymens put it, 'The Dutch catch more herrings, and prepare them better, than any other nation ever will, and the Lord has, through the instrument of the herring, made Holland an exchange and staple-market for the whole of Europe.'

DECLINE

This happy state of affairs was never going to last. The Netherlands' actual and, perhaps over-trumpeted success in waters so close to the Scottish and English coasts was always bound to end in tears. See **British Fisheries** and **Sovereignty of the Seas** for the background to the first three, herring-linked Anglo-Dutch Wars. Wars aren't good for fishermen. Even though the Dutch won many of the battles and, on points, could have been awarded victory in two of the wars, the disruption alone was enough to wear down the Grand Fishery. Add in the War of the Spanish Succession and you have more causes than anyone would need for a decline.

While not downplaying the significance of wars and piracy, Bo Poulsen adds a few more bad luck factors. Over the seventeenth century the annual per capita demand for herring in Europe had fallen from 0.9 kg to 0.4 kg. In the eighteenth century the Norwegians and the Scots (who, ahead of the English, had finally begun to get their quality control act together) increasingly took advantage of the diminished state of the Dutch fleet to challenge its former market monopolies.

Nations had, meanwhile, begun to introduce high import tariffs, which made the trading environment harder, particularly when your business model was extensively built on premium prices. On top of this, Poulsen suggests that, in the run of fluctuating herring populations, the 1720s probably saw an increase in the shoals close to the Scottish coast, which negated any advantage the 'high seas' fishing capacity offered the Dutch busses. The seventeenth-century Bohuslän period, and especially the late eighteenth/early nineteenth century one, flooded the market with cheaper herring. By 1850 the Dutch had only 5% of the European salt herring market.

Beaujon's analysis had been influenced by Adam Smith and the Dutch seem to have been influenced too. The *College van de Grote Visserij* was abandoned; deregulation and the abolition of subsidies were the order of the day. It worked. Perhaps it created the magic sense of a changed environment which, in turn, attracted back the investors, who'd previously lost faith in the herring industry.

The great advantage the Dutch had when they began to rebuild their herring fishery was an enthusiastic home market for salt herring. In the boom times you can manage without one, but sooner or later the lack will catch up on you. In a sense, the story of twentieth-century herring fisheries has been the gradual move towards an updated version of the Dutch buss model. Barrels of salt have been swapped for freezers; today's large pelagic trawlers can go anywhere, hoovering up quotas and Total Allowable Catches wheresoever they might be. The IJmuiden-based *Cornelis Vrolijk* company and its 1988 pelagic trawler of the same name bought 94% of the English herring quota (there's little sentimentality when quotas have been awarded to hedge companies). The Dutch company has acquired a range of fish processors in both the Netherlands and Belgium, all of which takes things back to the way they were, without the need for anyone to kneel at the fictional tomb of Willem Beuckel.

DUTCH & FLEMISH ART

People talk of the Golden Age of Dutch and Flemish painting, but when it comes to herring, Flanders had considerably less to paint about.

Hanging in Amsterdam's Rijksmuseeum, Adriaen van de Venne's *Fishing for Souls* (1614) marks the separation by water of the Dutch Republic and Flanders (or Belgium).

It's as if God's Protestants have crossed their own Red Sea and are standing on the left bank with their feet nice and dry. Their righteous fishers, with the help of their Bibles and their nets labelled *Faith, Hope and Charity*, are calmly pulling out those few who weren't quite prompt enough when they were called to leave Egypt. You wouldn't give much for the chances of the ones in the water towards the right bank: those ham-fisted Roman Catholic fishers can't even control their boat and, when you're drowning, incense just doesn't cut the mustard. If you want seamanship, Calvin's your man.

See **Dutch Fishery**, but herring industry expertise was overwhelmingly focused in the new republic. There are Flemish paintings with herrings, but Flanders' herring fishing never really recovered after the separation. Calvin's boys, of course, went from strength to strength and, in the extensive exhibition catalogue for *Fish: Still Lifes by Dutch and Flemish Masters, 1550–1700* (Central Museum, Utrecht, 2004) herrings feature in considerably more of the Dutch paintings.

'Although herring was the Dutch fishing fleet's most important product [...] they are rarely prominently included in fish still lifes,' the catalogue says. The age produced beautiful herring buss drawings and paintings by the yard, each vessel celebrating and allegorically representing the fish's entrepreneurial role in the Dutch economic miracle. Piled high on tables or market stalls, it produced still life cornucopias of fish, by the last. They mirrored to the wealthy of the Netherlands the element of water over which, by drainage, fishery, empire and trade, God had granted them such power.

Do you want herrings on your wall, though? I would say yes, but the Dutchmen who bought or commissioned fishy works at this time had a complex, even conflicted relationship with the herring. They were cheap, there was the smell, there were the common people. Herrings were unquestionably God's reward to a virtuous nation: Amsterdam, after all, was built on herring bones. They were intrinsic to the nation's wealth, but, at the same time, they were every bit as comic as they were on the other side of the North Sea.

In the *Fish* exhibition catalogue, there are two paintings of *Pekelharing*, the stock character, red-nosed, boozy clown, his red doublet in off-the-shoulder disarray, a mug of beer in his left hand, a salt herring in the right—Hendrick ter Brugghen's *The Merry Drinker* (c 1625, see second image section) and Gerard von Honthorst's *The Thirsty Eater* (1625–1630) are fine examples. Salt herrings were given out at taverns because—even more than the peanuts and crisps of this lesser age—they made you thirsty. Christiaen van Couwenbergh's grinning *Man with Herring* (1655), his doublet open, has a knife in his left while he holds the herring in his right, ready to attack it with an earthy enthusiasm only emphasised by the phallic depiction of both. Gottfried Schalken's *Woman Selling Herring* may be wearing pearl earrings, but the salt herring she dangles fresh from the barrel is accompanied by a look that seems to invite more than just the purchase of fish. Herring may not be of the destitute poor, but it has something of the joys of a *demi-monde*.

For an exhibition headlined simply *Fish*, the curators themselves may not have been working to a proportionate herring quota. Both smoked and salted, they have included a few, but while they were prime wealth generators, they may not have conveyed the display of wealth the rich wanted on their walls. Smoked and dotted with capers, Pieter Claesz's *Still Life with Herring, Wine and Bread* (1636) lifts his fish from its low life status with a perfectly-lit glass of white wine, a few grapes and a foregrounded, spiral-peeled lemon. You could equally view the herring as comically grounding any undue airs and graces. In Jan Davidsz de Heem's *Still Life with Glass of Wine and Herring* (1653) the herring is cut into bite-size pieces and the small glass of wine is only going to afford a sophisticated sip or two, although a glass of beer stands ready to wash down the salt. A Red Admiral is perched on the vine leaves attached to the grapes, a regular symbol of transformation. Perhaps it supports the wine's position in a higher plane—the beer, peeled lemon, bread, onions, prawns and herring belong resolutely lower.

Joseph de Bray's *Praise of Pickled Herring* (1656, see first image section) captures the ambiguities of praise and mockery to perfection. On a white tablecloth, the herring is placed in the foreground on a humble wooden platter. It is cut ready to eat with rye bread, thickly smeared with butter, a small plate of onions and a choice of beers: as recommended in the poem of the same name, which is inscribed on an ornate memorial, behind, itself bedecked with more herrings. The verses, encircled with a wreath, are by de Bray's uncle, the poet, physician and preacher, Jacob Westerbaen. The rough and ready placing of the food on the rumpled tablecloth contrasts with the monumental quality of the memorial; the lovingly detailed painting of the food and drink contrasts with the joyful vulgarity of the poem.

PRAISE OF PICKLED HERRING
Jacob Westerbaen (1633)

Salt herring from the vat,
so full and long and fat,
that head dispatched so neatly,
the backbone and the gut -
that deftness in the cut -
the skin removed discreetly;

Thus cleaned, it is no fiddle,
raw or from the griddle,
an onion slice for relish
and 'ere the night is out
there's very little doubt,
a fish will be demolished.

So let's not muck around,
a hunk of rye to help it down,
the butter spread so thickly:
no snake oil cures for me,
I'm happy as can be
and not amongst the sickly.

To clear a salty throat
a beer perhaps of note,
a Breda, Delft or Haarlem
all do the job just right
and in the next day's light,
sure, one more drink's no problem.

What? You don't feel so good?
That head's a block of wood?
Imagine pickled herring
beside your breakfast pot
to clear away the snot
and set away your morning.

A shit comes nice and easy
and piss, but may I say?
the farts might well be stinkers.
Just let the winds blow free:
in jolly company
toast food and fellow drinkers!

AFTER THE GOLDEN AGE

The low life popularity of herring stayed with the Dutch and their artists, although, in the nineteenth century, the paintings became more straightforwardly celebratory of its egalitarian charms. A young Piet Mondrian, learning his craft many years before he shifted into the less clupeid-friendly possibilities of the abstract grid, painted the naturalistic *Still Life: Herring* (1893), its fish spilling from a bowl on to an unadorned wooden table.

Van Gogh, possibly the greatest smoked herring painter of all time, was already pushing the possibilities forward. Particularly fond of a fish smoking shop in Schevingen, he painted

Bokkingen, summer 1886. Bokking is the Dutch word for Buckling. Van Gogh's impasto techniques don't always lend themselves to product identification, but in Paris, that same summer, he painted *Still life with herrings, napkin and glass*, which are probably the cold-smoked hareng saur—the paintings suggest the traditional drier variety (red herrings rather than the less-smoked bouffi or modern bloater). 1887 saw *Three harengs saur and a garlic bulb*. In January 1889 he painted *Still life: two harengs saur* and *Still life with harengs saur on yellow paper* (see first image section) and here the specific product is important.

After cutting off part of his ear, just before Christmas 1888, he felt he'd been unsympathetically, if not badly treated by the police. In French, *hareng saur* is slang for gendarme. He gave the beautiful yellow paper one to his friend Paul Signac. In his smoked herring paintings Van Gogh may have been influenced by the **Hareng Saur Monologues** of Le Cros (1873), Huysmans (1874) and Richepin (1886). The great French actor Coquelin Cadet regularly performed Le Cros' monologue in Paris.

Meanwhile, Flanders (or Belgium) came back with a late challenge by James Ensor and *Skeletons fighting over an hareng saur* (1891, see first image section), the herring possibly representing the artist himself as he is torn apart by the critics.

ETYMOLOGIES, EUPHEMISMS, NAMES

ETYMOLOGIES
Herring, Haring, Arenque, etc
Variations on herring predominate in the English-speaking world and, while not in Finland, Scandinavia or in Slavic languages, in variations across much of Europe south of the Baltic. Estonian is a geographical anomaly, surrounded by *sild* variants but opting for *heeringas*. The word herring was thought to derive from the Germanic root words *heer* or *heri*, meaning *army*. This was plausibly assumed to be a reference to the size of the herring shoals (see **Grand Migration**/Thomas Pennant).

In his blog for Oxford University Press, Anatoly Liberman, Professor of German Philology at the University of Minnesota, writes of nineteenth-century etymologist Karl Müllenhoff having pursued this theory and having identified the same root word in *har*bour, *har*angue and *har*ry. In the late nineteenth century, Otto Schrader proposed the alternative German root word *hero* (Old High German *haring*, Old Slavonic *seru*, Indo-Germanic *kero*) meaning *blue grey*. He also compared *herring* and *hoar* (as in hoary or hoar frost), which, in turn, derives from *har*, grey-haired or grey white. Blue-grey, grey or grey-white all work with herrings, but Liberman then notes an alternative connection with *hair* (Old English *haer*), pointing out that the Dutch *haar* means fishbone. He dismisses any connection, however, because 'the bones of the herring are neither too thin nor particularly fine'. It's hard to know on which finer-boned fish he is basing his implicit comparison, but some would argue herrings would be considerably more popular if he was right. The Welsh warn their herring-eating children with *Govalus o'r blew*—mind the hairs. Nevertheless, today Schrader's hero/blue grey theory tends to hold sway.

Sild, Silli, Sledz, etc

In Danish and Norwegian, the word for herring is *Sild* and there are many variations of this around the Baltic and to the East. There are few certainties here, but it is thought to derive from the words for herring in Northern Saami (*sâlled*) and/or Lule Saami (*sâllet*). Sild has been much used in English since the time tinned juvenile herring could no longer be called Sardines (see **Sardine Litigation**, but call it anything other than herring if you want the English to buy it). *Sile* was already a little-used English word for young herring, possibly introduced into Old English by the Vikings.

Sgadan

The words for herring in Celtic languages tend to be variations on *sgadan*, but here again there is also an Old English word for herring, *Sceadd*. This will probably have come from a British usage, but it gave us the word for the herring's relative, the shad.

Kipper

The word *kipper* comes with a range of etymological possibilities. In Old English *cypere* is a male salmon and the kippering, particularly of spent males, long predated the kippers we know today. *Cypere* may have come from the Old English *coper* (copper). Others point to the kip of a male salmon, the hook it develops on its bottom jaw in the breeding season. Another line links it to Old Norse *kjapt* (briskly, impetuously), *kippa* (snatch, pull, jerk) and Middle English and Dutch *kippen* (seize, catch, grip). In Middle Low German, *schippere* is apparently cognate to skipper, which would have the kipper in charge of the boat which catches the herring it once was. (See **Bloater** for its own separate derivations.)

EUPHEMISMS

The *Silver Darlings*, which gave their name to Neil Gunn's 1941 saga of North East Scottish fishing communities after the Highland Clearances, went by many other names.

Sailors, whose reluctance to eat fish at sea would flower into obstinate superstition at the drop of a hat (see **Luck**), were responsible for several euphemisms. The resilience and cheapness of smoked and salted herring made the fish attractive when provisioning voyages, so they became *Yarmouth capons*, *Billingsgate pheasants*, *Digby chicks* or *Digby chickens*. Digby is a fishing port in Nova Scotia.

The term *Digby chicken* was first recorded between 1915 and 1920 and probably grew out of the earlier English usages. The more widely known surviving example of this kind of euphemism for preserved fish is Bombay duck, which is dried bombil or bummalo. Some say this was named after the *Bombay Daak*, the mail train, which once carried it to the city, but dried bombil in Marathi is the reversed but similar sounding *takh bombil*, which I think provides a much more likely explanation. Sailors also used to call red herrings *sodgers* (soldiers), drawing on the army's red coats. This probably has nothing to do with the suggested Germanic root words *heer* or *heri*, but along this line, they were also known as militiamen in East Anglia. In Scotland, on the other hand, picking up on red robes, they were called *Glasgow magistrates*.

In Japan herring (*nishin*) is known as *Harutuge'ou*, the spring-announcing fish. The Algonquin words for herring, *aumsûog* and *munnawhatteaûg* seem to mean 'they give life', which sounds great except that it refers to their use as fertiliser in the growing of corn. The same words are used for a really oily clupeid, the alewife or menhaden, a much more suitable fertilizer.

NAMES

Algongquin	*aumsûog, munnawhatteaûg*
Arabic	*smk mumlah*
Catalan	*Arengades*
Danish	*Sild*
Dutch	*Haring*
English	*Herring*
Estonian	*Heeringas*
Finnish	*Silli, Silakka* (Atlantic, Baltic)
French	*Hareng*
Gaelic	*Sgadan*
German	*Hering*
Greek	*Rénga*
Greenlandic	*Angmagssagssuaq*
Haida	*Íinang* (Pacific herring)
Icelandic	*Sild, Hafsild*
Inuktitut	*Ammassassuaq*
Italian	*Aringa*
Irish	*Scadán*
Korean	*Cheong-eo* (Pacific herring)
Latvian	*Siļķes*
Lithuanian	*Silkė*

Japanese	*Nishin* (Pacific herring)
Norwegian	*Sild*
Polish	*Śledź*
Portuguese	*Arenque*
Russian	*Sel'd'*
Serbo Croat	*Herring*
Spanish	*Arenque*
Swedish	*Sill, Strömming* (Atlantic, Baltic)
Tla'amin	*Tchlagat* (Pacific herring)
Tlingit	*Yaaw* (Pacific herring)
Turkish	*Ringa*
Welsh	*Ysgadenyn, Pennog, Penwaig*

EYVINDR 'SKÁLDASPILLIR' FINNSSON

Laurels for First Herring Poet go to Eyvindr 'Skáldaspillir' Finnsson (910–990 CE). There appear to be no rival candidates. It was over two hundred years before Alexander **Neckam**, writing in Latin, became the first English one and he isn't in the same poetic league. Eyvindr was the last of Norway's major skaldic poets and had flourished at the court of Haakon the Good. His relationship with Erik Bloodaxe's son Harald Greycloak was more problematic and he went into exile. Only a few of his works survive but they include two which, in the absence of court patronage, arose from a herring expedition undertaken as a money-making venture in the late 960s. *Skáldaspillir* (poet (de)spoiler) is often translated 'Plagiarist', but that is pejorative. His knowledge of the skaldic tradition enabled him draw on its spoils, expecting listeners to appreciate this; his skill had enabled him to compose a tribute to Haakon the Good, which at the same time subtly mocked a tribute to Bloodaxe. Poets can be their own worst enemies.

I

Out of the North,

may our ocean-steed race

upon oar-hooves for promised plenty:

the tail-fin-feathered terns of the long nets!

Fortune! Say that this slow sea-pig

may rootle up a silver harvest,

find a ready market and

make friends fat.

II

The Icelanders sent me a silver cloak pin

I had to spend on the fjord-herd

and worse than that,

see, I sold

my arrow hoard:

Egil's leaping herrings

for these thin, sorry sea-arrows.

Hunger lay at the heart of both actions.

NOTES

The poems are *lausavísur*—namely of a single stanza. *Lausavísur* can be sets of unconnected stanzas, but these two are clearly connected: the setting out and the disappointment, a classic before and after pairing. The first appears in its entirety, the second in part, in Snorri Sturluson's *Heimskringla or History of Norway's Kings* (c 1230 CE). I referred to the complete literal translations, which can be found at the excellent online *Skaldic Project*. As with Anglo-Saxon poetry, the Old Norse tradition worked through alliteration and kennings, figurative word compounds—*ocean-steed* and *sea-pig* for ship, *fjord-herd* for herring shoals etc. I have sometimes made these more explicit, e.g. *oar-hooves* for the literal *sea-feet*. The poor man's George Herbert, arrowhead concrete poetry has nothing to do with Old Norse skaldic verse, but seemed appropriate in translating such an intensely visual oral tradition.

1. *Out of the North*—Eyvindr had burnt his bridges at the court of Harald Greycloak, but the king's rule, based at Avaldnes between Bergen and Stavanger, did not extend beyond Western Norway. Coming back from Iceland, Eyvindr probably based himself further north. He may be referring to the dangers undertaken in passing through waters from which he'd been banished. The great Icelandic warrior poet Egil, who appears in the second poem, had been shipwrecked on the North East English coast and only escaped execution at the court of Harald's father, Erik Bloodaxe, by means of an insincere but, obviously, extraordinarily good praise poem.

2. *Tail-fin-feathered terns of the long nets*—Both herrings and terns have forked tails: the shoal of herrings seen by Eyvindr mirrored the terns' acrobatic flight. The kenning prefigures the play with arrows in the second poem. The long nets may have been drift nets.

3. *Slow sea-pig*—In the first half of the first poem, he may be picturing a longship. For a fishing expedition a karve is the more likely vessel, similar in structure but broader in the beam, slower and far less graceful to the mind of a high-ranking courtier.

4. *The Icelanders sent me*—In exile, Eyvindr went to Iceland. He wrote a poem about just how good the Icelanders were and they liked it a lot. After he had returned to Norway, they sent the silver cloak pin as a token of their appreciation.

5. *Egil's 'leaping herrings'*—Eyvindr was celebrated for the wit of his borrowings from other poets. It is possible Egil had made such a kenning. Other arrow kennings such as *battle-blizzard* or *hail of the bow-string* picture a mass of arrows in the sky: a herring shoal, given the forked tails and the shared direction is richly apt. The

thin... sea-arrows might suggest *spents*, post-spawning herrings which would not have fetched much of a price; my addition of *sorry* follows this suggestion.

6. *Hunger lay*—the *Skaldic Project*'s literal translation is *famine causes both things*, 'both' could refer to two pairs of actions, *a*) to selling the cloak pin and selling the arrows and *b*) the Icelandic flattery which led to the cloak pin and the dubious investment in a herring fishing expedition. Both pairs refer to the precarious lot of a skaldic poet without a patron.

FARTING

Call it a squeak, call it a sneeze, call it a Fast Repetitive Tick (FaRT), herrings can make a noise when lifted from the sea. This has been known, probably for as long as fishermen have caught them. Neucrantz, in *De harengo* (1654) writes a whole chapter, 'Concerning the squeaking of herrings whilst they do not breathe':

> All fish have this so-called voice, coming either from their gills, which contain little bristles, or from the innards gathered around their stomachs, because air is held in these places and, when the fish are rubbed or shaken, sounds are squeezed out.

Samuel, in *The Herring; Its Effect on the History of Britain* (1918), writes:

> There is a belief among fishermen that a herring when caught articulates a sound similar to the word "cheese." This sound is caused by an escape of air from the air bladder, or a movement of the gills. Fishermen, indeed, frequently state that the herrings "sneeze," just as Aristotle says that gurnards "grunt."

In 2004 the high-pitched herring sneeze was confirmed as originating from the air held in the swim bladder, which then produces the sound as it is squeezed out of the anus. In their paper, 'Pacific and Atlantic herring produce burst pulse sounds', researchers Ben Wilson, Lawrence Dill and Robert Batty show no evidence of having read Neucrantz or A.M. Samuel, let alone discussed the matter with herring fishermen, but they identify a purpose.

Their research herrings did not use the sound when the smells of predators were introduced to the tank. They tended to make them at night. Wilson, Dill and Batty therefore suggest the little raspberry is rooted in nighttime shoal communication, when the herring's eyes are of less use. 'Here I am,' they are saying to each other. Some of them obviously continue their here-I-ams even as the net is lifted over the side of the boat.

The researchers identified pulses of 1.7 to 22 kHz lasting between 0.6 and 7.6 seconds. They could have called these sounds squeaks or sneezes. They could have said they sounded like *Cheese*. They decided to call them something for which FaRT would serve as an acronym. Herrings rise from the seabed twice during the night as part of their feeding routines. The reason not all the hauled-in herrings farted is because the frequency of their farts diminishes as their swim bladders gradually deflate. Upon reaching the surface, they are able to gulp in more air and fart again. Wilson, Dill and Batty earned an Ig Nobel prize for their troubles.

SOVIET SUBMARINES

Given the timing of their wind-breaking paper, they might have been made aware of clandestine research, which had been going on in Scandinavia...

In 1981 a Soviet, Whiskey Class submarine S-363, redesignated as U137, became stuck on rocks, a few miles from the Swedish naval base of Karlskrona. It became known as the *Whiskey on the Rocks Incident*. Swedes can enjoy a joke, but their military took the matter seriously, instituting a programme of hydrophone recordings, which, throughout the 80s and early 90s revealed extraordinary levels of submarine activity in Swedish waters.
There had been six prior incidents between 1962 and 1980. Depth charges were fired during some of them. During an incident in 1982, 44 depth charges and 4 naval mines

were used. There were a further eight incidents before the fall of the Soviet Union, but all the submarines escaped. There was also the one in 1990 which turned out to be a West German submarine, but alarmingly, the ones which couldn't be traced to friendly nations did not stop with the triumph of capitalism. In 1992, Swedish submarines nearly sank one of their own corvettes while dealing with an incursion. 'Where is the peace dividend?' they could have been forgiven for asking.

None of the incidents had delivered a captured submarine or tell-tale wreckage on the surface of the Baltic Sea and at some point in the mid 90s, it was discovered that one of the regular recorded sounds—something not unlike a propeller—was made by swimming mink. There were others though, notably regular bursts of clicking.

Just to be certain, the military called in biologists Hakan Westerberg and Magnus Wahlberg. Herring shoals. Thousands of herring squeezing air from the swim bladder, out through the anus. 'Here I am...' 'Here I am...' 'Here I am...' And there, indeed, they were.

The price of democracy is eternal vigilance and I like to dream of all the filled filing cabinets; all of the audio analysts, each at the bottom of a chain of command, eyes narrowed in concentration as they meticulously logged the interacting herring farts; all the natural habitat data through which Wilson, Dill and Batty could have expanded our understanding of the conversational world of herrings.

FASTING

Fishy Friday is an institution, even though England has technically been a Protestant nation since 1534; even though Protestant-resented secular fish days went out with the seventeenth century. In the public imagination, Fishy Friday is inseparable from the batter-fried cod and haddock introduced to us by the Sephardic refugees from Portugal's *Reconquista*. If you want to find a logic for fasting, do not look to the Church and

1. **Y is for Why?** et seq., *Rudder Requiem* and **A is for A Beginning** et seq.
2. *In the memory of gannets*, Will Maclean (courtesy of the artist), See particularly also **Two Contemporary Artists.**

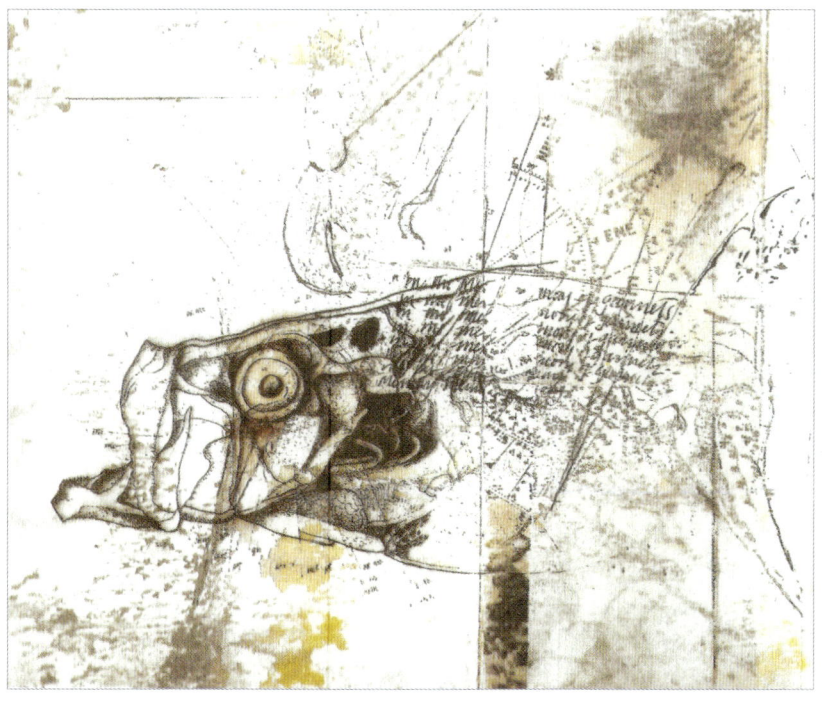

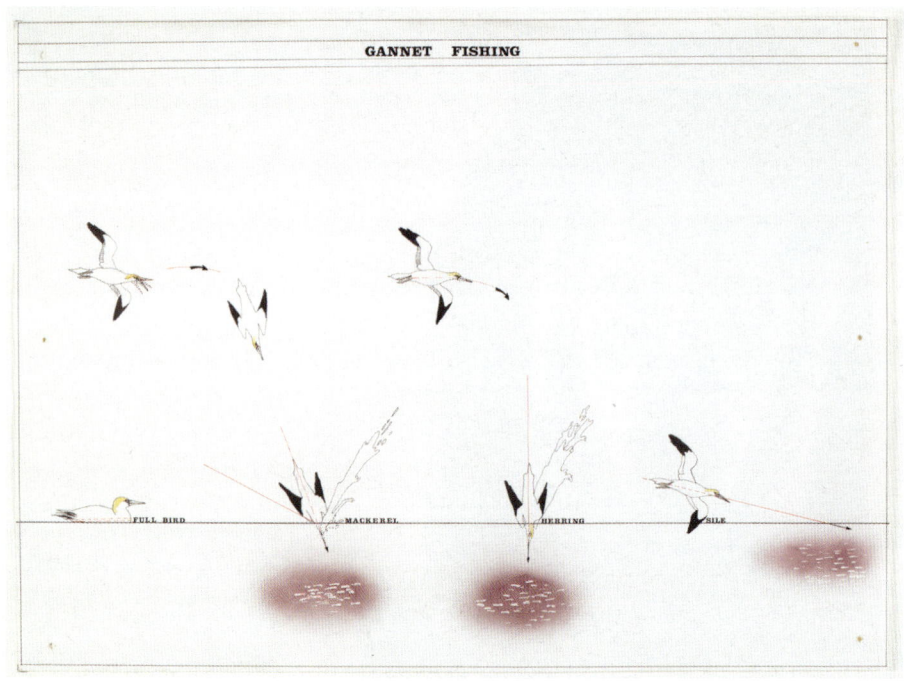

3. Appearances & Signs. *Gannet Fishing* (from *The Ring Net*),
Will Maclean. (National Galleries of Scotland. Purchased 1980).
See also **Two Contemporary Artists.**

4. & 5. Atlantic Herring et seq., *Ma heid's fair fu' o'
fish* and *The Herring Kiss* (2019), Keith McIntyre
(courtesy of the artist)

6. Atlantic Herring. Pacific herring spawning, Vancouver Island (Rolf Hicker Photography/Alamy). It looks much the same with Atlantic herrings and satellite phototographs have been taken of both Pacific and Atlantic spawnings.

7. Atlantic Herring. Herring shoal in a cave, Scotland (photo: José B. Ruiz/Alamy).

8. Cooperage. Cooper making a herring barrel in Lowestoft, Suffolk (Alamy).

9. Baskets. Arthur Beech's basket making tools (photo: author).

10. Caribbean & West African Food. Trinidadian dumpling stuffed with stir fried red herring, served on stir fry. The cockles of your heart are warmed, not least by the use of Scotch bonnet chillis (photo: author).

11. Documentary. Jeanie Wilson & Annie Linton (1843), David Octavius Hill & Robert Adamson, from *The Fishermen and Women of the Firth of Forth* (Alamy).

12. Dutch Fisheries. *Dutch Indiaman Passing Herring Busses* (late seventeenth century), Bonaventure Peeters (Alamy). The painting associates the growth of Dutch trade and empire with the herring buss fishery on which they saw the nation's wealth having been built. See also **British Fisheries**, **Dutch & Flemish Art**, **Pampleteers** and **Sovereignty of the Seas**.

13. Dutch & Flemish Art. *Praise of Pickled Herring* (1647) Joseph de Bray (Alamy). Taking delight in the day-to-day beauty of the fish, the salt herring bedecked poem behind celebrates its earthy joys. See entry for translation.

14. Dutch & Flemish Art. *Two Smoked Herrings on Yellow Paper* (1889)
Vincent van Gogh (Alamy). Painted in Arles just after the incident with the ear,
smoked herring in French is 'hareng saur', also slang for gendarme.

15. Dutch & Flemish Art. *Two Skeletons Fighting over a Smoked Herring* (1891), James Ensor
(Royal Museums of Fine Arts of Belgium, inv. 11156, photo: J. Geleyns). Both Van Gogh and Ensor
were probably aware of the **Hareng Saur Monologues** of Charles Cros, J.K. Huysmans and Jean Richepin.

16. Fasting. *The Fight between Carnival and Lent* (1559) Pieter Breughel the Elder (Alamy). Carnival, armed with meat on a spit, rides a barrel; Lent on three-legged chair and trolley is armed with two herrings on a paddle.

17. & 18. French Fisheries. Fécamp Herring Festival, November 2024 (photos: author). A nation at ease with its herrings.

19. Ganseys & Guernseys. Left: gansey, moss stitch diamond pattern on sleeves, knitted by Mary Muir Murray of Cellardyke for her husband Peter, twentieth century.

20. Right: gansey, step pattern on body and sleeves, knitted by Margaret Shirran Lowrie of Aberdeen, a herring gutter who followed the fishing fleet around the coast, gutting and packing the fish, 1949. (Courtesy of Scottish Fisheries Museum).

21. Herring Boats. Left: *Nordlandsbåt* (1998) Stig Tobiassen, the North Norwegian boat that according to Mike Smylie (see **Herringism**) is said to be 'the last boat in Europe working under a square sail.' Two years earlier Lofoten artist Stig completed a world record 10,012 paintings in one year (author's collection).

22. Herring Boats. The *Adenia* (LK193), midwater trawler built in 2019, one of Shetland's pelagic fishing fleet, moored at Lerwick harbour (Alan Morris / Alamy).

23., 24. & 25. Herring Boats. Top left: William Campbell, Lossiemouth, 1909, designer and owner of the first zulu, *Nonesuch* (INS 2118) in 1878 (courtesy of Scottish Fisheries Museum). Top right: Richard Padwick with his model of the zulu *Muirneag* (SY486), begun 2022, completed 2025 (photo: author). Bottom: the zulu *Cellandine* (BF737) and a fifie (BK234) entering Great Yarmouth harbour (courtesy of Scottish Fisheries Museum).

26. Herring Boats. *Skye Fisherman, in memoriam*, Will Maclean (1989), a collage using a fish box from the pelagic trawler *Antares*, lost in 1990 with four crew members off the Isle of Arran, pulled down when her trawl line was caught by the Royal Navy nuclear-powered submarine HMS *Trenchant*. (Courtesy of the artist).

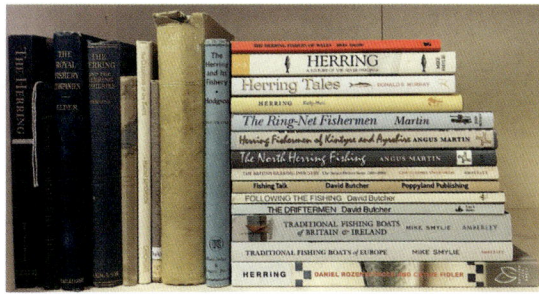

27. & 28. Herringism. Left: the mobile smokehouse of Mike Smylie, notable herringist (photo courtesy of Mike Smylie); right: a selection of herringist works from my bookshelves (photo: author).

29. Herring Lasses. Penelope Payne with her work *Scold Vixen Harpy Shrew*, Middlesbrough Art Weekender, MIMA, 2022 (photo courtesy of the artist). The words of the title are those most commonly used to describe fishwives. See also **Two Contemporary Artists.**

30. & 31. Herring Lasses. Two postcards, top: *Packing Herrings*, location unspecified, but postmark suggests Scarborough; bottom: *Scotch Girls Gipping Herring*, Yarmouth, early twentieth century.

32. Icelandic Fisheries. The boat house at the Herring Era Museum, Siglufjördur (photo: author). The building had to be constructed around the boats.

33–38. (from top, left to right) **Iddis.** Royalty sells Norwegian sardines. Among other things, the promise of sophistication, women in fast cars and women in love with very large herrings also work. (Courtesy of MUST/Norwegian Canning Museum, Stavanger).

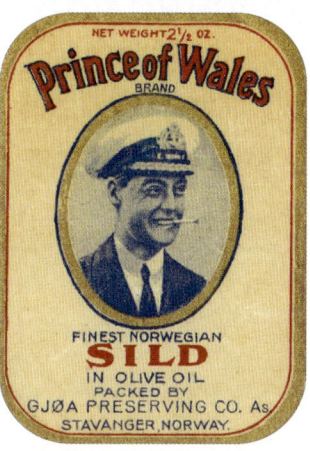
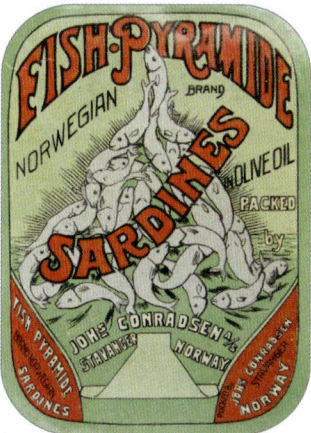

39. Herring Industry Board. Four versions (and there are more) of what was more-or-less the same booklet, some attributed to Mrs Arthur Webb, others to Mrs Stanley Wrench. (Author's collection).

40. Jewish Food. Chopped herring or *forshmak*, garnished with grated egg and dill, which some might include in the mix (photo: author). It is served on a Dutch tourist-ware dish in a tribute to the opportunities for Jewish involvement with the herring trade, which might have come with the rise of the Dutch Grand Herring Fishery.

certainly do not look to people. Technically, traditional, chip shop dripping would rule out fish and chips on a fast day (and hot cross buns should wait until Easter Sunday). Long before the sanctification of fish and chips, herring was the universal fish of fasting.

Pieter Breughel the Elder presents *The Fight between Carnival and Lent* (1559, see first image section) as a mock joust, supporters pushing the contenders towards each other. Carnival is a fat butcher astride a barrel of beer, his lance a spit laden with roasts and a sausage, a pie precariously balanced on his head, a crow's legs sticking out of the crust. Lent, a sorry-looking nun on a trolley-drawn, three-legged chair, is armed with a couple of herrings on a baker's paddle. She looks close to death and unable to knock anyone off his chosen perch; he looks so preoccupied with the pie on his head, it would take only the slightest touch to unbalance him.

In England, John Gladman was crowned Norwich's King of Christmas in 1444. Along with a representation of December, carried before him there was an effigy of Lent, dressed in red and white herring skins: *you're feasting now, but just you wait!* Arthur Samuel includes this beautiful herring fact in *The Herring: Its Effect on the History of Britain* (1918). He also refers to the sixteenth-century Bavarian writer Thomas Naogeorgus and his long poem, *Popish Kingdome*, which was *englyshed by Barnaby Googe* in 1570. It describes an Ash Wednesday custom in those parts:

> The Wednesday next a solemn day, to Church they early go,
> To sponge out all the foolish deeds by them committed so,
> They money give, and on their heads, the Priest doth ashes lay,
> And with his holy water washeth all their sins away:
> In wondrous sort against the venial sins doth profit this,
> Yet here no stay of madness now, nor end of folly is,
> With mirth to dinner straight they go, and to their wonted play,
> And on their devil's shapes they put, and sprightish fond array.
> Some sort there are that mourning go, with lanterns in their hand,

While in the daytime Titan bright, amid the skies doth stand:
And seek their Shrovetide Bacchanals still crying everywhere,
Where are our feasts become? Alas the cruel fasts appear.
Some bear about a herring on a staff, and loud do roar,
Herrings, herrings, stinking herrings, puddings now no more.

To this day, at Christmas, Catalan children beat the bums of their gift-shitting log, *Caga Tió* and sing:

Please don't shit us herring,
It is too salty tasting!
Shit us nougat,
Better by far!

Religions like to ordain fasting, because it humbles what is usually their chosen opponent, the physical appetite; because it thus cleanses the body and focuses the spirit. It has been common to ritual observance since time immemorial. The sanctioning of fish-eating on fast days is not universal. The various Orthodox churches of Eastern Europe grade their fasting—on some fast days one is allowed fish, some not. Fish fasting's main proponent was the Catholic Church. It recognised an exceptional virtue in eschewing fish, but did not require it. The provision of fish for regular weekly fasting and for Lent became a major business opportunity and underpinned the growth of Northern Europe's herring fisheries, which could supply accessibly cheap fish in bulk. The significant proportion of herring-based cultural information, feeding this encyclopaedia, is rooted in a love-hate relationship which developed out of over-familiarity.

WEEKLY FASTING DAYS

Fridays were Christian fast days from the beginning, but in the competitive religious marketplace of the Roman Empire, one day a week was never going to be enough. Thursdays and Sundays were specifically ruled out because they'd been taken by the

Manichaeans. A combination of Wednesdays and Fridays was fixed upon under Emperor Constantine and there is no better authority for the reasoning than St Augustine of Hippo, writing in 396 CE:

> The reason why the Church prefers to appoint the fourth and sixth days of the week for fasting, is found by considering the gospel narrative. There we find that on the fourth day of the week the Jews took counsel to put the Lord to death. One day having intervened—on the evening of which, at the close, namely, of the day which we call the fifth day of the week, the Lord ate the Passover with His disciples—He was thereafter betrayed on the night which belonged to the sixth day of the week, the day (as is everywhere known) of His passion… the Lord suffered on the sixth day of the week, as is admitted by all: wherefore the sixth day also is rightly reckoned a day for fasting, as fasting is symbolical of humiliation; whence it is said, 'I humbled my soul with fasting.'

Saturdays were also considered but abandoned except for Ember Days. Originally pagan cleansing days with which the four seasons were greeted, the Church fixed Ember Days on the Wednesdays, Fridays and Saturdays following St Lucia's Day (December 13th), Ash Wednesday, Whitsunday and the Exaltation of the Cross (September 14th). So: Wednesdays, Fridays, Ember Days and then, on top of that, Lent.

THE DEVELOPMENT OF LENT

Friday commemorations of the Passion may, in the early days, have been considered an alternative to an annual event, but fasting during Lent was an established practice by the early fourth century. The seeds were sown in the second century, towards the end of which, St Irenaeus explained that, during the Holy Week, 'Some think they ought to fast for one day, others for two days, and others even for several, while others reckon forty hours both of day and night to their fast.' The forty hours came from the time Jesus spent in the tomb; the later forty days from the time he spent in the wilderness.

By 331, St Athanasius was recommending forty days light fasting, prior to a strict fast during Holy Week itself. Eight years later, he was telling the Alexandrians, 'While all the world is fasting, we who are in Egypt should not become a laughing-stock as the only people who do not fast but take our pleasure in those days.' Observance varied in the different Christian communities from eight weeks (forty days with weekends off) to three weeks light and three weeks hard, or even just a straight three weeks. In Rome things initially settled on thirty-six days inclusive of Holy Week, but then, in the seventh century, one of the Pope Gregories added a further four to make forty.

From Ash Wednesday to Maundy Thursday is forty-four days, but putting aside those hot cross buns, truth be told, the fasting requirement doesn't come to an end until the painted eggs of Easter Sunday. It's best to abandon logic, but it does allow Pancake Day to be a Tuesday, Mardi Gras. And three of them are Ember Days, when you would have been fasting anyway, maybe even if you were a pagan.

46 (weeks per year minus Lent) x 2 days per week + 44 days (Lent) + 3 days (Ember Saturdays outside Lent) = 139 days or roughly 38% of the eating year. Feast days falling on a Wednesday, Friday or Ember Saturday might take precedence, but this is the market into which the herring fisheries played.

WHY FISH?

Many people have questioned why, on fasting days, you were allowed to eat fish but not meat. What's the big difference? Well, it tended to be justified on the dubious principle that fish have cold blood. Nothing to do with whether fish feel pain or not, the basic problem is sin. Gluttony is the sin most associated with the joys of animal fat, but Lust, Wrath and even Pride are also deemed to be hot-blooded. The Church drew on St Paul's *First Letter to the Corinthians* (Chapter XV, Verse 39): 'All flesh is not the same flesh: but there is one kind of flesh of men, another flesh of beasts, another of fishes and another of birds.'

FASTING

Constantine, Emperor of Rome's western provinces, came together with Licinius, Emperor in Byzantium, and in 313 issued the Edict of Milan, which officially tolerated Christianity throughout the empire. Licinius was a backslider, who resumed low-level, anti-Christian persecution before he was defeated by Constantine in 324 and hanged. At some point between the Edict of Milan and then, he had decreed that on certain days only salt fish could be eaten.

This may have been driven by a purely economic desire to boost the fish trade, but by the fifth century, church historian Socrates Scholasticus noted that on fast days, 'Some abstain from every sort of creature that has life, while others of all the living creatures eat of fish only.' There may be a hint of Socrates' disapproval when he writes, 'Others eat birds as well as fish, because, according to the Mosaic account of the Creation, they too sprang from the water.' He paints a picture of a genuinely diverse practice, including abstinence from fruit with hard shells and eggs, total abstinence and the eating of dry bread only.

It does not explain why fish became so central to the practice of Catholic fasting, but there are stranger seas in which to swim. There is a tendency in Church explanations not to probe the relationship between eating fish on fast days and using fish as a symbol of Christ—ICHTHUS, Greek for *fish*, as an acrostic for *Iesous Christo Theou Uiou Soter* (Jesus Christ of God, the Son, the Saviour). The symbolic, simply drawn outline of a fish was widely used by early Christians and has more recently been adopted by evangelicals.

Born-again pagans and anthropologists point to even earlier uses of this fish design, for example the intersecting, thin crescent moons (waxing and waning) which refer to the Goddess-Mother and her vulva. The Chinese Great Mother *Kwan-yin* is represented as a fish, the Hindu *Kali* is the Fish-Eyed One, the Egyptian *Isis* is the Great Fish of the Abyss, but fish-mothers can be followed through several incarnations: *Innana* to the Sumerians becomes *Ishtar* to the Babylonians becomes *Astarte* to the Phoenicians.

Ishtar/Astarte is often claimed to be the etymological root of *Easter*, but it more likely originates in *Ēostre*, a Germanic spring goddess associated with bunnies. *Astarte* is, however, associated with the Greek Aphrodite and the Roman Venus, from which we get *dies veneris* and *vendredi* (Friday).

When the Woden-worshipping tribes of Germany bought into the Roman seven-day week they allocated Venus' day to the more-or-less equivalent goddess *Freya*, from which *Freitag*, *Fredag* and Friday. The Germanic tribes also celebrated Freya with fish-eating and, at this point, it would be remiss to omit the story of a sea goddess, *Aphrodite Salacia*, once celebrated on Fridays with fish and orgies. You can almost hear the early Christians saying, 'You can keep the fish if you lose the orgies,' and it is possible to imagine the Salacians were grateful.

Moving towards the phallic, there is the intriguing origin of a bishop's mitre in the fish head costumes of the *Apkallu* or *Abgal*, the seven demigods created by the Sumerian god *Enki* to bring civilisation to mankind. Late in his career (around the fourth century CE), the Semitic god *Dagon* took to wearing a fish head. For theorists of the Erich von Däniken school (*Chariot of the Gods*, 1969, etc), *Dagon* and the *Apkallu* were unquestionably amphibious extra-terrestrials.

Did early Christians place their simplified fish design over the swollen belly of the Virgin Mary? Some accounts talk of this, suggesting they not only wanted to move the symbolic vulva away from the scene of the crime, but to translate it into a God/Christ/bishop/extra-terrestrial symbolic phallus controlling the otherwise independently fecund female form. Suspiciously, none of the accounts seem to illustrate this with any kind of evidential example.

There are so many logics to the association of fish with fasting but maybe, at the same time, none that would quite justify the generation of such herring resentment over the centuries. In the early Middle Ages there was a spirit of tolerance around fasting, which declined. Gruel was acceptable, but fish-eating on fast days gradually took on the force of injunction and herring fishermen were ready and waiting. The abandonment of fast days was one of the key popular attractions of the Protestant Reformation and the market for herring dropped throughout Northern Europe, especially in England (see **British Fisheries** and **Dutch Fisheries**)

In 1966 Pope Pius VI modified the requirement and this then informed the 1983 *Code of Canon Law*. These days, from the age of fourteen until you're sixty, you're expected to fast on Ash Wednesday and Good Friday and all other Fridays unless they correspond with a *Solemnity* which isn't restricted to Sundays (Christmas, Epiphany and Ascension Day). You can get an exemption, but you always could. Erasmus (c 1466–1536) wrote asking for one, because he really did not like fish. In some territories, episcopal conferences have allowed the eating of meat on Fridays other than Good Friday as long you substitute fasting with a pious act.

FILLETING & STUFFING

With herrings, you are never going to fillet out all the finer bones, even with a pin boner. Learn to live with them. Getting rid of the vertebrae and the main bones could not be easier. Decide whether you want heads and tails to remain attached for aesthetic reasons: if you do, find a sharp knife and a pair of kitchen scissors; if you don't, the sharp knife will suffice.

Having scaled the fish, press the tip of your knife into the anus and then pull it through the belly towards the head. You can now clean the belly cavity (save any roe, soft or hard and see **Roe**). Extend the line of the cut towards the tail, open the herring out and lay it on your board skin up. Press your thumbs down hard along the herring's back: you will feel the vertebrae and main bones coming away. Press the fish flat to loosen things, then turn it over. If you've cut off the head and tail, grasp the top of the vertebrae and lift it out of the fish. If you've left the head and tail on, take your kitchen scissors and snip through both the top and the bottom of the vertebrae and then pull from the top. You'll see the bones remaining on the belly flaps: slide your knife under them, as close to the bone as possible and lift them out. Trim off the belly cavity if you want a neater fillet—you'll want to cut off the anal and ventral fins anyway. If you have no plans to stuff the herring, slice either side of the dorsal fin from top to bottom and you'll have two neat fillets.

If you intend to stuff your herring, maybe trim off the dorsal fin with the kitchen scissors. Herbs are good, parsley and tarragon excellent; spices are too—a curry-spiced stuffing works. Breadcrumbs, cooked rice or potato with finely chopped onions or shallots make for good forcemeat bases. Caerphilly features in several recipes and most crumbly cheeses will do the trick. Lemon or orange zest is good. Bacon is great. In Sweden, one can get tubes of cod roe with which to stuff herring. A bit of mashed potato, some crispy fried soft roe, some herring caviar, shallots and lemon zest and you're laughing!

FISH FINGERS

There really was a Captain Birdseye. Well, maybe not a captain and he never said, 'Only the best for the Captain's table,' having died in 1956 (TV adverts for fish fingers were only screened from 1967 onwards) but he was a key figure in the story of frozen food and fish fingers. Meanwhile, one of the prototypes for the Birds Eye Fish Finger was a *Herring Savoury*.

CLARENCE BIRDSEYE

With an elder brother called Kellogg, Clarence Birdseye was, perhaps, all his life, a brand waiting to happen. He was a naturalist, but he dropped out of college when family fortunes took a dip in 1908. He went to work for the United States Agriculture Department and in 1912 while on an assignment to Labrador was taught ice fishing by the local Inuit (either the Nunatsiavut or the NunatuKavut). On the ice, he noticed that at -40°C fish froze immediately. Even more importantly, he saw what the Inuit had long known: when thawed, the fish retained its texture and flavour. Freezing food, including fish, was not new, but the existing slow freezing technology allowed ice crystals to form, which damages the tissues and consequently the quality.

Experimenting with fast fish freezing, Clarence set up Birdseye Seafoods in the early 1920s, but by 1924 the company had gone bankrupt. It had not generated sufficient interest in superior frozen food. He persisted, and came up with the double belt freezer. In 1925, he established the General Seafood Corporation in Gloucester, Massachusetts.

It was 1926 when Marjorie Merriweather Post's yacht sailed into Gloucester. Her father, once a patient at John Harvey Kellogg's Michigan sanitorium, had invented a wheat and molasses drink he called Postum and set up his own company to market it, along with the cereal Grape Nuts, which he also invented. He invented a rival corn flake called Elijah's Manna, which fared poorly. Elijah had been fed bread and flesh by ravens, rather than manna, which everybody knew was a Moses/Exodus thing. The business did well enough for Marjorie to have a yacht.

In Gloucester she was served fish and was told it had been frozen for six months. She liked it so much she bought the company. Postum and General Seafood became General Foods, and Clarence, continuing to work for them, developed more products. In 1930 he invented the multiple plate freezer. General Foods set up the Birds Eye Frozen Food Company, which launched fish sticks. Clarence was involved in the product development; herring seems originally to have been involved, but not exclusively.

BIRDS EYE FISH FINGERS

Birds Eye's British operation developed the product for the UK at its Great Yarmouth factory, market testing its fish sticks between 1953 and 1955. The Great British Public was represented by focus groups in South Wales and Southampton. Would they go for the oil-rich, tender-fleshed delights of herring or the bland alternative? Cod it was, which came to represent the acme of British culinary invention. The decision to call them fish fingers came after a vote by the women on the production line, although the first recorded mention of a *fish finger* had come in a recipe for a shaped and breadcrumbed fish and rice patty, published in the *Tamworth Herald* of Saturday, June 30th, 1900.

In 1953, General Foods sold the British Birds Eye operation to Unilever (formerly Lever Brothers), who had form with fish. William Lever, Lord Leverhulme had set up Mac Fisheries in 1918 with herrings on the logo, but, when he died the board had sold off both it and the port of Leverburgh on the Isle of Harris. Here they were, back, and at the Great Yarmouth plant, the development of the new Herring Savoury was undertaken by H.A.J. Scott. It wasn't just because the rival cod fish finger was blander. When it emerged, it was marketed with the slogan, 'No bones, no waste, no smell, no fuss.' How could it fail with the Great British Public?

In a stroke of genius, even though they were selling cod fish fingers, Birds Eye still followed the unwritten clupeid marketing law: you need someone with a beard. Angus Watson had brought the bearded fisherman in his sou'wester to his *Skippers* brand; Raskin's had a bearded Jewish grocer for their schmaltz herring; Captain Birdseye duly arrived in 1967.

Until 1998 he was played by John Hewer. Birds Eye tried killing him off in 1971, even placing an announcement in *The Times*:

> Birdseye, Captain. On June 7th, 1971, after long exposure, life just slipped through his fingers. Celebrity and gourmet. Mourned by Sea-Cook Jim and the Commodore, in recognition of his selfless devotion to the nutritional needs of the nation's children.

The British Public was having none of it, and they had to bring him back in 1974. When Hewer retired they tried a makeover, bringing in the designer-stubbled Thomas

Pescod, but they realised the error of their ways. Elsewhere in Europe, Captain Birdseye is known as Captain Igloo. This may or may not be a recognition of the role played by the Inuit in the development of frozen fish products.

HERRING FISH FINGERS

History could have been so different. In a rare window of herring availability, I set up my own production line: a tasty treat for any *Fishy Friday*, which could be cooked straight from the freezer—'No bones of any substance, no waste, no fuss and the gentle aroma of fried herring!' I served them to my grandchildren.

'Oh, Grandfather!' they cried. 'What do they know of fish who only know the focus groups of Southampton and South Wales?'

FRENCH FISHERIES

According to Roger Vaulthier (*Le Chasseur*, 1949) Charlemagne founded Hamburg as a herring port in 809. Vaulthier's account finds support on the website of a California canned fish company, but most accounts just say Charlemagne ordered the building of a castle there to secure pagan Saxon conversions. Vikings may have burnt Hammaburg to the ground, but they're also credited with founding Normandy's herring ports. The Norsemen loved the Alabaster Coast and had been raiding it since the late eighth century. Around the time they were burning Hammaburg, a number stopped going home at the end of the raiding season.

The Gauls and the Franks might already have had a herring fishery. Roman fish sauce amphorae show it was being caught in Belgium and England. If the Belgae were at it, it's hard to imagine their fellow Gauls were not too. There was, however, a widespread fish-eating decline after the Roman Empire collapsed. France has never been a major herring power, but its herring industry has its roots in a combination of Viking settlement and the wider *Fish Horizon Event*, which saw marine fish consumption increasing across Northern Europe from the tenth century.

The distinctive sense of traditions in Normandy and England both favour cold smoked over straight salted white and this inevitably draws on cultural sharing between the Norman Conquest and the end of the Hundred Years' War. Yarmouth already had a Herring Fair by the eleventh century. Denied the English throne, in 1088 William I's eldest, Duke Robert of Normandy, established one at Fécamp.

A French innovation which didn't catch on in England was the *Chemin de la Tide* or *Route du Poisson*. From at least the early fourteenth century relays of horses secured the rapid transport of herring and other fresh fish from the Normandy coast to Paris. The third of Claude Debussy's *Trois Ballades de François Villon* (1910) sets to music a fifteenth-century text celebrating the beauty of Parisian language above all others, asking us, if we needed proof, to listen to a couple of *harengères* (herring wives) selling their wares on the city's Petit Pont. The innovative route offered the poet first dibs on fish wife jokes (see **Herring Lasses**).

Exactly when cold smoking of herring began is unclear, but it appears in the literary record from the fifteenth century, as **Red Herring** in English and *soret* or **Haring Saur** in French (see the Villon-influenced **Life of St Herring**). There was also a traditional Parisian street vendor's cry: 'Hareng soret, haring de la nuit', the latter being fresh (as in last night's catch).

The conclusion of the Hundred Years' War may have led to a greater herring culture separation, exacerbated by the Reformation. As well as the resources of the Channel, France's herring fishers followed the Dutch in exploiting the North Sea shoals from Shetland down, but the French were also partial to the herrings caught by others, particularly the ready-barrelled Dutch ones. History does not relate the tonnage of herring brought into Dunkirk by its privateers. Dutch investment in naval escorts suggests it was substantial.

In *Dutch Herring*, Poulsen laments the lack of French historical sources before the 1788 government survey of its fisheries, which found 330 boats involved in herring fishing. Many would have been small and local, but the figure included 180 larger vessels operating out of Fécamp, St Valéry and Dieppe. With their larger boats, when close to home the French would land catches for curing, when fishing at a distance they'd salt and barrel on board like the Dutch busses. As with all major sea-going conflicts the Napoleonic Wars had a detrimental effect, but, even with recovery, the French herring fishery stayed relatively modest in size. Poulsen calculates 4,000 metric tonnes annually in the second half of the eighteenth century and between 1814 and 1850.

Walking round Fécamp's excellent Fisheries Museum—a treasure house of boat models and paintings—a continued cultural exchange, across the Channel, between fishermen was particularly evident. Drift netting continued as the prime method of herring fishing through until the 1930s. Just as French luggers had provided the example out of which British **Herring Boats** largely developed from the mid-eighteenth century, there was reciprocal influence in the nineteenth century. Model after painting after model presented a boat the French called a *dundee*. Looking it up in Mike Smylie's *Traditional Fishing Boats of Europe* (2013), it turned out, just as lugger (*lougre*) technically refers to a lug sail rig, when the French copied the dandy-rigged boats (*dandies*) increasingly favoured by the British herring fleet, they took the name too. Maybe they misheard it while fishing off the East Coast of Scotland. And, just as in some British ports dandies were still called luggers, so, even when the French changed rigs some still called their boats *dundees*.

French fisheries policy today places a higher priority on the sustainability of fishing communities and smaller, inshore fleets, than successive British governments have. I visited Fécamp during its November Herring Festival (see first image section). The museum is on a set of quays thrust out into the harbour, which were filled with scores of pop-up community stalls and bars—herring fresh off the boats and on to the grill or for sale by the kilo in the fish market. There were herring galettes, a Ukranian woman had brought **Shuba** as an offering to the stall where they were selling *Salade Fécampoise* (smoked herring, onions, potato, oil). There were trays upon trays of salt herring fillets. There were kippers. There was an excellent, cigarette smoking, Dutch artisanal hot herring smoker (see **Zuiderzee**). In the interest of balance, I should point out that there are also November herring festivals at Le Tréport, Lieurey, Dieppe and Saint-Valéry-en-Caux. The sense of affection for herring is palpable; of a community at ease with its fish.

(See also **Processions & Celebrations**.)

GANSEYS & GUERNSEYS

Who'd not want a gansey? As well as being the classiest workwear known to man, it's the only jumper ever to be designated as Sunday best, knocking any suit within a hundred yards into a cocked hat. Knitted (not always, but enough) by mothers, sweethearts or wives, the gansey carries an implicit love in each loop of the yarn. You don't have to be a fisherman to wear one, but it helps. In Rae Compton's *The Complete Book of Traditional Guernsey and Jersey Knitting* (1985), there's a photograph of a lion tamer wearing a fine example and nobody would have argued with him—although his mum did come from Sheringham.

Gansey, guernsey. It is commonly said they originated in Guernsey, hence the name, and they may have. Guernsey has a simple frock-knitting tradition which goes back to the fifteenth century, although, beyond this and the name, there is no proven narrative of connection and ganseys glory in complexity. Some have suggested the name comes from the Norwegian *genser* (sweater), but others point to *genser* coming from gansey. The word may come from *garn*, Old Norse for yarn—*gearn* in Old English. The vowel shift might account for the split in what they're called around the British Isles. The way etymologies go, it is entirely plausible guernsey (as a jumper) came from gearnsey, which, the *ea* sounding like or even shifting towards *ue*, led to an assumption, even in

Guernsey, that they came from Guernsey. Speaking *Guernésiais* or Guernsey French, the subtleties of Old English may have been lost on them.

Whichever word is used, the important thing is they unquestionably became the jersey (don't start!) in fishing ports and villages around Britain's coast, not to mention the coasts of other herring fishing nations (see first image section). They are particularly associated with herring fishing. Usually made for a specific person, the yarn has it that the individuality of the patterns were so a community, wife, mother or sweetheart could identify the body of drowned fishermen washed ashore. Apart from the fact most bodies did not wash ashore, it also seems unlikely given how superstitious fishermen are (see **Luck**). Too much like tempting fate. Gansey knitters could and can identify their own work, but the idea comes hand-in-hand with a picture of different communities having their own patterns.

There are unique motifs and it's plausible, in the era of predominantly small boat fishing, such degrees of idiosyncrasy were possible, but even then a knitter would have noted the detail of a stranger's knitwear and copied it. From the mid nineteenth century, the different communities' **Herring Lasses** all mixed together, knitting as they walked along the quays of the British Isles and learning patterns from each other.

Another myth corrected in various books and on various websites is that ganseys are waterproof. Many years ago, when I had a motorbike, I concluded that waterproof clothing was in itself a myth, but ganseys are just water resistant. The higher oil contents in handmade yarn will make them more water resistant, but not proof. The tension in the knit—thin needles delivering high stitch counts per inch—also increases resistance beyond that of many sweaters.

They're strong, not just from the strength of the yarn, but because they are knitted in the round on four wires, plus one for casting off. The needles are sometimes called wires, because they were originally made from steel wire, cut to length and the ends hand-smoothed. Knitting in the round means the gansey has no seams which would provide a weak point. There are no separate pieces, even the sleeves are knitted in. The knitter judged the size of the recipient and varied the number of seed stitches between patterns to accommodate girth. As someone who never moved beyond cotton reel bobbins, there is an air of the miraculous about them, even before you come to the patterns.

Di Gilpin and Sheila Greenwell's *The Gansey Knitting Sourcebook* (2021) identifies and provides diagrams for 150 patterns, broken down into herringbones, zigzags, steps, trellises, basketweaves, cables, ridge & furrows, sandbars, heapies (little turf piles), diamonds, flags, anchors, hearts, stars, starfish and trees of life. Top prize for the number of individual patterns goes to Eriskay. Who knows, but an outburst of creativity might yet be traceable to the 1941 sinking of SS *Politician* with its 28,000 cases of whisky on the rocks there.

GERMAN FISHERIES

Whole books could have been written on the Baltic peoples who might once have exploited the herring spawning grounds of Greifswald Bay, but the traces of Old Prussian historical memory were mostly eradicated in the enthusiasms of Christianity. In Samuel's *The Herring; Its Effect on the History of Britain* (1918) he quotes a Polish poem on a battle at nearby Kolberg in 1105 CE, 'They brought us herring and stinking fish, and now our sons are bringing them to us fresh and quivering.' He doesn't identify the poem itself, however. The rise of the German fishery there came with their twelfth-century expansion into Wendish lands, in which Germans came as new boys to what had been a Danish/Wendish struggle for control of the coastline.

Edging out the Wends, the Germans formed the Hanse out of an alliance between their different towns, taking on and continuing the struggle through the next 500 years in a series of alternating conflicts and collaborations with Denmark. As well as fishing, the Germans developed curing and trading skills which then helped to inform the massive growth of the Scanian fishery (see **Danish Fisheries**). It is impossible to say how much of this was informed by earlier Wendish practice.

Strangely the German North Sea ports did not seriously pursue herring possibilities until the sixteenth century. For an origin story, the Sonntags' *Heimathafen Emden* (Home Port Emden, 1998) draws on Ubbo Emmius' *Rerum frisicarum historia* (Of Frisian History, 1592–1616) to pinpoint 1552 as the date of its first five herring busses. They go on to explain how this had come out of the Dutch Revolt.

> In the middle of the sixteenth century, a number of Dutch refugees, escaping the conflict in their homeland, settled in the city on the Ems. As merchants, shipowners or boatmen, they continued their business under the neutral East Frisian flag and now let their trading ships sail from Emden.
>
> Other refugees, with experience, ships and equipment for herring fishing in the North Sea also saw Emden as a new home port and set up shop here. It obviously made sense that Emden's own merchants and shipowners should also take part in its new citizens' maritime trade and fishing expeditions. In no time Emden had a fishing fleet of up to 40 busses, along with other ships suitable for herring fishing.

When the independence struggles of the new Dutch Republic settled down, most of the refugees returned to the Netherlands, but for a while the momentum continued. It will have been hard to compete with the energy and investment of the liberated Dutch economy, however. The Emdeners had adopted Dutch fishing and curing practices, including the commitment to quality control, but by 1643 there was only one cure-master left in the town. A complaint about this provides the last mention of Emden's herring fishery for over 100 years.

In 1744 Emden was annexed by the Prussian State. It would be yet another 100 years before Prussia saw the creation of the Bismarck herring, but it was already resenting the cost of its salt herring imports. In 1768 it asked Emden to rebuild its herring fleet. At first Emden merchants were unwilling, preferring to invest in the new opportunities of the China trade. When Prussia refused to license new overseas trading companies and began herring fishery negotiations with a town further up the River Ems, Emden's merchants had a rethink.

The herring fishery took off again, only to collapse once more in the difficulties of the Napoleonic Wars and the period of poor catches and low prices which followed. In 1806 Bremen initiated a herring fishery, which collapsed for the same reasons. Things had to wait until German unification in 1871 and the economic dynamism which that precipitated. *Heimathafen Emden* says that, between 1872 and 1913, fourteen German herring fishery companies were established, benefiting from state boatbuilding support, catch bonuses and subsidised rail transport.

After World War I the Treaty of Versailles created hard currency problems, but ultimately this acted as an encouragement to the development of Germany's own herring fleet. National Socialist policies in the 1930s saw renewed commitment to its modernisation, which continued in post-war West Germany. In 1987, in an exchange with the East German DEFA films, Newcastle-based Amber Films documented Rostock in *From Marks & Spencer to Marx and Engels*, alongside other subjects looking at its Fischerei Produktion Genossenschaft (FPG), a worker-owned cooperative bringing together the local fishing fleet and a fish processing works where excellent rollmops were produced. It did not survive Reunification. The filmmakers returned in 2013 to make *From Us to Me*, finding the old works now a quayside restaurant. If DEFA had survived it might have captured the fancy architect-conversion of the smokehouses on North Shields' quay.

Today, most German vessels currently fishing for herring are under 10 m long. There are two pelagic trawlers working the shoals as part of its long distance fleet.

GERMAN SPIES

The maatjes-loving Dutch have their own way with a salt herring. In *The Humble Dutch Herring* (1944), the ever-unreliable Preger (see **Beuckel, Willem**) claims that, in World War II, this had been used in the identification of German spies who might have been pretending to be Dutch:

> Only recently an escapee from Holland who, because of his unusual accent, aroused suspicion, was tested by being given a herring to eat by the Netherlands authorities in London who were interrogating him. All suspicion vanished when, with three expert movements, he filleted the herring in true Dutch style.

Picturing a little crowd gathered around a herring stall, he describes how each would 'grasp the two ends of his herring's tail between the thumb and forefinger of each hand. Then, flipping the herring over its own axis, a firm wrench would remove half the flesh from the bone. This was eaten with zest. The other half would then be filleted with another firm movement, and consumed with gusto.' Delicious.

I have a Dutch herring dish (see **Objects of Desire**) designed for the tourist market, on which the happy Netherlanders dangle whole herrings above their mouths, heads and all. Obviously, the original image might have been developed as part of a wartime programme of disinformation. We may never know how many German spies were caught out by such cleverness.

GRAND MIGRATION

Early herring theory pictured an annual grand migration from the North: a single superpopulation. It went hand in hand with a belief in a nationally-directed divine providence. Even in these faithless days, it's not unusual to find people explaining the sequence of herring fisheries down the East Coasts of Scotland, then England through this imagined phenomenon—no matter that it was scientifically dismantled in the late eighteenth century. The concept almost certainly originated in the exploitation of that sequence by the **Dutch Fisheries** from the early fifteenth century. The xenophobia in conflicting projections of which people were the intended recipients of God's favours probably helped the concept take a firm hold of the public imaginations.

Natural philosophy had flowered with the Renaissance and it had a fairly free range. Patronised by Europe's emerging nation states, it's not surprising to find nationalist constructs of the natural world extending into the oceans between them. Internationalist fishery visions only really took off with the Soviet Union and then only because it had its eyes on everybody's fish.

THE DUTCH

In the sixteenth century the Dutch were locked into a Calvinist struggle with the interchangeable (or indistinguishable) forces of the Anti-Christ and Spain. A nation in the making, the Dutch identified themselves with the Children of Israel led out of captivity: they felt intimate with the hand of God and knew lots about floods and the separating of waters. The Red and North Seas became twinned playgrounds of manifest destiny. Appetites for both learning and herring came together in an account of the new nation's history, Hadrianus Junius' *Batavia* (1588). It traced the epic annual journey the fish made towards the grateful nets of Dutch fishermen.

The providential herrings came out of the Arctic, gathered off the Shetlands and then progressed down the North Sea. This vast migration could only be understood in terms of God's recognition of Dutch righteousness. Herrings were its reward.

ENGLAND & SCOTLAND

With the most prolific of the North Sea grounds being off the coasts of Scotland

and England, Hadrianus Junius' claim did not go unnoticed. "'Tis almost incredible what vast gains the Hollanders make by this Fishery on our Coast,' wrote the English historian and antiquary William Camden in 1607. He had originally published his *Britannia* two years before *Batavia* and hadn't felt it necessary to mention the herrings. Elizabeth I had been more herring-relaxed than her successors. This was the considerably expanded sixth edition, fully taking account of the fact that the Stuarts were anything but relaxed about them (see **British Fisheries** and **Sovereignty of the Seas**). Camden wanted it made clear: if there was to be talk of providence, there was a more likely candidate for its recipient in the joined (if not yet united) kingdoms of England and Scotland:

> These herrings (pardon me if I digress a little to shew the goodness of God towards us) which in the former age swarmed only about Norway, now in our time, by the bounty of divine providence, swim in great shoals towards our coasts. About Mid-summer, they draw from the main sea towards the coasts of Scotland, at which time they are immediately sold off, as being then at their best. From thence they next arrive on our coasts; and from the middle of August to November, there is excellent and most plentiful fishing for them all along from Scarborough to the Thames-mouth. Afterwards, by stormy weather they are carried into the British sea, and there caught till Christmas; thence having ranged the coast of Ireland on both sides, and gone round Britain, they convey themselves into the Northern Ocean, where they remain till June; and after they have cast their spawn, return again in great shoals.

EARLY QUESTIONS

In *De Harengo* (1654) Neucrantz adopted Camden's account, but wanted to know, if it was a single grand migration, why did it choose to spawn in so many different locations? Neucrantz's splendid work may not have enjoyed the greatest circulation, but, either way, no one followed up on this excellent question. The super shoal continued its stately progress through the seventeenth and eighteenth centuries, as did a comfortably overt linkage between religious belief, science and nationally-focused economics. In the first half of the eighteenth century it was popularised in *Atlas Maritimus et Commercialis or a General View of the World so far as related to Trade and Navigation* (London, 1728).

JACOBITE REBELLIONS & AMERICAN INDEPENDENCE

Questions began to emerge again. The German writer Johannes Anderson, in his *News from Iceland, Greenland and the Davis Straits* (1746), ascribes the herring's migratory flight south less to God than to an escape from whales and other predators. Six years later, in the United Kingdom and with Scotland on the post '45 Rebellion naughty step, James Solas Dodd is found narrowing Camden's sense of British providence:

> If the Importance or Dignity of a Subject can warrant the Choice, none can deny but that which I have chose is sufficiently warranted; the Herring-Fishery is an Undertaking that will redound endless Honour to the Promoters here, as well as unspeakable Emolument to the English Nation.
> *An Essay Towards a Natural History of the Herring* (1752)

The Welshman Thomas Pennant opens it up again, etymology inspiring the military metaphors of the herring discussion in his lavishly illustrated *British Zoology* (1766). I do not think it is fanciful to see the redcoats of post '45 pacification contributing to his vision, but it's the most beautifully imagined of all Grand Migration accounts.

> This mighty army begins to put itself in motion in the spring. We distinguish this vast body by that name; for the word Herring is derived from the German Heer—an army, to express their numbers. They begin to appear off the Shetland Islands in April and May. This is the first check this army meets with in its march southward. Here it is divided into two parts: one wing of those destined to visit our coasts takes to the east, the other to the western shores of Great Britain, and fill every bay and creek with their numbers; others proceed towards Yarmouth, the great and ancient mart of Herrings; they then pass through the

British Channel, and after that in a manner disappear. Those which take to the west, after offering themselves to the Hebrides, where the great stationary fishery is, proceed towards the north of Ireland, where they meet with a second interruption, and are obliged to make a second division: the one takes to the western side and is scarcely perceived, being soon lost in the immensity of the Atlantic; but the other, which passes into the Irish Sea, rejoices and feeds the inhabitants of most of the coasts that border on it. These brigades, as we may call them, which are thus separated from the greater columns, are often capricious in their motions, and do not show an invariable attachment to their haunts.

As the herring root word, *heer* was soon disputed (see **Etymology**), but it worked for Pennant. Migration theory, however, achieved its grandest exposition in the newly independent colonies in the Americas. Determined that Providence should not be seen as exclusively European and certainly not exclusively British, John Gilpin was inspired to one last all-encompassing vision in his *Observations on the Annual Passage of Herrings* (1786):

By August, the shoals, having come down from the Arctic along the east and west coasts of the British Isles, assemble in the Channel. From there, they cross the Atlantic, travelling westerly in November, a little more northerly in December, arriving off the coasts of Georgia and Carolina in January. In February they reach Virginia, where in the bays and estuaries they spawn in March and April.

Mindful of an unresolved Baltic question, he explains the presence of shoals there with a group of the smaller herrings turning left at the Skagerrak for an annual or biennial excursion. It was a grand vision, but Gilpin did not know its underpinning theory was already dead in the water.

BLOCH

Before Gilpin had published his speculations in Philadelphia, the great German Jewish ichthyologist Marcus Elieser Bloch had already published his *Economic Natural History of Germany's Fish* (1783).

Bloch wanted to know why the herring was found in many places throughout the year. He wanted to know why it was that smaller herrings chose the Baltic, while larger ones stuck with the North Sea. He wanted to know why, if it was on their route anyway, the shoals visited the coast of Iceland some years and not others. And it would be impossible, he argued, for the herring to perform such an epic journey in so short a time.

Taking up cudgels with his fellow German, Anderson, he also wanted to know why, if their flight was an escape from whales, they felt the need to travel so many hundreds of miles further than necessary. And how was it such large shoals were found where whales were hardly ever seen? If they originated in the Arctic and travelled south from the spring onwards, why were there such large shoals throughout the summer off the coast of Norway? And why had their return to the Arctic never been witnessed? If lack of food drove them south why could their arrivals be timed with such precision?

These were fair questions and Bloch knew he had the migrationists on the ropes. Such migrations as did exist, he suggested, came about from the herring's desire to find suitable banks upon which to spawn. The spawning season, he argued, was most likely to be dependent upon the weather and the temperature of the water.

Nobody likes a smartarse and so it was that the Grand Migration continued to enjoy its popular currency long after Bloch had been forgotten, but any scientific basis it enjoyed had been discredited. With the exception of the Norwegian spring spawner, a great traveller, the herring had been reduced from world explorer to workaday commuter. Any *sturm und drang* awakening of latent nationalist susceptibilities had to wait for Friedrich Heincke's **Racial Theory**.

HARENG SAUR

English translations of *hareng saur* can be confused, *saur* (meaning sorrel) mistaken for *sauer* (as in *sauerkraut*), leading to it becoming pickled herring. In *Seafood* (2001) Rick Stein describes it 'as the French equivalent of kippers, gutted and salted aboard the boat then smoked at a factory close to the landing point.' The French kipper can be called *hareng saur*, *kipper* or *safate*. Technically, the closest translation is red herring, sorrel meaning reddish-brown (the French fifteenth-century poet François Villon calls them *sorets*) but if the hard smoked, hard salted *hareng saur* is still produced in France, I've not seen it. Essentially, as with red, it's just about the colour achieved through its cold smoking.

Whereas, in the world of English herring smoking, the descendants of red herring are only known by their individual names (see **Kipper** and **Bloater**), *Hareng saur* is an overall term, equally used to denote a hard-smoked red, *un kipper* or *un bouffi* (the lightly smoked modern bloater). Under the same hareng saur heading, a traditional salted and smoked, filleted product is made by J.C. David of Boulogne, using only the herrings from the Channel. These are referred to as having been prepared *à l'ancienne* (old style). Their website talks of the herrings not being dried before smoking, which obviously then takes slightly longer, but the description also differentiates them from the *hareng saur* made, like most British kippers and bloaters, with larger Norwegian, Scottish, Icelandic or Russian herrings (see **Smokehouse Tale** for Will Buckenham's Lowestoft red herring preferences).

As to which came first, red herring or *hareng saur*, it's impossible to say, although Samuel, in *The Herring; Its Effect on the History of Britain*, notes that loves, the batons going up the sides of the smokehouse on which the *speats* or spits for reds or bloaters are supported, comes from the French *louvres*—louvers, as in louvre doors. This may hint at some of the smokehouse technology originating in France. Both red herring and *hareng saur* appear as terms in the second half of the fifteenth century (see **Life**

Hareng Saur production, *General Treatise upon Fisheries and History of the Fish they provide, both for the subsistence of Men and for several other Uses relating to Arts and Commerce* by 'Henri-Louis Duhamel du Monceau (1769). From the author's copy of A.M. Samuel's *The Herring* (1918).

of St Herring), but probably originated earlier. The later adoption of the Railway Age's *kipper* and *bouffi* (may have originated in the breakfast demands of English holidaymakers at Normandy's late nineteenth-century seaside resorts: *kipper* is clearly from the English; *bouffi* (see Bloater) results from a mistranslation.

HARENG SAUR MONOLOGUES

In the fifteenth century **Hareng Saur** inspired both Villon and the anonymous poet of the **Life of St Herring**. In the late sixteenth the **Red Herring Joke** was shared by three of England's greatest writers. In the nineteenth *hareng saur* is credited with giving us the modern French monologue or *le monologue fumiste* (smoker's monologue).

During Prussia's 1870 Siege of Paris, people were famously reduced to eating rats, cats, dogs and worse. As with red herring, *hareng saur*—the original hard salted and smoked variety—was the food of sieges and one of the better offerings around. In the mix of affection and over-familiarity, its comic, even proto-surreal potential inevitably came to the fore. The poems, by Charles Cros, Joris-Karl Huysmans and Jean Richepin may also have influenced paintings by Vincent van Gogh and James Ensor (see **Dutch & Flemish Art** and first image section).

CHARLES CROS' LE HARENG SAUR

The inception of Charles Cros' poem is remembered in the autobiography of Mathilde Mauté, seventeen years old at the time and recently married to the poet Paul Verlaine. With the Prussians at the gate, in an apartment on the Boulevard Saint-Germain her mother played piano for a Bohemian group of poets, artists and musicians hosted by Mathilde's stepbrother.

> It wasn't formal, but they'd often invite themselves to dinner, bringing their bread ration and whatever else they'd been able to get hold of. One day, Villiers de L'Isle-Adam turned up with a red herring. Having spent the night on the ramparts, he asked if he could lie down on one of the divans. Charles Cros, who came in while he was asleep, hung the herring on a string above the sleeper's head; then, while the golden fish swung back and forth, he took a sheet of paper and wrote: Le Hareng Saur, Once there was a high white wall, bare, bare, bare, etc.

The poem first appeared in Cros' slim volume, *The Sandalwood Box* (1873), most of which, Mauté says was written at her mum's place during the siege. Others suggest the original version had been a prose piece, which he then developed for publication as a poem.

It became famous, learnt at school by generations of children. By the 1870s, the milder kinds of **Hareng Saur** might have been being produced in Normandy, but Cros is specific about the dryness and implicit about its durability. He may have been aware of the metaphorical use of red herring in English: it would be consistent with the poem he wrote and William Cobbett had popularised this understanding in *Rural Rides* (1830). Cros later dedicated the poem to his son Guy, born in 1879, to whom he quite often read it at bedtime.

LE HARENG SAUR

Once there was a high white wall—bare, bare, bare,
Against the wall a ladder—high, high, high,
And, on the ground, a red herring—dry, dry, dry.

Here he comes and in his hands—dirty, dirty, dirty,
A heavy hammer, a large nail—sharp, sharp, sharp,
A ball of string—large, large, large.

So he climbs the ladder—high, high, high,
And bangs in the sharp nail—tap, tap, tap,
Right at the top of the high white wall—bare, bare, bare.

He drops the hammer—which falls, which falls, which falls,
Ties to the nail the string—long, long, long,
And, at its end, the red herring—dry, dry, dry.

He climbs down the ladder—high, high, high,
Carries it off with the hammer—heavy, heavy, heavy,
And then, he goes away—far, far, far.

And ever since, the red herring—dry, dry, dry,
At the end of that string—long, long, long,
Swings slowly—always, always, always.

I made this story up—simple, simple, simple,
To annoy people—so grave, grave, grave,
And entertain the children—little, little, little.

An inventor as well as a poet, in 1867 Cros had developed a theoretical method of colour photography a year before Ducos du Hauron patented his. Ten years later he designed but never made the *Paleophone*, a phonograph, eight months before Edison patented his method. He was a key member of *Le Cercle des poètes zutique* aka *Les Zutistes* (from the French expression *zut*, as in *zut alors!*). Established in 1871 out of a nostalgia for the comradeship of the siege, it included Verlaine and Rimbaud, composer Ernest Cabaner and illustrator André Gill.

Cabaner set *Le Hareng Saur* for musical monologue performance and Cros' own delivery was celebrated by those who witnessed it. The performer Coquelin Cadet made it famous and placed his own contribution to its success next to that of Cros:

> The monologue is one of the most original forms of contemporary entertainment; an extraordinarily Parisian ragout, in which the French farce smoker and the musical saw meet the shock of America; in which the implausible and the unexpected gambol playfully and peaceably around that which is serious; in which reality and the impossible find their bases in cold-eyed fantasy … I speak of that monologue to which Charles Cros gave birth, I myself,

if I may say, playing midwife; that monologue, that oddly-shaped child, whose earliest stutterings were le *Hareng Saur* … In that moment I saw the dawn of the modern monologue. Never have I been so curiously impressed as when, with the gravity of a man reciting Châteabriand or Lammenais, Cros delivered his incomparable *Hareng Saur*. Little did I imagine this small fish would grow so large, that it would be so relished by the crowds of Café-Concert goers, that it would so charm that ocean they call Paris.

You can almost feel his reluctance to pay Cros royalties, but it led to a falling out. Coquelin Cadet left line by line instructions as to how he felt it should be delivered:

Announce Le Hareng Saur in a strong voice. Do not move; be absolutely still. When giving the title, the audience should feel that it is a black line, standing out against a white background. Once there was a high white wall—bare, bare, bare: one senses the straightness and solidity of the wall, its boring monotone, so break the monotony: lengthen the sound of the third bare, it makes the wall bigger, almost giving the audience the experience of its dimension. Against the wall a ladder—high, high, high: use the same intent and intonation as for the first line and, to impart the idea of height, bring in a falsetto (out of the blue) on the last high, which will make you laugh, entirely in keeping with the fantasy. And, on the ground, a red herring—dry, dry, dry: point to the ground and say red herring with a sad expression which draws attention to this unfortunate herring, the voice, of course, very dry for the three adjectives, dry, dry, dry… etc.

JORIS-KARL HUYSMANS' LE HARENG SAUR

By way of a reply, the year after Cros first published his *Hareng Saur*, J.K. Huysmans published a prose poem of the same name in his first, Baudelaire-influenced slim volume *Le Drageoir des Épices* (The Spice Box, 1874). It was not performed as a monologue —he saw it as a still life—but it is written as a performative piece. Huysmans' poem is a demand to look more closely at the smoked fish: an example of the extraordinary

The musical monologue, *Le Hareng Saur*. Note how the writer gets the smallest billing.

everyday. The intensity of the colours he discovers, as with Cros' poem, also suggests the highly smoked red herring. Huysmans, who worked as a civil servant, was called up during the Franco-Prussian War, but was invalided out with dysentery. In his writing career, he moved from naturalism, through decadence to Catholicism and is most famous for *A Rebours* (Against Nature, 1884) and *Là-Bas* (Down There, 1891).

LE HARENG SAUR

Your gown, O Herring, it is the palette of setting suns, the sheen of old copper, the burnished gold of Cordovan leather, the sandalwood and saffron shades of autumn!

Your head, O herring, blazes like a golden helmet, and your eyes are like black nails driven into rings of copper!

All the sad and dreary colours, all the shining, joyful colours, by turn they dull and they illuminate your gown of scales.

Beside the bitumens, the Judean soil, the Cassel earth, burnt umbers and Scheele's greens, the Van Dyck browns and Florentine bronzes, the tints of rust and dead leaves bring out the radiance of the green-tinged golds, the yellow ambers, stonecrops, brown ochres, chromes and iron oxides!

O, shimmering and smokey, when I behold your coat of mail, I see the works of Rembrandt, I can picture his superb heads, his sunlit flesh, his jewels flickering on black velvet, I can picture his shafts of light in the dark, his trails of golden dust in the shadows, his bursts of sunlight beneath the vaulted blacks!

JEAN RICHEPIN'S L'HARENG SAUR

Richepin apostrophises the *Le*, a creeping onset of modernity which he shares with the first verse's *soubriquet cocasse* (funny nickname), which appears to be a reference to the *bouffi*, the more recent, mildly smoked modern bloater. It's made overt in this translation.

The poem was published in 1886 in Richepin's collection *Le Mer* and was intended from the start to be a monologue, playing to the market opened up by Cros, Cabaner and Coquelin. In the Franco-Prussian War, Richepin had fought as a *franc-tireur* or free-shooter, an irregular. He'd worked with André Gill on a play, *The Star*, in 1873 and had collaborated with Cabaner, who died in 1881. His first volume of poems, *La Chanson des Gueux* (The Beggars' Song, 1876) saw him imprisoned for offending public decency. The music for the monologue was composed by Désiré Dihau and the published sheet music illustrated by Henri de Toulouse-Lautrec.

L'HARENG SAUR

No blushes please, no carcass-shame,
Old pal o' mine they call the bloater.
Guard that crazy name they gave you
Like a treasure.

Let 'em laugh, that sainted crew –
Fine fellahs all, etcetera.
For ugliness you're nowhere near
Their la-di-dah!

For all those blessed airs and graces,
How long it takes to scrub 'em bright!
Flesh as limpid as the air
And ermine white.

Bath tubs ready every morning
As they tumble from their bedding:
Hands appear, all soap and lather,
For the scrubbing.

That precious skin of theirs is like
A blown-up bladder dubbed with lard:
Give me the leather riches of
Your old tarp.

It's just anaemia, you know,
That grants that mannered sheen like silk,
That pretty-as-a-petal pink,
Bathed in milk.

Is your hide clean or not? Who cares?
Its grain is noble to a fault:
Weather-beaten, it won't shun
The curer's salt.

Pulling on those offshore breezes,
Cooking, dreaming in the smoker,
While, beneath, those horses charge
With blood like silver.

Kit, caboodle meld and settle
In the patina of time:
Strange metals, rare tones
That gleam and shine;

And proudly on your solid neck,
That old phizzog: its monkish cast
Holds my gaze, as if a bust
Of gold and brass.

HERRING BOATS

Dismasted, rudderless, sides agape
She lies upon the beach a wreck -
She that was wont, a lovely shape
To sail with beauty on her deck
        from *The Old Sail-Boat*, Francis Charles MacDonald

The oldest boat discovered so far is the Netherlands' *Pesse canoe*, which goes back to between 8040 and 7510 BCE: we're talking a hollowed-out Scots pine log nearly 3 m long. 'Dutch?' you're thinking. 'A herring boat?' Unfortunately, it's thought to have been used in rivers and lakes, but a modern replica has been pronounced seaworthy. Faced with ancient boats hauled out of the mud, remarkably few archaeologists ask the question, 'Could this have been used for herring?' They tend to get more excited about whether they might have been used for trade or colonisation, but even the most coast hugging and estuarially-focused boats would have seen shoals of herring.

The ancestors of the Orkney vole arrived by boat, probably from Belgium, between 3455 and 3100 BCE, possibly carried as snacks: the vole-fed paddlers would have coast-hugged their way and, line or net, they had to supplement their diet. It is hard to imagine surplus voles making it to Orkney otherwise. We know herrings were being eaten in Denmark before 3000 BCE (see **Archaeology**). Notwithstanding the other options provided by **Nets & Weirs**, it's reasonable to speculate that, at some point between, say, 8000 BCE and then, boats began to be involved in herring fishing.

EARLY SEAGOING BOATS

Hollowed-out logs enjoyed a good run and, depending on the weather, were useful in inshore waters. Lime trees were popular, as were oaks. Split, controlled fire was used to burn out the centre of the trunk and, as the technology developed, to manipulate shape and extend the width of the boat. Tools were also used to notch and split off lengths within the trunk and to smooth surfaces. Planks could be used to raise the sides of these boats; prows could be raised and pointed. Log dugouts were still being constructed in England as late as the tenth century CE. It's been suggested, one reason for their demise in Northern Europe was the demand for oaks by plank, beam and keel shipwrights.

The earliest surviving, entirely plank-built hull is the 40 m Egyptian *Solar barque of Khufu* (2500 BCE), but it was made for a funeral and you don't get herrings in the Mediterranean. At Ferriby on Humberside, between 1937 and 1963 the remains of three plank boats were discovered: *Ferriby Boats 1* (1680 BCE), 2 (1940—1720 BCE) and 3 (2030 BCE). Their planks were sewn, as the Solar barque's had been. Boat 1 gives almost the complete bottom of a 13 m vessel, Boats 2 and 3 were more partial finds. Whether they were capable of sea voyages is debated. The most vociferous denials come from Dover, where the Dover Bronze Age boat (1550 BCE) was discovered in 1992. A section of just over 9 m was excavated, but the boat had been longer than this. It was also a wider vessel than Ferriby Boat 1. Strictly speaking, like the Solar barque, it also had been used for a funeral, but Dover Museum claims it as the earliest surviving example of a seagoing boat.

KARVES & FAERINGS, YAWLS & COBLES

Romans in Belgium and Britain were eating herring, if only as a substitute for the range of Mediterranean oily species, in their beloved fish sauce, *garum*. Did they fish for it themselves or rely on local fishermen? Did they bring their own fishing boats north or not? Civilisations have come and gone without expressing the slightest interest in these questions.

For an account of an actual herring fishing expedition, we have to wait until the 960s and two poems by the great Norwegian skald, **Eyvindr 'Skaldaspillír'**. He and his crew probably cast their nets somewhere in or near to the Skagerrak, possibly from a *karve*, a shallow-draft version of the *knarr*, the Viking's sea-going trade workhorse.

Both were similar in form to the longship, but shorter and broader in the beam. He could have fished from a *faering*, the smaller, four-oared Norse fishing boat, later versions of which are still found in Norway (and in the Shetlands, where it is known as the *fourareen*) but he calls his boat a *sea-pig*, which suggests something slower (*faerings* and *fourareens* are still raced today). Longship, *knarr*, *karve* or *faering*, however, they were all clinker built, all used square rigged sails (or could) and oars.

According to E.W. White's *British Fishing Boats and Coastal Craft* (1950):

> All the available evidence concerning the eastern coastal areas of both Scotland and England supports the conclusion that all the small boats owe their origin to the Norwegian Yawl or Yole. This was a light double-ended open boat, such as has been associated with the larger longships of the Vikings.

Norsemen may have taken the jewel-encrusted covers to the *Lindisfarne Gospels*, but they left us with their boat designs. There are *Yawls*, *yoles* and *yolls* of various descriptions, general fishing boats which also caught herring. The Scarborough Yawl was specifically developed as a herring drifter, but that came later.

Meanwhile, around the same time as Eyvindr's expedition, in Chester-le-Street, Aldred the Scribe was adding his gloss to the rebound *Lindisfarne Gospels*, translating its Latin into Old English. For *navicula*, a small ship, or boat, he suggests *cuople*. You can almost hear the Geordie inflection in what is thought to be the first mention of the coble, an open, clinker-built boat traditional to Scotland (from Caithness down), Northumberland, and Yorkshire. Like the karves and the faerings, the coble was a generalist, used for coasting cargoes and fishing. These days, surviving cobles are mostly used for crabs and lobsters. Documentation of Scottish cobles suggests they were mainly used for salmon netting, but the English coble was used extensively for herring fishing and will have been in the tenth century.

Sadly, Aldred did not offer a gloss on his gloss, describing the coble as it was in his day, but those of the nineteenth and twentieth centuries generally range from 3 to 12 m, with a length/beam ratio of around 4:1. With a flat bottom above a flattish lateral curve to the hull, it's held by a centreline plank called a ram. As the sides rise, they curve slightly inwards again in what is known as a tumblehome. A square stern slants backwards and the slightly curving upright prow is raised. It has three very shallow keels towards the aft, allowing it to sit flat on a beach. A deep rudder helps to compensate for this at sea. It has a single, backward slanting mast with a lug sail. This was a development from the square sail, before the mast, of the Viking longships: the spar holding the top edge instead running across the mast, slanted up towards the aft, the sail reshaped to follow the new line and broadened at the base. Aldred's cobles probably kept the sail square, but nothing is certain. There were also two-masted cobles and double ended ones, the sides shaping inwards to a raked sternpost. Sometimes the lug sail could be joined by a jib sail coming down to a long bowsprit.

Despite E.W. White's confidence, there is a debate as to whether Aldred's cobles derived from the stretched skin Irish curragh (perhaps via the monks of Iona who had founded Lindisfarne), from the Viking longships or from some other passing vessel (with or without voles).

HERRING BUSS AND VENTJAGER

All the boats so far have been generalists, used for herring when it was locally in season, but in the Middle Ages, fishermen began to travel considerable distances to noted herring grounds, such as those off Yarmouth or Scania at the western end of the Baltic (see **Danish Fisheries**). The French, the Flemish and the Dutch were Yarmouth regulars, possibly going back as far as the seventh or eighth centuries. The Welsh, English and Scots, along with others, were certainly active at the Scania fishery from the thirteenth century; small medieval cogs may have been used in some of the North Sea crossings, but relatively small open vessels will have formed the bulk of fishing boats at Scania, allowing considerable maritime design exchange. At Yarmouth, Scania and elsewhere, curing took place on shore, ensuring foreign fishermen were subject to local regulations and taxes.

The Dutch herring buss was the first true specialist. The Dutch were strongly involved in Scania, but they had also been buying herring as far afield as the Shetlands and the Hebrides by the fourteenth century. They discovered a sequence of herring seasons on the Scottish and English coasts, which, between them, could sustain eight months of continuous herring fishing and thus specialisation. Essentially a factory ship, gutting, salting and barrelling on board, it did not require negotiated access to anybody's shoreline. Bluff-bowed and broad of beam, the herring buss was built not for speed, but stability and had three masts. The main was square-rigged and also carried a topsail; the fore could be square or jib-rigged (a triangular sail also attached to the bowsprit); the mizzen (the one at the back) was generally gaff-rigged (a spar attached at a slant carrying a four-sided sail, the side to the rear longer than the side attached to the mast). The main and mizzen masts could be easily lowered, facilitating the shooting of the nets. It was developed out of the medieval cargo ship called a *buzza*, probably in the early fifteenth century. By the late sixteenth and early seventeenth centuries, herring busses would typically have a keel length of 15 m and a beam width of between 4.5 and 5.2 m. Crews numbered around fifteen and included coopers and picklers, along with the fishermen, who also acted as gutters. Generally, a buss could carry up to thirty-five lasts (13,200 herrings per last), although some carried considerably more.

Dutch buss success with the herring led to admiration and resentment. Their buss fleet was the largest, but other nations built their own and joined them. **Pamphleteers** actively advocated a British buss fleet, but such boats weren't without their problems: carrying up to thirty-five lasts of herring, gutted, salted and barrelled up, they became an easy target for any piracy. They were, nevertheless, demonstrably successful, although it wasn't until the eighteenth century that the Scottish and English herring fishing industries achieved anything remotely resembling a successful buss operation—by which time, they'd begun to understand, with their own coastline so close, they mostly did not need factory ships.

PICAROONER

A small herring boat, particularly associated with Clovelly in Devon, legend has it the picarooner originated in the cockboats or shore tenders carried by the galleons of the Spanish Armada. The Spanish word *picarón* gives us the English *picaroon* (pirate, pirate ship, rogue or curved spike). The suggestion is that Spanish sailors referred to these boats as sea-thieves. The earliest known use of the word in English is not until 1624—the verb, *to picaroon* or act like a pirate came the following year. Supposedly, one of these little cockboat-pirates was washed overboard and found at the North Devon fishing village of Clovelly, whose locals appreciated its construction.

A couple of Armada wrecks took place off the south-west tip of Ireland: if one of the galleons' unmanned tenders managed to overcome prevailing currents and make its way to Clovelly, it would have deserved appreciation. A manned cockboat would better account for the transfer of the name. Meanwhile, the captured *Nuestra Señora del Rosario* was taken to Dartmouth in South Devon, where its cockboats could have been examined by an unknown Clovelly boatbuilder, aided by a bilingual Spanish prisoner.

A good shipwright can shape a tradition, but styles will always continue to change. Whether or not picarooners came from Spanish cockboats, they will have developed since. They can be longer but are commonly around 4 m long with a beam width of roughly 1.35 m. A smooth-planked open boat, it has a straight stem, curving back below the waterline, while its flat stern angles in only slightly. By the time its design was properly recorded in the nineteenth century, the picarooner was lug-rigged.

LUGGERS AND DANDIES

The word *lugger*, as a type of large sailing boat, refers to the lug rig of its sails rather than a particular design. Between the eighteenth century and the 1870s, most of the various larger herring boats around the British Isles became luggers. From the 1870s most adopted the dandy rig. Such are the ways of language that they were often still referred to as luggers, particularly in Lowestoft. The lugger and its name (from *lougre*) came from France via

Brixham and the South West. The possibilities it brought obviously then influenced hull design, usually in response to the needs and conditions of individual coastlines.

Both the Hastings lugger and the similar Yarmouth one had straight-stemmed bows and modestly raked sterns, whereas the Yorkshire luggers of the early 1800s would typically have a curved bow, and a more sharply raked stern. Initially they all had three masts. In the eighteenth century there was considerable state encouragement to build busses for the herring fisheries. The luggers could provide similar scale, enabling more ambitious exploitation of the offshore herring shoals, but they were also built for speed and, abandoning the busses' factory ship approach, could reach shore-based curing yards quickly. They could also outrun the cutters of excisemen. Edgar March (*Sailing Drifters*, 1952) writes:

> By the 1750s it was a moot point whether many a fisherman on the South Coast was a smuggler in off moments, or a smuggler who went fishing in his spare time, and I think it is quite likely that the need for speed for this nefarious occupation influenced the change-over from the clumsy square-rigged buss to the fine-lined three masted lugger.

Finer and finer lines in luggers eventually saw state prohibition of the fastest designs, but smuggling was in decline by the 1840s. It may be a coincidence, but it was also around that time that fishermen began to dispense with the mainmast altogether—with speed not quite as critical, it got in the way of shooting the nets.

Scarborough Yawl

Clinker built, fully decked and designed from the start as two masted, the first Scarborough yawl was just over 10 m long and was built in 1833 by Robert Skelton. His foreman, John Edmond, later said it was influenced by the boats of North Norfolk. Lug-rigged on its foremast and mizzen (and therefore also a lugger) it sported a jib sail too. It had what is known as a lute stern—flat and raking inward before straightening out to accommodate the rudder neatly within the overall length of the boat. Narrower than the standard Yorkshire lugger, it could be handled by a smaller crew. The Scarborough yawls grew in size to between 14 m and 18 m.

Lug v Dandy

Essentially, having effected the 90° shift of the busses' square sails, the lug sail shape moved to an irregular trapezoid. There was a single mid-sized one on the foremast, a larger one on a slightly angled-back main mast (which also sported a small topsail) and a small one on the more angled-back mizzen. The spars for each sail were rigged dipping towards the prow.

For herring drifters, the dandy rig was a post-smuggling era innovation; an adaptation to having dispensed with the main mast. The gaff for the main sail, which was now on the foremast, was rigged behind it with a triangular bonnet replacing the topsail. A triangular jib was rigged to the fore of the mast—with an extended bowsprit there were sometimes two jibs. A smaller version of this, with or without the jib and/or the bonnet, was rigged from the mizzen. The dandy rig is sometimes called the gaff or ketch rig, although there are some minor technical differences. It took hold in the herring fleet in the early 1870s and, coinciding with the popular development of photography is overwhelmingly the rig of documentary record. Dandies became the *dundees* of the **French Fisheries**.

Scaffies

Double-ended (pointed both front and back) and clinker or clench-built, scaffies grew out of the traditional open herring boats of the Moray Firth—the kind of boats imagined in Neil Gunn's early nineteenth-century-set novel *The Silver Darlings*, but see also **Miller's Letters**. Also known as Buckie boats, scaffas and scaiths, they were similar to the line-fishing sgoths of Scotland's west coast. With a curved bow and a raked stern, they adopted the lug rig and increased in number as grants or bounties were extended to the small boat fishery (see **Smith, Adam**). Numbers increased further as the busses themselves faded in popularity. They were light, not just from design but because they were often built with larch, which also made them cheap.

As well as growing in length in the mid-nineteenth century, Scaffies were developed in both half-decked and fully decked versions, which increased their safety as they went further and further afield (up to 30 miles offshore), but they weren't as stable as the innovative fifies which also began to appear from the 1850s and they were gradually replaced.

Fifies

Double ended like the scaffie, but with upright perpendicular stems fore and aft, the fifie is named after its origins on the Firth of Forth and its Fife coast. Mostly two masted and also rigged with lug sails, it was designed around the needs of beach launches and the shallow harbours around the South East coast of Scotland. It had a reputation for what sailors call 'weatherliness'. The stable design was adaptable. Generally speaking around 11 m long by the mid-nineteenth century, by the 1880s they were being built at 18 m and over 21 m by the early twentieth. The 1870s saw experimentation with half-decked and fully-decked versions. *The Chatham Directory of Inshore Craft* (1997) says:

> From the mid-1880s onwards the fifie became a supreme herring catching and sailing machine, capable of taking dozens of tons of fish in its 2000 yards of (seventy-eight) drift nets in a night and, in favourable conditions, delivering them fresh to market at speeds approaching 10 knots.

Baldies

Like the currant biscuit, which also originated in the 1860s, the name of this Scottish East Coast boat celebrates the popular Italian radical nationalist Giuseppe Garibaldi. Once again developed from Scotland's traditional open boats, baldies were decked, but had a large open section in the middle of the vessel. They shared the fifie's double-ended hull and could be both clinker or carvel-built (the planks of the hull's sides abutting rather than overlapping). Baldies were between 7 m and 12 m in length, although the structure varied as both fishermen and builders responded to government encouragement and economic logics. It is also known as the Leith Baldie, after the town where the first one was built.

Zulus

The story goes that William 'Dad' Campbell of Lossiemouth liked the fifie with its straight stems, whereas his wife liked the raked stems of the scaffie. Some question this account, but either way Campbell ended up building a double-ended boat with a straight-stemmed bow and a rake-stemmed stern. It was 1879. Britain was at war with the Zulu nation and possibly in honour of an anti-colonial struggle—certainly honouring its perceived bravery—his boat was called a zulu. It was slightly cheaper to build than a fifie and gave a bit more deck space at the stern. This raked stern protected the rudder in what were often crowded harbours. By 1900 there were 480 zulus registered at Buckie.

A glory of the late nineteenth century herring fleet, the zulu was supremely fast and elegant in the water. Initially clinker built, it shifted to a carvel build. The introduction of steam capstans allowed an increase in size to over 24 m.

Nickeys & Nobbies

The Manx nickey and nobby were developed in the 1870s, modelled on the Cornish luggers which came up into the Irish Sea in pursuit of mackerel and herring. They had broadly similar hulls, a more-or-less perpendicular stem and a lute stern. Their different rigs made the nickey faster, the nobby easier to handle. Some say the nickey got its name from the fact that most Cornish fishermen were called Nick, presumably after St Nicholas, the patron of sailors and fishermen. He's also patron saint of pawnbrokers, which might have helped during poor fishing seasons. Nobby may have derived from the Scottish *nabbie*, although it has also been attributed to an unspecified Manx old codger, commenting on one of them, 'That's a nobby looking craft, there.'

LOCH FYNE & THE WEST COAST OF SCOTLAND

The smacks and skiffs of Loch Fyne and the West of Scotland were gaff-rigged and single masted. The smacks, developed in the 1850s out of earlier open boats, were half-decked and associated with traditional drift netting. Even as they emerged, a bitter struggle was taking place with Loch Fyne's innovative ring-netters, who, against considerable opposition, gradually took over most West Coast herring fishing. The ring-netters, who largely worked in pairs, came to favour a standing lug-rigged skiff.

In the early 1920s the Campbeltown ring netter Robert Robertson introduced two canoe stern skiffs, *Falcon* and *Frigate Bird*, which at over 15 m were 3 m longer than most of the Loch Fyne skiffs. The style was named, predictably enough, after the stern's canoe shaping. They had wheelhouses, paraffin engines as well as sail and were better able to venture out into the open waters of the West Coast when the skippers of standard skiffs were less keen. Meanwhile, in his wonderful 1970s documentation of ring net fishing, artist Will Maclean (see **Two Contemporary Artists**) includes a picture of *Acacia*, designed by a fisherman from Kyleakin on Skye and built in 1926, the shape of its hull based, after a lifetime's observation, on the line a herring gull makes sitting on the water.

STEAM, PARAFFIN & PETROL

There's a short sequence in the **Documentary** radio ballad, *Singing the Fishing*, which captures the transition from sail to steam. Sam Larner, one of the great traditional singers, had gone to the fishing as a boy in 1892, first as a cook, then, after four years, as a deckie. Ronnie Balls of Yarmouth was from the next generation.

> Sam Larner: There's something 'ooman about a sailing boat, how they answer—and they talk to them. 'Go on, old girl, you'll do this, he'll do it…' They talk to a ship just as they would talk to a human being. But as regards the work, that was like heaven when we gang to the drifters, the steam drifters, absolutely like heaven.
>
> Ronnie Balls: Ah, the steam drifter, the loveliest ship for the job that was ever built.
>
> Sam Larner: I went in the Larty, that was the first steam drifter I went in, in October 18 and 99 and that was the first start of the good seasons. 1899.

Steam powered boats go back almost to the invention of steam engines. The herring industry took a while to be convinced. The first uses of steam were to aid in the hauling of the nets. In 1877 David Allan & Co of Granton built *Pioneer*, claimed to be 'the first screw-propelled steam trawler'—not a drifter, but additionally equipped with seven drift nets for herring fishing. There were several Scottish experiments, putting steam engines into existing drifters as well as purpose-building, but costs were high and boat-owners cautious. The traditional perception of the herring shoals as sensitive to noise may have contributed to concerns, but whether or not they resisted change, fishermen often had a developed sense of where it was leading—David Butcher in *Fishing Talk* (2014) records *herring slaughterer* as a name for steam driftermen.

In *The British Herring Industry—The Steam Drifter Years 1900-1960*, Christopher Unsworth dates a change in attitudes to the success of an English prototype, *Consolation*, in 1897, which places Sam Larner's experience in the very early days. There were sixteen English steam drifters in the year he went on the *Larty*. By 1908 there were 385, 90% of them registered in Yarmouth or Lowestoft, the rest in North Shields.

Many used the fifie design with its reputation for stability, but eventually there were changes, such as rounding the stern to allow more space. The boats averaged around 25 m long and 6 m wide, giving more storage space for the herring, but also requiring space for both engine and coal. The zulu design with its sloping stern and its prow raised under sail was deemed less easy to convert. Purpose-built steam drifters generally got bigger, the economics of them requiring the larger catches they were able to get.

Meanwhile, from 1906, smaller boats, fifies, zulus and others, began to be fitted with lighter weight paraffin petrol motors (petrol was used to warm the motor to the point where it could run on the paraffin). Taking the shaft for the propeller through the sloping stern of the zulu was considered problematic, but at the Buckie and District Fishing Heritage Centre, John Addison drew me a picture of how they took it, towards the stern, through the side of the boat. He assured me the converted zulus handled perfectly well. Checking in Joseph Reid's *The Mighty Zulu* (2012), John's grandfather's and father's zulu, *Rosebank* BF 830, built around 1903, had an auxiliary motor fitted in the early 1920s. For whatever reason, however, having dominated the herring fleets at the beginning of the twentieth century, it's a sad fact that only a handful of zulus survived beyond the 1960s.

POST WAR

Robert W. Gear's *An Eye to the Windward, the Development of Shetland's Pelagic Fishing Industry* (2016) provides an account of the changes in herring fishing after 1945, which can stand as a model of modernisation, not just because Shetland is now a pelagic industry leader in the United Kingdom, but because, at the end of the war it wasn't. With most of Northern Europe's herring fishing nations having, at some point over the previous 700 years, followed the Dutch in exploiting Shetland's shoals, its own fishing fleet was relatively small and had received little investment. 'In the 1946 season,' Gear writes, 'there were 26 vessels over 45ft, 20 under 45ft and two steam drifters.' This was partly because they were still waiting for the Admiralty to return the boats which had been conscripted into Royal Navy service. Shetland was also the last working fishery for a number of East Coast fifies and zulus built in the late nineteenth century.

The fifie, *Swan*, now a sail-training vessel, was retired in the late 1950s; the zulu, *Research*, which can be seen at the Scottish Fisheries Museum in Anstruther, was by 1960 the only one of the old-style drifters still active. Initially, after the war, the buying up of secondhand drifters continued, but increasingly they were replaced by the rounded, cruiser stern, dual-use boats (for both herring and white fish). One of the reasons for the decline of UK herring fishing from the 1920s onwards was the drifter's inability to compete with the purse seiners of Norway and Denmark. In Shetland, they moved towards the purse seine model from the mid 60s. They also started to buy second hand Norwegian boats, before investing in newly commissioned ones, some built in Scotland, some wooden, but increasingly from Norway and steel-built.

With larger and larger boats across North Sea fleets, increased catch capacity, refrigerated or chilled seawater tanks and echo location, herring stocks collapsed and the boats shifted towards mackerel. In the late 1990s, with the stocks recovering, there was a move to the new method of pelagic trawling: a new generation of specialist, steel vessels began coming in at over 67 m in length (over 200 ft). There are fewer of them, but they can go anywhere and catch a lot of herring.

NOTE

Whole books have been written on this subject by people far more knowledgeable. I am deeply indebted to Edgar March's *Sailing Drifters* (1952), *The Chatham Directory of Inshore Craft* (1997) and Mike Smylie's *Traditional Fishing Boats of Britain & Ireland* (2011). Beautifully written, deeply knowledgeable and accessible, Smylie's book would be a good starting point for further research.

It is always worth visiting a herring or a fisheries museum, wherever you are, but, quite apart from its many other delights, the Scottish Fisheries Museum at Anstruther has a 70 foot (21 m) fifie, *Reaper* FR958, and a 30 foot (9 m) baldie, *White Wing* ME113, both of them seaworthy and in the harbour just outside the museum entrance. Sadly, their zulu *Research* LK62 is not seaworthy, but inside and in a special gallery. At 78 feet (24 m) it was the last remaining, first class, working zulu. See also **Yarmouth's Greatness** for Time & Tide Museum and the steam drifter *Lydia Eva* YH89.

HERRING INDUSTRY BOARD

There may have been one or two others, but in 1935 three major problems faced the British government: i) the small home market for fresh and salt herring was diminishing; ii) herring catches had fallen from a 1913 high of 540,000 tons to just over 250,000 tons, but a collapse in exports had led to unsold surpluses; iii) Britain's herring fleet needed modernisation. Before World War I, Russia and Germany had, between them, taken 80% of Britain's salt herring exports. Both now had hard currency issues and the efficiency of Scandinavian purse seiners enabled the Soviets, in particular, to play hardball on prices.

The Herring Industry Board was established, shaped by Ramsay Macdonald's Minister of Agriculture and Fisheries, the Scottish Unionist MP, Walter Elliot. Two weeks later MacDonald resigned and Elliot became Stanley Baldwin's Secretary of State for Scotland. Herrings were seen as 'a Scottish issue' (its curers controlled the trade and therefore held the politicians' gaze). In the 1937 parliamentary debate looking at the Board's progress, Elliot's under secretary, Henry Scrymgeour-Wedderburn addressed the first problem:

> I do not know why herring are not more popular. I do not know enough about cooking, but I believe that cooking is one difficulty. They take a long time to cook, and also people do not think that they are good for children to eat because they have so many bones. If that is so, the best way of proceeding is to try to overcome that prejudice, and advertisement is one of the best ways of doing it.

The Herring Industry Board could not be accused of slacking on that front.

EAT MORE HERRINGS!

For direct simplicity and straightforward good sense, there can be few better slogans than 'Eat More Herrings'. It derived from the 'Eat More Fish Caught By British Fishermen' used by the Empire Marketing Board to accompany the release of Grierson's 1929 **Documentary**, *Drifters*. There was even a large hand-painted version in Great Yarmouth (see second image section). Britain's housewives had been losing their sense of what to do with herring, the Board thought. Between 1935 and 1938, it produced at least four versions of a recipe booklet. Featuring a recipe from Buckingham Palace's own chef (*Harengs frit—sauce moutarde*) the first, *Herring Cookery*, is attributed to Mrs Arthur Webb, the 'well-known BBC Cookery Expert'. Minus the royal recipe, but otherwise barely changed, the second, *The Herring Book*, is strangely credited to Mrs Stanley Wrench.

The New Herring Book, still pretty much the same, is credited to Mrs Webb again and comes appealingly with the tagline. 'Aren't herrings delicious? Says London Films star Merle Oberon.' Mrs Webb may or may not have been personally involved in 'the herring cookery demonstrations held at Great Yarmouth, August 15–19, 1938' for which its souvenir second edition was published. (See first image section.) Sweating their assets, the Board then produced *In Search of Silver Treasure*, using the souvenir edition's cover photograph, rehashing some of the material and dropping both cookery writers from the credits. Educators were targeted in *Lecture Notes on the Herring*.

Parisian fish restaurateur Madame Simone Prunier, who'd opened a London restaurant in 1935, launched the Prunier Trophy for the boat with the largest single shot herring catch of the year. Charles Robinson Sykes, who'd designed Rolls-Royce's *Spirit of Ecstasy*, sculpted the trophy (it can be seen at the Lowestoft Maritime Museum). Each year's winners received £25 and an invitation to dine at Maison Prunier. Her chef Maurice Cochois created *Filets de Harengs Trophy* and she included his recipe in *Madame Prunier's Fish Cookery Book* (1938):

> Fry fillets of herrings in clarified butter, and serve them in this way. Two fillets on each plate, roughly chopped tomatoes tossed in butter on top, then another fillet to make a sandwich. Cover with a light Sauce Thermidor, and brown lightly.

After World War II, the Board experimented with monthly recipe sheets and a set of ten monthly leaflets, *Have Herrings* (a spring issue covered March to May). Convenience was the watchword and whereas, pre-War, there'd been diagrams of how to fillet, there were now regular canned herring ideas. The Board developed several experiments in fish freezing technology and probably encouraged Birds Eye in its herring **Fish Fingers** prototypes. A feature in the Co-operative Wholesale Society's *Family Fare* recipe book (1960) suggested A Herring Dish for Every Month of the Year, eight of them taken from HIB publications, but with Co-op margarine, chutney and salad cream substituted for original ingredients.

The Board's 1961 Annual Report reveals experiments with packs of kippers 'suitable for dispensing from coin-operated machines,' but the world wasn't ready for the Vend-O-Kipper. The report admits, 'herring and kippers are not, unfortunately, items which appear either regularly or, indeed frequently in every housewife's shopping-list.' A new edition of *The Herring Book* came out in the 1970s with colour spreads and entirely new recipes. The interesting educational facts were repackaged and updated in *The Story of the Herring*, but with populations collapsing, the marketing fervour came to an end with 1977's moratorium on herring fishing.

SURPLUSES

Back with the 1937 debate, the Hansard transcript is peppered with jokey MPs each claiming the best herrings were to be found in their constituencies, but the serious contributions are gloomy, angry or defensive. The Board's Annual Report had given little ground for optimism. Robert Boothby offers a ray of hope in the increasing exports going to the USA and Palestine. Mostly growing out of Poland's encouraged Jewish emigration, these would probably have been better described as location shifts than new markets.

Lowering salt herring production had reduced temporary storage solutions for surpluses and the occasional gluts. There are disagreements about how much this was happening, but catches had been thrown overboard. In the 20s and 30s, hunger was an issue with political traction and the senselessness of this waste exercised the political left.

Walter Elliot was a productivist: catch as many herrings as you can and create the markets to accommodate oversupply. At MAFF he'd been the man who'd introduced free school milk to address gluts in the dairy industry. Urged in the debate to do likewise, he stood firm: 'You cannot feed necessitous children on raw salt herring. I can imagine nothing which would upset a child more.' Not even hunger, presumably.

To cope with their indiscriminate catches Sweden, Norway, Denmark and Iceland had long since developed reduction plants for the production of herring oil and fishmeal (see **Måløy Raid**). After the war, the Board encouraged the development of the UK's own fish processing plants, mostly in Scotland. The surplus herring was transported from port to plant by road and rail, but there were problems. Complaints about the smell meant they had to go to the unplanned expense of sealed steel containers. After all the investment, in the late 1950s Peru's anchovy shoals undercut European fishmeal. The Board did its best to keep going with the reduction plant strategy, but in the 60s, it became increasingly untenable.

MODERNISING THE FLEET

The Herring Industry Board had taken a break during World War II, much of the fishing fleet commandeered by the Royal Navy and directed towards mine clearance. The experience with echo location technology played its role in herring population collapses, but that came later. In the late 30s, the Board had invested in decommissioning, equipment loans and setting up an unsuccessful scheme supporting new boat purchases, but the fleet was still mainly made up of steam drifters—many of which were then lost on naval service, along with their crews. Wartime boat-building strategies included replacements for these, designed with a view to post-war sales.

The signs of overfishing were there between the wars. Drift net herring fishers had identified the danger back in the mid nineteenth century, when they fought against the rise of ring netting on Scotland's West Coast. In 1943, the visionary fish scientist Michael Graham published *The Fish Gate*. At the heart of it is what he calls The Great Law of Fishing:

> Fisheries that are unlimited become unprofitable. Perhaps it is necessary to have a version for the socialist state of mind. If so, we might put it: Fisheries that are unlimited become inefficient.

A couple of pages earlier, he'd written:

> One of the strangest and most sardonic effects is on the position of the inventor. His invention is first hailed as just what is required, to remedy the fallen catch per ship with the old gear. The novelty produces excellent trips of fish at first. Those who use it say, 'You must be up to date'. But soon everyone has it; and then, in a year or two, it reduces the stock to a new low level. The yield goes back to no more than before, perhaps less; but the fisherman must still use the new gear. He was better off without it; but, owing to the depleted stock, he could not manage without it now. He needs the additional fishing power that it gives, in order merely to stay where he was before it came in, so he has to accept the expense.

Surprisingly, the British weren't the prime culprits: its fishermen had resisted the key modernisations. Honours go, instead, mainly to Norway, Denmark, Iceland and the Netherlands. Between the wars, they'd invested in diesel, pelagic trawls and purse seining. Britain came late to the party. By the early 60s, the once great East Anglian herring fleet had more-or-less gone, blaming trawlers for its ills. The Scottish industry, on the other hand, enjoyed a short-lived, minor boom on the back of Board-supported investment in new boats and equipment.

The mesh of a drift net is designed to catch mature herrings, allowing juveniles to swim through. With echo location, mid water or pelagic trawl nets and purse seine nets can precisely surround the reduced dimensions of modern shoals. As the nets are dragged through the water, the weight of the fish already caught blocks escape to all, juveniles included. As Michael Graham argued, efficiency generates inefficiency.

The Icelandic herring fisheries collapsed in the 1960s, so there'd been plenty of warning, but it's clear the Board could see what was happening. There's a remarkable passage in the 1961 Annual Report:

> The herring fishermen of this country are not directly affected by what happens to the Scandinavian herring stocks, only the fringe of which they touch by

chance on rare occasions. They are well aware, however, that a great increase in the amount of trawling around Norway has been accompanied by a fall in the yield from the principal Norwegian herring-fishery just as catastrophic as that which has taken place in the North Sea.

Having regard to these misgivings, it may seem strange that, in 1961, the Board sponsored and supported financially experimental herring-trawling voyages by British craft and that they aim to repeat the exercise—on a larger scale—in 1962. The policy stems from two considerations. If trawling has no harmful effects on the stocks, it is proper to engage in it because of the possibilities which are claimed to be inherent in the method, of thereby reducing costs of catching and increasing profitability. If on the other hand, trawling for herring is harmful, we, in this country, are likely to be no worse off by joining others who fish in this manner and taking all we can get while the going's good. Indeed, so doing and thereby threatening to bring so much nearer the time when there won't be enough herring left to make fishing for them worthwhile, is likely to make all concerned far more eager than they now appear to be to agree upon and introduce measures of conservation. As Dr Samuel Johnson so cogently observed: "Depend upon it, Sir, when a man knows he is to be hanged in a fortnight's time, it concentrates his mind wonderfully".

If anybody happens to be in the market for a post-war UK herring industry opera, this should be the basis for its big aria, an acceptance of fate almost as moving as Hamlet's 'There is special providence in the fall of a sparrow.'

Initially led by Britain, in 1977 there was a European Community ban on herring fishing in the North Sea. The fishery on the West Coast of Scotland was closed the following year. In the Southern North Sea and on the West Coast, fisheries reopened in 1981, in the rest of the North Sea two years later. Herring populations have recovered variously, but, notwithstanding the low pre-moratorium base and the noble efforts of the Herring Industry Board, the home market for it never has. In 1981 the Herring Industry Board was merged with the White Fish Authority to form the Sea Fish Authority. It's hard to argue based on the Board's track record that the fish needs such a body to fight its corner, but even though herring fishing started up again, fewer and fewer have found their way to British fishmongers' slabs.

HERRINGISM

I wanted a word for herring enthusiasm, for the ardent affection which has broadly shaped so many of the stories at the core of this encyclopaedia. Until the late 1990s, academic historians in Britain mostly ignored the herring. Certain writers in the late nineteenth and early twentieth centuries did the hard yards, uncovering key narratives. The National Fisheries Exhibition of 1883, largely driven by the fishing industry and the rapidly developing field of marine science, encouraged some historical perspectives. Perhaps the most significant was Anthony Beaujon's *The History of the Dutch Sea Fisheries*, but it seems to have been mostly the herringists who took notice of it.

I am a herringist. I stand on the shoulders of those early giants. I had to: in the late 1990s there were few new accounts in print, but the online secondhand book trade was getting going. Little did I realise what an addictive phenomenon it would become. In my first search, A.M. Samuel's *The Herring: Its Effect on the History of Britain* (1918) stared back from the screen. 'Buy me!' it said. Brought up in Norwich, Samuel wrote a book steeped in love for the fish, particularly for bloaters, but possibly drawing on the food cultures both of Norfolk and his Jewish heritage. He was one of the great herringists.

If a copy of *The Herring: Its Natural History and National Importance* by John M. Mitchell (1864) had been listed at the time, I would have been torn. Samuel had obviously nicked the idea for his title, but in the context of his legacy it seems a minor peccadillo. In 1998 I'd been working in **Documentary** for over fifteen years, but I'd never heard of Samuel, a Tory who became an MP the year his book was published or his crucial role in the field when Finanacial Secretary to the Treasury. A proper historian could not have written his book. Loosely structured around priceless nuggets of beautiful information, it was the perfect introduction. And there are rabbit holes on every page.

The herring histories of the nineteenth and twentieth centuries carry forward the spirit of the antiquary. Mitchell was an active member of the Society of Antiquaries of Scotland. His book set a template for ones to come. Book I provides a *Natural History of the Herring;* Book II is on *Fishing and Curing;* and Book III provides *A Chronological History of the Herring Fishery.* The history is focused on British experience. His cutting and pasting of complete parliamentary acts and reports are rich pickings, even when they sometimes remove one's will to live. It ushered in herringism's golden age.

The Herring and the Herring Fishery by J. W. de Caux (1881) is tighter and includes a chapter on the future of the fishing to remind us that conservation concerns are nothing new. On the title page de Caux introduces the Lacépède quotation about nations' use of the herring deciding *the destiny of empires* (see **British Fisheries**), much cited by later herringists and even in recent academic publications. Significantly he clarifies a narrative, beginning in East Anglia, then Scotland, moving to Scania (see **Danish Fisheries**) and the **Dutch Fisheries**, before returning for the painfully slow rise of UK domination. He also includes an inaccurate translation (by a friend) of Alexander **Neckam**'s thirteenth-century Latin herring poem.

John R. Elder was a *bona fide* Scottish historian, but his wonderful book, *The Royal Fishery Companies of the Seventeenth Century* (1912) has also been largely ignored by all except the herringists. He provides a beautifully detailed picture of Stuart monarchs' long obsession with the herring. My secondhand copy had been discarded by the University of Aberdeen's History Department. It carries a personal dedication by Elder to a Professor Terry, who'd 'evinced the greatest interest in my research'. Terry had obviously slit the pages of the preface and the acknowledgements before handing it over to the department library, on the shelves of which it remained for around a hundred years without anyone bothering to slit open the rest.

The starting point for herringism isn't always history, but its enthusiasm has often led writers to stray from their specialist field. James Travis Jenkins was a Scottish ichthyologist, but *The Herring and the Herring Fisheries* (1927) presents one of the strongest versions of de Caux's narrative. It's a well-written, well-structured book, although some may want to sidestep his sideline enthusiasm for anthropometry and Heincke's **Racial Theory**. To his credit, he seems to have been the first to point to Adam **Smith**'s disingenuous herring statistics in *Wealth of Nations*.

Nestling next to Jenkins in the photograph (see first image section), is Naomi Mitchison & Denis Macintosh's *Men and Herring: A Documentary* (1949), which reimagines six days with the ring-net fishers of Loch Fyne, their conversations perhaps leaning somewhat towards those of Neil Munro's Para Handy stories or a pitch for an Ealing comedy. This masks the radical nature of locating a book in the lived experience of herring fishing. See **Miller's Letters** for an early essay on this and **Documentary**, again for the Radio Ballads' *Singing the Fishing* (1960). Mitchison's 1939 poem *The Alban Goes Out* (included in *The Cleansing of the Knife*, 1978) is, in many ways more interesting than *Men and Herring*. And while on poetry, George Campbell Hay's *Wind on Loch Fyne* (1948) includes a number of herring poems, including, outstandingly, *The Fisherman Speaks* and *Seeker, Reaper*.

Edgar March's *Sailing Drifters* (1952) is a discursive wonder. Its subject is the history of the different kinds of craft which evolved to deal with local conditions and the lure of the herring. His knowledge is wide and allows him to wander freely, although he expects readers to know their nautical terms.

Another marine scientist, W.C. Hodgson, is among my favourite herringists. He produced a couple of shorter, more research field targeted herring works in the 1930s, but in 1957 he brought things together for a more popular audience in *The Herring and the Herring Fishery*. He acts as a counterbalance to the terminology choices of Jenkins and Heincke, but he also comes across as just incredibly likeable. There are moments in his queasiness on the idea of herring 'races', when he sounds like Kenneth More (*Reach for the Sky*, *The Thirty-Nine Steps*, *Sink the Bismarck!*). It's as if he's taking a pipe from his lips and poking Heincke in the chest, 'Look here, old bean, you may get away with that kind of tosh over there, but it won't wash here.'

The herringist tradition has continued. A selection is piled up in the photograph, next to their forebears, many of them bringing their own specialism or focus to the tradition's enrichment. In this regard, the sheer scale of David Butcher's, Angus Watson's and Mike Smylie's work deserves special recognition. I'd also particularly recommend Christopher Unsworth's book, not least for the way he structures his material. It would be impossible to bring together a coherent exploration of all the locally-produced booklets enthusiastically opening up on this territory—my personal favourite (see **Herring Lasses**) is Susan Telford's *'In a World a Wir Ane': A Shetland Herring Girl's Story* (1998), but it's always worth keeping an eye open for them—and a few turn up among the online secondhand books.

With the universities now on board, we're living through a second golden age of herring research, its new complexities, contradictions and corrections enriching the field almost daily (see **Z is for Zeno's Paradox**). It would be a full-time task, just connecting the work emanating from historians, marine scientists, archaeologists, geneticists, women's studies departments and more: perhaps the greatest contribution of herringism has been looking at the herring in the round, to shine its different lights on to the silver scales, enabling us to follow the unexpected reflections.

HERRING LASSES

The gutters, salters and barrel packers, who worked the *farlins* or *farlans*, the long troughs filled with herring; who worked the different herring seasons around the coasts of Britain and Ireland: they were never herring women or herring wives. From teenagers to grandmothers in their seventies they were *herring lasses, herring girls* or *herring quines* (the Doric or North East Scots equivalent).

From the late nineteenth century they were overwhelmingly thought of as Scottish, although many weren't. A substantial proportion of the curers who employed them were, however, and before the start of each season the Scottish curers hired in the fishing communities of the Hebrides, Shetland, Orkney and mainland Scotland. The reputation of the Scottish lasses was such, even East Anglian-based curing companies would source gutters and packers from the same communities. As with fruit picking, it might have been hard to meet the intense needs of the herring seasons from areas where alternative, year-round employment was available. The work ethic and the work rate among these fisher women were both remarkable.

FISHWIVES & FISHER LASSES

Fishwives, fisher lasses, fishlasses belong to a different context from that of the herring girl. A terminological confusion stems from the fact that a woman could be a fishwife or lass as well as a herring lass. The former belongs to work in and from a specific community, mending nets, baiting lines, carrying ballast, selling different fresh fish over the whole year. Herring lasses were a more modern phenomenon, required by the curing trade from the mid-nineteenth century, as operations moved from port to port. They took the curers' hiring fees because their home, family fishing operation could spare them—in some cases because the fishermen themselves were following the herring seasons. The cash that could be earned became an important addition to the family income. The skills and the preparedness to work in such hard conditions, which the curers relied upon, grew out of those of the fishwife.

Technically, a fisher lass became a fishwife when she married, but the male gaze sometimes made exceptions on aesthetic grounds. They were artistically projected as exemplars of a strong and independent-minded beauty. Fishwives were, perhaps, a little too independent and, proverbially, they grew coarser the older they got. Fishwives were a bit scary (see Penelope Payne's *Scold Vixen Harpy Shrew* in first image section).

In her article, 'A Partnership of Equals: Women in Scottish East Coast Fishing Communities' (1992), Margaret King describes a culture which placed a high value on a woman's physical strength as well as her skills in financial management. In a community where beach launches were necessary, a wife might carry her man to and from the boat to avoid the illnesses potentially caused by fishing in wet clothes. Crucially, she took responsibility for the business side of things.

She had to carry a large basket of fish and sell its contents on the streets of nearby towns and cities. She had to be forward enough to secure those sales before having to make the fine calculations between price and a deteriorating surplus. She had to be canny enough to come out on the top of any deal and to make the figures add up. She had to be able to take care of herself and had to teach her daughters to do the same. Sharp knives and sharp tongues were tools of the trade.

In early nineteenth-century Scotland, when most fishermen were still working out of undecked boats, wives would often go with them as they fished further and further afield. They would stay onshore in tents, huts and bothies to cook hot meals and help with the gutting when the catches came in. It is out of these contexts that the archetypal Scottish herring lass came.

In April 1881 the American painter Winslow Homer came to Cullercoats, a couple of miles to the north of the Tyne. Off England's North East, the herring season is in August and September. He was in Cullercoats for eighteen months, during which time there would have been two seasons when he could have painted the work of herring lasses on nearby North Shields quay. His focus was on Cullercoats, its lasses looking out to sea, gathering on the beach as a storm threatens, carrying their baskets or young siblings, even catching a ride back from Tynemouth in the family boat. It was

HERRING LASSES

Herring lasses (location unspecified) at the farlins, on a break and knitting as they walk along the quay (see **Ganseys**), from *The Sphere*, 1913, a peak year for the British herring industry.

never on the farlins, where Cullercoats women and girls would certainly have deployed their skills. In one of his paintings the presence of a steamer hints at change, at the arrival of the modern age, but he was not going to paint it.

THE INDUSTRIAL AGE

Herring lasses, pictured in herring ports on a thousand postcards from the 1870s onwards, were an industrial development. Women had long been working for curers, gutting, salting and barreling during a local herring season, sailing or walking as appropriate when spawning or feeding grounds shifted. It was in the 1860s that the Scottish fleet first sailed south to exploit the season off Great Yarmouth and Lowestoft. The Scottish curers invested in herring processing facilities and took advantage of the expanding railway network to bring the women they felt they could rely on to deliver on the Scotch Cure's brand quality.

The main sequence started in May in Shetland and moved down the East Coast of Scotland, to the Tyne and Tees, to Scarborough and the Yorkshire Coast, to Great Yarmouth and Lowestoft. The traditional Yarmouth season had run between the very end of September and the second week of November, but the industrial season lasted longer. Some would then go on to the Channel season, which went from the end of November into January. It was the extended run of seasons pioneered by the **Dutch Fisheries** from the fourteenth century, but like the Dutch, it also went down the West Coast of Scotland and over to Ardglass in Ireland. By the early twentieth century most herring ports and their local newspapers looked forward to the annual 'invasion of the Scottish herring lasses'.

THE WORK

Like all industrial operations, the work narrowed from the range of the women's traditional skills. Gutting and packing were all the curers wanted—along with skill, speed and remarkable stamina. The herring lasses worked in teams of three: two gutters and a packer. Whoever was tallest and therefore best able to reach the bottom of a barrel generally got to be the packer. Left-handers also got the job, as it was deemed prudent for all knives to be moving in the same direction. Members of the same family or a friendship group, a team would tend to come from the same community. Having signed with the curer off-season for a fee (*earlas* in Gaelic, *airleas* or *arles*—a pledge) everything they needed was packed into a *kist*, a wooden trunk or box that was loaded on to the train and/or boat transporting them to each destination.

The work was hard and, unless the fishing was poor, it was long. 6am to 6pm was standard. Carrying on until 9pm was regular; it was not unusual to work into the early hours of the morning.

There was an allowance for food and in most ports they were provided with basic accommodation. In Shetland this could take the form of long shed dormitories. In the seaside resorts of East Anglia they were paid an allowance for lodgings. After summer visitors had gone, landladies would strip out the rooms and cover the walls with brown paper or newspapers, protecting their properties from the scales, guts and pervasive fish smells that came with the herring lasses.

Some quayside jobs were on an hourly rate, but gutting and packing was piece work, a payment at the end of the season for all the barrels passed by the inspectors and the buyers. A higher rate was paid for gutting than packing, although many teams chose to share the money equally. In return for the lasses' 'keep' money, it was not unknown for landladies to feed them on herrings they had picked up from quayside spillage.

Before World War I, interviewed by David Butcher for *Following the Fishing* (1987), Annie Watt, originally from Peterhead, remembered being paid 8 shillings a week for food and lodgings and 8 pence a barrel. In a memorably good fishing week at Gorleston, near Yarmouth, she remembered her team gutting and packing 288 barrels between the Tuesday and the Friday. A barrel took between 900 and 1,200 herrings, depending on the size of the fish, so that week probably would have seen over 150,000 fish for each gutter—37,500 per shift. And it was only after the First World War that the curers raised the farlins to a more ergonomic height, avoiding the back-breaking requirement to pick fish up at shin level.

In the 1920s the signing-on fee was 10s, the weekly living allowance 15s and they were paid 1s per barrel. The gutters had to sort the herring by size and quality, at speed. In Scotland there were seven categories—*Large Full* (not less than 11¼ in or 28.5 cm, full of milt or roe), *Full* (not less than 10¼ in or 26 cm, milt/roe), *Large Spent* (10 in, post-spawning), *Filling* (10¼ in, maturing), *Medium* (9½ in, maturing), *Matfull* (9¼ in, milt/roe), *Mattie* (9 in, young maturing). There were fewer categories in East Anglia and this speeded the work up a little.

Salt was scattered on the herrings as they were tipped into the farlins, obviously helping with the preservation, but as importantly making it easier for the lasses to pick them up. In her booklet *Dear Gremista*, Margaret Bochel recalls, 'As soon as we took a herring in oor han's we kent its size and the tub to put it in.' A short, sharp *gipping* or gutting knife, known as a *futtle*, was used, guts and gills removed in one deft movement. The average rate for gutting and throwing into the appropriate tub was forty fish a minute, but some managed sixty or more.

The packer, working from the tubs, had to fill each barrel with neat layers of herring, tightly fitted and belly facing upwards. The top and bottom layers were crucially important, because the slightest visible sign of bad packing would lead to an inspector emptying the whole barrel. They did not always look deeper, but this could not be relied upon—sometimes they emptied a packed barrel to keep the lasses on their toes.

The filled barrels were left for a few days to *pine*—the herrings shrinking in the brine. The salt pickle was drained off, but it was kept: the flavour it had acquired was crucial. The barrels were then topped up with new layers of herrings and the pickle poured back in, before the lid was put back on. The lasses were paid 6d per hour for this work.

The sharpness of the futtles and the speed of the work meant accidents were common. The constant contact with salt could make even the slightest wound agonisingly painful. The first lines of defence were the *cloots* or *clooties*—strips of cotton, usually from flour bags, which were tied around each finger at the beginning of the day ('Get up an' tie yer fingers,' was a standard wake-up call). The Red Cross and assorted church and women's organisations provided first aid stations. Blood poisoning signalled the end of a girl's season. Rubber gloves came in just before World War II. The lasses covered their hair to stop the herring muck getting into it. They wore long oilskin aprons and the rubber boots which had replaced the leather ones of the early days.

KNITTING & SINGING

The Scottish fleet did not fish on Sunday and even though the English fleet did, there was some respite. The herring lasses would mostly go to church on Sundays, services were also provided in tents, missionaries travelling between the different herring seasons too. When there was any spare time, such as when the catches were poor, they would knit. There are photographs of whole lines of herring lasses, walking together along the quayside, knitting. They would dance, either at the local Palais or just in their sheds and brown-papered lodgings.

There was always singing. The fishwives and fisher lasses of Edinburgh had been prodigious singers, memorably recollected in 1820 by Professor John Wilson:

> Saw ye them ever marchin hamewards at nicht, in a baun of some fifty or threescore, down Leith Walk, wi' the grand gas-lamps illuminating their scaly creels, all shining like silver? And heard ye them ever singing their strange sea-sangs—first half-a-dizzen o' the bit young anes, wi' as saft vices and sweet as you could hear in St George's Kirk on Sabbath, half singin and half shoutin a leadin verse, and then a' the mithers and grandmithers, and ablins great grandmithers, some o' them wi' vices like verra men, gran' tenors and awfu' basses, joining in the chorus, that gaed echoing roun' Arthur's Seat, and awa over the tap o' the

Martello Tower, out at sea ayont the end o' Leith Pier? Wad ye believe me, that the music micht be ca'd a hymn—at times sae wild and sae mournfu'—and then takin a sudden turn into a sort o' queer and outlandish glee? It gars me think o' the saut sea-faem—and white mew-wings wavering in the blast—and boaties dancin up and down the billow vales, wi' oar or sail, and waes me—waes me—o' the puir fishing smack, gaun down head foremost into the deep, and the sighin and the sabbin o' widows, and the wailin o' fatherless weans!

Meg Hyland's article, 'The Innovative Work Songs of Gaelic-Speaking Herring Gutters', points to a rich vein of traditional song which is only now beginning to attract the study it deserves, but it wasn't only Gaelic singing. Hymns were popular in both Gaelic and English. *The Quartermaster's Stores* was another favourite, particularly if they were still at the farlins as midnight came and went:

> My eyes are dim, I cannot see
> I have not brought my specs with me…

Hyland records one source saying, 'We sang a lot at work: I sometimes think we sang to stop ourselves crying.'

BOLSHEVISM & TEA SETS

The Transport & General Workers Union organised the herring lasses after World War I and there were several strikes. They were usually successful, because no one could afford to leave the herrings to rot on the quayside.

As with their sisters, the *sildarstülka* of the **Icelandic Fisheries**, it was hard to argue too much with the long hours—to achieve the Crown brand mark of quality the herrings had to be cured on the day of the catch (even when technically it might have been 3 o'clock the next morning). They fought to up barrel rates and hourly rates and for improved conditions (a roof over the gutting farlins, for example, or just three lasses sleeping in each hut).

In Susan Telford's *'In a World a Wir Ane': A Shetland Herring Girl's Story* (1998) the author's grandmother, Christina Jackman (née Leask) talks of a strike in Lerwick over the hourly rate for shifting the barrels and salt that came in on the stock boat:

> We only got fower pence an oor first, working da stock boats, an dan we gied on strike for six pence. We gied on strike whan da stock boats cam in. Wir boss called wiz da Bolsheviks, an aa da names he could lay his hands on. We worked wi Bloomfields aa da time. Dey called wiz aathing, but we got it just da sam. Dey hed ta pay wiz tuppence because we stuck together. It was early ida twinties, somewye.

Christina Jackman also describes a slightly more enforced solidarity in Yarmouth in the 1930s:

> Wan year we gied on strike. We got fifteen an six shillings a week, an aabody gied on strike to get anidder half-a-crown onta wir wages. In Yarmouth dey wir dis tree women, an dey gied round aa da yards, aa da fishing yards, an took oot aa da women. God help dem at didna come oot. Dey wir nae black legs in dem days. Naebody dared geng back ta work, because dey wid be mauled. We wir frightened o dem because dey wir huge. Dey took aabody oot on strike… Da strike only lasted tree days. We just walked up an doon da river at Yarmouth. Dan, ida end da curers hed ta gie in because dey wir so much herring. We got half-a-crown, so dat brought wiz up ta seevinteen shillings. But we needna bothered because da landlady pat up wir rent a shilling, so whit we got wis only wan an six pense ida end.

Herring lasses brought money back into families and communities. However equal they might have been in traditional Scottish fishing villages, it gave them a new leverage and independence and played into the development of the Highlands and Islands. They also brought back any number of 'A Present from Yarmouth'-style tea sets and toys for the bairns. Buckie and District Fishing Heritage Centre on the Moray Firth has a beautiful display of the tea services.

The way of life declined with the industry. In 1920 there were 9,000 migrant herring lasses, by 1938 4,500. By 1962 there were only ten Scottish women working the Yarmouth season.

HERRIN'S HEID

The Herring's Head is a cumulative traditional song often thought of as Scottish in origin, although this may be more to do with predominating versions in the early days of the folk revival. Making the most of its Bristol Channel coastline, Somerset apparently claims the most versions. In Scotland and the North East of England you lose the *g* and swap the *a* for an *i*. *Herrin's Heid* is the version my children learned at school and is therefore the one which sticks in my *heid*, but there are many other variations of substance.

HERRIN'S HEID

What'll we de wi' the herrin's heid? [or red herring's head]
What'll we de wi' the herrin's heid?
We'll mak' it intae loaves o' breid! [or feather beds]
Herrin's heid, loaves of breid
And all manner o' things! [or And all such things or And all sorts o' things]

> *And of all the fish that swim in the sea*
> *The herrin' is the one for me!*
> *How are ye the day? How are ye the day?*
> *How are ye the day, me hinny-o?*

[or:
> *The herring is the king of the sea,*
> *The herring is the fish for me!*

HERRIN'S HEID

> *The herring is the king of the sea,*
> *Sing wack-faloodle-day!*

or:

> *The herring is the king of the sea,*
> *The herring is the one for me!*
> *Sing fa-la-la-la-lie-do!*
> *Fa-la-la-lie-do!*
> *Fa-la-la-la-lie-do-lie-day!*

or:

> *The herring is the king of the sea,*
> *The herring is the fish for me!*
> *The herring is the king of the sea,*
> *Sing fol the do or die!*

or:

> *Of all the fish that swim in the sea,*
> *Red herring it is the fish for me,*
> *And all such things!*]

And what'll we de wi' the herrin's eyes?
And what'll we de with the herrin's eyes?
We'll mak' 'em into puddin's 'n' pies
Herrin's eyes, puddin's and pies
Herrin's heid, loaves of breid
And all manner of things!

[In no particular order, the verses accumulate]

Herrin's gills / physical pills
Herrin's scales / a ship wi' sails [or a ship that sails or staples and nails]
Herrin's back / a fishin' smack [or a lad called Jack]

Herrin's fins / needles 'n' pins

Herrin's guts / a pair o' byuts [or of course boots, but the rhyme isn't as good]

Herrin's tail / a barrel o' ale [or Newcastle Brown Ale or a ship o' steel or sharks and whales]

Herrin's belly / jams 'n' jelly [or jars o' jelly or a lass called Nelly or a colour telly]

In the version from North East England with the line in the chorus repeating 'How are ye' the day,' this can be accompanied by the action of shaking hands with the person standing next to you. For a song celebrating the rich and varied community benefits of the herring, it is a great addition, reaffirming the neighbourliness of the community so blessed. The chorus versions where the herring is celebrated as the king of the sea certainly have a history. See **King of Fishes** and **Red Herring Joke** for stories of how it became King of Fishes. The version with red herring, collected by Jim Eldon and Steve Gardham in 1972 at Aldborough in a range of versions (involving sources Alan Grey, Lesley Smith and John Hodson) also has a narrative introduction:

> A fisherman was taking his son for the first time out fishing and as they were pulling away the son said, 'What are we catching today, Dad?'
>
> Dad says, 'We're catching red herrings today, lad.'
>
> 'Why are we catching red herrings, Dad?'
>
> 'Because of all the fish that swim in the sea red herring it is the fish for me.'

Meanwhile, working to the same broad principle, there's a *Herring Song* in the repertoire of the great Eliza Carthy, with a completely different tune, seeming to originate from both sides of the Irish Sea:

There once was a man who came from Kinsale,
>   *Sing aber o vane, sing aber o linn*
And he had a herring, a herring for sale!
>   *Sing aber o vane, sing aber o linn*

>   *Sing man of Kinsale, sing herring for sale,*
>   *Sing aber o vane, sing aber o linn;*
>   *And indeed I have more of my herring to sing,*
>   *Sing aber o vane, sing aber o linn.*

So what do you think they made of his head?
The finest oven that ever baked bread!

>   *Sing herring, sing head, sing oven, sing bread... etc*

Aber is Welsh for river or estuary but, although there were estuarial herrings in Wales, none swam in ones by the name of *vane* and *linn*. Think *wack-faloodle-day*. Before the days of **Reduction Plants**, if *heids* or guts were removed prior to curing, they generally went to farms for fertiliser. The herring is traditionally useful in all its parts.

ICELANDIC FISHERIES

As to the herring interests of the Irish monks who first came to Iceland, we know nothing. Norse settlers arrived in the late ninth century CE, but it took them a thousand years to get serious about the plentiful shoals which gathered around their coasts. Even then, they preferred to export it. Iceland had never had much in the way of forest, but by 1300 its trees were a limited and valuable resource: far too limited and valuable for smoking or heating salt pans. White fish, such as the cod and ling which were also plentiful, dries well without imported salt.

THE HERRING ADVENTURE

In the 1870s Norwegian fishermen began to exploit the herring shoals on Iceland's eastern and northern coasts. They drew on their own traditions, in particular working land-based seine nets, which they stretched across the Icelandic fjords. By the early 1880s, a fleet of 187 boats from seven Norwegian towns were mostly purse-seining. There was an investment in coastal property and infrastructure, but pack ice during a series of cold years put an end to things from 1883.

In 1902, when the ice had receded, the Norwegians returned to test the waters. They found herring in abundance on the northern coast and the fleet returned the following year. The potential of Siglufjörður as a base for processing and shipping had already been identified—at least in the Norwegian town of Haugasund. Both coming from Haugasund, curer Tormod Bakkevig and skipper Henrik D. Henriksen showed up in 1903 and set about building what was needed.

The Norwegians were probably responsible for bringing the distinctive curing mix, which Iceland adopted: salt, red sandalwood and cinnamon. The principle behind the recipe seems to have originated on the Danish island of Bornholm, the spiritual home of **buckling**, but the infrastructure of the Icelandic fishery they established was modelled on that of Norway. Lasting less than seventy years before overfishing brought about a collapse, the North Coast fishery is seen in Iceland as the Herring Adventure. Henriksen's station, opened in 1904, survived in family ownership through to the end.

THE VISTARBAND

To appreciate the profound social impact of this herring fishery, some knowledge is required of the Icelandic feudal system known as the *Vistarband*, which operated with only limited changes from 1490 through until 1894. Without property you could not be a free worker in Iceland. The landless had to belong to a farm. Each year, you could sign up to another farm, but you could not leave it without permission.

You were fed and clothed, but any outside earnings for your labour belonged to the farm, which contracted you out. With no earnings and therefore no possibility of buying land, it was hard to break free, particularly for women. 25% of the population was landless.

The *Vistarband* ended less than ten years before the start of the Herring Adventure. As with slavery elsewhere, its broad economic culture persisted even though the system had been outlawed. Local merchants met with Bakkevig, Henriksen and the other incoming curers and exporters, offering to provide contract labour, but the Norwegians said that they would pay their workers themselves.

Understandably, this was a popular move among Iceland's landless: the first time they had had their own money. In the season, they flocked to Siglufjörður and the other herring station towns along the north coast. The Norwegians were popular in other sectors too. Traditionally, the northern fishermen had concentrated on sharks, probably catching them after the manner recreated by Flaherty in *Man of Aran* (1934). Ready money can be a powerful force in cultural change. As well as the new work for fishermen, jobs on the quayside proliferated: gutting, salting, barrelling and, later, jobs in canning, fish oil and fishmeal factories.

By 1916, Icelandic involvement in this herring fishery had become greater than that of the Norwegians, but the patterns of labour organisation had been established. It was Iceland's first major experience of industrialisation and, however sentimental some owners might have felt about the old feudal ways, the economic potential of the herring generated greater enthusiasm.

THE HERRING GIRLS

If the *Vistarband* had been particularly bad for women, the herring fishery was particularly good. Men on the dockside tended to be waged, but the *sildarstülka* or herring lasses were on piecework and they became very quick at gutting, salting and packing. A skilled *sildarstúlka* could out-earn the men on the quayside, which gave them economic leverage in the home at the season's end.

Unsurprisingly popular culture responded with stories of moral decline, but these were not enough to undermine a growing sense of unity among the women. Whereas they had been quite isolated on the farms, throughout the herring season they worked together in teams for mutual benefit; lived together in company accommodation; socialised together. Before too long they began to organise together.

In 1920 they set up a *sildarstúlka* union. In 1925 it brought them out on strike for one krona a barrel. As with herring lasses elsewhere, they knew their power. The herring are there for a certain period: you either catch them or you don't. Once landed, they must be processed immediately if you want to fetch a decent price: with fish rotting on the quayside, the owners caved in. As with the **Herring Lasses** of the United Kingdom, the frequently long hours were determined by the scale of the catch and the union couldn't do much about that, but pay and conditions steadily improved. The strike had been a pivotal moment. A major shift had been achieved in women's status and political power.

CATCHING THE HERRINGS

Working away from the fjords, the earliest Norwegian herring fleets off Iceland were drift netters, but catching technologies were already advancing. The Herring Era Museum at Siglufjörður has early film footage of ring netting, which had been developed in Loch Fyne in the West of Scotland in the 1830s (see **Nets & Weirs** and **Ring Net Struggle**). The Norwegians became early adopters of purse seining, which had been developed in the USA. This enabled offshore pelagic or mid-water trawling. Within a very few years, the hugely efficient new technology dominated.

The grounds off Iceland are at the colder end of what herrings find acceptable. The North Coast fishery saw a mixed population: Icelandic summer spawners, Norwegian spring spawners and Icelandic spring spawners—the Norwegian spring spawners migrating to feed there. Herrings adapt to spawning in colder waters by increasing the number of vertebrae and therefore length. At 25–30 cm, the adult herrings caught there are large and fat and popular with buyers, particularly in the hugely significant Russian market.

SELLING THE HERRING

Coming late to herring fishing, Iceland benefitted from Norwegian expertise—and that of other nations. Quality was tightly controlled from the start. Magnus Vagnsson's instructional *Handbók—Sildverkunarmanna* may not have brought any radical shift from the curing methodologies developed by the Dutch between the fourteenth to sixteenth centuries, but it was not under any circumstances to be shared with competitors.

Prime quality adult herrings were mostly salted and barrelled for export, but, again following Norwegian practice of the time, **Canning** factories took these, as well as the juveniles, which purse seining also caught and which were marketed as **Sardines**. All surpluses or damaged fish were sold at a lower price to reduction factories, separating oil from the fishmeal, which was then used for livestock feed and fertiliser. European herring fisheries suffered badly during both world wars, but Iceland was a neutral country. The British had dominated both Russian and German markets and Iceland benefitted from its difficulties. German demand for herring oil in the production of high explosives was a bonus.

OVERFISHING

Purse seine nets can surround a whole shoal. Unlike with drift nets, dragging the catch through the water creates a weight of fish which blocks the possibility of escape by the juveniles. The market responded to this, not only by finding value in juveniles, but in spent herrings and surpluses. It would not have taken much to recognise the dangers. There were a series of poor catches around 1950, but like many other nations, the Icelanders carried on regardless.

The folly was compounded by the Norwegians, who were fishing a significant proportion of the same Spring Spawners in their own waters, the fjord-feeding juveniles actively pursued by the sardine canneries of Stavanger. Norway was also a world leader in fish reduction plants. In 1969 the boats set out for the northern Iceland herring grounds, but the herrings did not meet them there.

COLLAPSES & RECOVERIES

The impact of a simultaneous collapse in the three herring populations involved was profound. At its peak the Herring Adventure had delivered between 40% and 50% of Iceland's export income, half of that coming from the processing businesses of Siglufjörður, which had become the country's second-most important town. The factories and quaysides were abandoned. A way of life ended.

Cod populations off the southern coast were showing dangerous signs of collapse. The herring populations of the North Sea, which collapsed a few years later, were already in decline. Over the twentieth century, fishing had assumed enormous importance in Iceland's economy. Its response to the crisis was ruthless. There was a ban on herring fishing, but, even more significantly, Iceland took control of its fishing grounds.

The country had achieved independence from Denmark in 1944. In 1949 it had extended its fishery limits off the northern coast to 4 nautical miles, but the British had not traditionally involved themselves in the herring fishery there, so there had been no Herring War. A general increase to 12 nautical miles in 1958 led to the First Cod War. In 1972, three years after the collapse of the herring fishery, the limit was extended to 50 nmi (Second Cod War). After three more years Iceland set the fishing limit at 200 nmi (Third Cod War).

The Icelandic Spring spawning herring population did not return. The other two populations have recovered but relocated to the East and South Coasts. Strict quotas have been introduced for all the countries participating in the fishery—Iceland itself, Russia, the Faroes, Norway—and there is a partnership with Norway addressing the conservation of the population they share. So far, the approach has achieved a sustainable fishery. There are only ten to fifteen vessels involved today, but each one with the capacity in a week to catch what seven boats would once have caught over a whole season.

With herring fishing having gone in northern Iceland, Siglufjörður is now home to The Herring Era Museum, a splendidly rich and informative exploration of The Adventure. Housed in a set of abandoned herring industry buildings, with a new one built around its beautiful boat collection, it's well worth the five or six hour drive from Reykjavik.

IDDIS

Preserve food in a bottle or jar and clear glass alone allows the world to see what is inside; cans (see **Canning**) require labels. The Norwegian for label is *etikett*, which, on the streets of Stavanger, became *iddiket*—and Stavanger was the capital of Norwegian **Sardines**. Demand for sardine can labels was so high Stavanger also became capital of Norway's design and print industry and *iddiketts* became *iddis*. These days it's Norway's oil industry capital, but it is still the capital of Norwegian sardine label collectors and home to IDDIS, the Norwegian Printing & Canning Museum, where the idiosyncratic beauty of Norwegian sardine can labels can be explored. Why is this important in an encyclopaedia of the herring? Because Norwegian sardines are herrings and sprats.

A LITTLE BIT OF HISTORY

Norwegian canning took off in the 1870s, a wide range of mostly fishy contents identified with printed strips of paper. From the 1890s it rapidly grew around the enormous success of Norwegian sardines, which were undercutting the French ones (which are pilchards). The overwhelming majority of *iddis* were created for the *1/4 Dingly*, the classic sardine tin with a lid measuring 75 mm x 105 mm. In their heyday, most labels were vertically formatted.

The labels enabled a proliferation of brands. The size of the fish can vary, but similarly sized sardines in olive oil can taste quite similar. Across the markets of Europe, the USA and beyond, grocers liked to present themselves as knowledgeable: 'Sardines? Have you tried these?' The novelty of a good label could help; labels inventively designed around individual interests and self-perceptions could transform a grocer into a magician. Persuade your customers' children to collect labels and you were on to a winner. Competing canneries each produced numerous brands and, like cigarette cards, collectable sequences within each brand.

On top of this, labels could be created for different wholesalers and/or their perceived markets. A wholesaler in the American Midwest targeting growing Jewish communities could have a *Dr Herzl Brand*, celebrating the founder of the World Zionist Organisation. A British Tommy could decorate a *Conquerors Brand*, just as a World War I German soldier had once speared a sardine from a tin, using his bayonet, just as the first tank crossing the battlefield of the Somme became the *Tank Brand*, just as the 1934 German European pole vault champion Gustav Wegner seems to have inspired the Aryan hero depicted on the *Sieger Marke* or Winner Brand. And there were kings, queens, princes and princesses; Vikings and Normans; cars, trains, ships and aircraft; happy healthy families and happy healthy children; seductive women, wholesome women, honeymooning women offering their husbands opened cans of promise...

Bjelland's were responsible for what is seen as one of the earliest, a *Nansen Brand* from 1896. Fridtjof Nansen had crossed the icy wastes of Greenland in 1888 and his *Fram* expedition had just reached the closest yet to the North Pole. The polar bears he encountered also became a persistent theme, sometimes sitting on an icefloe eating sardines right out of the can. Later Norwegian polar explorer Roald Amundsen was also *iddis*-ed, along with his airship *Norge* and his friends the polar bears.

Collecting *iddis* started as a children's hobby, probably in the late 1890s. It was certainly in full flow by the early years of the twentieth century. In 1910 it entered the public record in the *Stavanger Aftenblad*, when the President of the Norwegian Stamp Collectors' Club, Bertrand Middlethon announced his intention to collect a full set. It is not known whether this ambition was ever realised, but several albums were produced, each methodically organised by image type.

The use of lacquered paper gave a stiffness which meant, as well as collection and swaps, the youth of Stavanger could make (small) model boats and aeroplanes. *Iddis* also became a kind of scrip for gambling on games of marbles. The big players on the scene developed *sjeining*: throwing large numbers into the wind, just to watch children less fortunate scrambling for the treasure. Stavanger had its wild side. In the same year Middlethon had legitimised these new collectibles, *Stavanger Aftenblad* also broke the story of a printers' boy robbed on the street of an 8,000 label delivery:

> The regular thefts label printers report result from this collecting craze. Parents must be aware of the temptations this craze is spawning. It is clear such quantities of labels can only be obtained by devious means.

Unaware that they were corrupting their own children, some printworkers may have fuelled the craze with discards and excess production. IDDIS houses a collection of around 11,500 different labels. Records suggest 30,000 or more different designs may have been created. The heyday lasted from the early 1900s to World War II. Rationalisation of the canneries and their promotional efforts had begun in the 1930s, a response to the arrival of self-service grocery stores, then supermarkets. When customers themselves selected from a shelf, familiarity moved to the fore in label design. The horizontal format became more favoured because cans displayed on shelves are more stable on their sides and the new width increased legibility.

The 60s and 70s herring population collapses coincided with the arrival of oil. There are no longer working canneries in Stavanger. The market leader, Bjelland's King Oscar Brand became part of Norway Foods in 1981 and in 2014 it was sold to Thailand's

Union Group. These days, the sardines are packed in Poland. *Iddis* remain, however, a testament to an extraordinary flowering in the history of commercial design.

IRISH, MANX & WELSH FISHERIES

> The herring are not in the tides as they were of old;
> My sorrow! for many a creak gave the creel in the cart
> That carried the take to Sligo town to be sold,
> When I was a boy with never a crack in my heart.
> From *The Meditation of the Old Fisherman*, W.B. Yeats (1889)

Why not just call the entry Irish Sea Fisheries? Well, for a start, the Atlantic coast sees winter and spring spawners from Sligo to Donegal, not to mention autumn spawners from Galway to Kerry; then there's the Celtic Sea, plus St George's, the Bristol and the North Channel, all with their own herrings. There is a range of populations even more diverse than the fishermen who have exploited them (the Irish, Manx and Welsh, of course, but Scots, Cornish, other English, Dutch, Spanish, Russian and more). There's history in these waters, but it hasn't had the focus granted to the North Sea or even Scotland's West Coast.

There are reasons for this: herring fishing survived much longer as a seasonal option for farmers; there were lower levels of investment; different stocks are quite localised and tend to be smaller sized. Distance from the political centre and the herring concerns of kings and governments will also have played its part. As with the West of Scotland, the boom times came with the slave plantations of the Caribbean and the accessibility of a provisioning trade which sailed from the Shannon and the Mersey.

With a number of different spring and autumn spawning stocks, the Irish Sea and its channels see herring seasons which run from July to September and October to January, providing good opportunities for specialist fishermen equipped for longer voyages.

IRISH FISHERIES

The narrator in Yeats' *The Meditation of the Old Fisherman* is probably referring to the tides around Howth, near Dublin. The fishermen there had abandoned herring for haddock in the 1850s, but then the haddock abandoned them. Inspired by the Cornish and the Scots who started using Howth harbour for herring around 1860, the fishermen had gone back to herring and the fishery boomed in the 1860s before a decline set in from the mid 1870s. Yeats picked up the old boy's lament in time for *Crossways* (1889), his first collection of poems: by then the town's herring fishing was more or less over. There's a timeless quality to the poem, given the collapses in the Irish herring fisheries over the centuries.

There's no agreement about when herring fishing began in Ireland, but it must have been active by the fifth/sixth century CE when either a wealthy pagan in Roscommon or the magician Mannan in Donaghmoyne tried to kill St Patrick with one or more poisoned herrings. A serving maid (possibly Christian) warned him, either by singing, 'a herring was never caught by its belly' (in Gaelic) or by saying to him, 'Musha my seven loves to the fish that was never caught for his appetite.' In what was clearly another herring miracle (see **Aquinas**) Patrick understood what she meant and got away.

The Danes have been credited with getting the herring fishing going in Wexford, but first mention in the records comes with the *Annals of Loch Cé* for 1217 when, 'All the fishermen of Erinn from Port Lairge [Waterford], from the south and from Loch-Carman [Wexford] northwards to Doire-Choluim-Chille [Derry] went to Manainn [Isle of Man] to fish. They committed violence in it and were all slain in punishment for their violence in Manainn.' By 1258 there were enough Irish fishermen again to be selling herring to the English army in Wales, although these could have been fishers from within the Pale, the Anglo-Norman enclave which included Howth.

Collapses could happen for a range of reasons. The military struggles for control of Ireland could boost and damage fortunes. Carlingford, in the Pale, had a strong herring fishery in the fifteenth century, substantially supplying the English army, but when this market left at the beginning of the seventeenth century, the town fell on hard times. The number of small herring populations encouraged quite localised fisheries and a preponderance of small boats. In a similar way to some on the Scottish West Coast, they could be vulnerable to shifts in the currents on which the plankton drifts.

Some Irish fishermen pursued the herring further afield, possibly better behaved than those in 1217, but the smaller boats tended to fish their local season and switch to other fish in the rest of the year. This made them vulnerable to the sixteenth-century opening up of European fisheries off Newfoundland. English participation was limited, but from the 1580s they seized large numbers of Spanish fishing boats and Ireland will have provided the easiest market at which cheaply to offload the stolen cod.

Patrick Hayes at Dublin's Trinity College Centre for Environmental Humanities sees the international nature of involvement in Irish herring fisheries as one of its unique aspects. The history of the North Sea is one of international herring competition. With limited investment and infrastructure, the Irish may have had a more positive view of other nations' boats, maybe not least because the English were so keen to chase off the French and Spanish.

Ardglass served as one of the major herring ports from the early thirteenth to the mid seventeenth centuries. Its fishery was recognised in a 1470 decree of Edward IV that, 'fishermen may lawfully draw and throw their nets for herrings at all times according to their will.' It continued to serve the Irish market through the eighteenth century, before benefitting from the development of its harbour by the local landowner. Economic redevelopment through the building of harbours had become fashionable with post-Jacobite regeneration in the Scottish Highlands and with the Clearances. The success of Ardglass' new harbour came with its attraction of Cornish and Scottish boats, which substantially built the scale of operations there. The Scotch Cure came with the Scottish curers and Ardglass benefitted from its market reach.

The twentieth century story, similar to elsewhere, saw a shift away from drift netting to, first, ring netting, then mid-water trawling; over exploitation leading to the establishment of quotas, although Ireland did better out of these under EU allocations.

MANX FISHERIES

The most notable herring fisheries in the Irish Sea are off the west and south west coasts of the Isle of Man and, at least from the thirteenth century they attracted boats from Ireland, Wales, England and further afield. The history of the island's own herring fishing, like that of Ireland, has been bedevilled by less ambitious approaches of farmer/fishermen, lack of investment and poor access to markets. From the nineteenth century tourism became a competing focus.

They always seem to have eaten a lot of herring on the Isle of Man, but the changes between original Manx, Irish Manx, Dublin-based Viking, Norwegian, Scottish and English masters did not leave much of a record as to trade. *The Smuggling* or *Mischief Act* of 1765 suggests herring, salt and other commodities were finding their ways across the waters, both in and outbound. In 1785 the duties on Manx herring imported into the mainland were abandoned and the barrel bounty payments available on the mainland were introduced, normalising the herring trade. Two years later, boat bounties for herring vessels of less than 20 tons also benefitted the Isle of Man.

Boats increased in both number and size: by 1826 the Manx fleet consisted of 250 boats, averaging 28 tons. This was extended by the number of Scottish and Cornish boats operating there. The development of Ardglass on the northern Irish coast, together with the Abolition of Slavery, led to a decline, but there was a revival from the 1850s, an increasing number of the men involved being full time fishermen. Fortunes rose and fell again although the boats themselves generally improved. Before World War I there were 35 of the larger nickeys and 22 nobbies (see **Herring Boats**); by 1922 the respective figures were 9 and 16.

The Isle of Man is known for its kippers. *A Manx Life* article from 1973 suggests, 'they have been making kippers at Peel for at least a couple of hundred years,' which would precede the supposed invention of the **Kipper** by seventy years, but there seems to be a confusion with **Red Herrings**, which were obviously being made on the island in 1765, when import duties of 1s 8d per barrel were abolished. What was unique about Manx kippers was that they were only produced in the herring season and therefore from locally caught fish. Elsewhere in the UK, before the days of freezing, smokehouses had come to rely on the railways to deliver year-round supplies. There were once seventeen kippering smokehouses in Peel. Moore's, which dated from 1882, was the last traditional one, the oak dust and shavings lit on the floor and each batch contributing to the black tar of the smokehouse walls. It closed in 2023. You can get kiln-smoked Manx kippers by post from Devereau's, which opened in 1884.

When the UK left the EU, Irish Sea herring quotas began to be readjusted. The Isle of Man, which, since the collapses of the 1970s had been excluded from fishing the recovering stocks, was awarded a share from 2023. The following year they even reinstated the ceremonial role of Admiral of the Manx Herring Fleet.

WELSH FISHERIES

Mike Smylie is a herring man mentioned elsewhere. Among his many books, there is *The Herring Fishers of Wales* (1995), which takes the reader round the coastline identifying historic sites from Tenby to the Mersey: a lament for what has gone.

There are twenty or so fish weirs in the Menai Straits alone and herring was caught there from the first century CE. The most prominent, Ynys Gorad Goch (Red Weir Island) supplied the monasteries of Amlwchy, Penmon and Holyhead with both fresh and smoked-on-the-premises red herring. In 1590, its tenant paid rent of £3 pa plus a barrel of herrings. It had new weirs built in 1824. Smylie identifies other weirs around the coast, some of which continued to catch herring into the twentieth century.

A range of different herring populations performed to fickle type, although historically the shoals have supported not just local demands but healthy exports. Tenby (Dinbych-y-Pysgod or Little Fortress of the Fish) was the export herring capital of the south coast in the medieval period. The mid sixteenth century saw some bad years in Pembrokeshire, when there was a need to import from Scotland. Visiting Tenby in 1724 for his *A Tour Through the Whole Island of Great Britain*, Defoe commented on it having 'a great fishing for herring in its season.' From the 1750s, however, there was another decline. The herring came back in the nineteenth century, but by then boats from Devon had taken control of the harbour. Beyond the fickleness of the shoals, Smylie points to shortages of capital. Without the investment in larger boats, fishing communities were more vulnerable to localised shifts in shoal movements.

A unique sub species exploited *Clupea harengus*' euryhaline tolerance of brackish to fresh water, spawning 10 miles up the Cleddau Waterway, supporting strong herring stations at Llangwm and as far up as Hook from the late eighteenth/early nineteenth centuries. By the early twentieth the stock seemed to be in decline. The fishery came to an end, although line fishermen talk of there being plenty of herring off the coast there.

Aberystwyth had a successful herring fishery, the early fourteenth century *Brut y Tywysogyon* (Chronicle of the Princes) describing how, in 1206, 'God gave an abundance of fish in the estuary of the Ystwyth, so much that there was not its like before that.' In the eighteenth century, if not before, there was an active trade in both fresh and cured Aberystwyth herring, certainly selling to Shrewsbury and the West Midlands. The shoals disappeared in the 1840s. The solicitor for Aberystwyth Corporation denied that it had anything to do with pollution in the river destroying the herrings' estuary spawning grounds.

Nefyn, a few miles up the north coast of the Llŷn Peninsula from Porth Ysgadan (Port Herring) was North Wales' herring capital. It thrived and survived from the Middle Ages until the early twentieth century, *'Penwaig Nefyn'* ('Nefyn herring') being a popular cry. The population included larger herring than were prevalent in the inshore shoals of the other side of the peninsula, which may have helped build the product's fame. It came to an end with the outbreak of World War I. There had been a decline in the population, although not necessarily one that was terminal.

Similar stories run along the coast from Holyhead to Conwy, the quality reputation of the fish having declined by the time you get to the River Dee. The great Welsh naturalist, resident of Mostyn and herring man Thomas Pennant (see **Grand Migration**) noted, 'Herrings in this sea are extremely desultory... Great quantities are taken and salted but they are generally shotten and meagre.'

Welsh herring fishing continued into the 1960s, but its economic significance was long gone. As elsewhere, some of the populations may have disappeared due to overfishing or the destruction of spawning grounds, but the collapse of the home market for herring over the twentieth century probably had more effect on the decline.

JEWISH FOOD

Sephardic refugees from Portugal brought batter-fried fish to Britain, but the Ashkenazis of Central and Eastern Europe may claim the historic honour of being top herring champions. Laments for a youth losing the taste for it, however, go back at least to 1928. 'As to the ham sandwiches, well, they are the logical downfall of a generation that knows not herring,' wrote F.F. Cooper, editor of the *Canadian Jewish Review*, noting the food offer at a dance hall. 'Keep the stomach Jewish when the mind has wandered away,' he tells his people.

What did the herring initially offer, to have played such a part in Jewish food culture? As fish go, it is upfront with its fins and scales. It has always been cheap and the *shtetls* of Eastern Europe were mostly poor. Christian **Fasting** played a part in supporting availability, but from lasts of barrels to a single salt herring, it could accommodate a trading culture in Jewish communities which operated at every level. As discussed elsewhere, the herring has always had a character suitable to ironic humour.

In the twentieth century, the herring was drawn into the antisemitism of both the UK and North America. This may have been helped by its declining role in Anglo-centric eating habits. Between the wars a distinct herring market segment was sometimes, depressingly and disturbingly, referred to as the Jew Boy trade. In World War I, when herring imports from Europe were difficult, Jewish herring merchants saved New Yorkers by sourcing supplies from Nova Scotia and Alaska, only to find themselves specifically excluded from a fish trade agreement with the Canadian Government. 'This is herring anti-Semitism and it must be called out,' cried the New York Yiddish daily, *Der Tog*.

HISTORY

Histories of Jewish herring engagement are patchy, but several of them have it dating back to the sixteenth century and the opportunities provided by the triumphant **Dutch Fisheries**. The major growth of Jewish communities in the Netherlands dates from the sixteenth century arrival of Portuguese Sephardic refugees. Jewish presence in German lands goes as far back as far the fourth century, but it was not until between the eleventh and thirteenth that it coalesced as the *Ashkenazim* and began the development of Yiddish. Hanseatic involvement with the Scania herring fishery (see **Danish Fisheries**) dates from the thirteenth century and both German and Dutch towns were centrally involved. The German Hanse barred Jews from active participation in trade, although in practice this may not have been rigorously enforced everywhere and restrictions were increasingly loosened as its power waned in the sixteenth century.

SCHMALTZ HERRING

What is schmaltz herring? It is Yiddish for salt herring—although you can get smoked varieties. As to the origin of the term, *schmaltz* is rendered chicken or goose fat and some suggest it originally referred to salted herrings which had been packed in this for enhanced preservation. These days, it is often sold in oil (as is much Eastern European herring), but there seems little evidence of *echt* traditional products packed in poultry fat.

Some have argued this would not have been kosher, anyway. Both the Talmud and Rabbi Jacob ben Asher's thirteenth/fourteenth century *Yoreh De'ah* argue eating fish and meat together can cause skin problems and/or damage to the hair (*tzaraath*). Counterclaims that this only concerns cooking practices fall flat in the face of the Talmud's *Chullin 97b* in which Samuel of Nehardea is quoted as saying, 'A salted food item is considered like a boiling hot food item, and a food item marinated in vinegar, brine, or the like is considered like a cooked item.'

There is room for debate (and the Talmud is full of it), but a close reading of *Chullin 97b* suggests the lack of a sciatic nerve in herrings gives one a little flexibility—and the Ashkenazim have a track record of this with fish. The most plausible origin story for schmaltz herring, however, comes from those who identify it with fillets of maatjes and full herring: those caught as they approach spawning grounds, at their most fatty richness.

Claudia Roden in *The Book of Jewish Food* (1996) steers clear of the arguments, saying no more than that schmaltz herring 'can be cured by being covered with coarse salt and left with a weight on top for up to 4 days.'

CHOPPED HERRING

Lovingly treasured herring dishes are to be found in most Jewish recipe books, but the dish of dishes, with each argued-over recipe a statement of identity, is chopped herring or *forshmak*. Chopped herring is a translation of the Yiddish *gehakte herring*, which is what Polish and Lithuanian Jews tended to call it. *Forshmak* is from Old German—*Vorschmack*, foretaste or appetiser.

The Soviet historian of Russian cuisine William Pokhlyobkin (1923–2000) traces its origins to East Prussia and a medieval fried herring dish, the recipe for which the Ashkenazim then carried east, transforming it, as they travelled, into the many versions of the classic, chopped herring, cold paté. On the basis of the name, *forshmak*, the revered American Jewish food historian and founding editor of *Kosher Gourmet* Gil Marks suggests a German, rather than a specifically East Prussian rissole and most historical accounts follow this sketched narrative migrating from a fried to a cold snack.

The following, from Paul Neucrantz's medico-historico-zoological treatise *De harengo* (1654) suggests an alternative story:

> Some fillet salt herring and grind the flesh with onion and apple and sprinkle it with oil and vinegar. Ulisse Aldrovandi thinks there is no better way of serving fish and I'm with him on this, surprised such an easy, healthy and delicious dish is practically ignored in Germany—after all, we have no shortage of freshly pickled fish. I combine carefully filleted and finely chopped salt herring with a slightly larger quantity of chopped apple. I add a little bit of onion at the last moment—the timing is key—along with a small amount of oil and vinegar. This is a dish to revive weak or lazy appetites. Sharpness is softened in the combination, taking away any potential harmful effects. Some prefer adding a pepper salad to stimulate the palate and to encourage the desire to drink, but this is putting taste above health.
>
> *De harengo*, Ch XII, 'Concerning herring preserved with salt'

A comic spirit runs throughout Neucrantz, but he knew his subject. *De harengo* is a summary of seventeenth-century herring knowledge, based on exhaustive reference to classical and contemporary sources. Aldrovandi (1522-1605) lived in Bologna, where they may have already been chopping their herring for a hundred years.

'Practically ignored in Germany' might suggest a popularity only in limited circles—such as, perhaps, the Jews who had migrated north from Italy. Neucrantz, a doctor and an academic, was at ease with Jewish textual sources and may have been as relaxed with the growing community in Germany. The key understanding is that the dish was more common in the Mediterranean, to which salt herring had been exported by the Hanse from at least the thirteenth century (see **Aquinas**). There is no question Neucrantz is describing something much closer to chopped herring than Pokhlyobkin and Marks' rissole, but they probably had not come across his treatise—few have. There is also a Greek recipe (see **Mediterranean Food**) mixing chopped red herring, apple, spring onion and olive oil. It may be a more modern phenomenon, but England was exporting reds to the Ottoman Empire by the sixteenth century. It all speaks of a range of southern chopped options.

The sixteenth- and seventeenth-century Jewish migration from Italy and Southern Europe was extensive and, if they had already been eating Aldrovandi's favoured recipe there, it seems more than likely they would have brought it with them to Germany. The Yiddish name *forshmak* comes from German, but it may just have been because it meant appetizer—the prime function of the dish in Jewish culture.

CHOPPED HERRING RECIPES

It has to be said, *forshmak* or *vorschmack* recipes, particularly in Russia and Ukraine, can also be hot and rissole-ish and, spelt with a *v* the term spreads far beyond the Jewish community. It can use meat rather than herring—appetites are appetised in so many ways. Chopped herring has spread far and wide too, but its diversity within the diaspora alone is enough to keep anyone going. Salt herring, apple, onion, oil or butter and vinegar or lemon juice are pretty much constant (although some recipes go for rollmops & Bismarcks—marinated herring which then lets you drop the additional vinegar). Maatjes can be specified—and they're so beautiful, who wouldn't use them if available? Usually, tart apples are suggested. The onions can be mild, yellow or spring (scallions).

The next most common ingredient is the hard-boiled egg, chopped or grated. One recipe insists the egg should be soft-boiled so the yolk can more effectively colour and flavour the mixture. Almost as common as the egg is bread. One recipe suggests brown, but most specify white. Crusts are always removed. It's usually soaked in water and then squeezed before mixing it in. The bread element can also be supplied by *matzo* crackers, crumbled ginger biscuits (Poland) or marie biscuits (South Africa). The dish is also served with or on bread (including the Jewish bread *challah*). It may even be served on lettuce. Some recipes include a teaspoon or more of sugar, black pepper, salt or sour cream. Some fusion foodies in the USA add chilli.

There's considerable debate about blenders. Some recipes use them without a thought, but, although you would not want large chunks of herring, the joyous texture of the salt fish is lost in what the Jewish Food Society refers to disparagingly as 'homogenous paté'. Personally, I'd mash or blend any egg, matzo/bread, oil/butter and vinegar/lemon juice and use it to bind the finely chopped salt herring, apple (rubbed in lemon juice to keep the colour) and onion. I don't think there are many occasions when herring needs sugar and I might do the **Shuba** thing and grate egg white and yolk separately, using them more as a decorative garnish (see first image section). I don't think I want to know about ginger or marie biscuits.

KING OF FISHES

The herring is the King of Fishes. Some claim salmon is, but they're just riparian hobbyists. History is clear on the matter: many versions of the **Herrin's Heid** acknowledge his majesty, but it's not just in British and Irish tradition. Enkhuizen's coat of arms goes back to the fourteenth century, sporting three herrings each with a crown. French tradition asserts its royalty. In Lübeck **Neucrantz** saluted the herring as Emperor of Fishes, but the city was still in the Holy Roman Empire and he probably just wanted parity of respect. We have the word of Thomas Nashe (see also **Red Herring Joke**) that Vigilius, Pope from 537 to 555 CE, paid homage to the herring's credentials.

There are reasons and there are stories. The fundamental reason lies at the heart of the *Herrin's Heid*: an historical sense of it underpinning the economies of community and of both home and competitor nations. Herring touched the lives of all. A silver darling it is, perhaps, but it is regularly associated with gold—and tied to that the miraculous quality captured in the anonymous fifteenth-century French poem, **Life of St Herring**. Kings have always traded on a supposed sense of divinity.

As the result of a race, it appears in *The Sole* from the collection of the Brothers Grimm:

> The fishes had for a long time been discontented because no order prevailed in their kingdom. None of them turned aside for the others, but all swam to the right or the left as they fancied, or darted between those who wanted to stay together, or got into their way; and a strong one gave a weak one a blow with its tail, which drove it away, or else swallowed it up without more ado. "How delightful it would be," said they, "if we had a king who enforced law and justice among us!" and they met together to choose for their ruler, the one who could cleave through the water most quickly, and give help to the weak ones.
>
> They placed themselves in rank and file by the shore, and the pike gave the signal with his tail, on which they all started. Like an arrow, the pike darted away, and with him the herring, the gudgeon, the perch, the carp, and all the rest of them. Even the sole swam with them, and hoped to reach the winning-place. All at once, the cry was heard, "The herring is first!"
>
> "Who is first?" screamed angrily the flat envious sole, who had been left far behind, "who is first?"

"The herring! The herring," was the answer.

"The naked herring?" cried the jealous creature, "the naked herring?" Since that time the sole's mouth has been at one side for a punishment.

from *Household Tales*, tr Margaret Hunt (1884)

The story of an election, befitting an island claiming the oldest continuous parliament, can be found in *Manx Fairy Tales* by Sophia Morrison (1911).

The old fishermen of the island say that years and years ago the fish met to choose themselves a king, for they had no deemster to tell them what was right. Likely enough their meeting place was off the Shoulder, south of the Calf.

They all came looking their best—there was Captain Jiarg, the Red Gumet, in his fine crimson coat; Grey Horse, the Shark, big and cruel; the Bollan in his brightest colours; Dirty Peggy, the Cuttle-fish, putting her nicest face on herself; Athag, the Haddock, trying to rub out the black spots the devil burnt on him, and all the rest. Each one thought he might be chosen.

The Fish had a strong notion to make Brac Gorm, the Mackerel, king. He knew that, and he went and put beautiful lines and stripes on himself—pink and green and gold, and all the colours of the sea and sky. Then he was thinking diamonds of himself. But when he came he looked that grand that they didn't know him. So they said that he was artificial and would have nothing to do with him.

In the end it was Skeddan, the Herring, the Lil Silver Fella, who was made King of the Sea.

When it was all over, up came the Fluke, too late to give his vote, and they all called out:

You've missed the tide, my beauty!

It seems that he had been so busy tarivating himself up, touching himself up red in places, that he forgot how time went. When he found that the herring had been chosen, he twisted up his mouth on one side, and says he:

"An' what am I goin' to be then?"

"Take that," says Scarrag the Skate, and he ups with his tail and gives the Fluke a slap on his mouth that knocked his mouth crooked on him. And so it has been ever since.

And, may be, it's because the Herring is King of the Sea that he has so much honour among men. Even the deemsters, when they take their oath, say: "I will execute justice as indifferently as the herring's backbone doth lie in the midst of the fish."

And the Manx people will not burn the herring's bones in the fire, in case the herring should feel it. It is to be remembered, too, that the best herring in the world are caught in this place off the Shoulder, where the fish held their big meeting, and that is because it is not very far from Manannan's enchanted island.

Morrison was a key figure in the revival of the Manx language and traditional culture and while she has added her own embellishments to the story, the substance feels authentic. How far back the Manx story went is unclear, but interestingly her version finds correspondence with the herring's election in *Nashes Lenten Stuffe* (1599). **Nashe** probably never visited the Isle of Man, but he knew Ferdinando, Lord Strange, the 5th Earl of Derby, who was also Lord of Man. Strange commissioned Nashe to write the scurrilous poem *The Choise of Valentines or the Merie Ballad of Nash his Dildo* in 1592/93. It may be wildly speculative, but it's not the only element of *Lenten Stuffe*

KING OF FISHES

Make the most of "herring week"

FORTHCOMING HERRING WEEKS

November 19 to 24
OLDHAM · NEWPORT (Mon.)
NORTH-EAST LONDON

Nov. 26 to Dec. 1
NOTTINGHAM · OXFORD
PORTSMOUTH

December 3 to 8
WALSALL · SWANSEA
LONDON (CITY)

Now that meat is scarce, the fishmonger is the Nation's main food supplier. Herrings are plentiful, cheap and full of nourishment. What could be tastier than a juicy herring, a kipper or a bloater! This, then, is your BIG OPPORTUNITY. Make big displays of Herrings. Use the showcards. Hand out recipe leaflets.

THE KING OF FISH

Get your share of this season's bumper sales

ISSUED BY HERRING INDUSTRY BOARD

The King of Fishes celebrates post-war rationing with a Herring Industry Board opportunity for all fishmongers.

which might point to a beginning of his herring thinking in his time with Strange (see **Red Herring Joke** and **Life of St Herring**).

Nashe's version begins with the accidental release of a falcon at sea somewhere between Ireland and England. Coming down to the sea's surface, a shark 'snapped her up, bells and all, at a mouthful.' The birds declare war on the fish, although the ducks and waterfowl with the webbed feet, which might have carried the hawks into battle, decline to offer their services, 'having received so many high displeasures and slaughters and rapines of their race.' The puffin, meanwhile, 'that is half fish half flesh,' warns the fish of the hawks' plans, which is why the fish feel the need to elect a king. Reasoning similarly to the ducks, 'no ravening would they put in arms, for fear after he had everted their foes, and fleshed himself in blood, for interchange of diet he would raven up them.' They decide they need to choose a fish, 'whom they might depose when they list if he should begin to tyrannise.' They also want one who might bring sufficient numbers, if necessary, to 'bid base to the enemy with his own kindred and followers.' And so it was...

> None won the day in this but the herring, whom all their clamorous suffrages saluted with Vive le Roi, God save the King, God save the King, save only the plaice and the butt, that made wry mouths at him, and for their mocking have wry mouths ever since.

The title should not be confused with The King of Herrings, a separate crown which probably comes from the fact that the largest herrings are seen at the head of the shoal. This role is sometimes ascribed to the shad or demon herring and sometimes to the giant oarfish, the largest bony fish, the longest recorded coming in at 17 m.

KIPPER

Ah! The kipper!

Herring, gutted and split, lightly to moderately salted, cold smoked, sometimes to perfection: a breakfast of kings. There's a popular origin story of a fresh herring, for some reason ready split, left overnight in a room with a smoky stove. Or there's the one about a building which burned down and there it was in the morning. Smoked fish origin myths should all be well cured with salt. It has been widely acknowledged as invented in Seahouses, in 1843, by John Woodger.

But no! Woodger, yes, but not Seahouses! Not for nearly twenty years did kippers come to Seahouses. 1843? Quite possibly, but in Newcastle!

I had put a post about kipper history online and the historian George Muirhead replied. There are many gaps in the story, but he filled me in on an altogether more fascinating narrative.

GEORGE MUIRHEAD'S ACCOUNT:

Woodger was born in 1813, in Liss, in Hampshire. He arrived in Newcastle in the late 1830s. Nobody knows why. He was maybe an impoverished agricultural labourer going somewhere he thought he would get a job, but there's nothing definite. We know he was in Newcastle in 1841: he married a local woman, Sarah Elstob. Their only son died quite early and Sarah herself died in 1845. In 1843, I think he was landlord of The Ship in Newcastle's Drury Lane. The entry barriers to becoming a publican were quite low. About a year after Sarah died he married Eleanor Tweedie, who I think came from Tynemouth. We know of six surviving children. He was at the Plough Inn, in the Bigg Market, around 1847.

Woodger saw an opportunity to make money in Newcastle and the rest of his family, five brothers and, I think, his mother and father, all came up. Most people seem to agree, he came up with the idea of the kippered herring round about the early to mid 1840s. 1843 is the date everyone gives, but there isn't a letter or anything. The standard account is that he sent the first kipper shipments to London in 1846.

He kept the Newcastle operation going, but he moved to Newbiggin-by-the-Sea, which at the time was an important herring port. He was there between 1854 and 1858. It's a moot point as to whether he lived there or just came during the herring season, but he built what the locals called the Herring House, practically on the water's edge, in partnership with John Henderson, who was a publican and fishmonger. He later sold the Herring House to Henderson, around 1860/1 and it was only after that he moved further north to Seahouses, where he bought property between about 1864 and 1867. Seahouses and Berwick had become the most important herring ports on that coast and, to the south, North Shields was superseding Newbiggin.

In November 1877 his son, George Edward Woodger, gave evidence to the Buckland and Walpole inquiry into the herring fisheries. He says the family had been trading in Seahouses for 15 or 16 years, which fits. He also said his father invented the kippered herring.

According to Muirhead, the six brothers were all involved in fish processing. Two were active on the Berwickshire coast in the 1850s: Thomas at Eyemouth and Edward at Dunbar. Thomas also spent time in Liverpool, while Frank was a fish merchant in Scarborough. Another brother became a grocer in London. John Woodger, himself, moved to Great Yarmouth:

MUIRHEAD:

He was certainly active there by the early 1870s, but may have been curing there as early as 1863. He made Yarmouth his home and divided his time between there and Newcastle. In 1875 Frank Buckland, in his *Report on the Fisheries of Norfolk*, praised Woodger's enterprise for introducing the kipper to Yarmouth. By the time Woodger died, in 1876, the company owned curing premises on the town's South Quay, while he had a house and fifteen cottages. He was, as a Liberal, active in local politics and had been elected to the Board of Guardians. He died at his son's house in Newcastle in the November of that year and is buried in Elswick Cemetery in Newcastle's West End.

In the mid-1880s the company was being run by his sons, George Edward and Nathan Lamble Woodger. With production and trading premises near the railway station on Forth Street in Newcastle, they had what was called a Dried Fish Store on Northumberland Street, but the family firm was also active at Seahouses, North Shields, Great Yarmouth, Stornoway and Peterhead. A few years later, Buckie joined the list and at some point they had a yard at Wick.

Muirhead sketches a picture of a kipper empire: you begin to see how it spread through both the country and the national consciousness in ways the modern Yarmouth bloater, these days very much an East Anglian delicacy, never did. In 1919, this family empire was sold to Lord Leverhulme's Holman Colonial Fishing Company, which later became part of his Mac Fisheries operation and, consequently, Unilever.

THE LOGICS OF EXPANSION

Like the Yarmouth bloater, the kipper was a product both of the Railway Age and the rapid expansion, from the 1840s onwards, of Britain's herring industry. Mild cures depend on rapid transport. Red herrings or traditional bloaters, heavily salted and smoked, last a year or more, whatever the climate. Did Woodger, himself, make red herring as well as kippers? Muirhead says there is some evidence he produced both bloaters and red herring at Newbiggin. As you'd expect, there was a period of transition.

MUIRHEAD:

The evidence from the Fishery Board records points to production of the traditional cures, red herrings and bloaters, expanding first, because they were a traditional proven product. But they're not smoking them so long: the market begins to change as people appreciate milder cures with a higher moisture content than might have been the case in say the 1820s. Kippers could have ridden in on this. As the output of red herring and bloaters goes up, kippers become more important as a kind of staple product, but by the 1870s kippers may well have been the established product.

The Woodgers' smoking operation, simultaneous with the growing reach of the Scottish salt herring curers, was based initially on following the different seasons around the coast. As kippers caught the public imagination other curers began to produce them, but the rail distribution that had enabled a national market also enabled smokehouses to source fresh herring all year round. Before the railways, the Scots had supplied fresh herring to London, packed in carts with ice and straw, but now something new emerged. *Freshing* involved a light sprinkling of salt and a rail network. As well as year-round kipper production it enabled **Klondyking**, using steamers.

MUIRHEAD:

By the 1880s kippers were produced all the year round. And certainly, as far as the North East goes, Woodger's premises on Forth Banks, near the railway station, gave them options. They could send fresh herring to the market or cure it there for distribution in and from Newcastle. There were curers based in urban areas who bought fresh herring and smoked it themselves. Others produced it on the coast and sent the kippers out. While they shipped their own kippers out, Woodger's probably also supplied the *freshed* market.

Freshing was made unnecessary by the freezer, but the logic remained the same. In the Isle of Man, they stayed with seasonal production for longer than elsewhere, probably until freezers enabled them to preserve their own fresh fish, but throughout Britain and Ireland, smokehouses declined as specialist, year-round operations increased. These days most get their herring from Norway.

SMOKING KIPPERS

Smoked salmon produced from *kippers* or thin, spent fish was common in the eighteenth century. C.L. Cutting, in *Fish Saving* (1955) explains: 'When caught, the lack of fat and emaciated appearance of a kipper led to its being split and smoked to make it more palatable. It may have been, too, that on account of the low fat content there was less trouble with rancidity in a drying, as opposed to a pickling process.' Smoking was introduced as an aid to drying. The verb, *to kipper*, is a transfer from the subject of the process to the process, itself, of splitting and smoking. It wasn't used in connection with herrings until Woodger started producing his kippers, initially *kippered herrings*, giving a new noun entirely divorced from the spent fish connotation.

The glory of the kipper lies in its diversity. Beautiful examples are created, not only in Seahouses, Craster and Great Yarmouth, but along the South Coast, all the way up the East Coast, in Scotland, in the Isle of Man and down the West Coast of England and Wales. *Les kippers* are also produced in Normandy.

Used for kippers, bloaters, red, golden and silver herring, cold smoking places the fish at a distance from a slow fire, sufficient to prevent cooking of the flesh through heat. Traditionally this is provided either through the height of the smokehouse or through construction of a shallow sloped chimney. The slow, non-flaming burn uses both sawdust and woodchips; the temperature of the smoke does not normally exceed 85°F (29.5°C); Hardwoods are preferred.

Most traditional kipper smokers use oak and/or beech. Coniferous woods are avoided because of their high resin content, although, in the words of an old Lowestoft smoker I interviewed in the late 1990s, 'Oak-smoked covers a multitood of sins.' He suggested the ratio of oak to other woods could fall as low as 1:10. He himself liked to use a bit of pine in the mix, which gave his kippers an almost varnished appearance.

PAINTED LADIES

Most artisinal smokehouses emphasise their 'natural' kipper production. Depending on how long you smoke them, a beautiful reddish brown colouring can—and should —come just from the smoke. It is why red herrings are so named. You still see the often blotchily dyed versions. *Manx Style Kippers* is the most depressing description I've come across for them. The fullest account of the dyeing story I've read is Christopher Unsworth's excellent *The British Herring Industry: The Steam Drifter Years 1900–1960* (2013).

What was called the *Painted Lady* first appeared in World War I. There was a shortage of herrings; curers sold kippers by weight; reducing smoking time meant losing less moisture. They were able to get an extra 12½% by weight through less smoking, but the product was suspiciously pallid. The dye reassured customers they were the genuine article, even though they weren't. Originally this was widely done with a coal tar-based dye, *Brown FK* (For Kippers), but too much of this isn't good for you—EU legislation limits the ADI (Acceptable Daily Intake) to 0.15 mg/kg.

Dyed kippers today are coloured with annatto, a natural product derived from the seeds of the achiote tree. Brought to Europe from the Americas in the sixteenth century—and used in the making of Double Gloucester cheese since then—it may have been added by some herring curers from the early days of kipper painting.

SMOKEHOUSE V KILN

In recent years public tastes have moved towards ever milder salting and smoking. *Natural oak-smoked kippers* are sought after and their very pallor can be a signifier of natural process and subtlety. Some consumers eschew genuinely *natural*, but more heavily-smoked kippers, suspicious of their deeper colouring. In a sense this is a continuation of the process Woodger began: lighter and lighter cures are now supported by vacuum packs and refrigeration.

Another development has also facilitated this: the smoking kiln. With a stainless steel kiln, the process can be tweaked with precision to reliably produce something more and more mild. In a continuing decline in the number of smokehouses, fewer and fewer use the traditional smoking techniques. Some wonderful kippers are available from this kiln production, but the Michelin-starred Newcastle chef Kenny Atkinson laments the loss of the tarry smokehouse walls, sometimes a hundred or more years in the making, dripping their complex flavours down upon the herrings hanging on their tenterhooks (see second image section). For this reason (and because he's a Geordie) Atkinson only uses Crasters for the concentrated kipper stock, a distilled quintessence of Woodger, with which he flavours his kipper cream.

And while we're on the subject of the excellent Robson's of Craster, Rod Hlalo, Zimbabwean saxophonist of Newcastle upon Tyne, rhapsodises over the memory of the Craster kippers his shopkeeper father would sell to popular acclaim in the Bulawayo of the 1960s, probably transported by ocean liners (see **Monkey Business**). These days, whenever he goes back to Zimbabwe, he always takes some with him for his brother—vacuum-packed, of course, for discretion.

Some people don't cook kippers because of the smell. You can avoid this by cooking them in the oven, wrapped in greaseproof paper with butter and lemon, or you can jug them... But it is a beautiful smell, carrying the memory of a beautiful meal and so much nicer than that of air fresheners... A decline in kipper eating has come with the decline of cooked breakfasts. It is important to remember: kippers aren't just for breakfast.

KLONDYKING

Steam trains made kippers possible and from the 1830s steam packets did for the seas what steam trains did for the land. From the late nineteenth century steam drifters were increasing the catching power of the herring fleet and creating the need for new markets. Lowestoft fish merchant Benjamin Bradbeer identified the possibility of using steamers to supply fresh herrings directly to the German market.

The German fleet mostly trawled, which damaged the herring. *Freshing* (light salting) was probably already putting fresh herring on the trains for the expanding network of British kipper curers. Bradbeer started sending boxes, lightly salted and iced, by steamer to Altona in Hamburg, where the Germans could pickle and sell their own prime products. Before long Germans were employing their own fresh fish buyers to work the ports of Scotland and the East Coast of England.

The Klondike Gold Rush of the late 1890s was contemporaneous with the development of this new fresh herring trade and gave it its name. No one seems to know why the *i* became a *y*. Some typos make history. German buyers took herring from the port, but they also took it directly from drifters at sea, their own packers working in the steamers which would send the boxes to Altona and Bremerhaven.

There was an understandable break in the trade for World War I, but after it klondyking herrings picked up again. When the German mark collapsed, the klondykers played a role in the depression of the market for British cured herring and continued throughout the 20s and 30s.

The association of herring fishing with gold mines goes back to the seventeenth century and beyond. It was an enthusiastic identification, which Dutch, Scots and English promoters used in pointing the way to the untold national wealth it would bring. Herring Poet John Lockman was among the most enthusiastic (see **Pamphleteers**), but it was a commonplace. Whilst insisting, 'these are our goldmines,' the British pamphleteers saw adoption of the Dutch herring buss (see **Herring Boats**) as key to unlocking this source of gold. It seems likely that this played a role in coining the term for the new trade, but it's hard to find direct evidence.

These days, *klondyking* tends to refer to the operations of the large factory ships, particularly the, often aging, Eastern European fish processors which worked the Scottish coast after the collapse of the Soviet Bloc. They would also buy fish direct from smaller fishing vessels. With this meaning, *klondyke*, *klondyking* and *klondyker* appear in the *Dictionary of the Scots Language* as late twentieth-century usages.

LIFE OF SAINT HERRING

The anonymous northern French poem, *La Vie de Saint Hareng, glorieux martyr* (The Life of Saint Herring, glorious martyr) dates from the mid to late fifteenth century. It was written as a *sermon joyeux*, medieval French monologues growing out of *fête des fous* (festival of fools) carnival traditions. Performed without music to audiences ranging across social classes, they could be scatological, sexually explicit and/or mock society and religion. Food was a popular theme and hagiographies a popular form: there is also a *Sermon de Saint Jambon et Sainte Andouille* (Saints Ham and Tripesausage). The performers could dress up as members of the clergy. Herring was a natural fit.

The *Heege Manuscript*, copied from the *aide-memoire* of a fifteenth-century gigging minstrel in the East Midlands points to a similar English tradition. Cambridge academic James Wade recently discovered in a mock sermon that it has the first mention of **Red Herring**. Writing around the same time, the *Saint Hareng* poet talks of two kinds of herring—'L'un est sor, l'autre est blanc': red and white. White is salted, *sor* or **Hareng Saur** is salted, smoked and, literally, red herring.

In the fifteenth century herring was mocked in France as much as it was in England and elsewhere (see **Battle of the Herrings, Dutch & Flemish Art, Fasting, Pickelhering, Processions & Celebrations** and **Red Herring Joke**). There are different versions of *Saint Hareng* (or *Harenc*), suggesting it was widely distributed. Some stop at the proverb of the stinking herring. The version translated here was taken from *'St Hareng, Glorieux Martyr': Le poisson de mer de l'antiquité à nos jours* (2006), edited by Isabelle Clauzel.

Clauzel suggests the *Saint Hareng* poet's use of language indicates he was from the North West of France rather than Normandy, although it feels like he was performing to Normandy audiences. She also suggests he was consciously writing with at least an ear to the lowlife lays of François Villon. The *sermon joyeux* formed one of the influences on Rabelais, the great sixteenth-century celebrant of the grotesque. Traditionally written in tetrameter couplets with alternating male and female rhymes, the anonymous poet of *Saint Hareng* is not strictly observant. Some of his rhymes are loose but, anyway, English does not do male or female ones: this translation pays homage to a poet who knew what he could get away with in performance.

THE LIFE OF SAINT HERRING, GLORIOUS MARTYR
Anon. Fifteenth century.

Good people, listen to my sermon.

The season of Saint Grape is calling,
Pilgrims all must set off walking
To seek salvation from these days,
While out upon those salty waves
Between Boulogne and England's chalk,
Where there's no land on which to walk,
That's where began Saint Herring's ills,

LIFE OF SAINT HERRING

Worse than Lawrence on his grill[1],
This was his site of martyrdom.
Forty masters all as one,
Day and night their hard-fought wrestle
Hauled him to the restless vessel,
With their nets and with their lines,
Along with hundreds of his kind.
That's how we saw Saint Herring caught.
But winds blew up, so far from port,
So strong all feared that they would drown
Yet they came safe to Dieppe Town
Where they displayed his holy body.
Fresh from the inn, some drunk, O Lord, he
Spotted him by candlelight,
Took him back there in the night,
And ate him, roasted to perfection,
With an allium selection.
The rest were all packed off, of course,
To Paris by the fastest horse[2],
Where some were barrelled up in salt
While others, though without a fault,
To the smoke and flames were led:
The outrage turned our saint bright red,
Hanging from the smokehouse rafter
Like a thief gets his hereafter –
Except that thieves are rarely dressed
With vinaigrette and watercress.
But pay no mind, that's all as nothing,
This blessèd saint we've been discussing
Found himself minced up with onion

For two jokers' own consumption:
Before he knew, he found that they
Had turned him into Saint Paté.
In Lent, the season of our fasting,
Everyone cries out for herring:
In Paris he's deemed so delicious
The taste of him's considered precious;
Those whose phlegm could see them off,
His holy bones will make them cough;
And honest men know landlords bless
Saint Herring for his saltiness.
His bounty travels through the nation,
Not only granting meagre rations
To Carmelite and Augustinian,
But even to those Jacobin(ian)s[3].
Saint Herring visits every home
From here as far as far-off Rome,
A welcome sight where'er he wanders,
Across to England, up to Flanders,
In Burgundy and up the Seine,
And down to Portugal and Spain,
The mountains and the plains of France,
In Lombardy and in Provence,
In Normandy and in Lorraine,
In Berry and in Aquitaine,
By Loire in a wicker basket
He is carried to each market,
In procession through the world.
This saint, whose life is here unfurled,
Was born at sea: his holiness

LIFE OF SAINT HERRING

Allows no taint of bitterness,
Eat as many as you wish,
Each one will taste as sweet a fish,
But just as he once loved to drink,
On this he likes to make us think:
Saint Herring's eaters all must first
Consider how they'll quench their thirst.
As I have said, two ways of curing
Keep us all supplied with herring:
There's the red and white as well
And should you ask, yes, they both smell.
With all such questions of the nose
It's as the well-known proverb goes,
'Herrings stink, it's in their nature,
But ripe bouquets beget adventure.'
The poor cannot afford to question
Cheap fish offering salvation,
Yet he seems all just grace and ease
When on a plate and served with peas.
In Lent, when there's no fat for frying,
They all smell good or am I lying?
And village folk in every cottage
Cook their pots of herring pottage.
Alas, Saint Herring, he should be
Martyred quite so frequently!
But, from here to Angoulême,
Each time he burns it's just the same.
Saint Herring will be martyred still,
Whether we, upon the grill
Or on hot coals, inflict his pain.

His season, yet, will come again,

His miracles both strong and sure

And better than some snakebite cure.

Now you've heard Saint Herring's sermon,

It's time for us to beg God's pardon

For our sins in this past year

And all the years that we've passed here,

Three hundred years of pardons won

And ten more months: it's nobly done;

So let us now pray for the poor,

'Lord, compensate their lack of ore.'

In need to God they all have cried –

May it please Him turn the tide;

Now cardinals and bishops, who

Perhaps may need our prayers too –

Those first shall be the last ones through;

So let us fall upon our knees,

'O Lord, do not forsake us, please.'

These days of turmoil, good or ill,

Will surely one day count for nil:

'Amen' should be our only meaning.

Here ends *The Life of Saint Herring*.

NOTES

1. St Lawrence was martyred on a gridiron. He is reputed to have joked, 'You can turn me over, I'm done on that side.'

2. The poke at the Dominicans, also known as Jacobins, refers to the story of Thomas **Aquinas** and his failure to eat the miracle fresh herrings God had provided.

3. See **French Fisheries** for details of the medieval *Chemin de la Tide or Route du Poisson*, which delivered fresh herrings (and other fish) to Paris.

LUCK

It's not just fishermen. Superstition has always been magnified in the presence of waves: to swim is to fight with water—best not to learn how; eat fish and you end up with the fishes (see **Euphemisms**); women can calm waves by bearing their breasts—let's have a bare-breasted figurehead… Herring fishermen were, nevertheless, particularly susceptible.

FROM AN INTERVIEW WITH JIM MUIR (Achiltibuie, 2005)

The superstitions of the herring fishermen were legion. There were taboo words: *minister* was one, *salmon* was another. What else? Rabbit, oh you didn't mention rabbit. They called a rabbit a furry codling. What else? What were the other words? Nobody cares about these things now, but some fishermen were very, very superstitious. Pig was another you didn't dare mention. Minister, salmon, pig, rabbit. Women were a bit chancy. If you met certain women on a Monday morning, it wasn't good. Certain ones, by habit and repute, became unlucky. Not for any particular reason: somebody met them once, something happened and they'd keep away from them.

There were men from the East Coast of Scotland and on a Monday morning you wouldn't dare ask a man for a light or a match or anything like that, because if he'd give you a match or give you a light for a fag, you had his luck then for that week. You would steal their luck. They were very superstitious, much more in the olden days, because once it became electronic, they depended more on that.

If somebody committed suicide, there were places in the mountains that they had specifically earmarked, so that the suicide would be buried where the sun never shone. If this suicide was buried in sight of the sea, the herring would not come back anymore. There have been cases, not in this actual part, but in the West. Probably, the last time, it would have been after the First World War, in the 20s, that it happened. I think I know some of the relatives of those people. A man committing suicide and buried in a normal cemetery was dug up that night and taken to that place and buried out of sight of the sea.

It was very important to the people, of course, that the herring fishing wouldn't disappear. That was just a superstition they had, which they took literally, to the extent that they would dig somebody up. The relatives wouldn't be aware of it. The fishermen would do it at night and he'd be buried up there. Headstones would be put in the cemetery, but the body wasn't there. I think the herring fishery was more prone to superstition than the other fisheries.

AND THERE'S MORE

Notwithstanding the occasional usefulness of their breasts, in some parts it was considered bad luck to have a woman on board a fishing boat. It was bad luck to head out to sea on a Friday (Christ's crucifixion), but good luck to do so on a Sunday (Hallelujah! Christ is risen), except the Presbyterian Scottish herring fleet wouldn't fish on a Sunday—although this might have been to avoid discussing the *minister*.

In one of his works, Will Maclean (see **Two Contemporary Artists**) points to the dangers inherent in wearing anything yellow on board: the colour was produced from crottle (Gaelic: *crotal*), *Parmelia saxatilis*, a lichen which grows on rocks. What comes from the rocks goes back to the rocks.

Meanwhile, there's a board on *Bad Luck Words* at Eyemouth Museum, explaining how names, such as Ross, Coull or Whyte were sure to bring bad luck and there were others. In Cullen, a Mr Allan had to be called 'the man wi' the short airms' and a Mr Ross, 'the man abune the brae'; in Portnockie a Mr Anderson was *'the craiter'*, in Stonehaven, a Mr Todd, 'the man Sandy'. The board also describes how:

> In many districts, the word salt could never be mentioned when at sea. A story is told of an Eyemouth boat that ran out of salt in the autumn of 1905. The crew were fishing at the time and spotted a Yarmouth drifter close by. The skipper hailed the vessel, and called out 'We need something that we dinna want tae speak aboot!' In reply the English skipper shouted back, 'Is it salt you want?'
>
> The salt was handed over, but the Englishmen remarked that all the rest of the Scottish crew had disappeared below deck rather than hear the terrible word spoken in their presence. The cure for hearing any of the unlucky words used was to touch cauld iron. This would cancel out any bad luck.

COINS & WRENS

It was possible to appease the herring gods by fixing a silver coin at the base of the mast or concealing one in the ropes of your nets—in a complicated knot, for example. A silver threepence or sixpence was considered perfectly satisfactory: greed is not in the nature of the silver darlings. Otherwise, it just has to be a dead wren. Francis Day in *The Fishes of Great Britain and Ireland* (1880–84) reported that it was all because some sea spirit had had it in for herring fishermen, stirring up storms. Others say it was some sea goddess luring honest Manx farmer fishermen to watery graves. Either way when they'd got her banged to rights, she turned into a wren and flew away. You can't blame wren-kind for goddesses in wren costumes, but, for luck, Manx herring fishermen had to have a dead wren on board or at least a feather or two from a wren which had been certified dead. And with luck only lasting twelve months, fresh wrens had to be murdered every New Year.

To be fair, it wasn't just fishermen with the wren. The folkloric abuse of the bird could probably fill its own encyclopaedia. Some of my best friends promote and deliver folk culture, but wren persecution is a black mark and the record of the Irish, Welsh and Manx is especially egregious.

In Dundee, meanwhile, good luck was available to any member of the community prepared to dress a herring as a doll and hang it up in the house throughout the year. There have been recent attempts to revive the tradition, dressing up cut out, cardboard herrings, although it's hard to see what luck you're going to bring with cardboard: no pain, no gain.

Apart from all the above, as Jim Muir said in his interview, 'you'd set your nets and hope for the best.'

MÅLØY RAID

Between 1942 and 1943, World War II operations *Grouse*, *Freshman* and *Gunnerside* eventually destroyed the heavy water production capacity of the Vermork Norsk Hydro plant at Rjukan in Norway. My brother and I walked down to Uckfield's Picture House to see the story's full film treatment in *Heroes of Telemark* (Anthony Mann, 1965). As was the case after all great war films, we marched home. It starred Kirk Douglas, who had established himself as top Norseman *de nos jours* in *The Vikings* (Richard Fleischer, 1958). So where, you might well ask, was the Kirk Douglas film of 1941's Operation Archery, the Måløy Raid, the very first action in the war by Combined Operations? Herrings just do not get the respect.

Måløy is a town on the island of Vågsøy on the west coast of Norway, south of Ålesund and the raid's focus included other nearby locations. It involved 570 commandos, including a detachment from the Royal Norwegian Army (one of whom could easily have been played by Douglas). Four squadrons of RAF bombers and fighters were involved, two landing craft, a cruiser, four destroyers and the submarine HMS *Tuna*, which everyone will agree is a great name for a submarine. It was a reasonably sized operation and destroyed four herring oil production plants and a herring oil storage facility (see second image section).

The website, *combinedops.com* talks of there having been 'no significant strategic importance' beyond ensuring Norway tied up German troops otherwise able to be fighting on the Eastern Front. This is not true. Rjukan's heavy water would have been crucial to the development of a German atomic bomb, but it turned out, even by the end of the war they were nowhere near achieving one. Herring oil, on the other hand, was crucial to the continued manufacture of German high explosives.

The commandos landed at dawn and by 2pm a successful withdrawal had been initiated. Between commandos, Royal Navy and RAF, 51 died and 8 aircraft were lost. One Norwegian civilian died, having been hit by shrapnel. German losses stood at 150, while 102 prisoners were taken including 4 Quislings or collaborators. 9 ships were sunk by the British and 4 Heinkels were shot down. A complete copy of German naval code was captured and 70 Norwegians were evacuated. It became a model for later combined operations, Churchill hailing it as a 'letter to Hitler'. As a result the Germans withdrew 30,000 Wehrmacht soldiers from the Eastern Front to bolster their Norwegian occupation (for which the troops were, quite possibly, extremely grateful).

There is a museum dedicated to the raid in Måløy, which displays many of the images taken by the official photographers who documented the raid, boosting British confidence in the progress of the war. You cannot help but feel, with their Archers Film Productions, that Powell and Pressburger would have been the ideal filmmakers. They would have ditched the diacritics in Måløy, but just imagine what they might have done with herrings somehow swimming through their quirky British mysticism. The Glue Man in *A Canterbury Tale* (1944) would have had nothing on it.

MEASURING THE HERRING

Warp, maze, cast,

cran, mand, last...

There is beauty in traditional herring measurements and not only in the words. It is as if the fish were reaching out for the mathematics of variable constants; as if an English, a Scots, an Irish, a Welsh and a Manx fisherman were each asked how many they'd caught and they all answered with their own version of, 'Well, I wouldn't start from here.'

Herrings came in different sizes and that was a factor; came in numbers defying precision, scaly masses for which scales were impractical; came to different beaches, quays and harbours, each with different languages or accents, different histories and customs. On top of it all, exchange on shared fishing grounds and seasonally visited quaysides added hybrids, adoptions and adaptations. On top of all this some Anglo-Saxon tribes brought a mathematical culture working to a base of twelve rather than ten to the British Isles.

HERRING MEASUREMENTS IN ASCENDING SIZE ORDER

Tale or *Tally* = 1 herring used for counting: 1 per 100 in Wales (a tale), 1 per 2 score in the Isle of Man.

Pair = 2. Kippers are generally sold as pairs to this day.

Warp = 2 pairs.

Cast = 3 herrings. A cast might initially have been the same as a warp, but it changed over time. In the Isle of Man the term referred to the tally fish cast aside to mark the count (but then thrown in on top). Meanwhile a cast of mackerel was specifically 12

(2 scoops of two handfuls at 3 fish per hand). Cast fish could also be those which were laid out on the quayside as representative of the quality of a boat's catch, which were then also thrown in with the sale.

Hundred = 120 or 10 x 12, sometimes called a long hundred to distinguish it from 100 or 10 x 10, aka a small hundred (see **Past(r)y**). 10 long hundreds make a long thousand of 1,200. Red herrings were counted in long hundreds, fresh herrings could be counted in small hundreds, but were also counted long. Varying tallies were added, depending on approaches to counting, so in Whitby a hundred was 123 (3 x 2 score + 3 tally fish), in the Isle of Man it was 124 (123 + 1 to mark the 120, perhaps?). Elsewhere it could be 126 (6 scores + 6) or even 132 (12 tens + 12), but the mathematics of 132 could also have been developed to accommodate the addition of make-weights—on the principle that a hundred of mackerel was heavier than a hundred of herring.

Maze, meise and *mease* = 5 hundreds or 615 in a Whitby maze (a hundred being 123); 620 in an Anglo-Welsh meise (a hundred being 124); 660 in a West Cornwall mease (100 being 132).

Klondyke-box = 12.25 stone (approximately) or roughly 78 kilos. A nineteenth-century development, based on the size of boxes in which *freshed* or lightly-salted herring was exported, particularly to Germany, for pickling there.

Mand = 1,056 or 8 hundreds of 132 (Cornish). This should not be confused with the *maund*, a basket measure, also Cornish, but comprising 360 pilchards, 10 of which would make up a *hogshead* (see **Baskets**). A *mand* is pretty much a Cornish version of a *cran*.

Cran = fresh, uncleaned herrings sufficient to fill a 37.5 imperial gallon barrel, notionally 1,200 fish or a long thousand, but, depending on the size of the fish anything from 700 to 2,500. The figure was originally standardised in 1816 as 42 English wine gallons, but then increased to 45 English wine gallons in 1832. The direct conversion from that to 37.5 imperial gallons dates to 1852. The word Cran comes from the Scottish Gaelic *Crann*, which can mean tree or lot, but more specifically just means measure of herring. The cran goes back as a Scottish measure to the eighteenth century, at least, and was made a legal measure in England and Wales in 1908, reflecting the dominance of the Scottish herring industry. It derives from the principle of a bottomless 30 gallon barrel filled to overflowing. Any discrepancy between this and 37.5 imperial/45 wine gallons could be ascribed to an allowance for shrinkage in the pickling process and/or compensation for lost tallies and casts and/or buyers always wanting a bit more. The quarter cran is a basket which, in theory, holds 9.375 gallons and was used on board and in carrying herring, a full cran being impractical for the purpose. There's also a half cran, which could be a basket or a barrel but they disappeared because the different functions were best fulfilled between the quarter and the full. An eighth cran was used as a more generous form of the display cast.

Last = 12,000 herring, calculated as 10 long thousands or 12 barrels. The term derives, via Old English, from a proto-Germanic root word for *to place*, meaning a load or cargo. Lasts as measurement were determined by the product, so there would be differently sized and weighted ones for leather, flax and feathers or gunpowder. The Dutch last, which was also used for herrings, was more specifically a measure of shipping space.

AND TODAY

In 1908, when the cran was made the prime legal measure in the UK, it was established that, apart from this, only standard weights could be used for herrings: pounds, stones, hundredweights (112 lbs in UK) and tonnes. Increasing mechanisation delivered increased capacities for quayside scales and, as pelagic trawlers grew in size after World War II, on the larger herring boats. With a consequent standardisation of herring weighing, the shift from stones to kilogrammes was relatively easy. The standard plastic fish box now follows the EU model of 40 litres/25 kg (800 x 400 x 225 mm). Quarter cran baskets hang these days from the pub ceilings of traditional fishing towns and villages.

NOTE: This entry draws on a number of sources, but is particularly indebted to *A Guide to Fish Measures and Terms* by Tony Pawlyn, originally published in 1995 before being rewritten for the website of the National Maritime Museum in Cornwall.

MEDICINE & HEALTH

Herring is good for you! Among many Dutch herring **Proverbs**, a popular one could be translated as, 'a herring a day keeps the doctor away.'

Not as oily as their close relative the incredibly oily menhaden, they're more oily than sardines or pilchards. They have high levels of Omega-3 fatty acids, which are especially good for the heart. Over and above the basics, it has been said herring-eating protects against cardio-vascular disease and can reduce the risk of developing some cancers (including prostate), as well as the development of child asthma. It may be good for the nerves, the joints, mental health, cognition and motor development…

In 2025 the Rowett Institute at the University of Aberdeen published an article mapping seafood production and supply in the UK in the context of the mismatch between recommended and actual consumption of oily fish. In addition to the Omega 3 aspects it points to other nutrient deficiencies, such as Vitamin B_{12} which can be problematic for those reducing or eliminating meat consumption. Herrings—readily available in the waters around the UK—represent a low emission source (notwithstanding their reliance on **Farting** for communication) for most of the deficiencies in our national diet and yet our consumption of oily fish is less than half the recommended level. Herring, even though it contains more Omega 3 fatty acids than salmon or mackerel (and is tastier than both), is consumed far less than either of them. Most of the oily fish we catch is exported and even the miserable amount we eat relies significantly on imports. Eat herrings and you will be healthier, reduce the burden on the National Health Service and help to save the planet.

The only slight health downside to herring is the level of purines. Along with their oily colleagues, they're up there with liver, kidneys and sweetbreads. This is only a problem if you have gout, which unfortunately I do. 400 mg of Allopurinol a day, however, allows me to eat as much herring as I want. That's the way I look at it, anyway. And maybe, if I did not eat the herring, I'd be dead. It's been touch and go with the joints as it is. The good news is that Allopurinol was developed by Wellcome Research Laboratories and the Wellcome Library in London has a beautiful collection of work by the eighteenth-century English herring poet John Lockman (see **Pamphleteers**). I don't think they have a copy of **Neucrantz**'s *De harengo* (1654), but who knows? If I keep taking the tablets they'll be able to afford one. It offers several potentially useful research avenues.

Paul Neucrantz was a doctor of medicine and, as such, frequently prescribed herring. He thought salmon might just marginally edge it for taste, but he'd only eaten the wild stuff. Even so, in his opinion, when you take medical benefits into consideration, the herring knocks salmon out of the park. By the time he reaches Chapter XIV, 'On the medicinal and other uses of herring', he's not informing us from a standing start:

> I've already commented on the relief of nausea, stimulation of appetite, purging of the stomach and loosening of bowels. I have similarly commented on the salting of herring and the abundant production of juices. Salt, of course, is astringent: it dries. It is not the salt itself which produces the abundance, but its encouragement of thirst and appetite. In addressing these, the body secures the necessary liquids.

You could probably get herring brine from the salt herring buckets of any good Eastern European grocery and Neucrantz is an advocate as much for that as he is for the fish itself.

> A small piece of linen, dipped in the brine, is useful in treating snake and dog bites, but the flesh itself may be used to good effect. Paul of Aegina says the

same of salt tuna and, together with Pliny, reports on the efficacy of salty foods for snake bites. If there's no access to a cauterising iron or the means to drain the blood, it provides a swift and effective remedy for rabid dog bites.

Cornelius Celsus says salt can cure any animal bite, especially a dog's. It needs to be lightly pressed in, the hand laid across the bite and tapped with two fingers, the cure completed by binding something salty over the wound. Meanwhile, salt herring, spread across the infected area, cures mange on the chest and is also recommended for ulcers, as, according to Dioscorides, is garum, the fermented fish sauce of the ancients.

Herring brine mixed with myrrh is good for bruises, whilst my own experience suggests it can also be used with chilblains or recent burns. It works for dysentery and for stomach ulcers. Gout in the hips can be treated with a clyster pipe enema. Conrad Gessner, quoting Pliny, praises it for the treatment of mouth ulcers. Combined with honey and corn, it's an effective prescription for diarrhoea. It is believed that the smoke from burning a herring's head will induce births in the case of late pregnancies.

Gessner also advocated a scattering of dried, cured herring heads as a way of getting rid of bed bugs. Neucrantz reports Gessner's belief that urine retention in men and horses can be addressed with the application of nine silver herrings. Alexander of Tralles recommends salty foods for mild malarial fevers and, although Neucrantz is not suggesting 'promiscuous use of salt herring,' he does consider it to be, medically, the best salty food. 'In cases of chronic fevers,' of course, 'brined herring bound to the soles of the feet is highly effective and it is also good for drawing out corns.'

Neucrantz corresponded on the subject of herring with the celebrated Dutch surgeon, Nicolaes Tulp, a fellow enthusiast. He points people in the direction of Tulp's *Medical Observations* (1641), in which:

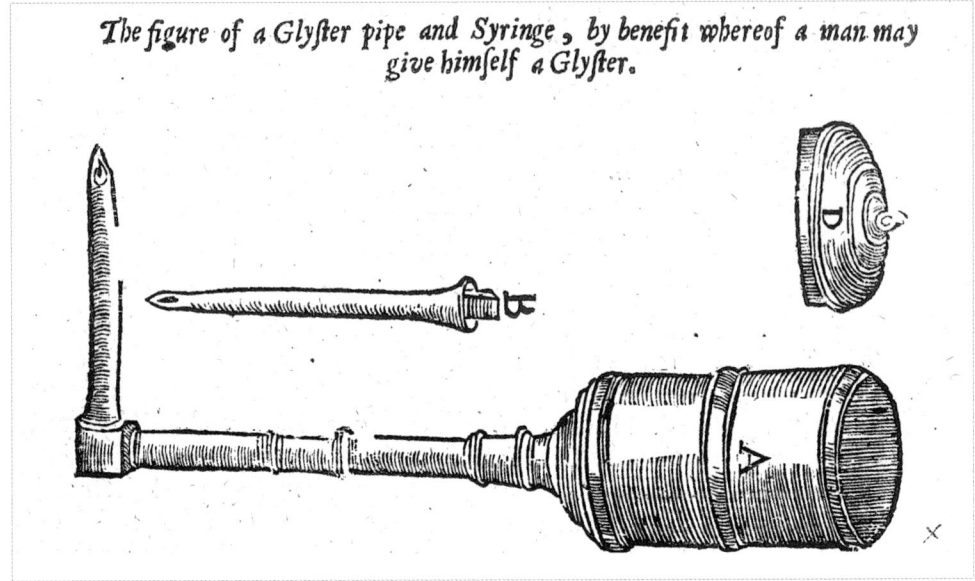

The figure of a Glyster pipe and Syringe, *The workes of that famous chirugion Ambrose Parey* (1649). Wellcome Collection, Public Domain

Dr Tulp remarks that doctors have fewer patients when herrings are in season. In the same book he tells the remarkable story of a pregnant woman, who craved salted herring so much, she ate a total of 1,400 before coming to term and had no stomach problems at all. She would have eaten even more, if she had not begun to worry about the baby.

There is plenty for Wellcome Research Laboratories to be going at, there...

MEDITERRANEAN FOOD

The popularity of smoked herring in Egypt, according to one food website, was down to it being 'a type of fish that is native to the Mediterranean Sea.' In *De harengo* (1654) **Neucrantz** exhaustively proves the herring was unknown to Classical authority specifically because it is not. In his red herring fantasia *Lenten Stuffe* (1599) Nashe, on the other hand, magics it into a central role in Greek mythology by playing on Yarmouth's longstanding trade with the Ottoman Empire.

In the late 1990s Great Yarmouth's H.S. Fishing Company was still producing the red variants, golden and silver herring for the Southern Mediterranean market—silver mostly to Italy, golden to Greece and Egypt. These days Greece and Egypt smoke their own *renga* or *ringa* using frozen Norwegian, Russian or Icelandic herring. They also now export their products to the UK—I have found it at Asian food stores in Newcastle and Walthamstow, which probably means it is everywhere. Imported renga is now the most commonly available red herring variant in British shops. History without irony is a rare commodity.

In Egypt renga is eaten particularly at *Sham Ennessim* (or *Sham al Nessim* or *Sham an-Nessim*) a festival which goes back to the time of the Pharoahs and which, perhaps surprisingly, has survived the enthusiasms of both Christianity and Islam (see second image section). Appropriately enough for a festival at which people eat red herring, the name means Smelling the Breeze: it is a celebration of Spring and takes place on Easter Monday. Given the lunar calculations which have always left most Christians uncertain as to exactly when Easter is going to be each year, this seems like a Coptic accommodation of the original pagan practice rather than a coincidence—although you can't rule out Pharaonic lunar calculations being lifted by the early church. Either way, that is when it is and Islamic conquerors let it pass, maybe because Egyptians simply love it for its non-denominational Egyptian-ness—and for the fish, of course.

The other cured fish associated with Sham Ennessim is *fesikh*, salted, fermented and dried grey mullet, which (see **Surrströmming**) is even smellier than red herring. Grey mullet is native to both the Mediterranean and the Red Sea and *fesikh* will almost certainly have been at the heart of the festival long before English red herring arrived. Its preparation requires care: fermented fish products are balancing acts between achieving the smell of death and generating it through botulism poisoning. Sloppy curing has been responsible for cases of food poisoning most years and in 1991 there were eighteen deaths. The smell is obviously important and red herring may have found a ready market because it too was smelly, but, at the same time, a bit less smelly. Herring shoals are much larger than grey mullet ones, so there is probably a price bonus as well as the reduced death count.

RENGA BEL TAHINI

The standard Sham Ennessim renga dishes seem to be dips or salads. *Renga bel tahini* involves loosening the smoked herring's skin by briefly searing both sides in a hot pan, filleting it and flaking or cutting the flesh into chunks, then laying it across a salad of diced red onion, tomato, bell pepper, spring onion, optional chilli pepper, oil and lemon or lime juice, served with a tahini sauce. The dip version simply involves chopping all these ingredients more finely and adding yoghurt before mixing it all up and serving with pitta bread. If you want a fancy canapé, you can also add chopped hard boiled egg yolks to the dip and fill the halved egg whites. It is Spring: the recipes are really invitations to experiment with new possibilities.

ARENGA

There seem to be versions of a dish, simply called *Renga*, in both Egypt and Greece: remove the skin and fillet the fish; chop it into bite-size chunks and mix with chopped spring onion, chopped apple and (a good quality) olive oil. Some recipes swap the apple for bell pepper. Personally, I love it with the apple. Eat it with a bread that will soak up plenty of the oil. It has got something about it of a deconstructed chopped herring (see **Jewish Food**). Another version has the chopped smoked herring with red onion, plenty of oil, vinegar and lemon juice. In Greece, renga can also be used as a bar snack, the saltiness of which encourages drinking (a tradition which once spread across the taverns, pubs and hostelries of Northern Europe).

ARINGHE

An H.S. Fishing Company leaflet marketing its silver herring included a simple

Northern Italian recipe, *fagiole aringhe*: filleted and served cold with boiled beans, olive oil and early new potatoes. Silver herring is strongly salted but barely smoked —just enough to dry but not colour it—a halfway house between salt and red herring. Antonio Carluccio specifies an origin in the German-speaking part of Italy's *Südtirol* for his *Aringhe alla Casalinga*, which brings together maatjes herring fillets with cooked new potatoes, finely sliced apple, onion and double cream. Meanwhile, at La Fattoria's Museum of Old Farming Traditions (halfway between Bologna and Rome) they remember the particularly economical practice of just hanging a smoked herring above the table, the family only having to rub their two pieces of bread either side for a bit of flavour: add a drop of oil and count yourself lucky!

MILLER'S LETTERS

Hugh Miller's *Letters on the Herring Fishery in the Moray Firth* (1829) were written to the editor of the *Inverness Courier*, the newspaper then publishing them in book form, 'in consequence of the interest they have excited in the Northern Counties.' Why are they of interest today? They capture an earlier age of herring fishery on the cusp of change.

There are Hill & Adamson photographs of Miller (see **Documentary**). In some he poses as a stonemason, the work to which he had been apprenticed at seventeen and from which, self-taught, he became Scotland's leading geologist and paleontologist. A founder member of the Free Church of Scotland, much of his geological writing is spent reconciling his beliefs with his discoveries. Apparently suffering from depression, he committed suicide in 1856, three years before Darwin published his *Origin of Species*.

Miller was twenty-seven when he wrote the letters, a witness both to the undecked small boats and the busses or luggers (which he refers to as *boat curers*). The period of the bounties (see **British Fisheries** and **Smith, Adam**) is coming to an end and he pictures a first Cornish fleet making the long voyage up to North East Scotland.

He draws on history and local legend, his conversations with fishermen and his own observations. Feeling the sufferings of his country, there is an arc to the letters, which imagine an educated fishing community, benefiting from the wider understandings of science and the humanities while not losing its rich knowledge of currents and tides, marine geography, boats and weather. It is the vision of a man who has stepped out of his class, but does not want to lose his birthright; who looks to a wider independence from the constant economic precarity herring fishing exemplifies.

LETTER I

Early on he differentiates between a feudally acquiescent, Gaelic-speaking Highland culture and his own Cromarty, where, 'on the contrary two-thirds of the people are marked with the unyielding independent Whiggism of the English and the Lowland Scotch.' At the same time, he projects a sense of Cromarty's lost golden age. Workmen at the end of the eighteenth century, exploring an abandoned herring merchant's house come across a ceiling rose as an archaeologist might uncover some Roman mosaic: 'a massy circular patras, round which a shoal of herrings exquisitely relieved, were swimming in a sea of plaster.' He recounts a tale of Latin-speaking fishermen:

> There is a tradition that one of the Urquharts of that time, when sauntering along the shore, accompanied by two guests, gentlemen from England, asked a fisherman he met, several questions in Latin, and to the surprise of the visitors received prompt answers in the same language.

This golden age was all in 'the era of the "herring drove"', the seventeenth and early eighteenth century, a time of prosperity, when there were 'not less than five three-masted vessels belong to' the Cromarty herring fleet: the Dutch-style busses Stuarts and Hanoverians had both encouraged, markers of ambition beyond the Moray Firth's uncertainties. This is juxtaposed with two local fishermen of the succeeding fallen age, who 'believed that at the distance of a few weeks sailing, the ocean was bounded by the horizon; and that all beyond was darkness; but though thus ignorant, not Virgil himself was better acquainted with the signs of the weather, or could tell more truly when storms or calms might be expected.'

After the Act of Union, 'the failure of the herring fishing completed its ruin' and we are left with folkloric interpretations of the disaster. Curers dealing with a huge catch are sanctioned to work through most of the Sabbath, but not only did they not come to the kirk in the evening, but when the minister (see **Luck**) came to remonstrate, some threw fish at him. He prayed, 'that the besom of judgement would come and sweep every herring out of the frith.' On the other hand it might have been the fracas between two fishermen whose nets had become entangled, a knife was drawn and 'Blood was spilt, unfortunately spilt, in the sea' (see **Sensitivity**). Either the fisherman with the knife or the one whose blood was spilt 'bore ever after the designation of "the bloody;" and there are men still living who remember having seen him.'

Miller binds this fallen culture to hints of a demoralised post-rebellion Scotland, mentioning his grandfather, 'who witnessed the smoke of Culloden from the hill of Cromarty.' From the 1740s he observes a moral decline; a lack of enterprise in the pursuit of herring. He doesn't mention the hoopla around the 1750 Act for the Encouragement of the British White Herring Fishery (see **Pamphleteers**) but he sees a small fleet setting out for the Caithness grounds. The men of Cromarty are easily discouraged by a few bad years. The herrings begin to return to the Morray coast from 1780, but not till 1816 did anyone risk the necessary investment in the home fishing ground. It fared well for several years, although, in recent seasons, he notes, the numbers have begun to decline again

LETTER II
The history aspect is completed in Letter II and there's another tale. 'A Cromarty boat had gone to the fishing. The night which was dark and foggy, set in before she arrived at the ground. When adjusting the fishing tackle, the crew were startled by a low frightful sound which rose from the sea.' Thinking some of the fleet had foundered,

they row to give assistance, when suddenly 'a boat under full sail was bearing down on them. The cry of "bear off!" had scarcely escaped them, when a tremendous crash told that the warning had been given too late. Their larboard bow was laid open to within three planks of the keel.' The crew move to the stern to keep the damaged prow out of the water, just one man sent to block the hole with the sail and bring the forward ballast back. 'The stem was then turned towards the shore and the oars resumed.' The key point of the story is made clear when a flickering blue light is seen. "'It is our death signal," said one of the crew, "I will strive no longer." "You may think of it what you will," replied another, "I for my part will consider it the omen of good." The confidence of this opinion was one cause of it proving such; for the fishermen doubled their exertions, and on the following morning had their boat, drawn up on the beach, below the town of Cromarty.' In the constant tension between Romanticism and pragmatism, Miller argues for a folklore less debilitating and able to work hand in hand with collective determination.

LETTERS III & IV

The next two letters are paired: the pragmatics and the Romantic vision.

'SIR, The Moray firth fishery commences in the middle of July, and the fish commonly leave the coast in the end of August, or first of September.' Letter III is a practical guide: the length, depth and number of nets required, the irregularities of the sea floor, the location of rocks on which nets are at risk. Particular attention is given to Guilliam, 'the long narrow bank which lies in the middle of the firth' below Shandwick, the favoured spawning ground. Miller is describing what seems to have become again, exclusively a small boat fishery and the letter ends with an account of a boat suddenly finding itself in the midst of plenty, a crew member calling out, 'We are in the middle of the largest shoal I ever saw in the Moray Firth, and shall lose our whole drift!'

The crew save their nets by throwing fish overboard to make room for those still to be brought over the gunnels. 'In this manner, taking in and throwing out alternately, they continued to labour until two o'clock in the afternoon, when the whole drift was hauled. They then made sail for Cromarty, and carried along with them twenty-five barrels of fish; having thrown out nearly thrice as much.' Miller never criticises the small boat fishery, but, together with the constant lack of sufficient salt and barrels, he pictures it leaving the community unable properly to exploit the herring in the firth. It's ill-equipped to pursue the herring further afield and unable to sustain itself through bad years.

Letter IV, in contrast, opens up on the transcendent beauty of a night spent with the herring fishers on the Guilliam bank, which took place when Miller was 17 or 18. In the deepening darkness after they've shot their nets for the first time, he hears the 'notes of a Gaelic song. "It's ane o' the Gairloch fishermen," said our skipper, "puir folk they're ay singing an' thinking o the Hielands'—a reference to the Clearances, which subtly picks up on the fractures in the culture of dependence referred to in the first letter. Miller's own Romanticism takes flight in a remarkable passage. After they've hauled in twelve barrels-worth of herring and shot the nets again, he goes to sleep in the discomfort of the space left to him:

> About midnight I awoke quite chill, and all over sore with the hard beams and sharp rivets of the boat. Well, thought I, this is the tax I pay for my curiosity. I rose and crept softly over the sail to the bows, where I stood, and where, in the singular beauty of the scene, which was of a character as different from that I had lately witnessed as is possible to conceive, I soon lost all sense of every feeling that was not pleasure. The breeze had died into a perfect calm. The heavens were glowing with stars, and the sea, from the smoothness of the surface, appeared a second sky, as bright and starry as the other, but with this difference, that all its stars appeared comets. There seemed no line of division at the horizon, which rendered the illusion more striking. The distant hills appeared a chain of dark thundery clouds sleeping in the heavens. In short, the scene was one of the strangest I ever witnessed; and the thoughts and imaginations which

it suggested were of a character as singular. I looked at the boat as it appeared in the dim light of midnight, a dark irregularly shaped mass; I gazed on the sky of stars above, and the sky of comets below, and imagined myself in the centre of space, far removed from the earth and every other world, the solitary inhabitant of a planetary fragment.

The vision is immediately disrupted by 'terrible threats of violence immediate and bloody' as the nets of two nearby boats become entangled, but it resonates with the fulness of ecstatic experience available from the fishermen's craft.

LETTER V

Letter IV sets up the final letter, in which herring drifting is compared with the reduced world available to the line fisher:

> Unfortunately for him, one of his employments, the procuring and preparing of bait, occupies much time, but requires so small an exertion of strength or skill as to be work for children. At an age therefore, when the children of mechanics are at school, those of the fishermen are either employed in baiting hooks, or in digging for the sand worm. When they become a little older the boys accompany their fathers to sea; and in their sixteenth or seventeenth year they are provided with the necessary tackle, and soon become such masters of the art of fishing as to be able to provide for their families. Early marriage is a consequence... The harrassing employments of the profession, and the cares of a family, prevent the fisherman when married from acquiring that education which he did not acquire when single, and he is thus shut up to a life of toil and ignorance.

The herring fisherman, on the other hand, 'is stimulated by hope; he ventures considerable property in the speculation; he reasons, he calculates. In short, by descrying advantage while yet distant, and in making preparations to secure it, he assumes and deserves the character peculiar to man.' It may be a tad unfair on line fishermen, but Miller is making the case for investment at precisely the moment when the bounties are being phased out. Across the wider employment herring fishing brings, Miller argues that society gets a perfectly reasonable financial return in taxes for the bounties, but they're necessary as a way of dealing with the uncertainties. And, on top of that, you get a better version of humanity. Meeting subsidy halfway, he suggests a scheme with the *Inverness Courier* for sharing information as to when the shoals are at Caithness and when in the Moray Firth.

The bounties ended and the town's herring fishery never recovered from their withdrawal. Elsewhere in the Moray Firth, the small open boats developed into the fully-decked wonder that was the zulu (see **Herring Boats**), which played such a huge role in the late nineteenth/early twentieth century flourishing of the **British Fisheries**.

MONKEY BUSINESS

Four stowaways on an ocean liner bound for New York, in *Monkey Business* (1931, see second image section), Groucho, Chico, Harpo and Zeppo Marx have hidden in barrels labelled *Kippered Herrings*. We never find out what has happened to the kippers they have displaced. As the film begins, the titles appear over a barrel. The opening credits illustrate their faces, superimposed on four barrels rolling down the gang plank and on to the New York docks.

Stowaways, the captain is told, have been heard in the hold, singing *Sweet Adeline*. We see the four barrels. We hear Groucho, Chico and Zeppo singing in barbershop close harmony. Some might doubt the likelihood of such a high class ocean liner carrying barrels of kippers, but they'd be wrong. A newspaper advert from 1913 illustrating Christopher Unsworth's *The British Herring Industry: The Steam Drifter Years, 1900 –1960* (2013) confounds the sceptics. 'YARMOUTH HERRING SEASON, SHIPPING ANNOUNCEMENTS. These steamers are specially adapted for the conveyance of HERRINGS.' Cunard Line's *Lycia*, Glynn Line's *Pontiac*, Wilson Line's *Carlo* and Cunard's *Pavia*. They are all advertised as calling at Mediterranean ports.

The liners made the fastest voyages and, with cool storage, could get kippers around the Mediterranean (or across the Atlantic) with shelf life left. See **Jewish Food** for the impact on the trade of World War I. Harpo, Zeppo, Chico and Groucho emerge from the barrels, regardless. They lift the lids off the barrels, and the mayhem begins.

It is not appropriate to intellectualise a Marx Brothers film—they themselves would have strongly disapproved—but from their first appearance there is a constant play between immigrant and all-American tropes. In the USA herring was and is strongly associated with the Jewish community; the Marx Brothers were the sons of French and German Jewish immigrants. Meanwhile, *Sweet Adeline* is a classic of the American barbershop tradition.

There are rival gangsters on the liner. Joe Helton is coming back from Europe with his daughter (providing the love interest for Zeppo), while Alky Briggs is trying to take over Helton's territory. His wife, Lucille (played by comedian Thelma Todd), has no fun at all as a gangster's moll: 'From the moment he got the marriage licence, I've led a dog's life.' 'Are you sure he didn't get a dog licence?' Like Groucho, she wants excitement; she wants the 'ha-cha-cha-cha.' Neither of the gangsters are Italian-background, as one might have expected, but then Chico is Italian enough for anybody... The Brothers' actual father makes a cameo appearance in the film, sitting on the luggage behind them when they make it to the New York docks (he was apparently paid $25 for two days work).

Producer Herman Mankiewicz warned the writers S.J. Perelman and Will B. Johnstone that the brothers were 'mercurial, devious, and ungrateful… I hate to depress you, but you'll rue the day you ever took the assignment. This is ordeal by fire, make sure you wear asbestos pants.' Groucho thought the first script stank and later said of Perelman, 'I hated the son of a bitch, and he had a head as big as my desk.' He considered

Perelman too intellectual for their kind of comedy. The Brothers actively did not want their films to *mean* anything. The thematic play with the idea of immigration feels like a surviving remnant of Perelman's work. The kipper barrels may have alluded to Jewish immigration in Perelman's mind, but they also provided a beautifully improbable visual gag, *Sweet Adeline* rescuing it from any suggestion of meaning, apart (see **Pickelhering**) from jokes which stink.

Perelman excised all mention of *Monkey Business* from his official publicity, but it's a great film, nevertheless. It has the distinction of having been banned in Ireland for fear it would encourage young people's anarchic tendencies.

N IS FOR NASHE & NEUCRANTZ

Thomas Nashe and Paul Neucrantz have been twin pole stars to the progress of this encyclopaedia. Nashe is simply the most inventive and fantastical improviser on herring possibilities ever; Neucrantz is happy in the knowledge that a treatise on the herring is not going to be taken seriously, but pushes on with a complete statement of seventeenth-century herring knowledge anyway. For their pains, they've both been largely ignored. *Nashes Lenten Stuffe* (1599) is generally misunderstood; *De Harengo* (1654) doesn't even get a byline. There is greatness, however, in these works.

THOMAS NASHE

C.S. Lewis suggested *Lenten Stuffe* was gloriously about nothing at all. The most thorough and engaging account of Nashe comes in Charles Nicholls' biography, *A Cup of News* (1984). He sees the work as:

> A hymn to the inexhaustibility of language, a quirky pageant of responses and reverberations. The red herring is, in the axiomatic sense, a complete red herring, and as such it is Nashe's metaphor for life itself. His 'prayse of the red herring'

becomes a paradigm for the mind's peripheral agitations around an elusive, perhaps non-existent, core of meaning. And if the red herring tells us life's secret, then that secret is the plain fact of survival. The metaphor doubles back: the herring is food on his plate, the 'stuffe' of life in a hard 'lenten' world.

I would agree with all of that and then add more on top, particularly on the subject of the **Red Herring Joke**, which drives the work and which, I'd argue, has only been partially understood. The details of Nashe's life, here, draw on Nicholls' book, which I'd recommend.

Originally from Lowestoft, Nashe knew about herring. Shaggy-haired with a gag-tooth, he was boyish-looking, skinny and verbally combative. He went to St John's College, Cambridge, gained a degree and left to make a living as a writer in the new and precarious world of pamphleteering. He had a journalistic eye, but he also seems to have had an electrifying capacity for sustained comic extemporisation; a manic and, maybe at times, scary ability to make endless connection between things apparently plucked out of the air. After he died, an anonymous friend/admirer wrote:

> Some things he might have mended, so may all.
> Yet this I say, that for a mother witt,
> Few men have ever seene the like of it.

Today he's best known for the picaresque novel, *The Unfortunate Traveller* (1594); in his own time it was probably for the richly imagined self-portrait, *Piers Pennilesse, His Supplication to the Divell* (1592). His pamphlets annoyed and were admired for their wild wit and energetic defiance, but he turned his hand to a range of genres. In 1593 he spent time in the patronage of Ferdinando, Lord Strange, 5th Earl of Derby, a man who walked the dangerous line between sympathy with England's Catholics and loyalty to his Protestant queen.

The only picture of Nashe comes from *The Trimming of Thomas Nashe, Gentleman* (1597). Glorying in his misfortunes after *The Isle of Dogs*, it was written by the Cambridge barber surgeon and friend of Gabriel Harvey, Richard Lichfield. The hobbling chains are wishful thinking.

Nashe fluctuated between the profound religious intent of *Christs Teares over Jerusalem* (1593) and the outrageous mockery found in his *Lenten Stuffe*. Nicholls suggests the first might have been written in a bout of melancholy or depression. The second suggests, at times, something of the manic, not to mention an atheism similar to that of which his friend Christopher Marlowe was accused. For Strange he wrote *The Choise of Valentines or The Merie Ballad of Nash His Dildo* (1592/3). It is tempting to imagine him in Strange's library reading a private collection of French *sermons joyeux*, poems in the lowlife/bawdy tradition out of which the **Life of St Herring** had emerged in the late fifteenth century.

It's generally agreed that Nashe collaborated with Shakespeare on *Henry VI Part 1* around 1591. Some have suggested he was a regular joke supplier. In Shakespeare's *Love's Labours Lost* (1594/5), the character of Moth, the argumentatively witty servant to Don Armado, is an affectionate portrait. Don Armado might be a portrait of Nashe's literary opponent, the writer and Cambridge academic Gabriel Harvey.

Robert Greene, Nashe's friend and mentor—the man who had labelled Shakespeare an *upstart crow*—had called Nashe 'young Juvenall, that byting Satyrist'. Greene's death in 1592 elicited mockery from the Presbyterian-sympathising scholar Gabriel Harvey. With *Strange News* (1593) Nashe bit back. Harvey returned with an attack on Nashe, *Pierces Supererogation or a New Prayse of the Old Asse* (1593), after which Nashe seems to have gone through a crisis of faith. In *Christs Teares* he apologised to Harvey, who came back at him anyway. Nashe did not reply for a while. His own explanation was that 'bitter-sauced invectives' did not pay the rent, but Harvey had asked for it and eventually got it in the devastating form of *Have With You To Saffron-Walden, Or, Gabriell Harveys hunt is up* (1596).

Nashe was an argumentarian and a consistent opponent of self-righteous Puritanism. He could be accused of prizing wit above caution. In the summer of 1597 he collaborated with the young Ben Jonson on *The Isle of Dogs*, a play which crossed the line as far as the authorities were concerned and was banned. The text is lost, but it almost certainly formed part of the red herring joke story, which had been initiated in Shakespeare's *Henry IV Pt 1*. Through it, anyway, Nashe acquired a new enemy in Henry Brooke. In the suppression of *The Isle of Dogs*, Nashe had to leave town. From the volume of material he draws on in *Lenten Stuffe*, it is possible he was already planning to do something inspired by the red herring, but the situation in which he found himself shaped what he wrote.

We don't know where Nashe was for a year or so, but he spent some time in Great Yarmouth. He claimed to have written most of *Lenten Stuffe* during Lent 1598, which he says accounts for the title, although that is one of the text's many evasions. Nothing in what was to be his last work can be taken at face value. In the constant multiplication of meanings, the whole text is the joke and, through it, much more besides. With its pastiche, linguistic invention, puns and ambiguities it looks forward to Lewis Caroll's *Through the Looking Glass* and Humpty Dumpty's insistence: 'When I use a word… it means just what I choose it to mean—neither more nor less.'

Nashe subtitles *Lenten Stuffe* as *the prayse of the red herring*. The sole bid he makes to posterity in his greatest and most extraordinary work is simply that, 'I am the first that ever sette quill to paper in prayse of any fish or fisherman.' It's the first literary work to draw on red herring as a metaphor and delivers a veritable shoal of them. Like a Soviet dissident poking the *Politburo* bear, he makes clear that any interpretations are, in advance, denied. Authorities can make up their own rules, however. Two months after its publication Archbishop Whitgift, seemingly under instruction, announced a ban on several works, including ones by Marston, Middleton and the dead Marlowe. He additionally ordered that 'all Nasshes bookes and Doctor Harvyes bookes be taken wheresouver they may be found and that none of theire bookes be ever printed hereafter.' Harvey seems to have stopped writing after *Have With You To Saffron Walden*, relying on a friend to pen *The Trimming of Thomas Nashe, Gentleman* (1597) which, possibly encouraged by Brooke, had gloated at Nashe's post *Isle of Dogs* misfortunes. For Nashe, who lived by his pen, it was a devastating decree. He died in 1601.

In 1995 an unpublished *Elegy dedicated by Ben Jonson in fond memory of his most beloved friend Thomas Nash*e turned up in the archives of Berkeley Castle in Gloucestershire. It begins:

> Mortals, that yet respire with plenteous breath,
> View here a trophy of that tyrant Death,
> And let the object strike your melting eyes
> Blind as the night, when you but read 'Here lies
> Conquered by destiny and turned to earth
> The man whose want hath caused a general dearth
> Of wit throughout this land; none left behind
> To equal him in his ingenious kind.'

The poet Charles Fitzgeoffrey wrote a Latin epitaph, interpreted as suggesting either Nashe died of a stroke or as a result of the poverty inflicted by authorities. A combination of the two is also possible. Translated, it reads:

> When Death, upon imperial Jove's command, obeyed,
> Extinguishing the vital spark of Nashe with night,
> First, with stealth, he seized those twin thunderbolts,
> That young man's battling tongue and fearsome pen,
> So he could move upon one naked and unarmed,
> Bringing back in triumph the poet as his trophy.
> Had pen or tongue been left available to Nashe,
> He would have struck the fear of death in Death himself.

The narrative of the Red Herring Joke shared by Shakespeare, Ben Jonson and Nashe between 1596 and 1599 is about writers and power, of reading and not reading the signs. *Lenten Stuffe* is, however, a great work, deserving far better than the misunderstanding and obscurity it enjoys.

PAUL NEUCRANTZ

In 1654 'the splendid council of the Republic of Lübeck' published Neucrantz's learnedly comic celebration of the fish he loved: *De Harengo exercitatio medica in qua principis piscium exquisitissima bonitas summaque gloria asserta et vindicata* (A Medical Treatise upon The Herring, in which the excellent virtue and supreme glory of the Prince of Fishes are presented and proved). He begins with an explanation as to why he has written it:

> O, magnificent, most noble, learned and generous amongst men, my masters, to whom all honour is especially due, until recently we had not discussed the virtues of the herring. At the recent wedding in Thurovia, however, Master D. Johannes Grakius gave us his thoughts On Herrings. He called them unpleasing and unhealthy fish.

Given to buying his fish whole and ungutted, he had eaten a fresh specimen, properly cooked, and suddenly he felt ill. There was a belching, there was a thunderous seizure of the bowels and then there came the diarrhoea, like a deluge. In the light of this, he has decreed his abstinence from herring. No matter how reasonably priced, it has been banished from his tables. In his address he told us also of those brave, but demoralised fishermen of Travemunde, how they may catch it but do not themselves like it, any other fish being preferred. And popular opinion seems to be with him, My Lords, when he argues that eating herrings can lead to the fever. This is why mistresses of the house are expected to order them carefully gutted, cooked, only lightly salted and then marinated in vinegar and horseradish, its harmful effects thus countered. Boudewijn Ronsse says the herring acquired this unjustified reputation in his lifetime. Likewise, Stephan von Schoneveld, in the chapter on herrings in his Book About Fishes, argues, as a soft fish, it is inclined to produce excrement and fevers among the incautious.

I had only recently asserted the exact opposite in my Book on the Treatment of Malignant Fevers. Having surveyed the commentaries of doctors and natural historians on just about any fish they have chosen to mention, I feel duty bound to stick to my own opinion, holding it to be well-founded, that the herring is a fish of the most commendable virtue. Were I not to undertake this present and necessary defence of the chief of fishes, I should be dismissed as some lick-spittle toad, a man who would deny the truth of anything.

Neucrantz was a Doctor of Philosophy and Medicine of Rostock, but lived and worked in Lübeck, very much a part of the medical, scientific and cultural scene. The city had a keen sense of the herring's role in its own glory days as capital of the German Hanse, but by the mid-seventeenth century this variable federation of European cities was crumbling. The Scania herring fishery, in which Lübeck had been so involved, was a mere shadow of what it had been. *De harengo* is a defence in fifteen chapters of a fish fallen from grace.

D. O. M. S.
PAULI NEUCRANTZI
ROSTOCHIENSIS,
PHIL: ET MED: DOCT:
DE HARENGO
Exercitatio Medica,

In quâ principis piscium exquisitissima bonitas summaq; gloria asserta & vindicata,

Ad Amplissimos Reipubl: Lubec: Consules.

LUBECÆ,
LITERIS GOTHOFREDI JEGERI,
ANNO cIɔ Iɔc LIV.
Sumptibus JOACHIMI WILDII, Bibliopol: Rostoch:

Title page from the photocopy of Neucrantz's *De Harengo* sent to me back in the pre-digital age. (From the British Library Collection, 1257.d.17.)

Witty and playful, its erudite arguments are determinedly out of all proportion to what such cheap food might have expected. He laboured over it, ensuring its academic credentials, but its origins are in an extensive speech he performed to an audience of his peers and patrons. Some of its performative qualities remain. He cannot help throwing in fascinating asides and little-known facts. He takes every opportunity to demonstrate his dazzling range of sources and authorities. In addition to those from the Bible, he refers to ninety-six different source authors, many cited for multiple texts.

After his introduction, the chapter headings explain themselves: 'In which it is demonstrated that the herring was unknown to both Greek and Roman authors alike'; 'In which the nature of the herring and its grounds is reviewed'; 'Concerning the squeaking of herrings whilst they do not breathe' (see **Farting**); 'In which it is shown that herrings do not live on seawater alone'; 'Concerning the boiling of herrings'; 'Proof of the herring's special virtues'; 'Demonstrating that a herring's value lies in its distinctiveness'; 'Proving virtue in the herring from the evidence of its fins and scales'; 'Concerning roast herring'; 'A review of conflicting evidence;' 'Concerning herring preserved with salt'; 'Concerning smoked herring'; 'On medicinal and other uses of the herring' (see **Medicine & Health**); 'A vindication of the herring, its inestimable value and its primacy among fish, together with a eulogy upon this treatise'.

Some of the questions he raises have only been fully addressed in the twentieth and twenty-first centuries. At 80 pages, the work is too long for inclusion in its entirety, but in addition to those entries pointed to above, see also, in particular, **Grand Migration** and **Jewish Food**.

NECKAM, ALEXANDER

Alexander Neckam, philosopher and poet, was the first European writer to describe the use of magnetism in navigation, was an encyclopaedist (bonus points) and wrote extensively on natural history. Knocking all of that into a cocked hat, he was the first Englishman to write about the herring. He wrote in Latin, but it should not be held against him.

Neckam was born in 1157 in St Albans on the same day as the future Richard the Lionheart. His mother was hired as royal wetnurse and in his early life he was raised as Richard's foster brother. Educated in St Albans, then in Paris, where he also taught, he returned to England in 1186. He joined the Augustinians, writing and teaching in Oxford before moving to Cirencester, eventually becoming Abbot in 1215. He died there two years later.

See **Aquinas, St Thomas** for the arguments around Roman Catholic adoption of pre/non-Christian philosophy, but the Augustinians were reasonably relaxed and Neckam was big on Plato, Aristotle and Avicenna (Ibn Sina). It is hard to beat the title of his encyclopaedia, *De naturis rerum* (On the nature of things) which was written around 1190. His ten lines on the herring form a small part of a longer work, *De Laudibus Divinae Sapientae* (In Praise of the Divine Wisdom), which was possibly completed around the same time.

NECKAM ON THE HERRING

The Herring lives on water[1], its mother and its home,
How much he has to teach, how sweet it is to learn!
O Neptune, I shall sing of all your precious gifts,
But he, amongst all fish, is he I love the best,
Escaping those who hunt by sheer size of shoal,
As swollen as your seas this fish appears to be!
O, who would turn a nose at herring on a plate?
And at the price? Its flesh, once dried by fires of salt,
Is fit for Caesar's table and his poor fisher host[2]:
This gift of Thetis[3] grants a happiness for all.

NOTES

1. Neckam uses the Latin *halec* for herring. The complete text of *De Laudibus Divinae Sapientae* is available online: search on *halec* to find the relevant lines. *Halec* or *Allec* were the most widely used Medieval Latin words for herring, seemingly drawing on Classical Latin uses for these, meaning sardine or pilchard and/or a cheaper version of the Roman fish sauce *garum*—in *De harengo* Neucrantz suggests they derived from misinterpreted references to the lees of a fish sauce. Neucrantz also counters the widespread Medieval belief that herrings lived on seawater.

2. Neckam refers to the story of Caesar knocking on the door of a fisherman called Amycla, which appears in Lucan's *Pharsalia*. The great man is treated to a fish supper, *fit for Caesar's table, but enriching that of Amycla*.

3. Thetis, a sea nymph or goddess was a *Nereid* or daughter of the sea god Nereus. If any unidentified nymph were to offer you a herring, Thetis would be in the frame, but she was famous, in particular, for being the mother of Achilles. By association Neckam might be spinning a bit of early *Guinness for Strength*-style herring promotion.

NETS & WEIRS

The realisation you could catch more than one fish at a time was one of the great turning points in history. So many problems have flowed from that moment, but also, indivisibly, so many ingenious solutions in curing technology, so much trade...

WEIRS & SHORE NETS

One of the constantly rewarding information sources I have followed on X/Twitter goes by the catchy name, *Underwater Cultural Heritage of Stone Fish Weirs*. Its mission is to tell the world about the historic, ecologically sustainable fishing practices of indigenous peoples. The photograph of a double-heart fish weir on the coast of Taiwan has been a particular joy, but there is an endless supply.

Currently, the oldest stone fish weir dates to around 9100 BCE, but it is early days yet with submarine archaeology. Identified in 2010 and properly explored in 2022, the weir is in Shakan Bay on the west coast of Alaska's Prince of Wales Island. This is traditional herring fishing territory for the Tlingit (see **Dried Herring**) and the island hosts one of the most spectacular, visible-from-space herring spawnings, the sea turned white with milky sperm. These are **Pacific Herring** (but see **Taxonomy**). Other fish may also have applied, but the gift of herrings will have inspired the earliest identified evidence of large-scale fish capture.

Conceptual thinking is a blessing and a curse. Mankind in the presence of visible resources will always consider exploitation. When an Alaskan fishery management plan restricted indigenous herring fishing, the Tlingit were quick to respond, 'There were no problems until you came along.'

Fish weirs work on straightforward principles: in a tidal context retaining walls or other barriers are created. They are low enough to allow incoming fish at high water, high enough to prevent fish exit on the ebb. The double heart weir allows the trapped fish to be driven into a further, shallower enclosure, where a concentrated catch can be scooped out even more easily. With some, the stonework provides a base into which branches or brush can be fixed. Weirs can additionally exploit strong currents, as at Ynys Gorad Goch (Red Weir Island) in the Menai Straits. The coasts of Northern Europe are littered with fish weirs, some of which continue to be used. Many different herring populations gather in coastal or estuarial waters, amply repaying the capital investment involved.

In 2018 what are thought to be ancient fish weirs of the Wabanaki people were discovered at Cape Porpoise in Southern Maine. Incoming European fishers were able to draw on both indigenous technologies and their own traditions. Further north in Fundy Bay, with, at 39 feet (12 m), the world's greatest tide differentials, the tallest weir structures were constructed in the nineteenth and twentieth centuries, primarily catching juvenile herrings for the boom in North American East Coast, canned **Sardines**.

The oldest net discovered only dates to 8300 BCE, but fibre tends to be less durable than stone. It was found in what was Finnish Antrea, now Russian Kamennogorsk, a Karelian lakeside community. Made of willow, it was roughly 108 feet (33 m) long, over four feet (1.2 m) deep and had a two inch (5 cm) mesh. Shore-based early seine nets were also extensively used in traditional herring fisheries, again working with the tides, particularly in estuaries, sea lochs and fjords. The use of swimmers and/or small boats could enable one end of the net to be taken further out into the water, especially where there were opportunities to identify shoal positions. In later-deleted lines from his poem *Fish* (1922), the American poet William Carlos Williams writes of the men on the cliffs above a Norwegian fjord calling out and blowing horns, guiding the boats towards the herring shoals they can see.

The poem was based on the memories of a friend, Carolina Benson of Vermont, whose early years had been spent in Norway. The use of vantage points from which herring shoals could be seen and fishermen directed will have gone hand-in-hand with the extension of fish weir and shore netting technologies and the development of boat fisheries.

DRIFT OR GILL NETS

With the shift to predominantly boat-based herring catches, the drift or gill net developed as the prime technology. Hook and line methods are efficient for larger and more widely spaced fish, but can't match the opportunities presented by vast, densely-packed shoals. Drifting involves a set of nets hanging vertically like a mesh wall, but not anchored to the seabed. The nets, shot from fishing boats, are suspended in a line from corks or buoys and weighed down below by a heavy rope.

The herring is a pelagic or midwater species, feeding on or near the seabed during the day, following the zooplankton in the evening as it rises to the surface. They follow again as the plankton descends halfway down at midnight and comes up again at dawn. The fisherman's prime target at sea was normally the adult fish and appropriate mesh sizes were established to allow juveniles to swim through. The larger herrings are caught by the gills as they swim up. It is a passive method of fishing: the nets are shot in the evening and the fishermen wait for the shoal on its upward diagonal path. If the fishermen think they have achieved a good catch on the midnight rising, they might haul in and shoot again.

The origins of the basic technique are lost in the mists of time. It seems likely that when **Eyvindr 'Skaldaspillír' Finnsson** talks of the long nets in the tenth century, he was talking about drift netting. The method was considerably developed in the fifteenth-century rise of the **Dutch Fisheries**: its histories record the first large herring net as having been made at Hoorn in 1416. Their busses (see **Herring Boats**) were bigger and had larger crews. They were able to handle the larger catches and the weight of hauling them. There are many stories, however, of smaller vessels capsized by the weight of herring catches.

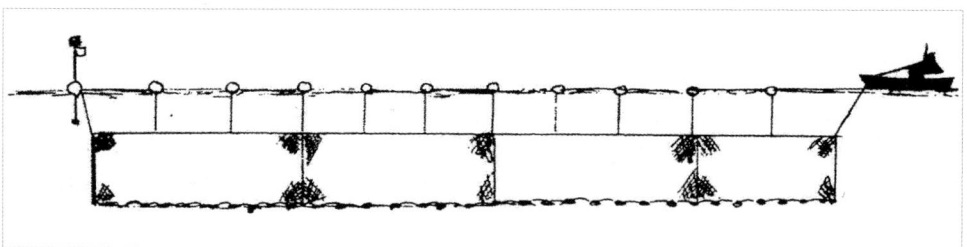

Drift netting: the vessel rides at the leeward end of the set to ensure the net is stretched; surface drift nets may extend, end to end, for several miles. (Courtesy of the Scottish Fisheries Museum.)

Scottish fishermen, incidentally, always shot an even number of nets, whereas the English stuck with odd numbers (and a more relaxed observation of the Sabbath). Concerned at the threats to sustainability inherent in other, more catch-efficient netting methods, both Scottish and English East Coast fleets largely stuck with drift netting until the 1950s and 60s, but other nations did not and the **British Fisheries** were increasingly undercut.

There are conservation arguments against drift nets too. While it was a reasonably sustainable method of catching herring, as populations declined (mostly at the hands of the purse seiners and pelagic trawlers) the line of nets became longer. Mechanical hauling overcame the natural limits otherwise imposed by human endurance. Around the world, in other fisheries, the lines of drift nets became even longer—up to thirty miles and more, creating what have been described as walls of death.

TRAWLING

Early trawling, which also developed in the fifteenth century, was seen as an efficient alternative to long lining (fishing with multiple hooks). Essentially a net weighted by a beam is dragged over the seabed stirring up and then catching demersal or bottom feeding fish. The seventeenth-century popularity of Dutch-style trawlers known as doggers gave their name to the Southern North Sea fishing grounds of Dogger Bank and consequently, ironically, to Doggerland, the prehistoric antediluvian plains which once joined Britain and the European mainland. Modern trawling developed from innovations in Brixham in the first half of the nineteenth century. Neither early nor modern demersal trawling were used in herring fishing: their significance here is focused on the damage caused by trawl beams to herring spawning grounds. Developments in marine science from the 1870s drew on the concerns of drift netters around both beam trawling and other trawl-based technologies.

RING NETS

The ring net was an early form of pelagic trawling involving two boats, developed in the 1830s in Loch Fyne, on Scotland's West Coast, out of shore-based methods, where the net was actively stretched behind a shoal feeding in shallow waters and then hauled directly on to the land. A boat was regularly used to manoeuvre the net, but the innovation of ring netting saw two boats working together, freeing the net from the shore and opening up the possibilities of the technique in deeper waters.

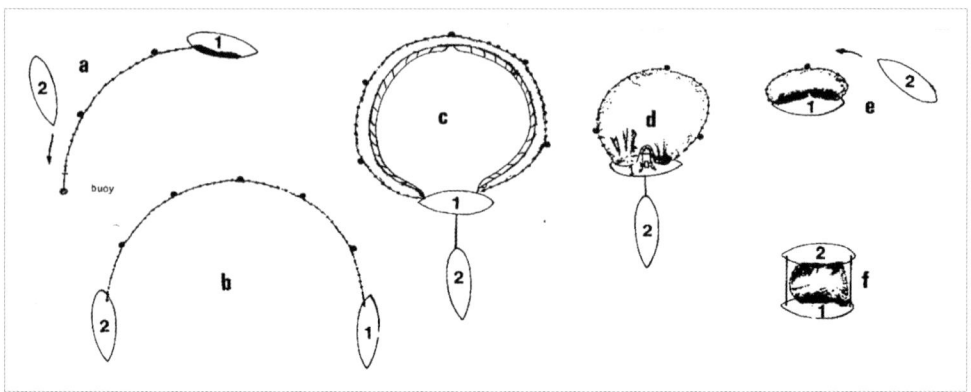

Ring netting: two boats manoeuvre the net around an identified shoal.
(Courtesy of the Scottish Fisheries Museum.)

The **Ring Net Struggle** with drift netters gets its own entry (see also **Two Contemporary Artists** for Will Maclean's documentation), but the argument centred on sustainability. A net mesh's ability to discriminate between adult and juvenile disappears when it is pulled through the water: the weight of fish caught at the back of the net prevents the escape of smaller ones. Working in partnership, the two boats could surround a shoal, trapping it by tightening the ring—a promise of things to come. A Scottish Fisheries Museum factsheet explains:

> A ring net consists of five panels—the wings, shoulders and bag, each with a canvas float attached. It hangs vertically in the water where the wings and shoulders serve to guide the herring into the bag. Two boats would sail to the fishing ground where one would remain at a certain point with one end of the net. The other would sail round in a circle, shooting the net as it went, until it rejoined the first boat. Both crews would then board one vessel to haul in the nets.

Drifting relies on identifying where the shoals might be; ring netting involves a more active pursuit and therefore more refined methods of identifying a shoal's size and position (see **Appearances & Signs**). Angus Martin's deeply knowledgeable and meticulously researched book *The Ring-Net Fishermen* (1981) is an invaluable resource.

The method spread to Scandinavia, where shore netting was active in the fjord fisheries of Norway. There are photographs from the early years of the **Icelandic Fisheries** showing ring netters at work. The technique could be deployed by one boat, but there was an increasing adoption of single boat purse seine trawling. In the scheme of things, ring netting was not primarily responsible for the herring population collapses of the 1960s and 70s, but it would be fair to say it was a step on the road.

PURSE SEINE NETS

With shoal-finding technology and little chance of escape, for herring the only hope offered by the purse seine net and the pelagic trawl which has, in turn, replaced it, lies in the fisherman's mercy. In 'History and Global Review of Purse Seines '(1971) Yunosuke Iitaka describes the purse seine as, 'almost rectangular in shape… The essential feature of this net is the closing by pulling a purse line which is threaded through a series of rings along the bottom so that the lead line is bunched or puckered.' Designed to stop the fish escaping out of the bottom of the net as the catch is hauled in, the purse line is so called because it pulls the net together after the manner of a purse's drawstring. The shoal is surrounded, the noose is pulled tight.

Shore-based seine nets go back to Ancient Egypt at least. Yunosuke talks of the writer Koziki referring to their use in sardine fishing in the early eighth century CE. Purse seining had already been developed in 1826 for pelagic species, specifically the menhaden fishery of Rhode Island on the USA's Atlantic coast. By the early twentieth century, notwithstanding the resistance of English and Scottish herring fleets, purse seining had spread worldwide. The efficiencies it brought to other North Sea herring fleets—and to new boys on the block, Iceland—played a significant role in the loss of crucial markets for the 'Scotch cure' in Russia and Germany between the two World Wars. By the time the British adopted purse seining the North Sea's herring populations were well on the way to collapse.

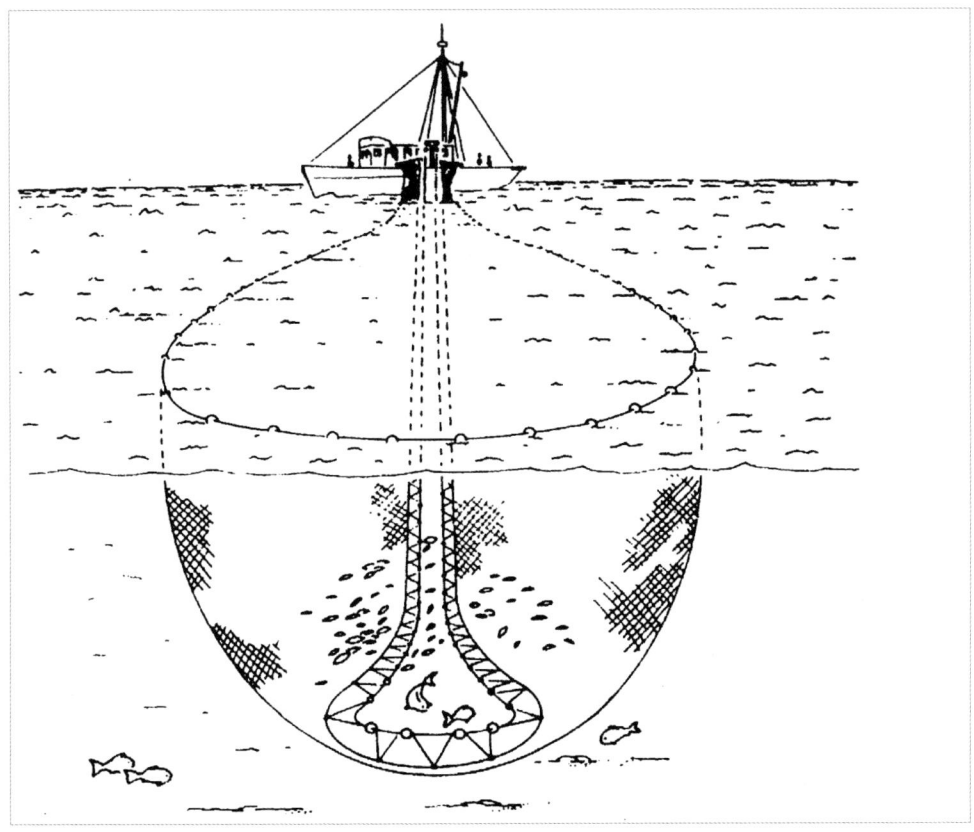

Purse seine netting or pursing: the lower edge of the net drawn together under the shoal like a purse. (Courtesy of the Scottish Fisheries Museum.)

Guided by sonar shoal identification, with active netting methodologies the scale of catches becomes far more regularly high. Together with the high proportion of juveniles caught this compromises shoal renewal. The initial solution to gluts was to develop herring **Reduction Plants**, which produced fertiliser, animal feed and herring oil. There was nothing new in using fish as fertilizer—the Algonquin word for herring refers to its use in growing corn (see **Etymologies, Euphemisms, Names**). Purse seining went hand in hand, however, with productivism, which, in fishing, aggressively finds markets for anything you catch: the pursuit of excess is normalised.

As Europe emerged after the war, fishing fleet renewal was a necessity. On mainland Europe it was supported by the Marshall Plan. The first commercial fish finders emerged around 1950. The hydraulic power block and net hauler (first produced in 1954) enabled even larger purse seine nets and even larger vessels.

PELAGIC TRAWLING

Modern pelagic trawlers are large—up to 144 m. They are factory ships like the Dutch herring busses of the fifteenth to eighteenth centuries, but work with freezers. The Dutch, Namibian-flagged pelagic trawler, *Cornelis Vrolijk FZN*, comes in at 114 m long. The net is of a straightforward conical design and, when the trawlers work in pairs, it can be wider. The herring shoal is identified, the net can be lowered to the appropriate depth: bingo! Where once there was a shoal, there is a shoal no longer.

Mid Water or Pelagic Trawling, which can also involve paired boats, extending the width of the net. (Courtesy of the Scottish Fisheries Museum.)

NORTH AMERICAN FISHERIES

Billy Bigelow and his friend Jigger may sneer at the hard-working herring fisherman Enoch Snow, but they are not going to amount to anything. When they have gone, in *When the*

Children Are Asleep, one of the great songs of Rodgers and Hammerstein's *Carousel* (1945), Enoch reveals his plans to fiancée Carrie Pipperidge. He may only have one little boat, but he's going to invest the profits in another one, then another, then another, until he's got 'a fleet of great big boats.' Carrie has a moment of doubt, wondering whether there's a market for 'all that herring'. Enoch has it all figured out, however. 'They ain't gonna be herring,' he tells her. He's going to put them in cans and call them sardines. He's going to start with a little cannery... At this point, in her heart Carrie just knows she's found her man.

European readers might wonder how Enoch Snow can so easily rename his herrings but see **Sardine Litigation**. The implicit key to his vision is his understanding that, if you want to make money, renamed they must be. His success, evident fifteen years later in Act 2, may be modelled on that of the Canadian Connors Brothers, Pat and Louis. (Herring) sardine canning in Maine goes back to the 1870s: the Franco-Prussian War having interrupted the supply of French (pilchard) sardines, importers started looking round for alternatives. Ernest Wentworth and Richard Wilbur's *Silver Harvest* (1986) identifies 'the greatest living authority on the history of the Maine sardine plants' as Mose Pike, who says, 'This business started in 1876 but by 1900 there was a factory on every beach up and down the shore. There were 13 factories in Lubec alone but many were so small and it was a very unstable situation.'

In 1889, the Connors brothers started out working a fish weir in their native New Brunswick (see **Nets & Weirs**), but they expanded rapidly, buying up several of the small canning factories in Canada and Maine. By the time they retired in 1923, they were selling a million cans a year and the company continued to grow, even through the difficulties of The Depression. One sardine factory seller in 1936, quoted by Wentworth and Wilbur, noted, 'the history of Connors Brothers buying out sardine plants is that after they've bought them out, there's no more smoke coming out of the chimney.' They also experimented with that old trick of paying their workers in vouchers which could only be spent at the company store.

They opened **Reduction Plants** and, as well as exploiting the juvenile herrings caught especially in the coastal weirs, they were also catching and processing adults. Their products expanded from just sardines, but their base in Black's Harbour, New Brunswick, nevertheless ended up housing the biggest sardine cannery in the world. They weren't the only herring fishers off the coasts of Maine, New Brunswick, Nova Scotia and Newfoundland (the potential of which had been identified by Robin Hitchcock in 1580—see **Pamphleteers**), but they illustrate the problem at the heart of Enoch Snow's vision: essentially following a model similar to that of Norway (juveniles, adults and reduction for anything the market otherwise couldn't accommodate) the fishery collapsed in the 1960s. Connors Brothers was itself bought up in 1967, although the name survives in the Connors Brothers Income Fund, which was sold to a British private equity firm in 2010.

As I write, the US National Oceanic and Atmospheric Administration (NOAA) is warning of an imminent collapse of the recovered Atlantic herring population. With both the USA and Canada there are also important West Coast fisheries of the **Pacific Herring**, which have experienced similar overfishing problems.

NORWEGIAN FISHERIES

With the world's first herring fishing poems under its belt (see **Eyvindr 'Skaldaspillir' Finnsson**), plentiful herring off its North Sea, Norwegian Sea and Barents Sea coasts and a heroic role in herring fishery research, Norway deserves its dominant role in today's herring fisheries. It has been a bit of an up and down story getting there and some say, as the country has become wealthier, Norwegians themselves have begun to favour fancier fish. They still catch and export a lot of herring.

Working against the blessing of its seas, Norway initially had two problems: the perennial difficulty Northern climates had with salt and the legendary unreliability of herring shoals. In a timeline presentation at Bergen's Norway Fisheries Museum, 1064 CE has two fishermen in a boat, each with question marks in the caption cloud bubbles coming out of their heads. 'Where have they gone?' it suggests they're thinking. 'When there is no herring it is known as "black sea"', we're told.

It happens again in 1858: one of the fishermen looks down into the waters, the other looks up to the sky. 'When the herring disappear, people look to religion and superstition.' By 1870, although the pastor is still telling them that, 'It is God punishing us,' the fishermen are dismissive: 'Yeah, yeah. But where ARE the herring?' As always with herring, ask a question and you get more than you bargained for, but Norwegian Fisheries Investigations had been established in 1864 and it's easy to imagine them smiling, 'Well, let's find out…' Norway was already committed to developing their marine science capacity.

There had also been a third problem, historically. Norway's farmer-fishermen extensively used shore nets and small boats in the fjords: this was substantially reliant on the herring coming to its nets. Specialist fishing villages were mostly landlord owned, creating problems with investment and incentive—the same problem had bedeviled the early development of the Scottish industry. When the herring came where they were expected, everything was fine and dandy, when they did not, it was not.

Bo Poulsen's account of the Norwegian herring fishery in *Dutch Herring* (2008) draws a picture more of occasional herring booms than of *black sea* droughts. The traditional herring fisheries were focused on the country's west coast, between Trondheim and Stavanger. Two herring populations are involved here, the larger spring spawners and autumn spawners. There was a spring spawning boom between 1518 and 1572 and an autumn spawning one between 1620 and 1650. As that declined, the spring spawners came back. There was a boom in salted herring exports in the mid eighteenth century, another decline, then a massive growth from the 1820s (from 10,000 to, in some years, 80,000 metric tonnes and more). The subsequent decline takes us to the black sea of 1858.

Increasing recognition of the importance of the herring as a resource developed as Norway agitated for its independence from Sweden. It coincided with a widespread, international interest in the opportunities presented by marine science, which fishermen themselves were keen to encourage. Support for the field by fishermen in the UK was a key driver in setting up an International Fisheries Conference in 1883. Along with the United Kingdom, Denmark, the Netherlands, Germany, Sweden, Finland and Russia, Norway was a founder member of the International Council for the Exploration of the Sea (ICES) in 1902. Its active commitment was led by Johan Hjort, who had become director of the Norwegian Institute of Marine Research in 1900. The understanding that they were dealing with different kinds of herring was considerably helped by the German zoologist Friedrich Heincke's **Racial Theory** of herring. Hjort was soon joined by another Norwegian giant of herring research, Einar Lea (see **Otoliths & Scales**) who took forward understandings of migration paths and age identification.

Norway's fishermen, exploring further afield, began to open up the **Icelandic Fisheries**, initially from the 1870s and then in the early twentieth century. Meanwhile, from the 1890s there was a boom in the Norwegian sardine industry, which used juvenile herrings and sprats (see **Iddis** and **Sardine Litigation**). Notwithstanding the extraordinary advance of Norwegian fisheries science, they failed to anticipate the problems which might accrue from heavily exploiting the same populations in their juvenile, feeding and spawning grounds. Their enthusiasm was compounded by an extensive development of herring **Reduction Plants**. Populations collapsed in Norwegian and Icelandic waters in the 1960s.

A new understanding of their herring resource's finite nature probably contributed to Norway's decision not to join the European Community, which would have opened their waters to other fishermen. In 1946, they had become the first country to have a Ministry of Fisheries, which in the context of the herring fishery collapse was well placed to develop the rigorous fishery management policies, which now inform what they hope to be a sustainable approach. Their system, which, like that of the EU, allows the buying and selling of **Quotas** has been blamed for pricing out the smaller boats and the inshore boats out of which their fishing industry arose. They are, however, one of the major Atlantic herring fishing nations. In 2015 they caught 312,959 tonnes.

OATMEAL

You can grill, boil, steam or bake a fresh herring, but it's hard to beat frying it in the pan. You could coat it in various flours, polenta, breadcrumbs or batter, but if you happen to have some oatmeal it's a marriage made in Heaven: the character to match it without in any way diminishing or distracting from the flavour. It draws the oils of the fish and the fat in the pan while toasting up a texture substantial enough to complement the sweet soft flesh.

In *The Scots Kitchen* (1929) F. Marian McNeill simply lists fresh herring, oatmeal, pepper, salt and dripping, specifying an ounce each of oatmeal and dripping for every two fish. She recommends two or three slashes either side of a seasoned, gutted and trimmed whole herring, tossed in the oatmeal, placed in the pan when the dripping is smoking hot and fried for between 5 and 7 minutes either side. She serves it garnished with lemon but notes that, 'In Buchan, vinegar and oatcakes are considered the perfect accompaniment to this dish.'

Theodora Fitzgibbon in *Traditional Scottish Cookery* (1980) more-or-less keeps everything else the same, apart from suggesting a plastic bag for oatmeal tossing and dispensing with the slashed sides. She sticks with the lemon wedges and adds parsley to the garnish. She specifies coarse oatmeal but also makes the case for a fine grade pinhead oatmeal, 'which imparts a particularly nutty and delicious character.' As an alternative, Fitzgibbon suggests painting the sides of the herring with English mustard before coating it with the oatmeal. She allows the possibility of cooking oil; personally, I'd stick with dripping and I like what rolled oats bring to the table.

Herring fried in oatmeal has a long history throughout Britain and Ireland yet is almost mythologically associated with Scotland. There should be some Celtic god of oatmeal, but it was the Romans who introduced it when they saw how few other crops would put up with the climate. It became the crofter's staple. Given its ready availability in Scotland's small fishing communities, it's reasonable to go with the idea that the recipe is Scottish in origin, although I'm drawn to the approach in Rick Stein's *English Seafood Cookery* (1988)—in particular to the addition of bacon, fried in the lard first to flavour it up a bit and then served on the plate with the herring. He bones the fish, which some might prefer. If only for the aesthetics, I'd go for Fitzgibbon's whole and unslashed fish. I would laud Stein's efforts, in later versions, to appeal to modern sensibilities, cutting the bacon into lardons and shifting from lard to sunflower oil, but it's hard to improve on perfection.

OBJECTS OF DESIRE

I grew up disliking Wedgwood Blue Jasperware. Despite its eighteenth-century credentials, it was of my parents' generation. The table cigarette lighter and its accompanying ash tray stick in the mind. Visiting the Wedgwood Museum at Barlaston was a revelation, not least for the discovery of the creamware herring plate. Serving herring to your guests? An eighteenth-century Queen's Ware herring dish is what you need. It's what I need too: an object of desire.

Wedgwood Queen's Ware is an early cream earthenware, which was being produced by the 1740s, but as well as developing his Jasperware Josiah Wedgwood took on the task of improving the cream stuff too. In 1765, George III's wife, Charlotte of Mecklenburg-Strelitz, commissioned a tea set, enabling it to be called Queen's Ware. The herring dish did not come along until the 1780s and, as far as I know, there is no record of Queen Charlotte extending her collection to include one.

The truth is, Josiah had not developed the line with a British market in mind: it would have been pearls before swine. He had a retailer in Amsterdam, where herring love knew no bounds. With a smile on his lips, Josiah referred to his British customer base as 'shoals of ladies,' but that was as far as it went.

Daniel Rozensztroch and Cathie Fidler's lavishly illustrated *Herring—a love story* (2014) is largely built around his collection of herringalia, notably some beautiful, mostly German, mostly china, nineteenth- and twentieth-century lidded *Marinierte Heringe* terrines, pretty much every one of which I'd happily accept. His collection also includes dishes, postcards, stamps, posters and more. For those who can't afford to buy their own herring still life from the Dutch Golden Age or even one of Van Gogh's it opens a sense of where a herring collector might go. **Iddis** are another beautiful option at the cheaper end of the spectrum.

I have a herring work by the artist Will Maclean, *Wind Knots* (see **Witches**). The kind woman who tweets on behalf of the Caledonian Oyster Co, near Oban, drew my attention to a Dutch herring dish, possibly from the 1970s, which she had seen in the window of a shop in Perth. There's a nineteenth century cast iron sardine can opener, I found on eBay (see second image section). They all give me inordinate pleasure.

OLIVIER, LAURENCE

Asked, in the making of a 1980 German television documentary, to name his greatest role, Laurence Olivier apparently 'placed one hand upon his forehead, stared meaningfully into the distance and intoned in that wonderfully modulated voice: 'Saving the kipper on the Brighton line."The filmmakers were following a day in the life of veteran *Daily Express* writer James Davies; a Class 86 electric locomotive was being named after the great actor and Davies was covering the occasion. The integrity of *Express* journalists is, of course, legendary, which is just as well, because we have to take his word for it. The priceless moment ended up on the cutting room floor.

What we know for certain is that Olivier led a campaign for the reinstatement of kippers on the Pullman car breakfast menu of the Brighton Belle. He'd moved to Brighton in the early 60s after marrying his third wife Joan Plowright and in 1970 had become Baron Olivier of Brighton. Having founded the National Theatre at the Old Vic in 1963, he'd become increasingly occupied with the development of its three stage complex on London's South Bank, which had a phased opening from 1976.

He was there for the topping-out ceremony before he retired in 1973, but over the decade leading up to that, he had been a regular on the Brighton Belle and in its Pullman car. None of the online accounts say why the kipper was withdrawn from the breakfast menu, but the sixties were a time of change. Memory suggests muesli went mainstream around 1965.

There is online confusion as to the date of Olivier's triumph: some accounts saying 1970, some '71, even '72. In one, a photograph is detailed as having been taken for the *Daily Mirror* on March 23rd 1970. Searching the British Newspaper Archive, the short article appears in the edition for Tuesday March 24th with the headline, SIR LAURENCE CELEBRATES HIS KIPPER VICTORY WITH SCRAMBLED EGGS.

> British Rail brought back the banished kipper on the Brighton Belle express yesterday. Not only that. They also served scrambled eggs, which are still officially off the breakfast menu.
>
> The eggs were for the commuter in the picture, Sir Laurence Olivier, who led the campaign to save the kipper after it was dropped from the menu last week along with scrambled eggs.

Sir Laurence had his eggs served on brown toast. He sipped coffee too, as the train sped through the Sussex countryside on its way to London's Victoria station. Savouring his victory, Sir Laurence said: 'I don't eat kippers all the time, you know. But I am very fond of them.

'I protested because I think this train, which is one of the finest in the world, should keep up its standards. I don't think its passengers should be limited in their choice of food.'

He added: 'I am extremely appreciative of the very gracious and dignified way British Rail have dealt with the whole thing.'

A British Rail spokesman accepted the compliment and said: 'I think our action shows that we take prompt notice of our customers' wishes.'

The spokeman went on: 'Although scrambled egg is officially off the menu, the chef obviously used his discretion. Whether we continue to serve it will depend on demand, and whether the chef has time to prepare it.'

Report: RONALD RICKETTS

The cultural advance of muesli notwithstanding, British Rail had obviously been too far ahead of the curve. Even though kippers had only been withdrawn for a week, in response to Olivier's letter to *The Times*, there had already been a petition and other letters demanding that the great actor should be able to select from a full breakfast menu.

There had been a Pullman Car Company from 1874 to 1962, but as part of Dr Beeching's modernisation of Britain's railways, the cars became the responsibility of British Transport Hotels and its British Rail Catering division, both based in the then rundown palatial splendour of St Pancras Station's former Midland Hotel. BTH's PR team provide the unseen actors in the story. Writing in the *Financial Times* in 2010, the chef, restaurateur and cookery writer Rowley Leigh records, 'A rueful restaurant manager from the train commented: 'It would not have been so bad but Sir Laurence never ate the kippers anyway.''

Olivier's son, Tarquin remembers him initiating the campaign: 'In anguish he wrote a letter to the London Times.' He remembers that, 'He looked forward to the train journey back to London and having breakfast in the Pullman carriage. Invariably he had kippers which they did so well.' In Olivier's moment of triumph, he also says, 'He picked up the menu, paused, and ordered porridge.'

There's no getting round the fact the photograph (see second image section) shows him eating scrambled eggs, but it's possible it had taken a day to organise the shoot and Olivier was reprising his obstinacy with a more photo-friendly breakfast. There's another photograph, taken shortly after the one used (slightly less scrambled egg on the plate). It reveals Joan Plowright looking every inch the modern woman BTH might have wanted to project as the kind of person you meet in a Pullman car (the *Daily Mirror* cropped almost all of her out of the picture they used). In the unused photograph the shadow of her coffee cup on the saucer indicates, what just might have been the greatest railway scene since *Brief Encounter*, was being lit from behind her left shoulder. There is yet another photograph of Pullman chef Arthur Evans holding a rejected plate of two kippers, which seems generous, even for a Pullman car.

Kippers had been saved, but the Brighton Belle itself was axed two years later along with all its breakfasts. In 1973 British Rail Catering became Travellers Fare. Advised by Prue Leith, they introduced poached haddock and grilled salmon to the dining car experience but even that couldn't save them from the rail privatisations of the 80s. Fresh from university, in 1974 I got a job as a Clerical Officer Grade 1 at BTH. Every morning, I'd go out of my way to use the old Midland Grand's magnificent staircase. After six months, however, the lure of the dole became irresistible. The building was reopened as St Pancras Renaissance London Hotel in 2011. It offers several breakfast options, none of them involving kippers.

OTOLITHS & SCALES

'Waiter, waiter, how old is this skate?'

'I'm sorry, sir, I couldn't possibly say… Rays have no otoliths.'

Neither rays nor sharks have them. They both have placoid scales. Luckily for the marine scientist, most bony fish have otoliths and either cycloid or ctenoid scales, all three of which have growth rings (a bit like trees only smaller). From the late nineteenth century, the otoliths and scales of herrings played a major role in the development of marine science.

Knowing a fish's age can contribute to many understandings, but it is crucial to stock management: the levels of recruitment to a year class can act as an alarm call. Scales are scales. Anybody remotely familiar with fish has dealt with scales. They each have two layers, the outer one mostly made up of hydroxyapatite and calcium carbonate, the inner one mostly of collagen. They protect fish physically and can provide camouflage: the herring's light-reflective silver can be very effective in this role. Overlapping from the front, each row of scales partially covers the one behind. Delivered by the same genes that give mammals hair and nails, the scales essentially record alternating summer growth with winter rings.

Otoliths are stones found in both of the fish's inner ear canals—one larger and two smaller in each. Like white peas, they are made of calcium carbonate and enable the fish to judge horizontal and vertical acceleration. Looked at closely, they have alternating opaque and translucent layers, which create grooves. The number of these indicates the fish's age. Unless you're a marine scientist, you could spend an entire life not bothering about otoliths at all.

The study of these fish age indicators has a history which is long and inevitably intertwined, but scales go back further. Aristotle first suggested their use in the fourth century BCE, but lacked the microscope with which he could have made good on his speculation. Huge respect is owed to the Dutch father of microbiology Antonie van Leeuwenhoek (1632–1723), who identified age rings on the tiny scales of eels and burbots. In 1836 Baron Cuvier glimpsed a potential for otoliths in exploring fish and their ecologies, but did not make the vital growth groove connection. In the 1890s C. Hoffbauer worked on aging big fish, specifically looking at carp scales, although you'd barely need a microscope for that.

Johannes Reibisch at Kiel University comes across as another lightweight. He was trying to apply Hoffbauer's principles to plaice, but couldn't hack how fiddly it was, so switched his research to their otoliths. Some great shifts in the development of science can simply be attributed to laziness. Nobody would call Friedrich Heincke a lightweight (see **Racial Theory**). He was a colleague of Reibisch at Kiel and he looked at everything, including otoliths and scales. In his great work *Natural History of Herrings* (1898) he measured the variations between what he then identified as the different types of herring. **Taxonomy** has yet fully to catch up with Heincke, but through this he radically opened up what could subsequently be identified by the otolith and scale boys. The heroic age of aging herrings began and it was primarily associated with one man.

EINAR LEA

Herring scales are neither too large for a marine scientist to garner any respect, nor too small to enable demonstrable productivity. In the autumn and winter of 1909/10 the Norwegian Einar Lea (1887–1969) personally examined 9,000 herring scales. With herring the most economically important catch in Northern Europe, marine science (and the study of herring scales) had found its hero. He never got a Hollywood biopic (*The Man Who Read Herrings* would have been a cracking title) but he had the respect of his peers.

William Hodgson, in *The Herring & Its Fishery* (1957), describes him as 'the founder of modern herring investigation from the scales… So intimate was his knowledge of the scales of the herring that he was able to tell almost at a glance from which part of the north European waters a herring had come, if he were in possession of its scale.'

Johan Hjort (see **Norwegian Fisheries**) had recruited Lea before he'd even graduated from the University of Oslo. A couple of years before, Hjalmar Broch and Knut Dahl had already established the principle that a herring's age was written in its scales, but Lea, with breakthrough papers such as 'On the methods used in the herring investigations' (1910) and 'A study of the growth of herring' (1911), established the case. There were naysayers. At ICES (International Council for the Exploration of the Sea) D'Arcy Thomson, who led a Scottish investigation of the herring, considered its scales altogether too variable for the confidence Lea was expressing, but Hjort simply organised a herring committee without D'Arcy Thomson. By 1912 Lea was demonstrating, from the scales, the migratory travels of the 1904 class of Norwegian spring spawners and what a strikingly bad third year they'd all had. He took over from Hjort in running the herring committee in 1920 and after 'Frequency curves in herring investigations' (1923) even the British were persuaded. 'The herring scale as a certificate of origin' (1929) was the *coup de grace* for D'Arcy Thomson and his pals.

Hodgson explains the fundamentals of Lea's methodology:

> The scale can also be used to study the growth of the herring, for it has been found that it grows at approximately the same proportional rate as the fish itself, so that if a herring is 25 centimetres long and has five rings (including the edge), the length of the fish at the time of the formation of each ring can be calculated, using the following equation:
>
> $$l1 = \frac{Lv1}{V}$$
>
> Where L is the length of the herring, V is the length of the striated portion of the scale, v1 the length of the scale up to the first winter ring, and l1 the length of the fish at the end of its first year.

If you have a microscope and manage to purchase an unscaled herring from your local fishmonger, you could try all this at home. Hodgson gives detailed instructions on the 'use of an "Anglepoise" type lamp' and the lighting of the microscope field. From a ring counter's point of view, the best scales come from 'a position just above the pectoral fins and immediately above the lateral line.'

At the Norway Fisheries Museum in Bergen, among the exhibits in a vitrine celebrating Einar Lea and his achievements (see second image section), there's a tiny heap, *Herring scales from the North Sea in 1914*: forget digital displays, that's what I call a proper museum exhibit. It's hard to imagine a more evocatively beautiful tribute.

RETURN OF THE OTOLITHS

With his 1951 article 'Racial Analyses of Icelandic herrings by means of the otoliths', Einarsson put them back on the map. In the late 1950s, Postuma and Zijlstra took things further, finding that the spawning season of a herring could be identified by the size of the sagittal otolith's nucleus. Some fish which don't have scales (for example monkfish) do have otoliths. For the observant marine scientist each otolith records an extraordinary range of important data on habitats, water temperature, migration patterns and more. For these reasons there has been a movement away from the use of scales, but they did do the hard yards.

PACIFIC HERRING

The hero of this encyclopaedia is the Atlantic herring (*Clupea harengus*). The Pacific herring is *Clupea pallasii*: same genus, different species. It is genetically different, but not as much as different Atlantic herring populations can be between themselves. It is just that two million years ago they swam the North East Passage without any thought to the implications this might have for **Taxonomy**. The Pacific herring includes two subspecies, the Chosa and the White Sea herrings, which swam part of the way back and some Pacifics which swam all the way back have been given joint parentship status in a stable hybrid population near Tromsø.

Pacific herrings have the same level of genetic variations as Atlantic herring populations: adaptations to the temperature and salinity at the spawning ground and as early juveniles. In the Bering Sea the Pacific herring gets to be 13" long (34 cm), but, moving south and genetically adapting to warmer waters, other populations can be 10" (26 cm), 9.5 or 9". For herrings, genetic variability is a constant.

A number of herring populations on the USA's western seaboard have been the subject of petitions under the Endangered Species Act, but these have been turned down by the National Oceanic and Atmospheric Administration (NOAA) on the grounds that they 'did not constitute a species, subspecies or distinct population segment.' These questions depend on what you choose to call a fish and on which levels of difference you are focused. There have been a number of disputes between the fishing industry (which tends to take a broad view of species) and First Nation/indigenous American fishermen (who tend to focus on their particular local populations). The way genetics is going suggests things may need to be weighted more towards the arguments of the latter. Substitute European inshore fishermen for First Nation/indigenous American ones and there are concerns in common. There's more on this in **Quotas, Racial Theory, Svetovidov** and **Taxonomy**.

The Pacific herring is found in similar latitudes to those of the Atlantic herring: from the Bering Sea to the Yellow Sea and to Baja California. It is fished by Russia, the USA and Canada, Japan, Korea and China. It spawns on shallow coasts and in estuaries, then migrates (or drifts) into deeper waters for feeding. It has suffered population collapses since the 1950s for much the same reasons as the Atlantic herring: mostly overfishing, particularly in order to supply **Reduction Plants**. Its milky spawnings, visible from space, can be even more spectacular than those in the North Atlantic, but that is due to its choice of shallow, clear blue spawning grounds in British Columbia and Alaska.

Variations in fat content across clupeid herrings contribute to subtle variations in flavour, but, broadly, you can say that they are all fairly similar tasting. If the Atlantic herring had just been called the common or northern herring, maybe they could all have been called that. Some European cultural and culinary responses to the herring have been carried over into the New World. Commercial production of dried and half-dried herring has survived among First Nation/indigenous American communities in the Pacific North West, as well as in Japan, South Korea and as far south as the Phillipines. Japan's use of fresh herring in sushi and sashimi deserves exploration (always mindful of the need to freeze fish for raw consumption). The bottom line here, however, is that any of the recipes included for Atlantic herring will work fine with Pacifics.

PAMPHLETEERS

The 1784 edition of *Wealth of Nations* blesses us with Adam **Smith**'s thoughts on the herring buss fishery: pearls of wisdom for the benefit of all mankind. Putting aside the question as to whether they are either disingenuous or dishonest, they show little sign of the great man having given more than a cursory glance at the pamphlets which had proliferated on the subject over the previous two centuries. The catalogue he ignores is impressive.

The first of the publications, Robin Hitchcock's *A Politique Platt for the Honour of the Prince, the greate profite of the Publique State, reliefe of the Poore, preservation of the Rich, reformation of Roges and Idle Persons, and the wealthe of thousands that knowes not howe to live* (1580), acts as a taste of things to come. Many of the themes are established, but strictly speaking Hitchcock was advancing the case for a Newfoundland herring fishery. It would, by necessity, have involved a fleet of busses able to cure the fish on board, but the main run of pamphlets which followed on from his was focused on the possibility of busses exploiting the herring off British coasts, which were, more effectively, being exploited by the Dutch. Before the House of Stuart came to the

English throne, herrings swam lower down the political agenda than the nation's relationship with its fellow Protestant power. In Scotland they came much closer to the surface (see **British Fisheries** and **Sovereignty of the Seas**).

JOHN KEYMER & TOBIAS GENTLEMAN

In 1601, with succession imminent and the election lights almost certainly about to fall on James VI of Scotland, the diligent economist John Keymer published *Observations on the Dutch Fisheries*. In 1612 he was back on the case. A conversation with the mariner and fisherman Tobias Gentleman led to a scheme for an English buss fleet to rival that of the Dutch. Nothing came of it, but despite his claims to be 'more skilled in nets, lines and Hooks than in Rhetorick, Logic or Learned Books,' in 1614 Gentleman himself joined the argument with *England's Way to Win Wealth and to employ ships and mariners or a Plain Description what greate profite it will bring unto the Commonwealth of England by the erecting, building and adventuring of Busses to the sea a-fishing. With a true relation of the inestimable wealth that is yearly taken out of His Majesties Seas by the Hollanders by their numbers of Busses, Pinkes and Lineboats*. Possibly exhausted by his own title, Gentleman then disappears from the historical record. With a slightly shorter title, his work was nevertheless republished in 1660 and, yet again, along with other *Scarce, Curious, And Entertaining Pamphlets And Tracts* in *The Harleian Miscellany* (1744 and 1808).

WALTER RALEIGH

In 1605, imprisoned in the Tower of London two years earlier for his part in the Main Plot (see **Red Herring Joke**), Sir Walter Raleigh had humbly presented his *Observations Touching Trade and Commerce* to King James and—knowing it was what James wanted to hear—it has a major section on the potential of a herring buss fishery. This was also the year of the Gunpowder Plot, which probably did not help with the mood music for his attempt at rehabilitation. Raleigh was eventually pardoned in 1617 before being executed the following year. His *Observations* weren't published for another thirty-five years.

SIMON SMITH

With Charles I on the throne (and even more obsessed with herring than his father had been) Simon Smith stepped up to make the case again in *A True Narration of the Royall Fishings* (1641). Recognising there were 'Divers Treatises published, that have sufficiently already invited unto the Herring-Busse-Fishings,' however, he also published *The Herring Busse Trade*, a practical handbook for anyone convinced enough to get involved.

He begins with the sixty-seven laws which had been enacted by the Dutch between 1622 and 1634: this was the kind of thing any serious herring nation needed, the prerequisite underpinnings of success. They include legislation aimed at preventing the 'naughtily salted' catches for which Britain was famous. He gives us *Directions for the building of a Herring Buss*, not only explaining that 'The stoage will be for 412 barrels,' but exactly where each of them should go. He details building costs of £500 and the equipping of the buss at £237 4s 4d. On the basis of a two month voyage (a Dutch average), he calculates the outlay on salt, gipping knives, wages, repairs, wear and tear, etc, then deducts all of it from the income from an imagined sale of 400 barrels. The profit on each such voyage would be £144 6s.

From the beginning of June, he details the locations of the Dutch fishery running down from Shetland to Yarmouth, the dates and the profitable length of time spent at each. He tactfully recommends leaving the English Channel to small fishing craft, probably because herring busses were such attractive prizes for the Dunkirk privateers. He notes the 'good fishing' in the lochs of Scotland's West Coast and at the Isle of Lewis, but again suggests leaving it to the locals—almost certainly mindful of the fate of earlier English herring fishing merchant adventurers. He outlines the grades of herring and how to deal with them, fishing methods, the number of crewmen and their duties, the necessary provisioning and a recommended approach to financing based in each major port. It is extraordinarily thorough.

ROGER D'ESTRANGE & JAMES PUCKLE

Sir Roger D'Estrange's *A Discourse shewing the Necessity, and proving the Practicability of establishing a British Herring Fishery* (1674) draws on Hitchcock and Raleigh for its figures and concentrates on the nation's will. There is nothing new about the idea: it is self evident, 'I That it is of Great and Certain Advantage. II That it lies fairer for the Subjects of his Majesty of Great Britain, then for the Hollanders. III That if it be Encouraged, and Established, it will prove the Foundation of an ample, and lasting Revenue to the Crown, and of Wealth and Prosperity to the Nation.' There's none so blind as those who will not see, and one by one he deals with the arguments they advance.

'Some indeed will have it that We want Men; Others, that our Men will never take to it.' Nonsense, he says, 'we have men enough, but they are idle.' Get them out of the poorhouse! In a burst of national pride, against the suggestion English seamen wouldn't put up with the food Dutch sailors did, he argues, 'the English can bring their stomacks... to the Grossest Food Imaginable.' He does admit, however, unlike the Hollander, an Englishman needs his 'Pease and Bacon' and he factors this into the costings. His plan, essentially, is for an investment in the necessary infrastructure with the Crown investing in the fleet for a third share in the profits. The Stuarts were keen on the profits, but tended to prefer others to foot the bill.

With a range of tweaked and retitled editions, James Puckle's *England's Way to Wealth and Honour, in a Dialogue Between an Englishman and a Dutchman* (1697) tackles the problem of the argument's familiarity, by introducing literary ambition. You have to feel sorry for the Dutchman, whose 'Good morrow Friend, what art musing on?' finds him immediately caught in one of those pub conversations with a stranger, the manic gleam in whose eye you unfortunately missed.

The Englishman's essential argument for the greatness of his nation's fishing industry centres on its capacity to be better than the Dutch if only it tried. The Dutchman settles comfortably into the role of straight man, feeding the lines through which England's latent superiority becomes plain. When the Englishman finally unveils his twenty-seven point plan for *Employing the Poor in a National Fishery*, the Dutchman is clearly impressed: 'Upon the whole, I confess, that England may out Fish us, but then you must have nothing to do with Companies, only make it every particular Man's Interest, and they'll soon make it their Business.' However mindful Puckle might be of the corrupt collapses of Charles II's English and Scottish Corporations for the Royal Fisheries, his Englishman hedges his bets with an 'It's Dangerous taking a Rivals Advice.'

Puckle's *mow-'em-down* approach to the arguments of foreigners found a further creative outlet in his designs for an early version of the Gatling gun, which he patented in 1718, but his hinted querying of corporate Britain's probity went unanswered. The story of herrings and corruption is a long one.

JOHN LOCKMAN, ENGLAND'S HERRING POET

There was a flurry of activity in 1750/1. There was a new edition of Puckle and *A Small Collection of Valuable Tracts Relating to the Herring Fishery* republished Keymer's *Observations* and D'Estrange's *Discourse*, along with the *Sentiments on the same Subject* of Johan de Witt. The Dutch statesman may have endeared himself to English readers through his having, together with his brother Cornelis, been murdered by an Orangist mob before having their livers roasted and eaten (cf D'Estrange's 'grossest food imaginable'). The major arrival on the scene, however, was the one-man herring pamphlet phenomenon, John Lockman.

The Society of the Free British Fishery had been established in 1749 to agitate around the parliamentary *Act for the Encouragement of the British White Herring Fishery* of 1750, which notably introduced a system of bounties to encourage the development of a British buss fleet. This state subsidy, modified by further acts in 1753 and 1755, lay at the heart of Adam Smith's subsequent counterblast. The act's name speaks of the independence Puckle had tentatively suggested, but Frederick, Prince of Wales, was its Governor, just as the future James II had been Governor of the earlier corporations —and as, when Frederick died, his son, the future George III, took over. It was the Hanoverian solution to Britain's still unfulfilled promise as a herring nation and John Lockman was appointed its secretary.

The coinciding republications have to be seen as linked to the Society's agitation, but 1750 also saw a new jig, *The Herring Buss*, included in John Hinton's *The Universal Magazine of Knowledge and Pleasure*. Lockman had written an opera libretto, *Rosalinda* (1740), knew his ballads and frequented the New Spring Gardens (later to become the Vauxhall Pleasure Gardens) where such topical music gained currency. He may even have paid the anonymous tunesmith with the Society's herrings (see below).

Lockman got to work promptly upon appointment with the pamphlet, *The Vast Importance of the Herring Fishery, &c. to These Kingdoms: as respecting the National Wealth, our Naval Strength, and the Highlanders. In Three Letters Addressed to a Member of Parliament* (1749). The MP was Slingsby Bethell, president of the Society.

The first letter is prefaced by a couplet:

> Hark! 'tis the FISHERY!—This powerful Name
> Must ev'ry British, Patriot Heart inflame.

It addresses the huge wealth that would be generated by a successful buss fishery, noting among other points, that, 'In a Dutch Placart, or Proclamation, published in 1624, the Fishery is called the Golden Mines of the United Provinces.' Comparing the herring shoals to the Spanish goldmines of the Americas was a commonplace of Dutch self-promotion.

The second letter addresses the argument (also encouraged in Dutch PR and taken up by D'Estrange), that the herring fisheries would provide a training ground for the Royal Navy, which in turn would deliver an empire and even greater wealth:

> BRITONS! wou'd ye the Ocean's Sway secure,
> Yourselves to the bold Fisher's Toils inure.

Letter three's couplet, succinctly suggesting a solution to Jacobite rebellion, looks forward to the role herring fisheries will play in Scottish economic regeneration and the Clearances of the late eighteenth and nineteeth centuries:

> In Fishing Arts the HIGHLANDERS employ,
> Then will their Swords no more our Peace annoy.

Lockman moves into song for 1750's *Britannia's Goldmine or the Herring Fishery for Ever* (to the tune of *There was a jovial Beggar*). Between its twenty verses it delivers British liberty, food security, wealth, trade and commerce. It pays off the national debt, supports regionally-dispersed industrial development and builds maritime power. It addresses the Scottish problem, unemployment and idle poverty, bringing peace in our time whilst dealing with the French and the Dutch.

Puckle envisaged a dialogue between an Englishman and a Dutchman, but Lockman goes one better, imagining a poetic conversation between *The Shetland Herring and Peruvian Gold-Mine* (1751). He tackles the key problem head on:

> This MINE our Herring thus addrest: -
> "Vile Fish! which the Polite detest;
> Refuse of Billingsgate profane,
> Where Scoffs, and Oaths, and Tumult reign!
> Thou Beggar's Cate, which Mopsa cries,

As daggled to her Stall she hies!
Thou, specious Lump of taudry Skin,
With a rude Heap of Bones within!
Dar'st thou with mighty ME compare,
Whose Bounty Kings are proud to share?
Who round the Globe triumphant run,
And dart like Splendors with the Sun!"

Needless to say, the Peruvian gold-mine's contempt proves to have been misplaced.

Later that year, William Hogarth's *Beer Street* features two fishwives avidly reading *A New Ballad on the Herring Fishery*. This is probably Lockman's *Flourish the Herring Fishery, a New Ballad*.

FLOURISH THE HERRING FISHERY

O THE Mighty Fishery!
Mighty Herring Fishery!
So long expected, So long neglected,
Will at last triumphant be;
Will at last triumphant be.
O the mighty Fishery!
Mighty Herring Fishery.

O the foreign Merchandise!
Various foreign Merchandise;
We the World ranging,
Herrings exchanging,
For every Thing that Mortals prize;
For every Thing that Mortals prize.

O the foreign Merchandise!
Various foreign Merchandise.

O the powerful naval Sway!
Powerful British naval Sway!
Commerce reviving:
The Nation thriving;
Bidding the World our Flag obey;
Bidding the World our Flag obey.
O the powerful naval Sway!
Powerful British naval Sway.

O how charming to behold!
Doubly charming to behold!
This Fish'ry flourishing,
Half the Land nourishing;
And our Pockets lin'd with Gold:
And our Pockets lin'd with Gold.
O how charming to behold!
Doubly charming to behold.

Lockman, a poet without honour in the British literary canon, turned to prose (mostly) in his last major herring pamphlet. He was defending his reputation against the accusations of L.D. Nealme, an officer of the Society who'd been sacked over the disappearance of £50. 1753 saw *A Proper Answer to a Vile Anonymous Libel written by L. D. N. Chiefly against John Lockman, Secretary to the Society of the Free British Fishery in a letter to Slingsby Bethell, Esq., President of the Said Society*. It may well be his finest work. 'Where, my little Jesuit, is the Petty Cash-book thou burnedst?' he asks. 'Our Tartuffe knows perfectly well that he was rebuk'd for daring to lay his sacrilegious paws on the Society's Shetland herrings before they were seen or tasted by the Royal Family, his master or the public.'

William Hogarth's *Beer Street* (1751) presents a contented nation, its fisher lasses reading the latest offering from England's Herring Poet, John Lockman. In its partner work, *Gin Lane*, everyone is, of course, far too drunk to be able to read anything. (Author's collection)

Nealme had accused Lockman of misappropriating the Society's herrings. In the New Spring Gardens and elsewhere, the great pamphleteer was indeed known for giving away salt herrings with copies of his poems, but, unlike Nealme, the Society's Board had allowed Lockman 'a Barrel of SHETLAND Herrings… pursuant to the Dutch Custom' (whatever that might have been). The sense of outrage will be familiar to anyone caught up in an organisational implosion, but Lockman—not only a friend of Hogarth, but an acquaintance of Alexander Pope—finishes with a flourish:

> N____e dip his brush, in soot, and filth and gall
> And draws his devil on a bog-house wall.
> Then as my picture, to the world 'tis shown
> But the strong likeness proves, that 'tis his own!

The Society collapsed in 1772, all its herring busses and effects sold at Southwold. Lockman had died the previous year.

PAST(R)Y

After the Norman Conquest, Beccles, near Lowestoft, saw a doubling of its annual render to the Abbey at Bury St Edmunds to 60,000 herrings. In his paper, 'Domesday Herrings' (2001), just focusing on some of the big ones, Prof James Campbell tots up medieval renders of over 200,000 herrings a year from various ports in Norfolk, Suffolk, Kent and Sussex. The king, the aristocracy, landowners, religious institutions: they all had dibs in the herring fisheries. Salted *Herring Silver* was as good as minted coin. On top of all that, Great Yarmouth's charter of 1286 required it to send 24 herring pasties for the king (Edward I at the time).

Sometimes, this render is presented as Norwich's, but, containing a hundred herrings between them, it was Yarmouth which sent them to the Sheriffs of Norwich, who, in turn, were required to deliver them to the Lord of the Manor of Carlton in Suffolk. He'd been granted thirty acres of land in return for then delivering them to the king, wherever he might be.

At this point, the mathematicians among you are possibly thinking, 'a hundred herrings? 24 pasties? Four and a bit in each? Why not 96?' The answer is (see **Measuring the Herring**), herrings were counted in long hundreds—120—five per pasty. 343 years after the granting of the charter, a complaint was lodged with the Corporation of Norwich by Charles I's secretaries of state: they hadn't each contained the right number; the herrings were supposed to have been taken from the first catch of the season, but the secretaries weren't convinced; in their view they hadn't been well-baked either. The complaint also refers to them as pies and mention is made of an unfulfilled requirement for 'good standing pastry,' which may suggest something more like a pork pie than a pasty.

In pursuit of herring knowledge I've made a number of different dishes, but best of all was the recipe for *Herring Pasties* from Ambrose Heath's *Herrings, Bloaters and Kippers* (1954, see second image section):

> Clean the fresh herrings, take out the backbones, leaving on the head and tail, and stuff the fish with ordinary veal or savoury forcemeat. Wrap each up whole in pastry, leaving the head and tail sticking out at each end, and bake in a moderate oven for half an hour.

The principle is similar to Cornwall's Starry Gazy Pie, which has pilchard heads and tails sticking out of the crust. As with that, this herring pasty has a feel of a recipe that goes back a few centuries. Heath leaves you room to personalise, but basically you gut the herrings and remove the fins: the heads and tails are for the aesthetics; you don't want crunchy bits inside the pasty. See **Filleting & Stuffing** for the method, but once you've separated the main bones from the flesh, take a pair of scissors and snip through the backbone at both ends.

I originally opted for a stuffing using fresh breadcrumbs, onion, chopped bacon and tarragon. Second time around I substituted anchovies for the bacon; Delia Smith has a stuffed herring recipe using capers. They all work—it's just nice to have an interesting salty tang in there. For pastry I used rough puff, which is relatively easy to make. Brush the pastry with an egg glaze. They look beautiful straight out of the oven, but they're really good cold, too. You simply break off the head and tail before eating.

It's hard to work out how you'd do it with five herrings, but whether for a pasty or a standing pie, the journey time would have prohibited extruding heads or tails. Preservative pastry depends on sealing contents in and the air out. Standing pies tend to use jelly as well and I've made an excellent five-herring pie with a prawn stock, agar jelly. The eighteenth-century cookery writer Hannah Glasse suggests that, traditionally, the pies were filled with butter. Effectively this gives you potted herring in a crust. Originally (depending on journey time) the crust might not have been eaten, but the concerns of Charles I's secretaries suggest that, by his time, they were. And who wouldn't want to eat a good, raised crust pastry?

Campbell says that by the fourteenth century the pies were elaborately spiced. I went for orange zest and dill, which was excellent. I did not have any horseradish to grate at the time, but I might add some of that. I might alternatively experiment with the *épices Parisienne* which **Dumas** uses on his herring roe gratin: salt, bay leaves, white pepper, black pepper, cinnamon, mace, nutmeg, ginger, cloves and thyme.

I fried off and skinned herring fillets in butter to reduce the liquid. I use a small, greased cake tin, working the pastry from a ball pressed into the removable base, up the sides. Break the fillets into the pie casing and add flavourings between each layer. Place a rolled, circular lid on top of the pie, crimp the edges and make holes through which to pour in the clarified butter, brush with an egg glaze and put it in the oven at 160°C for 45 minutes. Five herrings fit nicely in a tin 16 cm (6 in) across and 6 cm (2.5 in) deep. After half an hour you can push the pie out of the tin on its base and glaze the sides as well. Pour in the butter as the pie cools, letting it settle before adding more, until it's genuinely full. (See second image section.)

What can I say? It's as good as the herring pasty, which is high praise indeed. The pies were sent to the monarch each year until 1816. The then Prince Regent, later George IV, was possibly not a herring man, but, as my father used to say (quoting Thomas Wentworth, 1st Earl of Strafford), 'Put not your trust in princes.' Heath also includes a recipe for *Herring Pastry Rolls* (sausage roll, with a herring fillet and a little chopped onion instead). I would also put in a personal word for kipper tarts and for kipper, leek and potato pasties.

PICKELHERING

For pickled herring, see **Vinegar**. *Pickelhering* is German for pickled herring, but he is also a stock character of German clowning whose popularity lasted up until the nineteenth century. Pickelhering, in common with contemporary clowns, wore oversized shoes, trousers and waistcoat and a large ruff collar. The story goes, he was introduced by the troupes of English actors who were popular in Germany between 1592 and 1659.

In 1586, The Earl of Leicester had taken his own company of actors to the Low Countries, when commanding the English Army sent to support the Dutch Revolt. Shakespeare's large-bottomed dancer and clown Will Kemp had been in the company which performed for Denmark's King Frederick at Helsingör or Elsinore (see also **Prophecy**), but he split with the bard just before *Hamlet* was written (see **Red Herring Joke**). Shakespeare moved away from Kemp's comic improvisations and slapstick, clearly thinking of him in the Prince of Denmark's instructions to the players:

> Let those that play your clowns speak no more than is set down for them; for there be of them that will themselves laugh, to set on some quantity of barren

spectators to laugh too, though in the mean time some necessary question of the play be then to be considered; that's villainous, and shows a most pitiful ambition in the fool that uses it.

The influence of Shakespeare on a rising generation of Jacobean playwrights did no favours to Will Kemp or his fellow clowns, who became culturally surplus to requirements in England. They had found a stage in Germany, however. Speaking little or no German they presented simplified versions of plays with dumbshow explanations. Their slapstick was a trademark and the Germans loved it. Along with the obscene gestures, their pidgin English was littered with mispronounced Dutch and German words and phrases.

'Me, Pickelhering,' the clowns would announce. Preserved fish raised a cheap laugh in any language. Hans Stockfish was another of the popular English clown characters. An English eyewitness at the Frankfurt Fair of August 1592 wrote:

> The Germans, not understanding a worde they sayde, both men and wemen, flocked wonderfully to see theire gesture and Action, rather then heare them, speaking English which they understoode not, and pronowncing peeces and Patches of English playes, which my selfe and some English men there present could not heare without great wearysomenes.

There is truth in this account of the emergence of the German stock character, but complicating it is the fact that *Peckelharing* was also a Dutch clown. A heavy drinking buffoon, he sometimes carried a salt herring, suggesting he got his name from its famous use in encouraging the drinking of beer (see **Dutch & Flemish Art** and second image section). He might have similarly sprung from the same English clown acts, but he seems more likely to have been a homegrown figure of fun. The English clowns may have used the name because it was already known or they thought it might be. 'Dutch? German? Who cares?' you can hear them saying. 'I'll have another beer, thanks. You can be Hans Stockfish.'

POTATOES

Mashed, boiled, sliced in a gratin or even crushed, it's hard to beat the potato as an accompaniment to plainly cooked herring. Chips, roast, rosti and fondant potatoes may offer a little too much evident oil—the herrings bringing their own—but each to their own. The Scots' tatties an' herrin', like **Oatmeal**-fried, has mythological status. As the Victorian song goes:

> When the Queen wanted someone tae fecht wi' her foes
> It wisna awa tae the lowlands she goes,
> But awa tae the hills o' the brave and the darin'
> The lads that were brought up on tatties and herrin'.
> > *Tatties and herrin'! tatties and herrin'!*
> > *The lads that were brought up on tatties and herrin'!*

TATTIES AND HERRIN'

The entry for it in McNeill's *The Scots Kitchen, its lore and recipes* just offers a description of the dish by the Reverend Alexander Stewart. It is so beautiful, it would be tempting to agree with her decision that there is nothing more to say:

> The other day, landing from our boat, we went into a cottar's house just as the gudewife was preparing the family dinner. A pot of new potatoes was boiling on the fire. Looking now and again into the pot, and listening with inclined ear to the sound, actually musical in such a case, of its boiling and bubbling, she was ready at the proper instant to snatch it off the fire, and carrying it to the corner of the kitchen she poured off the water and immediately re-hung it over the fire, shortening the chain by which it was suspended by a link or two, that the fire might not, now that it was waterless, have too much effect upon it. She then got some half dozen fresh herrings, caught early that morning—herrings large, beautiful, and as silvery-scaled as a salmon—and drying them nicely with a

cloth, she placed them flatwise, side by side, on the top of the potatoes in the pot, the lid of which she was careful to fit tightly by means of a coarse kitchen towel, which served at once to cover the contents and to cause the lid to fit so tightly that the steam was effectively retained.

During quarter of an hour, perhaps, the wife kept an attentive eye on the pot, never once lifting the lid, however, but from time to time raising or lowering a link in the chain as in her judgment was necessary. All being ready at last, she took the pot off the fire and set it on a low stool in the middle of the floor. She then lifted the lid and the cloth, and the room was instantly filled with a savoury steam that made one's mouth water merely to inhale it.

Occupying a low chair, we were invited to fall to, to eat without knife, or fork, or trencher, just with our fingers out of the pot as it stood. It was a little startling, but only for a moment. After a word of grace we dipped our hand into the potato, hot and mealy, and with another we took a nip out of the silvery flank of the herring nearest us. It was a mouthful for a king, sir!

from *Nether Lochaber*, Rev Alexander Stewart (1883)

Fresh herring, as so finely celebrated by the good Reverend, was a seasonal ingredient: much of the year it was salt herring, which could just as easily be cooked in this way, but which also gave rise to another approach—layers of thickly cut sliced potato, onion, salt herring fillets, cooked in milk like a gratin. In truth, understandings of tatties an' herrin' probably encompass a range of possibilities.

JANSSON'S TEMPTATION

The first time I was served Jansson's temptation (*Janssons frestelse*) it was by the Tyneside Finnish documentary photographer and filmmaker Sirkka-Liisa Konttinen. She introduced it to me as a Finnish dish made specifically with salted **Baltic Herring** or *strömling*, the small subspecies adapted to the lower saline waters of the Eastern

Baltic and the Gulf of Bothnia. She showed me a large jar of salted strömling in oil which she'd brought back from Finland.

Jansson, the temptee, has a Swedish name, of course, but with Finland's 700 years of Swedish occupation, who would quibble? Particularly when the temptations include salt herring, potatoes, onion, butter and cream. It was only when I began to research the dish that contrasting Swedish claims became so insistent: *Janssons frestelse*, a dish to be made with *ansjovis* not strömling. Some say anchovies, which would taste fine, but it's a mistranslation. Ansjovis are tinned sprats and I was told on various Swedish food websites, you could get them at IKEA. Conquering an almost pathological aversion to IKEA, I tried its Swalwell branch and was assured they'd never heard of them.

But back to Jansson... Who was he? Some say Pelle Janzon, nineteenth-century food-loving Swedish opera singer. Others sneer and tell you there's no evidence he ever ate a plate of it. This seems harsh: I for one was brought up never to leave evidence on a plate. Referring to Wikipedia, the entry for *Jansson's Temptation* outlined an alternative claim made by Gunnar Stigmark. The name had been given to a dish created by his mum and the chef she had hired for some fancy dinner party. They'd wanted to differentiate it from a similar clupeid dish which included egg, so named it after the silent film *Janssons frestelse* (1928). A number of film websites describe the character Gunnar Jansson as the *archival* of Baron von Werner, as well as providing the love interest for the Baron's daughter Inga. It's quite possible nobody checked the texts they copied and pasted from the *Internet Movie Database* in which someone had probably intended to type *archrival*.

There was a 1936 remake in which Jansson was neither an archival nor a Gunnar, but a family man, John, employee of the banker (or possibly stockbroker) Holger Linder, who still had a daughter, but she was called Vera. At this point it seems only fair to point out, the Wikipedia entry for *Jansson's Temptation (film)* claims it 'takes its title from the Swedish casserole dish Jansson's Temptation.'

The earliest published recipe for *Janssons frestelse* dates from 1940, but it's hard to imagine Swedes taking so long to make the fundamental connection between potatoes, cream and their readily available salted herrings and sprats. There is a Swedish *sillgratäng* or herring gratin: some recipes for it involve egg (hardboiled or raw), but others don't. It seems most likely that Jansson's Temptation became a name for an existing dish, which, like the Scottish *tatties' an' herrin'*, comes with almost as many recipes as there are people who cook it.

Online Swedish recipes insist on the tinned *ansjovis* as part of the temptation, essentially coalescing around something like:

> 4 potatoes cut French fries-style; 25 g butter; 1 onion, finely sliced; 125 g tin of ansjovis; salt; black pepper; 300 ml double cream; 300 ml whole milk; 2 tbsp dried breadcrumbs.

> Set the oven at around 200° C. Bake the cut potatoes for 20 mins. Fry the sliced onion in the butter until soft. Mix with the potatoes and layer a casserole dish with half the potatoes and onions, then the fish. Repeat with second layers and season. Mix the cream and milk and pour over, sprinkling the top with the breadcrumbs.

Some suggest mixing the marinade liquid from the tin with the milk and cream. When I eventually managed to get some tinned ansjovis (online), the brine included, not just salt, but nutmeg, cinnamon and sugar. This is quite common in Swedish canned marinades and it has historical roots. For me, much as I love nutmeg, cinnamon and sugar, in a can they take on a flavour which does no favours to herrings or sprats.

I did a test: a) *ansjovis*, b) pickled Baltic herring (saltier, but similarly spiced) and c) salted herring. It confirmed my prejudices entirely. Salted herring makes the best Jansson's temptation. If you can get straight, salted Baltics or even sprats, go for it, if not

I'd suggest the plain salt herring readily found in Polish or Lithuanian grocers. If you've invited anyone likely to kick off, call the dish *Sillgratäng*... or even tatties an' herrin'.

PROCESSIONS & CELEBRATIONS

Public events celebrating the herring have been noted since the fourteenth century. 'Celebrating' may not always be quite the right word.

REIMS

In the Herring entry of his *Grand Dictionaire de Cuisine* (1873) Alexandre **Dumas** mentions Reims' *Procession of the Herrings*. It involved a game played at the end of Lent by the cathedral canons, mocking the fish they'd been eating for six long weeks. In the procession, each canon dragged behind him a herring on a string and tried to step on the one in front, while avoiding his own being trodden on by the canon behind. The reckless use of remaining stocks was probably seen as a bonus. Dumas had lifted his text from a Madame Clément, did not use a second paragraph which said it had originated in 1429 as a mockery of English victory celebrations for the **Battle of the Herrings**. Maybe he knew its origins were earlier. A piece about it on the website *La France Pittoresque* refers to the historian Varin, back in 1911, having traced its origins to 1300. Dumas and Madame Clément have it continuing until the sixteenth century, but it was banned by Regnault de Chartres, Archbishop of Reims in 1439. Regnault seems to have been as scheming a character as Dumas' Cardinal Richelieu and may be pictured with a gleam of sheer malevolence in his eye as he put an end to his canons' innocent fun. Pierre Desportes, in his *Historical Review of the Church in France* (vol. 85, no 215, 1999) opens up a wider, if equally disappointing, context:

> A reformist current began to grow, first noticeable in the 1372 decision that no church ornament should be lent for any theatrical events, even were the subject to be religious. Reform was motivated out of concern for the dignity of the clergy

and it was not long before the burlesque Procession of the Herrings ... began to seem intolerable, its antiquity notwithstanding.

CORK

Ian Duhig's poem *Paschal Anthem* (*The Lammas Hireling*, 2003), written to the tune of Ewan MacColl's *Shoals of Herring* (see **Documentary**) is a glorious voicing of Irish monastic Lenten herring resentment. He prefaces it with an epigraph from *An Duanaire: Poems of the Dispossessed* edited by Seán Tuama & Thomas Kinsella—'Until recent times processions and festivals were held at the end of Lent to ridicule the herring.' Maybe they were inspired by Reims; maybe it was the other way round, but Irish mockery wasn't confined to monks or the clergy.

Nathanial Grogan's painting *Whipping the herring out of town—a scene of Cork* (c 1800, see second image section) captures the kind of event to which Tuama and Kinsella refer, a wild procession in which a salt herring hanging from a pole is attacked by one and all to the enthusiastic encouragement of a fiddle player. Also hanging from the pole is a leg of lamb, maybe heralding the resurrection of the Lamb of God, but primarily the return of meat. It is suggested some of Ireland's herring-mocking processions were organised by butchers looking forward to healthy returning sales.

EYEMOUTH

The Herring Queen Festival at Eyemouth only properly came about in 1939, when herring action at Scotland's smaller ports was already in decline. Unusually, there is no mockery. The celebrations resonate with a shared past and its ability to hold a community together. There are tartan herrings, knitted herrings, silver paper herrings, but few real ones. Down by the harbour, the excellent fishmonger D.R. Collin has some nice looking filleted fresh herrings from Peterhead and gets his kippers from Robson's of Craster. The effort of making his own is not justified by demand, but he shows me his smokehouse. The tarry walls, which drip with what looks like well over a century of herring smoking, these days benefit his cold-smoked hake and haddock.

The Herring Festival grew out of a Peace Festival established in 1919 and it still involves that original drive, but with the clouds of war gathering again in 1939, it was felt a Herring Queen would bring in a stronger involvement from the town's young people. There are processions galore. Just for starters it kicks off with one for children, led by the town's pipe band. A parade of decorated boats sails to the quayside leading the Queen Elect, together with her court of maids-in-waiting and young sailors. The busy pipe band (who have made their way to greet her) then leads the procession as they all go up to the house of a once notorious merchant/smuggler. They then make their way to the Co-op Car Park where she is officially crowned.

She receives gifts from Eyemouth's tradespeople, she awards prizes for the best decorated shops and the best decorated boats, she officially and individually receives what seems like over thirty previous herring queens—in 2024 these went back to the early 1950s and at least one had come, especially, all the way from the USA. Among them, Holly Blackie received her own mother, Lynn, who had been Herring Queen in 1993. The pipe band starts up again and they are all off, processing to the war memorial and to the memorial for the 189 fishermen lost in the savage storm of Black Friday, 14th October 1881.

DUNKIRK

Back in France and leading up to Shrove Tuesday, Dunkirk's carnival is celebrated for its processions, including one with sixty musicians dressed as fishermen. The whole thing goes back to the seventeenth century and is supposed to have originated in giving the city's white fish fishermen a good send-off before they set sail on their long voyages to northern seas. It is also a *Mardi Gras* preparation for the long weeks of Lent in which salt herring and **Hareng Saur** will feature prominently. Dunkirk's curious herring event only dates from the 1960s, but it has true conceptual beauty.

On the Sunday before Shrove Tuesday, a procession comes to the city square. They all cry out, calling on the mayor in his city hall, 'Lib-é-rez les ha-rengs! Lib-é-rez les ha-rengs!' (release the herrings). From the balcony the mayor and his assistants then throw approximately 450 kg of vacuum-packed *hareng saur* into the crowd. Everyone scrabbles to get hold of their lenten provisions. It feels like both celebration and mockery, but that's the kind of love herrings inspire.

FÉCAMP

The prospective herring queens of Fécamp in Normandy dance through the crowd gathered outside an old smokehouse at the back of the beautiful Fisheries Museum. They pose for photographs and lead the crowd inside to join a crowd already being entertained by shanty singers. The annual election, part of the town's *Fête des Harengs* (see **French Fisheries**) is an extraordinary pantomime dame-style drag event. My French wasn't good enough to work out exactly what was going on, but all the contenders had to sing herring songs. One paraded with a raw herring clasped between her teeth like a Spanish rose (see second image section). Whoever caught the herring, thrown into the cheering masses, could also come up and sing a song, but the catcher yielded the privilege (and the herring) to his mate.

I have no idea how the winner was elected, but everybody was happy. Afterwards, they were at one of the festival's many beer stalls, together with the shanty singers. I met the elected queen later, on his way home. The tradition, he told me, had only been going for ten years, established by a group of friends at a nearby bar. It was a wild event, as joyous as anything you could hope for and the crowd loved it.

PROPHECY

In J. W. de Caux' *The Herring and the Herring Fishery* (1881) there's an account of prophetic herrings rivalling the writing on the wall at Belshazzar's Feast.

Two herrings were caught off the coast of Norway on November 10th 1587. Strange markings on their sides were thought to resemble Gothic print, maybe even Hebrew. Recognised as a wonder, they were taken immediately to Copenhagen to be presented to Frederick II. They may have been salted to preserve both the text and the fish beneath it.

Like Belshazzar, Frederick hadn't enjoyed an error-free reign. He had had an argument with Peder Oxe, Steward of the Realm, who had then gone into exile. He had initiated a war with Erik XIV of Sweden, but, without Oxe, had failed to take proper account of the finances. He made the common mistake of not paying his army, but luckily, Erik was deposed on mental health grounds and eventually poisoned. Frederick brought Oxe back and things had been beginning to look up. At his new castle of Elsinore he had only recently been entertained by Shakespeare's clown Will Kemp (see **Pickelhering**). Then the herrings turned up.

The prophetic but anatomically incorrect herrings caught in November 1587, as presented in Johann Faulhaber's 1632 *The Divination of Reasonable Creatures*. (From the British Library Collection, C.29.f.1)

Without a Daniel on hand, a range of Denmark's learned men offered their herring readings. The story turns up in both Raphael Eglin's *Prophetia Halieutica nova et admiranda* (New & Admirable Fish-Related Prophecy, 1598) and Johann Faulhaber's *Vernünfftiger Creaturen Weissagungen* (The Divination of Reasonable Creatures, 1632). Faulhaber claims one was caught in Norwegian waters, one in Denmark's, but Frederick was king of both, which only emphasises the likelihood that the herrings' message was addressed to him. Some of the wise men, of course, suggested the text referred to bad human behaviour and God coming in judgement. Others suggested, 'You will not fish herrings in future so well as other nations,' or 'Very soon you will cease to fish herrings as well as other people.' The common folk thought the herrings were just telling Frederick his time was up.

The **Danish Fisheries** did indeed radically contract from the late sixteenth century. Within five months of having been presented with the fish, Frederick was dead. Take your pick.

PROVERBS & SAYINGS

There are quite a few herring proverbs and sayings and this is by no means a comprehensive list. Which language proverbialises them the most? German. Which comes up with the best? Yiddish. It stands on its own and it's a corker, but generally themes recur and some of the proverbs cross languages, so I've organised them thematically. Inevitably there are some losses in translation.

WEALTH

'No herring no wedding' is admirably succinct and may have been common across the British Isles, but was, certainly, in the West of Scotland and the Isle of Man.

'Don't cry herrings until they're in the net' appears in both Scottish and Dutch versions. There is also a German variation, 'Catch your herrings before you salt them.'

'Better the herring on your plate / than the roasted fish another man ate' comes in German and Danish versions. In German, rather than plate the rhyme is *table* (tisch) and *fisch*; in Danish salt herring is opposed to fresh pike.

'If you would be a merchant fine / beware o' auld horses, herring, and wine' is a Scots warning, which works both as investment advice and how best to present oneself to one's customers.

'You sell more herrings on the market than sole' is solid French and German counsel on the profits available in selling to the poor.

'From bad debtors, spoiled herring' is Danish advice on credit and repayment schedules.

'When herrin' mauger [is thin] him bone show' is Jamaican, a kind of 'Well, what do you expect?' or 'You get what you pay for.' Going back to the slave plantations, much of the red herring sold in the Caribbean has been made with spents, the cheap, thin, post-spawning fish.

FOOD & FOLK

'Bad herring can make a good bloater, bad men good monks' is German (sometimes just the first half is used).

'Sour herring won't taste sweet' is another German truism.

'Herring is simple nourishment: / don't waste time on measurement' is German too.

'It takes a lot of herring to drive off a whale' appears in both German and Danish, playing on the scale of a herring shoal's strategy of sacrifice.

'Wash a herring in water or wash it down with beer' is German, but draws on the

41. Kipper. I Marshall's Smokehouse, North Shields, hanging kippers (1979), Nick Hedges (courtesy of the photographer).

42. & 43. Kipper. *All the lost kippers!* | Marshall's Smokehouse, North Shields (1979), Nick Hedges; The Smokehouses, North Shields (2025), Charles Bell - what was Marshall's is front right. (Courtesy of the photographers).

44. Måløy Raid. Also known as Operation Archery, 1941. The first Combined Operations action in World War II, it took out four herring oil production plants (Alamy).

45. Mediterranean Food. Cairo (2013), *Renga, Ringa* or golden herring on sale for the Egyptian Spring festival of Sham Ennessim - Smelling the Breeze. (Amr Sayed/Alamy)

46. Mediterranean Food. *Renga*, a Greek dish made with golden herring, apple, spring onion and olive oil (photo: author).

47. Monkey Business. Stowaways on a transatlantic liner, Groucho, Chico, Zeppo and Harpo (tacit) emerge from kipper barrels singing *Sweet Adeline*.

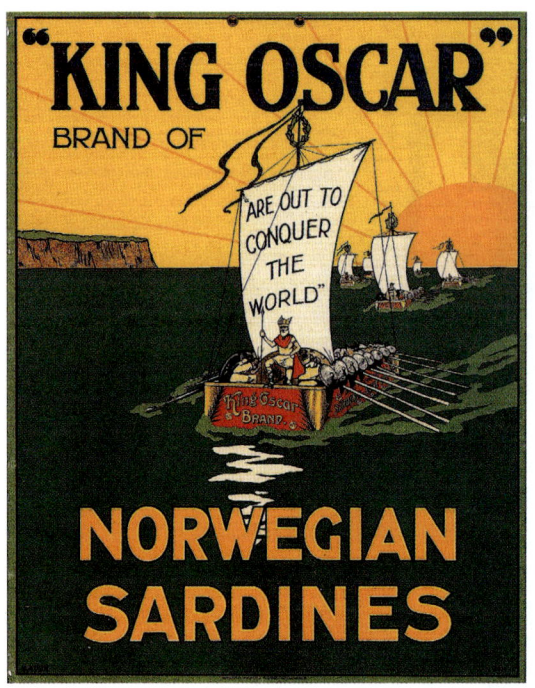

48. Norwegian Fisheries. Poster for the successful Norwegian sardine brand, King Oscar (MUST/Norwegian Canning Museum). See also **Sardine Litigation**.

49. Objects of Desire. Nineteenth-century sardine can opener (author's collection). See also **Sardine Litigation**.

50. Olivier, Laurence. Joan Plowright (mostly cropped out) and Laurence Olivier, March 1970, the successful conclusion to his campaign to save the kipper on the Brighton Belle (Alamy).

51. Otoliths and Scales. Herring scales, Norway Fisheries Museum, Bergen - a tribute to Einar Lea, who, over the autumn/winter of 1909/10, personally examined 9,000 herring scales (photo: author).

52. & 53. Past(r)y. A shoal of herring pasties and a herring pie fit for monarchs from Edward I to George III. *Halec Rex Piscium*, the pie says—Herring **King of Fishes** (photos: author).

54. Pickelhering. *The Merry Drinker* (c 1625) Hendrick ter Brugghen (oil on canvas; Collection Centraal Museum Utrecht, purchased with the support of the Rembrandt Association, 1955; photo: Ernst Moritz). With his tankard in one hand and a half-eaten salt herring in the other, the painting almost certainly refers to the Dutch comic character *Peckelharing*. In Franz Hals' Peeckelhaering (1628–30) the herring itself is tacit.

55. Processions & Celebrations. *Whipping the Herring out of Town—A Scene of Cork* (c. 1800) Nathaniel Grogan (Collection Crawford Art Gallery, Cork). See also **Fasting**.

56. Processions & Celebrations. Election of the annual Herring Queen, Fécamp Herring Festival, November 2024. The curly, bleached blonde contender on the right was crowned (photo: author).

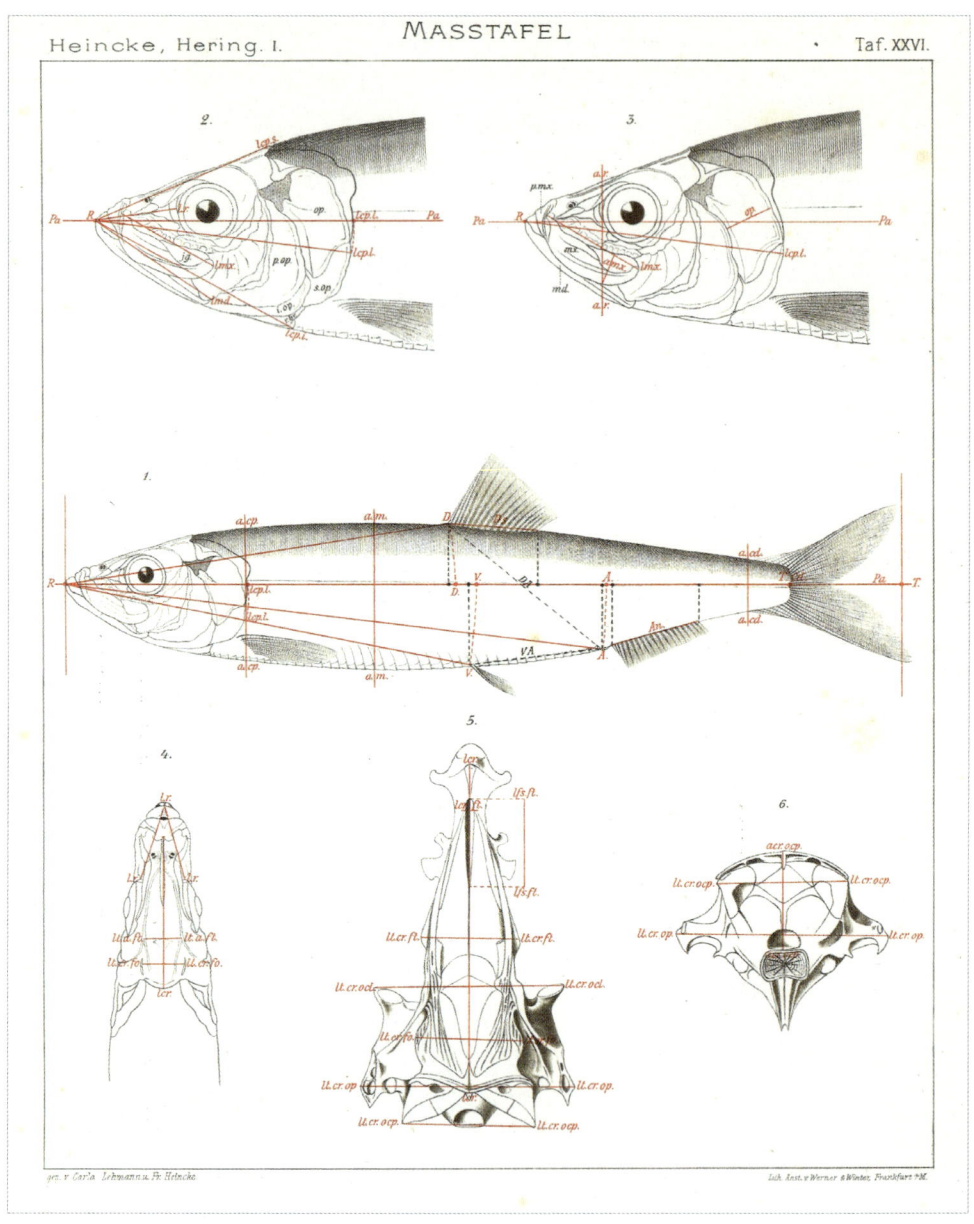

57. Racial Theory. An anthropomentry of the herring - measurements indicating its racial type, *Natural History of the Herring* (1898), Friedrich Heincke (Author's collection).

58. & 59. Red Herring. Hard-smoked red herring (top) and smoker Mike Kelly in the smokehouse, H.S. Fishing Company, Martin Figura (courtesy of the photographer). H.S. Fishing used to supply red herrings to the Caribbean and West African markets, as well as golden and silver herrings to the Mediterranean. It closed in 2018, the last smokehouse in Great Yarmouth.

60. & 61. Reduction Plants. Icelandic Post-Industrial—inside a former herring reduction plant and, outside, a herring oil holding tank (photos: Penelope Payne). The former works is now an arts venue, where Penelope Payne's *Horizons* was shown in 2024. See also **Two Contemporary Artists**.

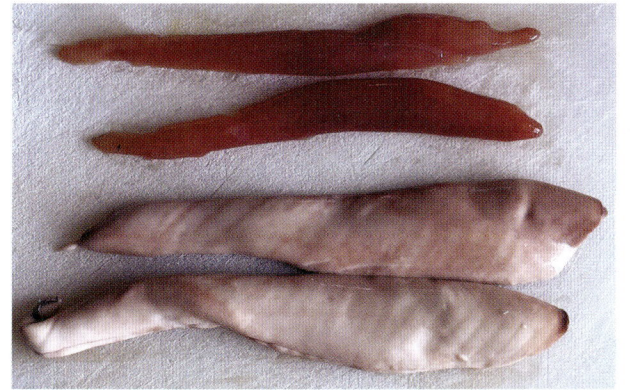

62., 63., & 64. Roes. Top: female and male roes. Middle: crispy fried soft roes with a herring caviar and sriracha mayonnaise. Bottom: mixed roe puffs with herring caviar. Where are the pea shoots when you want them? (photos: author).

65. & 66. Sardine Litigation. Strategies in defeat: no longer able, in Europe, to call sprats and herring sardines, Atlas describe their Small Sild, 'formerly known as sardines'. Tyneside sardine magnate Angus Watson squeezes an extra s into his popular Skipper brand, printing 'Norwegian Brisling' in black on dark blue. (Atlas, MUST/Norwegian Canning Museum; Skippers, author's collection)

67. Shuba & Sour Cream. Popular throughout the former Soviet Union, Jewish, Ukranian & Russian diasporas, Shuba or herring under a fur coat is one of the great herring dishes and is simple to make (photo: author).

68., 69., & 70. Smokehouse Tale. Will Buckenham in the yard of The Old Smokehouse, Raglan Street, Lowestoft; inside the smokehouse; speating up bloaters (photos: author). Dating from 1760 it was the oldest working smokehouse in the country and one of the last to produce red herrings. Will was unable to sustain the business during COVID and 261 years after it first opened the smokehouse closed. The loss is ours.

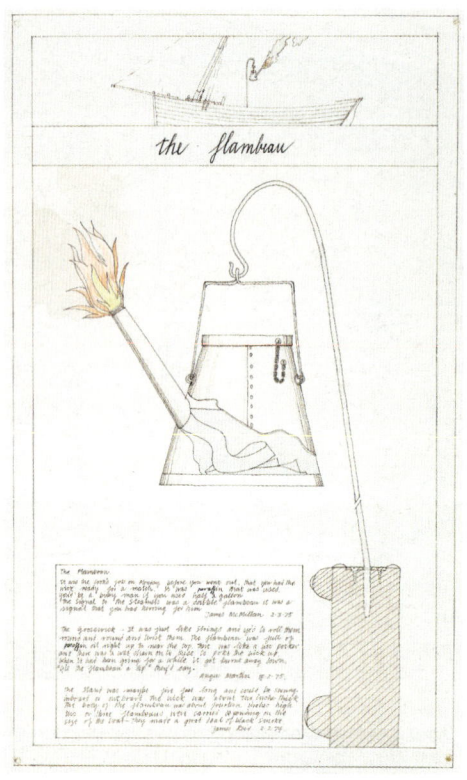

71. & 72. Two Contemporary Artists. *The Flambeau* and *Herring Chute*, Will Maclean from *The Ring Net*, 1973–78 (National Galleries of Scotland. Purchased 1980). Will Maclean developed *The Ring Net* from 1973 to 1978. See **Appearances & Signs** for *Gannet Fishing* also from *The Ring Net*. See **Y is for Why? A is for A Beginning** and **Herring Boats** for some of his later herring-related works.

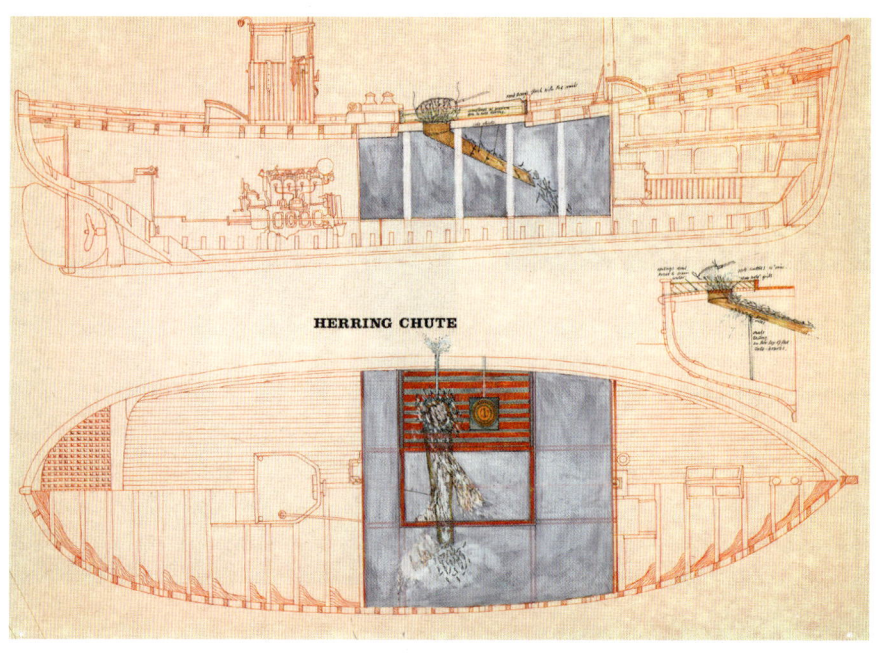

73. & 74. Two Contemporary Artists. *The Weight of Salt* at Cheeseburn Sculpture Festival, 2021 and *Horizons* at Cullercoats Bay, February 27, 2022, Penelope Payne (courtesy of the artist). Both works, together with *Scold Vixen Harpy Shrew*, grew out of a long term engagement with **Herring Lasses** and their stories.

75. & 76. Zuiderzee. The lost Zuiderzee herring, as recorded in Heincke's *Natural History of the Herring* (1898, author's collection) and the closing of the Afsluitdijk, 1932, after which it was no more (Alamy).

77. A message from Great Yarmouth (see also **Yarmouth's Greatness**): *Eat More Herrings* (Alamy).

widespread tradition in many countries, going back at least to the Middle Ages, of innkeepers offering free salty snacks to encourage thirst.

'He's been shot through the neck with herring' is a German way of saying 'he's a heavy drinker' (see above and **Pickelhering**).

'Where there's herring there's salt' is German, yet again.

SMELL

'Herrings stink, it's in their nature / but ripe bouquets beget adventure' is joyously French, a proverb quoted in the anonymous fifteenth-century **Life of St Herring.**

'The barrel still smells of herring' is an excellent French 'I'll believe it when I see it' response to any promoted claims of individual, commercial, organisational or political change.

'It's but kindly that the pock savour of the herring' is Scottish (you've got to expect the bag to smell of herring), a more philosophical version of the previous.

'What's the use of a herring that doesn't smell?' is a German way of saying you're complaining about a virtue.

'No better herrin', no better barrel' is a Jamaican critical, but more flexibly applicable, version of 'like father, like son.'

HEALTH

'A herring a day keeps the doctor away' is both German and Dutch, literally the proverb goes, 'when there's herring in the land, doctors are not required.'

SMOKING & CURING

'Let ilka herring hing by its ain head' is Scottish, but also exists in the English, 'Every herring must hang by its own gill.'

'Neither flesh nor fowl nor good red herring' is English, said of something beyond category to the point of uselessness.

'Give [someone] the red herring' is Dutch for taking someone down verbally.

'Done up like a kipper' and 'stitched up like a kipper' are English, referring to the gutting (see *gip*, below), splitting, even smoking of a kipper: left helplessly exposed and vulnerable; something a character played by George Cole might say ('You've proper stitched me up like…') but see *giddy*, below.

'Giddy little kipper' and 'giddy as a kipper' are English, originally Cockney phrases for a well-turned out young woman, from the 1860s, playing on the colour and display of the recently developed smoked herring product, they turned, in the twentieth century, into meaning prettily-dressed but maybe over-excitable. 'From a giddy little kipper' appears on countless postcards from smokehouse-filled coastal resorts.

'To gip' is English for 'to cheat'. Using a variant spelling, 'gyp', some suggest it derives from a racist slur on Gypsies and it has been used mistakenly but deliberately with this intended connotation. The usage derives, however, from the verb meaning to gut herring (specifically removing the gills, long gut and stomach)—something **Herring Lasses** could do in a second.

LITERARY

'"New herrings, new!" we must cry, every time we make ourselves public, or else we shall be christened with a hundred new titles of idiotism,' Thomas **Nashe**.

'Fools are as like husbands as pilchards are to herrings, the husband's the bigger,' William Shakespeare (Feste to Viola, *Twelfth Night*).

'How like herrings and onions our vices are in the morning after we have committed them' comes from the notebooks of Samuel Taylor Coleridge.

'A kind word is no substitute for a piece of herring or a bag of oats' is from Sholom Aleichem, pen name of Solomon Naumovich Rabinovich (1859–1916) Russian/Ukranian, Yiddish actor and playwright (the musical *Fiddler on the Roof* was based on his stories). Elsewhere he substitutes 'a wise word' and drops the bag of oats.

AND FINALLY

'Where no worthy man exists / herring also is a fish' is Yiddish (and the original, *Bemokem she-eyn ish iz a hering oykh a fish*, is enough to persuade anyone to start taking classes). The best herring proverb I've come across, you can feel your shoulders lifting into a philosophical shrug. It derives from two earlier proverbs, the Yiddish 'Where there's no worthy man, strive to be worthy' and the Russian 'If there are no fish, crayfish are also fish'. Bringing the two together delivers a surreal, stoic response to life's oppressions. 'Don't expect justice or even logic; eat your herring.' And maybe, implicitly, 'We all eat our herrings.'

QUOTAS

The late 1960s saw a collapse in Canada's Pacific herring population. The cod population on the American East Coast's Grand Banks collapsed. Three Icelandic herring populations collapsed—including the mighty Norwegian spring spawners. These shocks to the system provided enough of a context for the emergence of quotas, but the first response, naturally enough, had been complete bans on fishing for the threatened species in particular sea areas. The longer term projected solution of species quotas had to wait until the late 1970s, by which time herring populations in the North Sea and off the West of Scotland had also collapsed.

A BIT OF BACKGROUND

Informed by increasing understandings of fish movements, the need for international collaboration had become obvious by the 1870s. The world's oldest intergovernmental science organisation, the International Council for the Exploration of the Sea (ICES), was established in 1902. North Sea herring fishing was approaching its peak and not a main focus for concern, but in 1909 Friedrich Heincke, whose *Natural History of Herrings* (1898) had introduced **Racial Theory** to the herring world, presented a paper on plaice which considered protective legislation. Just before World War I this led to a ban on landing juvenile plaice.

Following a British unilateral decision to enforce trawl net mesh sizes, an Overfishing Conference was held in London in 1936. It was the first in a series of international considerations of the issue, which even continued during World War II and led to the setting up of a Standing Advisory Committee on Overfishing in 1947. Still focused on demersal fish populations, it took several years to extend the remit to include the pelagic fisheries. The standing committee evolved into the North East Atlantic Fisheries Commission (NEAFC) in 1980.

THE QUOTA

In principle, quotas promised a way forward. Essentially, they operate at three different levels:

1. Total Allowable Catches (TACs) set for particular commercial species in particular fishing areas;
2. Allocation of TACs to the different nations with claims to a share in those fishing areas;

3. Allocation of national quotas to what are called fishery producers—usually fishing companies and/or individual vessels.

Examining the state of fish populations, the standard approach to TACs has been that scientists (ICES/NEAFC) propose and the politicians dispose. In the European Economic Community (EEC), the necessary political negotiations should have been made easier with the 1983 ratification of the Common Fisheries Policy, but back in the early 1970s, with the imminent accession of Denmark and the UK (with their fish-rich waters) the EEC had coincidentally rushed through legislation which gave all its fishing nations mutual access to all its waters. This increased the number of nations at the table considering sea areas and species, whilst also increasing the possibilities of using fish as bargaining chips in separate, simultaneous negotiations on matters closer to the political heart of some nations (the regulation of the financial sector, for example).

Most fishing communities are situated away from the political centre of most nations, which sometimes means they are not always at the very top of government concerns. Some nations may seem more interested in, say their bankers and hedge fund managers, than their fishermen. From a politician's point of view, the great thing about this is the infinite flexibility it creates for the structuring of deals. Some quotas may, of course, end up in the hands of hedge funds too, but they are able to look at things dispassionately, judgements unclouded by sentimental concern for fish or fishermen's livelihoods. Adam **Smith**'s 'invisible hand' tells us whatever they decide will be in the best interests of everybody and, anyway, fifty years of political betrayal can always be re-presented as a question of maritime **Sovereignty**. Everybody wins.

ALLOCATION OF QUOTAS

Once the TAC has, by intergovernmental agreement, been divided into national quotas, each nation allocates its share. Some in the EEC/EU have paid attention to the Common Fisheries Policy's call to allocate with a view to environmental impact and impacts on fishing communities. England and Scotland both dish out most of their quotas to a handful of wealthy fish producers and once awarded a quota, a holder is free to sell it on. According to a 2018 article in *The Guardian* by John Lichfield, 'Small, coastal boats under 10 metres, which make up 77% of the English fleet, currently have the right to catch 3% of the total English catch of quota-controlled fish such as cod, haddock, plaice, sole, herring and mackerel. One super-trawler, Namibian-registered, British-flagged, but ultimately Dutch-owned, has the right to catch 94% of the English herrings taken in the Atlantic and North Sea.' This is why many English fishmongers, if they bother with herring at all, rely on small inshore populations and by-catch; why most English kippers and bloaters are made with Norwegian herrings.

Having said this Norway, which chose not to join the EEC over the fisheries issue, began allocating quotas to fishermen on the basis of the level of their catches, but, as the quotas have increased in value, the market has seen them increasingly sold off to the larger players. The administration of quotas has seen fishing inexorably moving out of the hands of the smaller inshore fishermen.

SUSTAINABILITY AND CAPITALISM

There has always been some tension between the assessments of the scientists and those of the fishermen, who tend to argue that, from their experience, stocks are in a better state than a recommended TAC suggests. The scientists counter-argue that their assessments are based on data from quite wide areas, whereas the fishermen go directly to those locations where the maximum fish numbers traditionally concentrate.

Another problem with quotas has been that monitoring has been based on landings: fishermen are able to catch more than is consistent with an allocation, discarding what they do not want. A scary 40% of the catch can be discarded and some suggest this is an underestimate. Norway banned discards in 1987. Iceland adopts an Individual

Transferable Quota (ITQ) system, which reduces discards by allowing a trade in species allocations between quota holders.

DIVERSITY AND BLUNT INSTRUMENTS

TACs and quotas are allocated on the basis of species. Populations of **Atlantic Herring** are, taxonomically, simply identified as the species *Clupea harengus*: we've long known the differences between populations (see **Racial Theory**), but choose not to make any distinction in catching them. Genetics is increasing our understanding of the extent of their diversity, the links between this and water temperature and the apparent link to the fish's immune system. System-advantaged larger-scale pelagic trawlers are capable of taking out smaller populations almost at a single scoop.

In the unpredictable effects of warming oceans, genetic adaptations of individual herring populations may well prove crucial to sustainability. The quota is a blunt instrument. There would seem to be a value in revisiting its broadbrush taxonomic principles with, at least, smaller inshore herring populations protected through the greater achievable subtlety of smaller inshore fishing approaches. In England, where fishermen and fishmongers have a hard time generating a market for herring, there have been attempts at promotion such as those around the *Silver Shore Herring*, the small-but-tasty Thames population. An investment in inshore fisheries and the support of such initiatives could see the rebuilding of relationships between local communities and herring.

'You may say I'm a dreamer...'

RACIAL THEORY

In his *Economic Natural History of Germany's Fish* (1783) the remarkable Bloch had dismissed the whole idea of the herring's **Grand Migration**. Perhaps some felt he'd been a little bit too aggressive, perhaps some did not like the fact he was Jewish, but the old thinking proved hard to shake. You still come across it. By the 1830s, though, even in Britain questioning voices had begun to appear. Not only were there different herring populations, some were distinctly different. Noting that there were apparently 'three species of herring said to visit the Baltic,' William Yarrell (*A History of British Fishes*, 1836) announced:

> The examination of considerable quantities of the various sorts of fish caught at the mouth of the Thames during winter by fishermen engaged in taking Sprats, has enabled me to select what I believe to be a second species of British Herring…

When the English marine biologist William Leach died in 1836, Yarrell pointed to the fact the great man had posited just such a thing. He proposed the name *Clupea leachii.* He went further, arguing that British herrings might not have stopped at just two species. Others elsewhere, he claimed, had also noticed differences.

RACES NOT SPECIES

Leach may have observed a Channel herring. *Clupea Leachii* was probably a Thames herring. In the development of the railways and the markets for fresh and mildly cured fish, awareness of herring varieties should only have increased, but there were counter arguments too. In his *History of the Fishes of the British Islands* (1878) Jonathan Couch dismissed Yarrell's discovery:

> This eminent naturalist does not appear to have been aware of the fact, which has been noticed by numerous observers, that the exact magnitude, minuter proportions of shape, and quality of the flesh in the Common Herring are so very different, even in districts not very distant from each other, that none of them can be regarded as signifying a different species.

Francis Day, however, in *The Fishes of Great Britain and Ireland* (1880–84) subtly shifted the argument, referring to herring races. He noted that the Baltic herring was 'a small and inferior race.'

Darwin's *Origin of Species* (1859) influenced a generation of social anthropologists struggling to find the magic principle behind innate European superiority. Evolution looked like a winner. Darwin's half-cousin Francis Galton encouraged the application of evolutionary theory to the study of human beings (*Hereditary Genius: An Inquiry into its Laws and Consequences*, 1869). The concept of herring races could have come directly from Darwin, but, from the start it seems to have gathered the anthropometrical baggage of Galton.

Differences between **Atlantic Herring** populations are part of the fish's genetic adaptability. Size, vertebral counts, the position of the dorsal fin, fat content and other measurable distinctions are environmentally determined, but those understandings came later. In Scotland, Cossar Ewart and Duncan Matthews were examining the territory; F.A. Smitt was similarly engaged in Sweden; there were many others, but it fell to Friedrich Heincke, Director of the Biological Institute of Helgoland, to construct a grand racial theory of herrings. He published his *Natural History of Herrings* in 1898, but had already been arguing his case for several years.

MEASURABLE CHARACTERISTICS

Heincke's theory represented a considerable advance in herring studies, but the talk of 'measurable characteristics', of anthropometry and the parallels to the study of man do give pause for thought. However unfair on his monumental work, it is hard not to see the callipers shifting from the length between a herring's ventral fin and anus to the lips and noses of passers-by (see second image section).

Nevertheless, there is a kind of heroism in Heincke's detailed and methodical differentiation of herring varieties. Impressed at his achievement, James Travis Jenkins (*The Herring and the Herring Fisheries*, 1927) noted that French scientists, faced with a similar problem classifying the races of man, reduced 102 measurable characteristics to a ready reckoning 20. For the herring, Heincke laid out a closely argued list of 65, which he then reduced to 26.

Length & Breadth: total body length; total length less caudal fin (tail); distance from dorsal fin to tip of snout; distance from ventral fin to tip of snout; distance from anus to tip of snout; length of the base of the anal fin; length of the base of the dorsal fin; length of head; length of top of head; length of lower jaw; upper length of cranium; breadth of cranium at rear of *ossa frontalis*.

Number: dorsal fin rays; ventral fin rays; anal fin rays; keel scales behind the ventral fin; vertebrae; vertebral series with closed blood vessel arches; vertebrae in front of the dorsal fin; vertebrae between dorsal and ventral fin; vertebrae between ventral and anal fin; vertebrae behind anus.

Combinations & Other Factors: average length of vertebrae 2 to 5, lying above, between and beneath ventral and dorsal fins; average length of vertebrae 2 and 3, lying above the anal fin; sex; degree of sexual maturity.

THE RACES

Over a twenty-year period, Heincke conducted and collated measurements on 5,106 young and adult herrings, 88 larval herrings, 432 sprats and 50 pilchards. They were taken from 99 different European locations, the full ton achieved by including 30 examples of *Clupea zunasi*, which had been preserved in alcohol and sent from Japan. Originally identified as *Harengula zunasi* by Bleeker in 1854, its life as a Clupea did not last. These days it is a *Sardinella*. Heincke, anyway, was focused on his European races. A closely argued and combative text is followed by 201 pages of tables, recording each individual fish and the batch from which it came. He includes 26 pages of illustrations identifying the heads, crania and full-length variations. However hard it is to shake off the feelings of unease, at the same time it is a thing of beauty.

Heincke identified fourteen races of herring: the Icelandic, the West Coast of Scotland, the East Coast of Scotland, the Norwegian spring spawning, the spring spawner of the Skagerrak, the spring spawner of Limfjord and the Belt and Rügen, the spring spawner

RACIAL THEORY

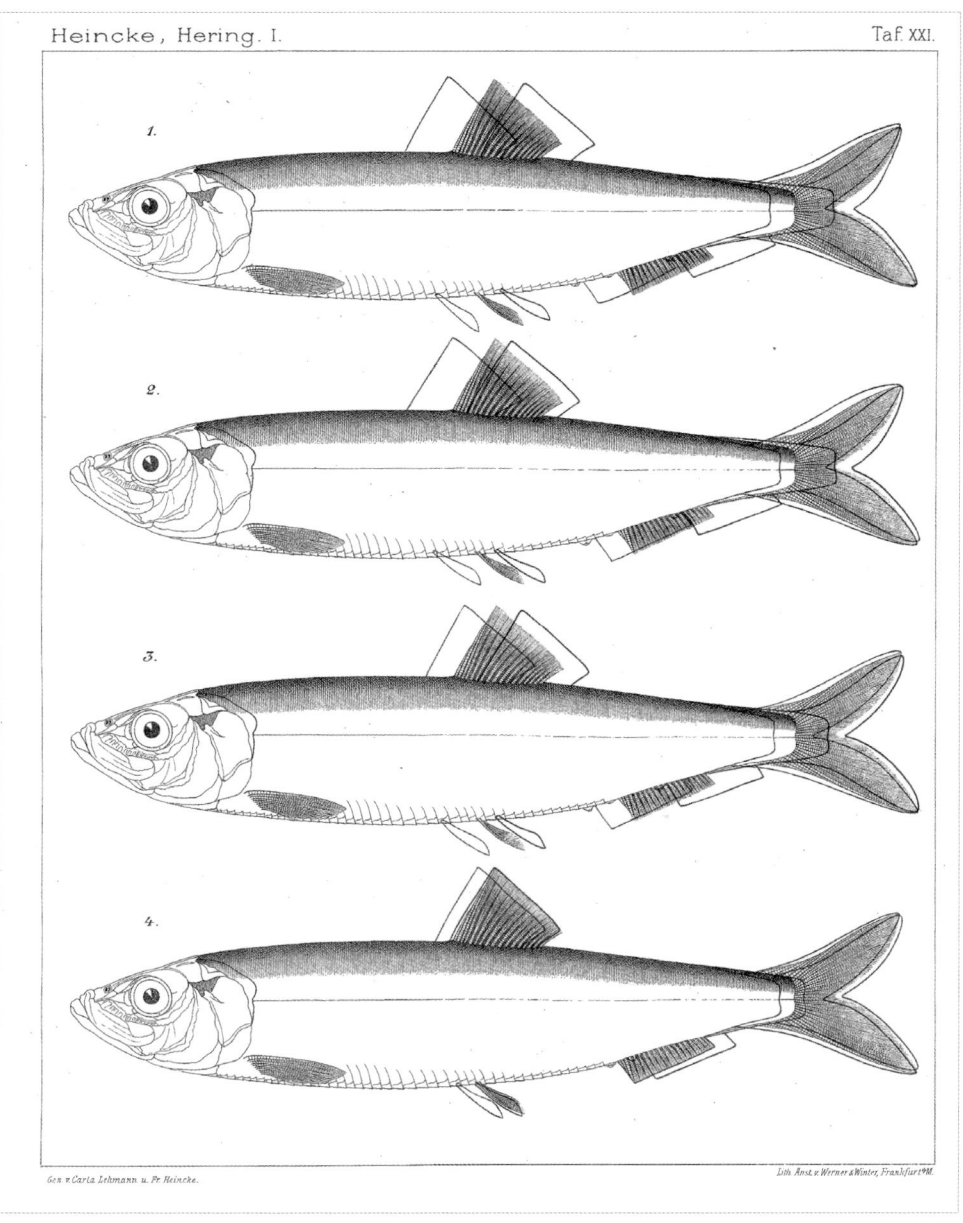

Differences between and within herring populations. 'Extent of Variation in the Position of the Dorsal Fin, Pelvic Fins and Anal, as well as of Body Length, excluding Tail Fin, in the Herring. 1. Extremes of Variation in sexually mature Herrings of all Local Forms. 2. Same for sexually mature herring within a Local Form, as well as for same size Herrings of a local form. Both are assumed to be equal. 3. Minimum for juvenile and maximum for all herrings within a local form. 4. Average Increase in the relevant Dimensions from Juveniles to Mature.' (Author's collection.)

of the Western Baltic and the Southern North Sea, the English Channel, the autumn spawner of the Southern North Sea, the autumn spawner of the Northern North Sea, the autumn spawner of the Kattegat and the Western Baltic, the autumn spawner of the Eastern Baltic, the strömling of the Eastern Baltic (identified by Linnaeus as a subspecies) and the White Sea (now seen as a Pacific herring subspecies). He then added five sprats: the English Channel, the Southern North Sea, the Skagerrak, the Western Baltic and the Eastern Baltic.

As Couch had pointed out, there was considerable variety within different populations, including the number of vertebrae, keel scales and other characteristics, Heincke determined the mean average for each of his varieties and used it to establish a racial ideal.

WHAT'S IN A NAME?

Jenkins's book is excellent, only marred by his casual acceptance of the intellectual context that comes with Heincke. He praises him as the man who 'first applied anthropometrical measurements to the distinguishing of these (herring) races.' In 1931, Schnakenbeck went the whole hog and suggested individually named subspecies: *Clupea harengus britannicus* (English Channel), *atlanticus* (southern entrance to the Irish Sea), *ivernicus* (the Clyde), *caledonicus* (west coast of Scotland), *scoticus* (Firth of Forth), *frisicus* (Zuiderezee), *cimbricus* (Jutland Bank), *scandicus* (Norway, form A), *norvegicus* (Norway, form B), *septentrionalis* (Faroes), *borealis* (Iceland, spring spawning), *islandicus* (Iceland, summer spawning).

Political temperatures were rising, however, and no matter how impressed ichthyologists had been with Heincke's science, the associations of herring racial theory were getting harder to ignore. In his Buckland Lectures of 1933, William Hodgson was noticeably less of an enthusiast for the language and ideas than Jenkins. He preferred the more accurate 'biometrical' to the suspect 'anthropometrical'. He cautiously accepted some aspects of the theory, while registering a hint of distaste for its baggage.

In the 120s Helmuth Lissner had become the herring specialist at Hamburg Marine Biological Institute, serving as one of Germany's representatives at the International Council for the Exploration of the Sea (ICES). When the Nazis came to power, he had to leave for England, where he published a summary of his thinking in the article, 'On Races of Herring' (1934): 'The characters used for the discrimination of races are not purely inherited but influenced considerably by external factors.' Summing up the summary, he suggests, 'Heincke's definition of race as a spawning community is no longer held to be true. A new definition is given in which several spawning communities or local forms of a geographically well-defined area are united into a race.'

Hodgson is even more specific in his critique: 'Variations in the number of skeletal components, such as vertebrae, fin rays, 'keel' rays, etc, are supposed to be caused by environment at the time the young larva is developing in the egg, and the intermixing of herrings seems to be an absolute certainty, at any rate in the southern North Sea.'

In his article, Lissner gave a final caveat that 'the opinion expressed here is only a working hypothesis.' In their different ways, Heincke, Schnakenbeck, Hodgson, Lissner and many more made extraordinary contributions to understanding the complexities of herring variation. All of them were long dead by the time of Pettersson *et al.*'s 'A chromosome-level assembly of the Atlantic herring genome' (2019) and the breakthroughs in genetics which are now opening up herring thinking.

RED HERRING

At this point in the encyclopaedia, you should not be asking, 'Is there really such a thing as a red herring?' but, in case you have just come straight to this entry, the answer is 'Yes'.

There is green herring (fresh or very lightly salted), white herring (salted) and red herring (whole—ungutted—heavily salted and cold-smoked for a long time). Red herring also includes a number of other colours and shades: golden (heavily salted, but cold-smoked a bit less), silver (heavily salted and cold-smoked a lot less), baconed red herring (heavily salted and smoked for a lot longer) and black herring (heavily salted and smoked for three months, by which time Hell would have to freeze over before it goes off). **Bloaters**, which are now lightly salted whole herrings, mildly cold-smoked like **Kippers**, were originally a variety of red and the terms could be interchangeable.

Red herrings were called so because smoking for a length of time naturally gives them a reddish colour. In France, the same thing was called **Hareng Saur** (from sorrel or reddish-brown). The degrees of salting and smoking were both to do with the need for food preservation. Both white and red herring had shelf lives of around a year, which made trade practical with an oily fish which otherwise, before refrigeration, could begin to smell quite unpleasant after two or three days (depending on the temperature). Black herring was produced for the plantation owners of East Africa, who used it to feed their workforces. Red herring at the baconed end seems to have been preferred by the slave plantation owners of the West Indies.

Red herring was never one thing. It was salted and smoked at levels adaptable to the needs, taste and possibilities of different markets. Less salted, less smoked versions will probably have been available for local sale long before the railways enabled the development of today's mild cures, but the success of these signalled the end of its production for British markets. The last traditional producer, Will Buckenham of Lowestoft (see **Smokehouse Tale**), who retired in 2022, had kept producing them for a small number of local afficionados until the previous year. With traditional UK smokers abandoning it, Sunshine Saltfish of Hull, established in 1998, began producing red herring (and other preserved fish) primarily for the Caribbean community market.

Smoking time for reds varied between two and seven weeks. Buckenham smoked his for ten weeks, but he was just leaving them up in the smokehouse between his kipper, bloater and smoked haddock firings. He used November's small inshore herrings and they were ready for the end of January. By Easter he'd pretty much sold out. Available at their best throughout Lent, this was not dissimilar to medieval practice.

Smoking fish goes back to the earliest times, initially an adjunct to the process of drying them. The development of the smokehouse is more recent. In Northern Europe, the smokehouses which gave us red herring and eventually the kipper seem to have developed from the thirteenth century. Just as Fécamp is central to the development of **Hareng Saur,** so **Yarmouth** is to red herring (see second image section), although which came first would be a difficult call. The quality of Yarmouth's red herring is recognised by **Neucrantz** (1654) and probably by **Dumas** (1870), but the technology spread throughout Great Britain and Ireland. If you want hard-smoked red herring today, search online or try Caribbean food suppliers; for golden buy your *renga* at Asian food stores.

THE METAPHOR

Yarmouth's red herring production is celebrated in *Nashes Lenten Stuffe* (1599, see **Red Herring Joke**) in which specific mention is made of the use of its strong smell to distract dogs from their pursuit—a simultaneous explanation of the endless diversions and frustrating hints of the extraordinary work. Reds got their first English literary mention in what seems to have been a fifteenth-century East Midlands' gigging minstrel's *aide memoire* for a mock sermon, *The Hunting of the Hare*. Around the same time, the French *sermon joyeux*, **Life of Saint Herring**, talks of both white and sorrel herring, as well as smokehouses.

William Cobbett is sometimes credited with initiating the metaphor of a false trail in his *Political Register, Vol XI* (1807), although he says little about it and he does not employ the metaphor himself, but more people read Cobbett in the nineteenth century than, probably, have ever read *Nashe's Lenten Stuffe*. He may well have been responsible for its later popularisation by Dorothy L. Sayers in *The Five Red Herrings* (1921) and by a host of other crime writers.

ADVICE ON COOKING

Red herring, like all cold smoked, hot smoked or otherwise cured fish need not be cooked. Some recipes suggest searing in the pan to loosen the skin. Steeping in water or milk is often recommended, particularly given the declining popularity of salty foods. In *A Plain Cookery Book for the Working Classes* (1852), Charles Elmé Francatelli, Late *Maître d'Hôtel* and Chief Cook to Her Majesty the Queen, helpfully offers the following advice:

> The cheaper sort of red herrings are always too salt, and unpleasantly strong-flavoured, and are therefore an indifferent kind of food, unless due precaution is taken to soak them in water for an hour before they are cooked. First, soak the red herrings in water for an hour; wipe and split them down the back; toast or broil them on both sides for two or three minutes, and having placed them on a dish, put a bit of butter and some chopped onion upon each herring; pour a little vinegar over all, and this will make a cheap and savoury dish to be eaten with well-boiled potatoes.

See **Caribbean & West African Food** and **Mediterranean Food** for alternatives, but Will Buckenham suggested just simmering them for six minutes and serving with mustard, which helps to counteract the salt.

RED HERRING JOKE

Why are Protestant martyrs like red herrings? Because they're hanged and burned. (Boom! Boom!)

That is the essence of the red herring joke. Everything suggests it was already out there—the germ of it is in the fifteenth century **Life of St Herring**—but this entry explores its use and consequences between 1596 and 1599 in the works of three writers:

William Shakespeare, Ben Jonson and Thomas Nashe. None of them crack it overtly, which may be why the critical establishment has largely missed the story, although a lamentable interest in herrings probably also plays a part. Among a range of sources, this account draws on Charles Nicholl's *Cup of News* (1984), James Shapiro's *1599, A Year in the Life of William Shakespeare* (2005) and Stephen Alford's *The Watchers* (2013).

FALSTAFF: THE STORY BEGINS

Shakespeare's company was the Lord Chamberlain's Men, but in 1596 the Lord Chamberlain, Henry Carey, Baron Hunsdon, died. The new one, an aging William Brooke, Lord Cobham, ended the patronage and introduced a more Puritan regime. Sir John Oldcastle, the original fat, old rogue in Shakespeare's *Henry IV Pt 1* had genuinely been a friend of the young Prince Hal, but he had also been an earlier Lord Cobham and it may also have been a poke at the new Lord Chamberlain. Word came down from on high that the character's name had to change. Oldcastle had been a proto-Protestant Lollard and in 1417, condemned for heresy by the Ecclesiastical Court, had been hanged and burned.

Shakespeare changed the character to Sir John Falstaff, recognised by critics and audiences of the time as Sir John Fastolf (who had briefly appeared in the earlier *Henry VI Pt 1*, on which Nashe was a collaborator). This was a double joke: *Fall-staff* was a gag about William Brooke's virility, but Fastolf (see **Battle of the Herrings**) was the herring's great defender and therefore defender of the Cobham family name. Oldcastle or Falstaff, the role was triumphantly taken by the great comedian Will Kemp, famous for his embellishments of the script. Falstaff was his most successful role.

William Brooke died in March 1597 and may not even have been aware of the joke, but his son Henry took up the cause. He had wanted to be the new Lord Chamberlain, but Henry Carey's son George got the job, and reinstated Shakespeare's company as the Lord Chamberlain's Men. Henry Brooke became Lord Warden of the Cinque Ports, but was obviously still agitating around the insult to his family, because the

Herbert Beerbohm Tree as Falstaff in
The Merry Wives of Windsor, 1889. (Alamy)

joke was retargeted at him. George Carey seems to have been happy with Shakespeare capitalising on Falstaff's popularity in *The Merry Wives of Windsor*, notwithstanding its little poke at Henry in the character Ford who, thinking Falstaff is cuckolding him, disguises himself as a man called Brook.

THE FALLOUT FROM THE ISLE OF DOGS

In the summer of 1597 Nashe and Jonson's satirical play *The Isle of Dogs* was banned immediately and all copies destroyed or lost. It may have made suggestions of a corrupt state, it may have referred to the Islands Voyage, led by the Earl of Essex and Sir Walter Raleigh. Henry Brooke moved in Raleigh's circle and Raleigh appears later in this story. From Nashe and Jonson's later contributions it seems clear that some references to the red herring joke were deployed. Jonson, who also acted in the play, together with two other actors, was imprisoned for three months. Nashe may have been warned: he left town in a hurry. His lodgings were raided and his books and papers taken.

Will Kemp reprised his Falstaff in *Henry IV Pt 2*, again to great acclaim, but there's a suggestion of someone having had a quiet word. There are two versions of an epilogue, both curious. In the first Shakespeare promises more Falstaff adventures in the forthcoming *Henry V*, in which 'for anything I know, Falstaff shall die of a sweat,' but he's keen to point out, 'Oldcastle died martyr, and this is not the man.' The second epilogue, specially written for a 1598 Christmas performance at Court, is more contrite: 'I was lately here in the end of a displeasing play;' he wishes 'to pray your patience for it, and to promise better.'

Audiences loved Kemp; Shakespeare famously came to want a clown who would stick more closely to his lines. This would not have been down just to whatever Kemp as Falstaff had done with the red herring joke, but something had upset the authorities and it seems likely this contributed to Shakespeare's cutting the big man out of *Henry V*. His death scene is reported in it and it is made absolutely clear there was no sweating or bodily heat of any kind. *Henry V* is a disappointing end to Shakespeare's history cycle: the big man leaves a big hole. Kemp, a shareholder in the Lord Chamberlain's Men, leaves the company. In the account of his dance from London to Norwich, *Nine Daies Wonder*, he calls Shakespeare 'Shakerags', an accusation of ineffectuality and cowardice not a million miles away from the fall-staff joke.

EVERY MAN IN HIS HUMOUR

We don't know which play had displeased Court, but Jonson's *Every Man in his Humour* upped the stakes with the red herring joke. The Lord Chamberlain's Men gave Jonson his big break either in the late summer or the autumn of 1598. In it, Jonson extends the red herring's target to include all Oldcastle's descendants. Shakespeare almost certainly acted in the new play, taking his customary role as the old man, but Kemp had taken the key role in delivering the joke, playing the water-bearer Cob (a reference to Henry Brooke as Warden of the Cinque Ports). 'The first red herring that was broiled in Adam and Eve's kitchen, do I fetch my pedigree from,' Cob says. 'His cob was my great, great, mighty great grandfather.' Later he laments his family fortunes:

> A fasting-day no sooner comes, but my lineage goes to wrack; poor cobs! they smoak for it, they are made martyrs o' the gridiron, they melt in passion: and

your maids do know this, and yet would have me turn Hannibal, and eat my own flesh and blood. My princely coz, [he pulls out a red herring] fear nothing; I have not the heart to devour you, an I might be made as rich as king Cophetua. O that I had room for my tears, I could weep salt-water enough now to preserve the lives of ten thousand thousand of my kin!

'Martyrs o' the gridiron' refers to St Lawrence (see **Life of St Herring**), who met his end on a large grill. Jonson may have been playing with the crowd-pleasing improvisations for which Kemp was already famous in his role as Falstaff.

THOMAS NASHE RETURNS

Along with all his other works, a couple of months after it was published in March 1599, *Nashes Lenten Stuffe* (see **N is for**) was banned and ordered to be seized. Unlike *The Isle of Dogs* it has survived. It was written to be deniable in every aspect, but the authorities obviously understood it well enough. As well as being England's first major celebration of the herring, it is a celebration of language and defiance and it is not just about the red herring joke, but, frequently misunderstood, it does begin to unravel once you engage with the joke's logics. Nashe hadn't produced anything since the *Isle of Dogs* scandal. He only seems to have returned to London a couple of months before publication, but various references in it show he knows what has been going on with the joke while he has been away.

Nashe announces his work as 'The Description and first Procreation and Increase of the towne of Great Yarmouth in Norffolke: With a new Play never played before, of the praise of the RED HERRING.' He is promising to undo any offence given to William Brooke's ancestors through a generous celebration of the hanged and burned fish, but Henry is excepted. 'The silliest millers thombe, or contemptible stickle-banck of my enemies, is as busie nibbling about my fame, as if I were a deade man throwne amongst them to feede upon,' he complains. The miller's thumb or European bullhead was also known as a cob, a small freshwater fish (a little fish of the brook, perhaps).

There are also various pokes at Yarmouth's old enemy, the Cinque Ports, to keep Henry in our minds, but he does not get to be the red herring until Nashe has had his fun with praising.

Great Yarmouth & The Royal Line

There's no getting round the complexity of Nashe's game and late on he talks of red herrings used to put dogs off the scent. There is, however, a logic to the text's different sections and its individual stories. As promised, he starts with Great Yarmouth as the 'principall Metropolis of the redde fish.' Born in the rival herring town Lowestoft, he is in the land of his enemies not just because of the red herring joke, but he is profusely grateful for Yarmouth's hospitality and with their Cinque Ports rivalry, his enemy's enemy is also his friend.

Henry Manship, historian of the town (see **Yarmouth's Greatness**) generously opened up his extensive papers to Nashe, who starts his history with Cerdic the Saxon, who in 495 CE landed on the sandbank which became Yarmouth. Cerdic is particularly important, because from his loins came the royal line of the House of Wessex and therefore of England's crown. From William the Conqueror onwards, Nashe finds a way of mentioning every English monarch apart from minors, those who lasted less than a year, Richard III (usurped by Queen Elizabeth's grandfather) and Henry IV (another usurper but also the subject of the play out of which the controversy had arisen). He uses the phrase *all the Henries* to

Sir John Oldcastle, hanged and burned in 1417, from Hollinshed's *Chronicles* (1577). In Shakespears's history plays and other works, Hollinshed's expanded 1587 edition was a major source (image digitised by the University of Pennsylvania)

get round any major break in the sequence and succession to the aging Queen Elizabeth is what he wants to put in our minds. There is an interlude in which he makes clear, he has recently spent time with 'some of the deftest lads in all Edenborough towne' (seat of James VI of Scotland, the prime succession contender). But then he's off.

Red Herring Exports

Having described the town, Nashe follows its red herring exports into Europe and beyond. The smoked fish is a Protestant warrior: 'to think on a red Herring, such a hot stirring meat it is, is enough to make the cravenest dastard proclaim fire and sword against Spain.' This prepares the ground for his later play with hanging and burning, but he doesn't linger. In the Levant trade, Reds were exported to the Ottoman Empire and in a whimsical reference to the original joke, he wonders 'whether those turbanto groutheads, that hang all men by the throates on Iron hookes, even as our Toers hang all their Herrings by the throates on wodden spits, first learnd it of our Herring men or our herring men of them.' And in case anyone thought he might just be making fun of a Protestant saint, he tortuously proves, etymologically, Shia Islam's Imam Ali, was 'a dead red herring, and no other.'

Since he's in the Levant, he takes the opportunity for an extended riff on gods and men in Ancient Greece. Golden herring is the favoured kind of red in Southern Europe (see **Red Herring** and **Mediterranean Food**) and it may have been then. Either way, his focus on their 'guilded' nature puns on their export value (guilders) and every classical mention of gold turns out to have been our friend the red herring. All those golden temple idols? Nothing more than 'a plaine golden coated red herring.' It was simply 'the strangenes of it (they never having beheld a beast of that hue before) in their temples inshrined for a god.' Red herring was, of course, the food of the Olympian gods and, unused to such 'delicates', Midas was just experiencing a little indigestion. Great Jupiter, 'raining himself down' into Danaë's lap in a golden shower, as well as in all his other 'slippery pranks', was again just a red herring. Before we know it, however, Nashe slips into the first of his four longer stories, 'Let me see, hath any bodie in Yarmouth heard of Leander and Hero, of whome divine Musaes sung, and a diviner Muse then him, Kit Marlow?'

Hero & Leander and the King of Fishes

The interlude in ancient Greece eases us into Nashe's version of his friend Marlowe's unfinished love story, the tragedy retold as a tavern joke. The two dead lovers at the end are metamorphosed, Ovid-style, into a phallic ling (Leander) and a tender-hearted herring (Hero), destined to meet again on every fast day table accompanied by Hero's old nurse: the gods, who cannot bear her tears, transform her into a mustard plant. Nashe even has Hero neatly swimming back, almost to where we started, to the seas by Lovingland near Lowestoft. An origin story for the herring, we are now in the build-up to the grand climax of the red herring joke, but it also points readers towards Marlowe, cut off in his prime in a tavern brawl. Officially witnessed by the 'intelligencer' or spy, Robert Pooley, Marlowe's death was as suspicious then as it is now. After *The Isle of Dogs*, Pooley was also placed in Jonson's cell to elicit confidences. Nashe may be reminding us of his own precarious situation, surrounded by enemies in the middle of his text. The next story is also of the live fish, Nashe's version of the folk tale explaining how the herring became **King of Fishes**. Its election of the least worst option as king serves as another reminder of the succession and James VI of Scotland.

How the Red Herring Became a Protestant Saint

And he's off yet again, 'King, by your leave, for in your king shippe I must leave you, and repeate how from white to redde you cameleonized.' His origin story for the red herring is his *tour de force*, a fantasia on Oldcastle as a Protestant saint. The miracle of its accidental creation in a Yarmouth fisherman's shed is set during the sixth century papacy of Vigilius (even more of a miracle because, as he has already established, the sandbank which became Yarmouth had, by then, not yet emerged enough even for a shed). The fisherman-peddler-trickster takes his red herrings and sets off for Rome, but having been robbed on the way, only has three left when he arrives. He baits the interest of the pope's caterer by announcing it as King of Fishes, eating the first two as the caterer balks at their rising price. Vigilius is adamant he must have the last one. The stink of our red herring roasting on the coals empties the Vatican of pope and cardinals, Vigilius canonising him in order to calm his turbulent spirit, Nashe inviting us:

> Looke the Almanack in the beginning of Aprill, and see if you can finde out such a saint as saint Guildard: which in honour of this guilded fish, the Pope so ensainted: nor there hee rested and stopt, but in the mitigation of the very embers whereon he was sindged, (that after he was taken from them, fumed most fulsomly of his fatty droppings,) hee ordained ember weekes in their memory, to be fasted everlastingly.

Oldcastle as red herring defeats Catholicism through an enaction of the joke of his own demise. It is praise in the form of savage mockery played to the guffaws of the crowd, as rude and rambunctious as anything in English literature. Before the action moves on, in one paragraph he uses 'cob' four times, including 'cobbing country chuffs' which brings Shakespeare, the 'upstart crow' to mind. A play with Roman (old) castles, a 'Castor' by Norwich and implicitly Fastolf's own castle at Caister (both have Roman ruins) seems to take a convoluted poke at Shakespeare's *Henry IV Pt 2* epilogue, 'This is not the man.'

The Return of Henry Brooke

Any suggestion that Nashe might have insulted the memory of Saint John Oldcastle has now been dealt with and it is time to let his descendent Henry return as 'but a cropshin, one of the refuse sort of herrings.' In the form of a spent red herring he steps forward. Nashe takes time to establish, once again, the foolishness of interpretation, commenting on the overpaid legal imbeciles who, 'out of some discourses of mine, which were a mingle mangle cum purre and I knew not what to make of my selfe, have fisht out of such a deepe politique state meaning as if I had al the secrets of court or common-wealth at my fingers endes.'

With a much stronger, directly allegorical feel than anything else in *Lenten Stuffe*, this tale of the red herring and *Lady Turbut* is altogether darker and yet is anticlimactic —Henry is so contemptible he doesn't deserve a climax. 'As compleate an adelantado as hee that is knowne by wearing a cloak of tuftaffatie eighteene yeare... to Lady Turbut there is no demurre but he would needs goe a wooing.' The cloak-wearing adelantado could be Henry's friend Sir Walter Raleigh. *Adelantado* was a military title in the gift of the King of Spain. Skip forward three years or so and both Henry and Raleigh were imprisoned in the Tower for their part in the Main Plot. Ultimately with Spanish funding it had supposedly sought to engineer succession to the throne by James' cousin, Lady Arbella Stuart. Henry's brother George was involved in the linked Bye Plot. The conspiracies were an unlikely and unholy alliance between Puritans (who wanted the freedom of conscience to worship outside the Church of England) and Catholics (who needed this too).

Lady Stuart/Lady Turbot is not a stretch. The timescale for the preparatory 'wooing' of Arbella is plausible. Henry was Secretary of State Robert Cecil's brother-in-law. Cecil and the Carey family were actively involved in ensuring the smooth election of James. There were secret communications between both of them and the Scottish throne. Cecil would have had intelligencers watching his own mother, never mind his brother-in-law. Nashe could easily have picked up rumours in Scotland or elsewhere. Cecil would not have felt free to move on the Main and Bye Plots, because Elizabeth still would not name her own preferred successor. She did not do so until she was on her deathbed and we only have Cecil's word that she finally plumped for James.

In Nashe's story, Lady Turbot refuses the *cropshin's* advances and for her pains finds herself literally in hot water: 'boyled to death... her posterity thoroughly sawst and sowst and pickled in barelles of brinish tears.' Yet again, Nashe challenges his readers, 'O for a Legion of mice-eyed decipherers and calculaters uppon characters now to augurate what I meane by this: the divell, if it stood upon his salvation, cannot do it.'

Cecil was known for playing a waiting game. Raleigh and Brooke were arrested in 1603 and put in the Tower. Henry Brooke implicated Raleigh, George Brooke implicated Henry, but it did not do any of them any good. George was immediately executed, Raleigh eventually in 1618. Henry was released in the same year, but only because he was already dying. Arbella was locked up in 1610 for marrying someone who was also too close in line to the throne and she died in the Tower five years later, but by this time Nashe was long dead.

To me, two months after *Lenten Stuffe* was published, 1599's unusual banning of so many writers' works (see **N is for**) along with everything Nashe had ever or even might one day write, looks like he, in particular, was being silenced (perhaps along with rumours of a plot with which Cecil could not yet deal). Nashe lived a precarious life at the best of times: denied a livelihood, he seems to have died in poverty in 1601, aged only 33.

The Ending
Nashes Lenten Stuffe is a joyous celebration of the red herring in its capacity to become anything he wants it to be. If it is more than an attack on Henry Brooke it is because it is through energy of invention that Nashe overcomes his tribulations. The richness of the joke is more important than its targets, just as Falstaff became bigger than Oldcastle. The fat man is still on Nashe's mind as he moves towards his close—'Be of good cheere, my weary Readers, for I have espied land.' As well as the succession and Jonson's *Every Man in His Humour*, there are references to Falstaff and, with Shakespeare writing *Henry V* at the time, it's tempting to hear something of Hal's 'Cry God for Harry, England, and Saint George' when Nashe finally gets there. It ends like a dangling fish head, a red herring's cob.

> My conceit is cast into a sweating sicknesse with ascending these few steps of his renowne; into what a hote broyling Saint Laurence fever would it relapse then, should I spend the whole bagge of my winde in climbing up to the lofty

mountaine crest of his Trophees? But no more winde will I spend on it but this: Saint Denis for Fraunce, Saint Iames for Spaine, Saint Patrike for Ireland. Saint George for England, and the red Herring for Yarmouth.

REDUCTION PLANTS

In *De harengo* (1654) **Neucrantz** laments Heligoland's use of herrings as fertilizer. The whole idea is an insult to the **King of Fishes**. In the mid-nineteenth century, in Aberystwyth, some blamed the disappearance of the shoals on the herrings having taken offense at such practices. The Algonquin, whose lands ranged across most of the herring fisheries of the North American East Coast, at least tried to appease them elegantly: 'Whilst you may be used as fertilizer, your sacrifice is life-giving and we name you Giver of Life for this reason.'

On the shores of Northern Europe such elegance was always in short supply. Unaware of falling prices ashore, fishermen hauled in as much of a glut as they could, then, laden to the gunnels, raced to get their catch to market first. Whales and other predators eat what they can, then stop. By introducing the split predator (fishermen, curer, market) capitalism's natural inefficiency meant millions of surplus herrings were dead before anybody even knew they were sated. What else were you going to do with all those herrings?

Even the smooth-talking Algonquin would have been appalled at the reduction plant, huge vats separating vast catches of herring into train oil and fishmeal. Where did it all start? The literature is vague. The US developed the reduction of, first Pacific, then Atlantic herring in the 1870s. In the 1970s Höglund identified where the herrings in the Bohuslän gluts came from (see **Swedish Fisheries**) by investigating eighteenth-century waste pits. This indicated industrial-scale reduction, but nothing similar earlier.

Out of the blue, a tweet from Swedish archaeologist Anton Larsson was talking of eighteenth-century Bohuslän workers drowning in vats of herring oil. It spoke of a technology in development, proper health and safety procedures not yet implemented…

AN INTERVIEW WITH ANTON LARSSON

It's a niche field. I'm not aware of anything in English on this and, in Sweden, I'm probably the one who knows most about it… But it's possibly one of the single most interesting episodes of eighteenth-century Swedish history.

The Development of Herring Reduction

We have four known Bohuslän herring periods, 1556 to 1589, 1660 to 1680, 1747 to 1809 and 1877 to 1906. As far as I know, there's no evidence for reduction in the first two periods. In 1747 the herring returns. It's a couple of years until they're able to get the fisheries going: you need new vessels and new equipment and it takes a while. So it's not until 1752 that things get going. In the early years it's mainly just salting the herring, but then there are smokehouses and gradually they're developing the tri-works or the oil reduction facilities. By the 1770s, this is a large industry.

The technology is a development rather than a brand-new invention. It's the same kind of equipment you're using to produce whale oil in Spitsbergen or Svalbard —or seal oil in the Baltic. Essentially, you have a large vat and you put fire under it and you reduce the herring. You have these scoops that you use to scoop off the oil from the top of the vat. The herring oil is called train oil just like whale or seal oil is. The Swedish word for a herring reduction plant is *trankokeri*—literally train boilery. The Dutch are doing it with their whaling industry in Svalbard and there are a lot of Dutch and German merchants on the West Coast of Sweden. If you look at the illustrations from Smeerenburg, the Dutch seventeenth-century whaling station in Svalbard, the technology is virtually identical. I think it's possible to see a trail. There are also a few of the industrialists in Gothenburg, experimenting with wooden presses, pressing the oil from the herring, but these are anomalies.

The Battle of the Train Oil Waste

It all gets even more interesting with something called the *Trankrympsstriden*—the Battle of the Train Oil Waste—a fascinating early environmental battle. The reduction plants were being established in two areas. In the inner fjords they were close to farmsteads and the industrialists had to negotiate with local peasants for access to land to build on. Everyone was quick to realise that the waste from producing the oil was a good, nutrient-rich fertiliser and they probably took it straight to the fields. Reduction plants were also being established on the skerries out in the Skagerrak. It was free to build there, because the skerries were owned by the Crown, which wanted to see them colonised. There was less access to farmland and, given fishing in the winter conditions was difficult, it wasn't worth the cost of transporting the waste to the mainland, so it was dumped at sea.

In the 1770s, you start to see reports about the negative impact of dumping tons and tons and tons of fish waste into very sensitive environments. The reports are of fundamentally two things. One is that fish stocks are disappearing. What happened is that they experienced a lot of what we see today—dump a lot of nutrients into a sensitive marine environment and you get oxygen depletion and so on. There were also reports from navigators, concerned that the dumping was causing a build-up of the sea floor, ruining shallow navigation points.

Nobody wants to see the herring go. The Crown panics and in 1780 they start to force factory owners, instead of dumping the waste, to take care of it. This crystallises in 1782/3, when the Crown mandates the construction of herring waste reservoirs, which are quite complex—you have a timber structure, then a stone structure which has to be walled with soil, so the waste doesn't spill out and poison the sea.

There's a major reaction from the industrialists, which is the 'Battle'. It's political warfare. They fund a scientific expedition of the disciples of Carl Linnaeus, who are going out to greenwash things. They produce a several hundred page report trying to show that, *No, no! Actually these industrial wastes are good for the fisheries.* It's a very hectic period, because the industrialists think it's very, very expensive to build these reservoirs. In the end the Crown decides it's going to insist anyway. The herring are a vital resource.

The Scale of the Industry

If you look at the whole picture of the herring industry at this time on the Swedish West Coast, there are around 1,000 works, of which 300 or 400 are specifically reduction plants. They vary vastly in size. You have ones that are essentially just a shack with a single vat, a quite small vat, and those would be usually operated by well-off local peasants or urban burghers in the smaller towns of the northern part of Bohuslän. Then you have them going up in size and usually, they will be in sets of two, so two, four, six, eight vats. The largest single factory was one that had thirty-two copper vats producing herring oil and we're talking big, big vats.

Bohuslän was already deforested, because in the Middle Ages and early modern period, it was Dano-Norwegian territory and this was where the Danish fleet got most of its timber. So they'd logged the province clean, almost. Then you had a rapidly growing population, so there was a lot of household need for firewood and so on. Then you have the construction of all these factories, each burning a lot of wood to produce the oil: it's massively worsening the deforestation. It gets so bad, in the 1770s there's a royal decree: you are not allowed to fuel the reduction plants with wood. You're allowed to start the fires with wood, but you're not allowed to keep them going with it. Instead you're mandated to use either peat, which is found locally, or, crucially, black coal, which is not produced in Sweden. You see hundreds and hundreds of British vessels coming in with coal from Newcastle and so on. This is the first industry in Sweden using coal *en masse*. Until then it was just isolated factories, sugar manufacturers and so on and the lighthouses.

We have no idea about how much of the herring oil was used for the domestic market. We only have statistics for exports from Gothenburg and in the single best year we know of, there were 50,000 barrels of herring oil being exported.

FROM THE MID NINETEENTH CENTURY ONWARDS

The herring waste reservoirs, which Larsson pictures being constructed are interesting because of their role in Höglund's work. The Battle of the Train Oil Waste is doubly interesting, because any mention of the waste pits in British herring histories presents them as driven by superstition around herring **Sensitivity**. The masking of their actual underpinning logic would appear to be a projection of its dismissal by the industrialists and the greenwashing members of the Linnaean Society.

Sweden's first major engagement with the Industrial Revolution can also be seen as having been generated because of the rapid increase in the market for train oil set in motion by the Industrial Revolution itself. The herring period in which we see reduction plants developing ended in 1809. Larsson talks of 'a complete reinvention of technology in the late 1800s, when the herring returned—they're trying out new kinds of gasoline-powered plants and they start to produce what they call a herring-based 'guano', a sort of powdered fertiliser.' Fishmeal.

Why herring reduction plants did not take off in the United Kingdom is unclear. Over the nineteenth and early twentieth centuries the British Isles became the major producer and exporter of salt herring. Even as North Sea populations showed signs of collapse, between the wars, there were parliamentary discussions on what to do with gluts. Reduction was taken forward by the United States, as well as back in Scandinavia. The North American West Coast took to herring reduction in the 1870s—just in time to influence the reinvention of the practice in the late nineteenth-century Bohuslän herring period. The East Coast took to it slightly later.

Worried about stocks, US authorities banned the direct use of fish as fertiliser, only allowing licence-holders to use fish for non-edible purposes. As these tended to be the owners of fish reduction plants, it did little to disrupt the industry. When the Norwegians established the **Icelandic Fisheries** they exported the technology (see second image section), the first plant opening at Siglufjörður in 1911.

Notwithstanding the brave actions of World War II British commandos on the **Måløy Raid**, reduction plants continued to flourish. In Mitchison and Macintosh's *Men & Herring* (1949) at one point the ring netters are grumbling at the lower price they will get for a catch sold for reduction. Post-war, the **Herring Industry Board** began to encourage the development of plants—just in time for the United Kingdom not to be able to claim any credit for its earlier abstinence. Herring reduction, developed to deal with gluts, created a regular market for catches that went considerably beyond humanity's need and/or desire to eat herring. To all intents and purposes, it created an infinite market for a resource which, in the second half of the twentieth century, was finally revealed as finite and rapidly decreasing. Höglund proved that the excess herrings in the Bohuslän periods came from Southern North Sea populations. The four known periods came roughly seventy years apart. Unsurprisingly, whatever glut had been pencilled in for the mid 1970s was barely noticeable.

Self-sacrificially, in the 1970s Peruvian anchovies came to the rescue of the herrings by beating them on price. In the UK, most of the recently established plants went bust, but population collapses off Iceland, Norway and in the North Sea led to herring fishing bans and then **Quotas**. Fish reduction continues, most efforts focused on species like capelin and sand eels—but apart from the Japanese, whales and puffins, who cares about them?

RING NET STRUGGLE

In 1833 two fishermen caught 6,700 barrels of herring by stretching their drift nets across a bay in Loch Fyne. A number of trials were initiated, experimenting with nets adapted for trawling and the ring net resulted (see **Nets & Weirs**). It was worked by pairs of boats, which actively surrounded shoals. There had been little room in the loch for the larger busses or the decked luggers to operate, but the ring nets began catching substantially more fish than Loch Fyne's traditional, small, open-decked drifters. Angus Martin's meticulously researched *The Ring-Net Fishermen* (1981) details the story in greater depth. By 1842 the Fishery Board was seizing ring nets, after responding to complaints, on the basis that they were illegal, even though the mesh size (1" from knot to knot) was as specified in the 1808 legislation.

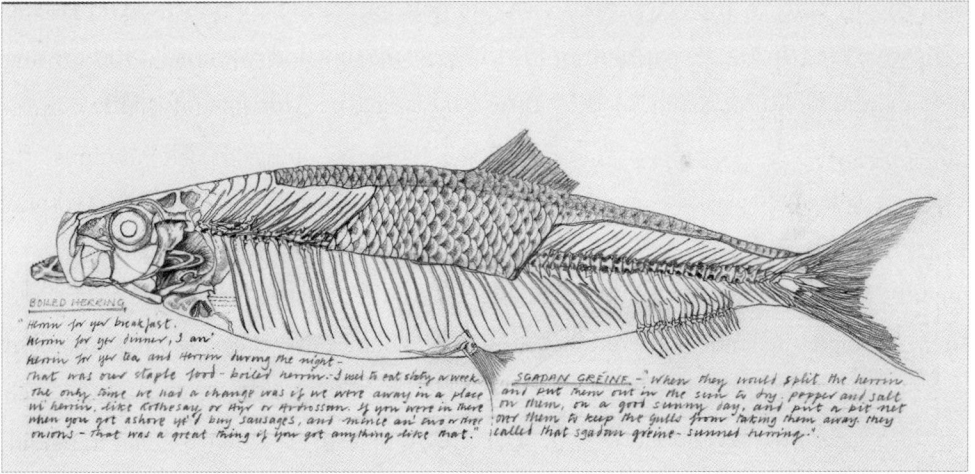

BOILED HERRING "Herrin for yer breakfast, herrin for yer dinner, I an' herrin for yer tea and herring during the night - that was our staple food - boiled herrin. I used to eat sixty a week. The only time we had a change was if we were away in a place wi' herrin, like Rothesay or Ayr or Ardrossan. If you were in there when you got ashore ye'd buy sausages, and mince an' two or three onions - that was a great thing if you got anything like that." SGADAN GRÉINE "When they would split the herrin and put them out in the sun to dry, pepper and salt on them, on a good sunny day, and put a bit net over them to keep the gulls from taking them away, they called that sgadan gréine - sunned herring." Ink drawing of a partially filleted herring with hand written text beneath. *Herring Cooking* (from *The Ring-Net*), Will Maclean. National Galleries of Scotland. Purchased 1980.

The ring netters were concentrated around Tarbert, towards the mouth of the loch. The drift netters further up, around Inverary, relied on the herring swimming up to where their passive nets had been set. They regarded such large catches in the lower reaches as ultimately destroying their livelihoods. They were also concerned about overfishing. A trawl of any kind traps young fish; the mesh size of a drift net was determined so they could pass through.

In 1849, petitions were sent to the Fishery Board by both drifters and ring netters. The driftermen argued that the new method destroyed the spawn and fry, led to over-catching and dumping, the rotting fish repelling the shoals. The ring netters were also interfering with the drift nets, stealing the catches. The counter argument was that it was free to everyone to change, and that ring netting was more efficient and generated higher incomes. The board's report supported the drifters and a parliamentary act of 1851 banned ring netting. The Navy was drawn into policing the fishery, nets were seized and guns were fired. In 1853 a patrol from HMS *Porcupine* shot and wounded a Tarbert ring netter called Colin McKeich. In 1861 Peter McDougall of Ardrishaig was killed.

Policing fishermen is hard at the best of times. The Loch Fyne ring netters knew the waters. Herring fishing takes place at night. The fish had to go to market by sea, anyway, and beyond the loch's mouth there were larger boats to take catches without them having to be landed. There was widespread defiance and the economic argument was persuading more and more of the driftermen to convert to the new method, which was also spreading beyond Loch Fyne. Eventually, in 1867, ring netting was legalised. The struggle continued to be played out in the fishing communities of the Highlands and Islands and on the East Coast. Steam, enabling greater manoeuvrability for larger boats, increased the efficiency.

The method spread to Scandinavia, where it was particularly suited to the fjord fisheries of Norway, but there was also an increasing adoption there of single boat purse seine trawling, which had been developed in the USA. This, in turn, led to the demise of both ring netting and drifting for herrings, which in turn contributed to the population collapses of the 1960s and 70s. The concerns of the drift netters of Inverary were mostly proven to have been justified. Angus Martin, himself from a ring netting family, finishing his book during the herring fishing bans of the late 70s, writes:

> The most profound and influential personal lesson of these five years of questioning and gathering has been this: that Western society, by its criminal contempt for the fellow creatures which share its corner of the planet, has brought itself to the edge of an ecological and moral crisis from which, without the exercise of immediate and unswerving restraint, there can be no withdrawal.

ROE

A hard roe is the ripe egg mass of a mature female fish, found in its ovaries. Soft roes are the testes filled with the male's sperm—also known as the milts or the melts. Herrings at their tasty best are caught just before spawning, which means that when herrings are in season, there is generally plenty of roe around. If you don't see it on many fishmongers' slabs, it is to do with the market for such things being in decline. If you do see fresh herrings, it is always worth asking.

There are more recipes for soft roe and they usually involve buttered toast. The softness of the roes, dipped in seasoned flour and fried (often also in butter), is given the hint of a crisp crust. Lemon juice cuts both the creaminess of the roe and the butter. In *Fish* (2011) Mark Hix gives a recipe which adds capers and parsley to this and it is a joy. For the most elaborate recipe, see **Dumas, Alexandre**. It brings together the milts of thirty herrings with a gratin and much more, creating a meal as hearty as anyone could wish.

In my grandmother's hand-written recipe book there's a recipe for steaming the milts and mixing them with a little cream, then cutting this mildness with olives and raisins.

For squeamish children, the 1930s *Herring Book* issued by the **Herring Industry Board**, suggested cooking in milk, then mashing it with baked potato and creamed spinach. In an approach which sounds like exposure therapy, it suggests starting with a teaspoon, building up gradually to a tablespoon's worth: nursery food, but not as we know it these days.

Hard roes are also floured and fried, or floured, dipped in egg, then breadcrumbs and then fried, but if your child has problems with both kinds of roe, you could try the *Herring Book*'s hard roe surprise, cooking one in salted water, putting it in a small, ovenproof dish lined with mashed potato, then covering the roe with beaten egg, salt and pepper, before putting it in the oven until the egg has set. Sprinkle with a little chopped parsley. They'll love it so much, before you know it, you'll be looking up the Dumas recipe for them.

There are herring roe caviar products on the market, for which the hard roe is both smoked and salted. Greece, smoking its own golden herring from imported, frozen fish, has diversified its production to include a caviar marketed as *arënkha*. It was originally called *avruga*, but the name was changed to avoid any possible confusion with *sevruga* caviar, made with sturgeon roe.

The Tlingit and the Haida of the North American North West traditionally collect the herring's fertilised eggs by laying hemlock branches in shallow spawning grounds. Although not quite the same, there are recipes which combine pre-spawning male and female roes (see second image section). The 1970s completely new edition of the *Herring Book* was sadly issued just before the North Sea population collapse. It never had the chance to educate a new generation, which is a shame, because its roe puffs could have become a chip shop favourite.

Take 8 oz / 250 gms of mixed herring roes and, together with a tablespoon of lemon juice, add to a thick batter made with 4 oz / 125 gms plain flour, salt, warm water and a tablespoon of oil. Fold in the thickly beaten whites of two eggs, then drop dessertspoons of the mixture into hot oil and fry until they are crisp and golden brown. Served with pea shoots, it might yet become a gastropub starter.

RUSSIAN FISHERIES

Herring fishing in the Russian empire has a long history and probable pre-history, but for the most part its main industrial significance was as a huge market for the different rising and falling fisheries of Western Europe. Herring travelled via Viking trade networks stretching East to the Kievan Rus and then via the succeeding Hanseatic routes. Scanian, Dutch, Norwegian, Bohuslän, Danish, British and Icelandic herring found its way into the vastness of this market of the interior.

Russia has coastlines on the Baltic, Barents, Bering, Chukchi, Kara, Pechora and White Seas, not to mention the Sea of Japan, all of which have herring populations. It has access to Atlantic, Baltic, Pacific, Chosa and White Sea herring stocks. Its difficulties were not just in the establishment of fisheries, but in the uninhabited nature of many of these areas.

'Herring fisheries in the White Sea in the C18th—beginning of the C20th' (Dmitry Lajus *et al.*, 2007) does not appear to have emerged in a crowded publication field, but it does identify a continuous tradition since at least the mid-sixteenth century. The earliest record is of the rich herring fishery near the Solovetsky Islands. As populations grew around the White Sea, there was an active local market, but Lajus points to customs records for 1634/5 showing 'as much as 500 barrels of herring... transported daily through the town of Vologda... to southern and eastern parts of Russia.' Vologda is 700 miles south of Archangelsk and 300 miles north of Moscow. That this trade grew alongside Russia's herring imports is testament to the scale of demand. It probably helps that in the Russian Orthodox Church fish is more of a benevolent dispensation during Lent, excluded on Wednesdays and Fridays along with meat.

Russia more than tripled its total fish catch between the mid-nineteenth century and 1913, but this was still overwhelmingly taken from inland waters. An intention to modernise its herring fisheries predated the revolution of 1917 and the establishment of the Soviet Union. Christopher Unsworth's *The British Herring Industry* tells the story of an initiative on the cusp of World War I, which saw Yarmouth-based James Bloomfield setting up a joint venture with Equerry to the Imperial Russian Court, Vladimir De Sivers. This company, Russian Northern Maritime Industries, began a methodical search for new White Sea herring grounds and training in drift net fishing techniques. 1913 turned out not to be such a good time for it, but Bloomfield sent Norfolk skipper 'Wee' Green (a big man) in the steam drifter *Pesha*, to work with Captain Spahde of Archangelsk. A Scottish cooper and his wife also participated in the venture, which was wound up in 1919, its £11,700 in rouble assets never heard of again.

In 1925 the Soviets sought to redevelop their fisheries, slowly shifting focus to its herring-rich northern seas. It took a while for them to invest in the larger vessels which would enable wider exploitation, but as its fisheries grew, they showed a similar commitment to underpinning it all with science. *Clupeidae* (1952) by the great systematist A.N. **Svetovidov** brought all the world's herrings together in the same book, possibly for the first time. Up until this point herring studies had been overwhelmingly rooted in national or regional perspectives—even Friedrich Heincke's **Racial Theory**. Svetovidov shared the distaste for Heincke's 'races' of herrings, replacing them with an impeccable internationalism, although, behind it, one senses a Soviet vision of the universal right of all fish to be exploited by its growing fleets.

In 1956 the 20th Congress of the Communist Party of the USSR committed itself to a fleet of factory trawlers, using stern launched nets, supported by the smaller vessels which would allow flexibility in the catching. It was these and others like them which, after the collapse of the Soviet Union, became the klondykers familiar on Scotland's West Coast. Capitalism's triumphalist Western advisors naturally encouraged the privatisation of Russia's fishing industry along with everything else and it has continued to grow. In 2024 VARPE (All-Russian Association of Fisheries Enterprises, Entrepreneurs and Exporters) announced that, as the Norwegians had reduced their own exports, Russian operators had increased theirs and the country was now the world's leading herring supplier.

Today Russia accounts for 80% of the Pacific herring catch and 27% of the Atlantic and Baltic herring catch. At the same time, Lithuania, supported by Estonia, Latvia and Sweden, is accusing the Russians of 'unsustainable fishing activities in the Baltic Sea, which are undermining our joint efforts to rebuild the biological resources of this sea basin in line with scientific advice.' There have also been suggestions of continued exploitation of herring in the West Bering Sea, contrary to a ban recommended by Russia's own scientists. In the overfishing of herring, the fishery practices of other nations may also apply.

SALT & SALTING

My sister, in love, once assured me, 'a kiss without a beard is like an egg without salt.' One of my earliest memories is my mother, in Bahrain, pouring a little heap of it in the palm of my hand to replace what I was losing, sweating in the relentless sun. It gets a bad press these days, but an egg without salt is still a matter of regret. Historically, salt was central to the preservation of food and the enabling of much food-based trade. It is an active ingredient in over a third of the entries in this encyclopaedia: without it herring could have been insignificant.

Plain salt herring is undervalued in the United Kingdom. Even its herring lovers tend to prefer fresh or salted and smoked. If you want some, try an Eastern European grocer. Whole salted herrings are often sold from a bucket of brine, but they're also usually available filleted and packed in oil. It is great: a maatjes held by the tail and lowered into the mouth, Dutch style; laid Swedish/Danish-style on a slice of thickly-buttered rye bread and garnished with any number of nice things; see **Potatoes** for the temptations of hot meal happiness. You also need it to make many of the classics: see **Jewish Food** for chopped herring; see **Shuba & Sour Cream**, both for herring under a fur coat and German red herring salad (beetroot coloured rather than red herring); see **Vinegar** for a range of marinated delights.

Archaeologists point to the earliest evidence of salt harvesting, more-or-less simultaneously in 6000 BCE, both in the Subcarpathians of Romania and at a salt lake near Yuncheng in China. There was then a 4,000 year wait before the Chinese came to the pleasures of salt pickled fish. It is enough to make you lose faith in the idea of innate human intelligence. It was also around this time the ancient Egyptians started illustrating their tombs with fish pickling pictures, but it seems likely that salt fish honours go to the Harappan civilisation of the Indus Valley, around 2400 BCE.

WHY SALT & WHICH SALT?

Herring is an oily fish, containing several polyunsaturated fatty acids which are good for us (see **Medicine & Health**), but unsaturated oils are also good at combining with atmospheric oxygen, meaning herrings go off quickly. Pickling in salt minimises oxidation. Salt also draws water from the fish by osmosis and in brine concentrations of around 20% kills off most dangerous bacteria. Tightly barrelling the brined herring further minimises the access of oxygen and gives you white herring, a product with shelf-life. A fish which comes in massive shoals and is then given shelf-life insists on the development of trade.

Salt and fat combine to make so many good things. Salt, fat and smoke is one of food's magic combinations, the smoke delivering tarry phenols, which also have antioxidant properties. Well-cured white herring has a shelf life of roughly a year, ample for trade and even for use as an alternative to currency in the Middle Ages.

As communities and nations competed for trade opportunities the quality of the salt became ever more important. The Scania fishery, then the Dutch led the way, although the French may have been ahead of the game with the ready accessibility of their bay salt. Purity could be a factor in both taste and shelf life, the English and the Scots always running from the back, too far back, like lazy schoolboys on a cross-country run. Salt whether from the sea or from brine pits was evaporated by sun and wind or by fire. Sand, silts and soot all presented problems, but there was a further one in *bittern*. With gourmet salts some trace elements are welcomed, but it is ultimately sodium chloride you are after. Evaporating seawater or the water from brine pits, you could get plenty of sodium chloride, but you also got calcium chloride, magnesium chloride, sulphates, bromides, iodides and more. In salt manufacture, these are called *bitterns* because they give a bitter flavour.

Scania

There were brine pits (see **Danish Fisheries**) but throughout the great herring fishery off the Skåne coast of what is, today, southern Sweden, it was predominantly the German rock salt of Lüneberg from the twelfth to the fifteenth century when the Scania fishery flourished. By the late fourteenth century the Dutch were shipping bay salt to the Baltic from France and further afield. It wasn't just the quality which led to its adoption, but the competitive costs of sea transport.

The Dutch

The factory ship that was the Dutch herring buss saw the salting and barreling of herring at sea. As well as this immediate curing, Dutch regulations increasingly insisted on better quality salt. Initially using the bay salt from Bourgneuf, they shifted towards their home-produced moor salt, then Portuguese Lisboa and salt on salt (see below). The Dutch somehow maintained access to Portuguese and Spanish salt even when they were locked in war with Spain, something the British never seem to have managed.

The British

Salt production is the most fully recorded industry in the *Domesday Book* of 1086, both sea and rock salt. Records of Scottish sea salt pans go back to the twelfth century, when Prestonpans was given a royal warrant. It continued production through until 1959. By the seventeenth century England's production was focused on Lymington's Portsea salt (it was shipped from Portsea Island at Portsmouth), the rock salt of North-, Nant-, Droit- and the other -wiches of Cheshire and Worcestershire, or the coal-dried sea salt of the River Tyne, notably at South Shields. Scottish production, which had moved similarly to the use of coal, was mostly based on the Forth, with pans at Culross, St Monans, Joppa and elsewhere.

Benefitting from its lower and less rigorous salt taxes, from the seventeenth century the Scots flooded the English market with smuggled salt, but the quality of both English and Scottish salt was generally poor and the English continued to import bay salt. Scottish salt production largely collapsed after the duty on salt was abolished in 1825. Lymington continued producing it until 1865, but it was ultimately disadvantaged by the cost of coal on the South Coast. Making the most of its local coal, its bitterns and its coaly by-products, Tyneside saw the growth of Britain's chemical industry, although this then moved to Teesside, helped by the discovery there of a rock salt deposit.

SEA SALTS

As John Collins says in *Salt and Fishery* (1682), 'Where the Sun shines hot, and the Tides vary but little, tis easie to have Salt enough.' Sea salt producers traditionally work with tidal difference, taking the water at high tide—spring tides by preference—and channelling it into shallow holding pools or salt pans. The less silt and sand you take in at this point the better, but the holding pools allow both to settle to the bottom. The pans take advantage of sun and wind.

Fleur de Sel, Flower of Salt in English, is a top of the range product, the artisanally-gathered crust of salt crystals that forms on the surface. It has been collected since

Roman times, is treasured by gourmets and has always been expensive. It is, in consequence, irrelevant to the salting of herrings.

Bay Salt is technically the sea salt of the Bay of Bourgneuf, near Nantes, particularly Guérande and Noirmoutier—the closest sun-evaporated production to the major herring grounds. The term came to describe any salt produced in this way—in Spain, Portugal, around the Mediterranean and, as trade expanded geographically with European colonialism, in Cape Verde and the Caribbean. When the Dutch banned Bourgneuf's own production, it was because of a high clay content.

Jerbo Salt is described by Collins so:

> At Jerbo, a place in Barbary, 30 Leagues to the Westward of Tripoly, is much Salt made, on a plain of red Sand, by the Sun's vigour: the Sea (which ebbs and flows but about a foot,) making its way through the Sea sandy-Banks into the Plain aforesaid. A Bassa seeing a Ship Arrive from Sea, and Anchoring on the shoales where is safe Riding, estimates her Bulk, and sells her Lading for about two Dollers a Ton, the which is carried on Board by Turks, or Moors into the bargain.
>
> This Salt is of so strong a Grain, that it will not readily Dissolve in fresh-water, wherefore if it be necessary the Marriners put fresh water to it, to wash out the Dirt and Sand, powring away the Liquor that will run.

Moor Salt was, for a while, particularly popular with the Dutch, who produced it by soaking and evaporating the ashes from burning salt-rich estuarial turf. It was purer than Bay Salt, but soon they found they did not have enough estuarial turf to cope with demand.

Salt on Salt was another way of dealing with impurities. Collins explains:

The Dutch above 50 years since finding the ill qualities and effects of French Salt, both as to Fishery uses, and for curing of Flesh for long Voyages, besides the discolouring of Butter and Cheese, Prohibited the use thereof by Law, and being at Wars with Spain, Traded to Portugal, St Tubas, and the Isle of May, for Salt granulated or kerned meerly by the heat or vigour of the Sun, and fell to the refining thereof at home by Boyling it up with Sea-water, and thereby cleansing it of the three ill Qualities, to wit, Dirt, Sand and Bittern.

Collins goes into detail on traditional salt making at both Lymington and South Shields. Lymington was a halfway house in its reliance on both sun and coal. At Shields they just used coal:

The want of Brine-Springs on the Eastern Coasts of England, begat the necessity of making much salt at sheilds, and in the Counties of Durham, and Northumberland.

The Pans there used are made of wrought Iron, of 18 or 19 foot long, 12 foot broad, and 14 inches deep; the Fewel being for the most part, a sort of crusty, drossy, mouldring Coal, taken from the upper part of the Mine, which if not spent this way, would be for little or no other use, to the prejudice of the Coal Miners, and be mingled with the better sort of Coals, to the great dammage of the Buyers, especially those of London.

The Sea-water they commonly at Spring-Tide let into Ponds called Sumps, from whence 'tis pumpt into their Pans, which are six or seven times filled, and half or more every time Boyled away, before it becomes Salt.

The poor quality of British sea (and rock) salt held back English and Scottish herring fishery exports, which sold to the cheap end of the market in Europe. The situation only improved with the quality control introduced initially by the Scots in the eighteenth century. The strong reputation of Yarmouth's and Lowestoft's red herring was probably because the high levels of smoking masked any salt defects. The slow movement from lead and iron to stainless steel salt pans eventually delivered gourmet products such as Maldon Sea Salt. Concerns these days centre on what we are depositing in the seas over and above the natural bittern.

ROCK SALT

Collins again:

> Of Salt made of the Brine from Pits
> One of the most Ancient ways to make Salt, is by boyling of Bryne from Springs or Pits; whereof the most Eminent are found in Cheshire, and Worcestershire... The Cheif in Cheshire are at Northwich, Middlewich, Namptwich, of which those at Northwich have the perheminence.

The natural brine combines fresh water with rock salt deposits—either salt domes or salt beds. In Cheshire and Worcestershire, -wich is a common place-name suffix for salt producing towns and villages. Collins provides an account of production at Droitwich:

> There are many Salt-Springs, particularly one in the great Pit at Upwich, of which is made 450 Bushels of Salt in every 24 hours, so strong that 4 Tuns of Brine make one Tun of Salt. The Brine is said to be so strong, that it cannot be Boyled in Iron-Pans, neither Cast nor Wrought, because the former breaks, and the latter is too soon Corroded... They say they are therefore driven to the use of Leaden-Pans, 5 foot and a half long, and 3 foot wide, whereof the sides and ends are beaten up.

> Their Fuel was formerly all Wood, but since the Ironworks in the Forrest of Dean have destroyed the Wood there, etc. they cannot at any resonable distance be supplied for one quarter of a Year, and are now forced to use Pit Coles, that are brought 13 or 14 miles.

Collins is a great advocate of the quality of Cheshire's and Worcestershire's rock salt. The problem it had in his time was that it was on the wrong side of the country for the major herring fisheries and land transport was expensive. Through over-fast heating it also produced smaller grains of salt, which can coagulate the surface tissues of the fish or flesh you're trying to preserve. This prevents further penetration and leads to what is called 'salt burn'.

Rock salt has been mined at Hallstatt in Austria since 5000 BCE and other salt mines have been exploited elsewhere, but it wasn't until the seventeenth century that the deposits in Cheshire began to be directly mined. With the development of the railways in the nineteenth century, transport economics and improved evaporation techniques began to shift arguments in favour of the UK's rock salt and this took over from sea salt as the prime herring curing product.

These days, the making of most salt in the UK is achieved by forcing water down a borehole into underground salt domes and salt beds. This creates what is known as *solution-mined brine*. The water is then vacuum evaporated (more reliable than sunshine in the UK), centrifuge-dried and then, for table salt, finished off by drier-coolers.

THE SUFFERING SALTWORKERS OF SOUTH SHIELDS

So sympathetic to their sad lot, Collins separately includes *A Short Narrative of the Sufferings And Case of the Salt-Workers of Sheilds, Northumberland, Durham, &C.* Beyond the greed of the English State (kings and Commonwealth), Church and the assorted tax farmers on the state's behalf, the English saltworkers' complaint focuses on unfair advantages both taken by the Scots and given to them. It is a sorry tale, but let us start with the good times.

In 1629 the French had banned the export of their Bay salt to England. The initial English response was to source their salt from the Spanish. Recognising England's need, the Spanish imposed an export tax which effectively doubled the price. In a burst of patriotic indignation, England decided to invest in its own salt production on the Tyne. But where would they put all the *Wharfs, Boyling-Houses, and Pans*? Maybe the Church could help? Why, yes, there just happened to be some 'spare neglected Church-Lands.' The Dean and Chapter would be happy for the salt producers 'to take Leases, and pay an annual Rent for the same.'

It was during the War of the Three Kingdoms (which includes the English Civil War) that, in 1644, Alexander Leslie, commander of Scotland's Army of the Solemn League and Covenant, laid siege to Newcastle upon Tyne. It was by way of being a friendly action, its military support to the English Parliament given in exchange for the promise of a civil and religious union of the Three Kingdoms on the basis of *Scottish Rules* Presbyterianism. Alexander Leslie was the Earl of Leven, in Fife and Fife was home to Scotland's salt producers. Would anybody notice if he 'dispossest divers of the Saltworkers of their Salt-Pans, by reason of their Loyalty to his Majesty, and pulled down and destroyed many others, pretending them to belong to Popish and Malignant Owners, on purpose to advance their own Manufacture of Salt?'

Leslie marched his Covenanters Army back to Scotland, but in 1648, before anyone had a chance to recover and rebuild the different saltworks, Oliver Cromwell's Commonwealth decided to put up for sale 'all lands belonging to Bishops, Deans, and Chapters,' including the derelict 'Salt Houses and Pans of the Saltworkers, that lived at South-Sheilds.' The new owners decided that all repairs and renewals would have to go through them and, for some reason, this radically increased the costs. Moreover, in the same year, 'Sir Arthur Haslerig, comming to Command at Newcastle, (to add to their Miseries,) laid on an arbitrary Imposition of 4 s. a Wey on Salt, and as much on a Chaldron of Coals, for the use of the Garrison.'

On top of all this, as indicated above, salt taxes were set at different rates in England and Scotland. Even more importantly, Scottish salt was taxed at point of sale, English at point of production. Both English and Scottish salt was a crystalline sludge from which a lot of the water would slowly drain away in transport. '20 wey [of salt] at

Sheilds, did not upon delivery make out above 12 wey at London, and sometimes less.' The Scottish producers would only ever pay tax on the delivered weight. And on top of this, taxing at point of sale meant the monitoring of production was unnecessary, which meant any amount of unregistered salt was available for smuggling.

With the smuggling of Scottish salt rife, there were various attempts at addressing the problem, but Collins notes the role of those making money out of it in maintaining the status quo. The argument was advanced by some that Scottish salt was of a better quality—others have said it was even worse. Both Tyneside's and Scotland's sea salt remained low grade products through until the technological advances of the Industrial Revolution.

Taxation of salt in the United Kingdom was abolished in 1825 as it was deemed essential to the interests of the Industrial Age and Scotland's salt production went into decline. It would be interesting to look at the capital accrued by Scottish salt in its heyday and its relationship to the dominance of Scottish herring curers throughout the United Kingdom in the nineteenth and twentieth centuries, but by then they no longer used Scottish salt.

HOME HERRING SALTING

Fiddle player and composer Chris Stout is from Fair Isle but grew up in Shetland. One ancestor, William Strong Eunson, is famous for having invented the fish filleting machine. As a child Chris went out with his dad netting the herring, although the salt herring they made was generally with fish which had come in on the commercial boats.

AN INTERVIEW WITH CHRIS STOUT

We'd rouse the herring with a sprinkling of coarse salt. As for gipping, we'd just slit under the head, take out the gills and the long gut. The gills damage the flavour and if they've been feeding, the plankton's too rich and makes the curing difficult. If you caught them, say, ten o'clock at night, you wouldn't need to take out the long gut, because they hadn't fed. If it was four o'clock in the morning, you'd maybe leave them in the net a bit, before hauling them in.

The process of salting was the same, whether commercial or for home use. For the home, it wasn't always in a barrel, it could be a box, as long as you could seal it. You'd lay them in the bottom, belly up and all in the same direction, sprinkling them with salt between each layer, building up the layers until the box or barrel was full, then you'd leave them a couple of days to settle down, before adding another layer. If you'd used a barrel you'd put the lid on and put it on its side, take the bung out and fill it with brine. Whatever else you'd used as a container, it was the same: you'd fill it to the brim with the brine and seal it, so there was no air. It would then last as long as you want—they'd all be finished before the next season, because you'd want to eat them.

To cook, you'd put them in a pan of cold water, bringing it up to the boil, then throw the water away. Depending on your taste, you could do that again, but then you'd let it simmer for ten minutes. You'd put the potatoes in the same water and that'd take away some of the salt—tatties 'n' herrin'. Beautiful! Just talking about it makes me want to go back and do it again.

SARDINE LITIGATION

> The difference which stands between
> The Cornish pilchard and sardine
> Is taxonomically nil,
> But geopolitically still
> A matter of which sardine you mean.

Why are sardines even in an encyclopaedia of the herring? Well, it is only in Europe that a herring cannot simultaneously be a sardine.

Who doesn't remember *Juicy* (1994), Biggie Smalls, The Notorious B.I.G., rapping about how, 'the opposite of a winner,' he 'used to eat sardines for dinner'? Biggie's sardines will probably have been juvenile Atlantic herrings. We don't know whether his West Coast rival Tupac ate sardines in the 'hood, but if he had, they would have been Pacific pilchards (*Sardinops sagax*). Back on the East Coast, maybe THE BEST HERRING SONG EVER is the funk/go-go Junk Yard Band's *Sardines* (1986). Their 'hood was the Barry Farm government housing project in Washington DC. 'I got sardines on my plate / I don't need no steak,' they sang. Their juvenile herrings were unconflicted signifiers of community; fish to feed the 5,000.

It's a quarter to four in the morning. The people are calling for more sardines. The singer asks his mother what he should do and she tells him he should 'do the go-go and give them some too!' Would the 5,000 have eaten them if they'd known they were herrings? (See **North American Fisheries** and Rodgers and Hammerstein's *When the Children Are Asleep*). After Europe-wide lawsuits, most of the canned sprats and herrings in the United Kingdom, which had previously been sardines, were respectively rebranded as *brisling* and *sild*...

THE GREAT SARDINE LITIGATION

Once upon a time almost any clupeiform in Europe could be pulled out of the sea and canned as a sardine. Even the English loved herring sardines. As long as they were in a can, they were OK. They liked French and Portuguese sardines too, but the Norwegian ones, imported by Tyneside grocery entrepreneur Angus Watson and sold under his Skipper brand, were cheaper. The French, Spanish and Portuguese canned juvenile pilchards, *Sardina pilchardus*; the Norwegians smoked and canned juvenile sprats and herrings, *Sprattus sprattus* and *Clupea harengus*, which often shoal together.

In 1911 the French went to court in London in pursuit of the principle that a canned sardine could only ever be a European pilchard and so it was sardine magnate Angus Watson was drawn into the Great Sardine Litigation. The Norwegians had, many years earlier, taken advantage of a collapse in French pilchard shoals to rebrand their brisling and sild products as sardines so maybe one shouldn't be too hard on the French. In his autobiography, *My Life* (1937), however, Watson looks back on the defence counsel running rings around the expert witnesses the pilchardists had called, who couldn't even recall the number of a pilchard's vertebrae or of a herring's scales—and, in one exchange, their own work:

> 'What is your view of that article?' enquired Counsel.
>
> 'It is sheer nonsense,' replied the witness.
>
> 'I gather you do not agree with the writer.' said Mr. Walter.
>
> 'Not at all,' replied the witness, 'he obviously has never given any study to the subject.'
>
> 'Would you be surprised to hear that he claims to have expert knowledge on the question?' queried Counsel.
>
> 'I don't care what he claims.' said the witness, 'I only know that he is entirely wrong in his conclusions.'
>
> Counsel paused for a moment, and then handed a slip of paper to the expert in the box. 'Look at that,' he thundered, 'it is the receipt for the payment of this article, and you have signed it, for the article was written by you.'

An initial ruling had found in favour of herring's legitimate sardineability, but in 1915, on appeal, it was finally settled in France's favour. Watson, however, had played a clever game with his *Skipper* brand. Featuring its iconic bearded 'Skipper', he ran newspaper adverts projecting it as an attack on the Englishman's right to eat his own sardines (see **Canning**). He later changed *Skipper* sardines to *Skippers*, keeping the bearded captain, but essentially renaming the fish inside (see second image section). I grew up eating *Skippers* on toast, never once thinking I was eating anything other than sardines.

The cases in London dragged on for nearly five years and, long before the EU, the French had had to pursue separate cases across Europe. Maybe the USA's entry into World War I seemed a greater priority; perhaps the French thought the Americans—with no European pilchards of their own—wouldn't have bought the hair-splitting arguments. Either way, the matter was not pursued beyond Europe. North American sardines are the way they are and elsewhere they can be all kinds of *Sardinops* or *Sardinella*. And Norwegian sild and brisling can be sold as sardines elsewhere too. The EU (Commission Regulation (EC) No 1181/2003) now recognises the following 'sardine-type products', as long as their taxonomic binomial is made clear on the label:

(a) *Sardinops melanosticus, S. neopilchardus, S. ocellatus, S. sagax, S caryleus*; (b) *Sardinella aurita, S. brasiliensis, S. maderensis, S. longiceps, S. gibbosa*; (c) *Clupea harengus*; (d) *Sprattus sprattus*; (e) *Hyperlophus vittatus*; (f) *Nematalosa vlaminghi*; (g) *Etrumeus teres*; (h) *Ethmidium maculati*; (i) *Engraulis anchoita, E. mordax, E. Ringens*; (j) *Opisthenema ogilinum*.

Watson sold his company to Unilever and the canned fish giant, John West, was formed in 1961 out of a merger with two other Unilever companies. They kept the Skippers brand, as well as selling canned sild and brisling. The sad truth is, canned herring and sprats only shift on supermarket shelves when they're called something else.

(See preface, **Y is for Why?** for the story of me and Angus Watson.)

SENSITIVITY

Herring shoals like armies could be measured in miles, but they were thought to be easily offended—by being used to improve farmers' fields, by spilt blood, by bad behaviours. During the Napoleonic Wars, the Swedes, who were waist-deep in herring fertiliser, became concerned at the detrimental effect of British warships' cannonfire on the Bohuslän herring period of the time—and it's worth noting it came to an end in 1809.

In his *Lenten Stuffe* (1599) Thomas **Nashe** reports herring sensitivity to wars and civil strife: they are a peaceloving sort. He has them upset at the unrest in Scotland following the death of Robert the Bruce, although he is vague on whether, in the late sixteenth century, they had been dismayed by the execution of several hundred Scottish **Witches** or that they'd just responded to the curses the executions had elicited.

Did they leave Tenby in the 1740s because local beggar Leekie Porridge had been beaten up or in response to his curse?

Who knows?

SHUBA & SOUR CREAM

Around the Baltic, salt herring salads bound with sour cream abound. The German *roter heringsalat* has nothing to do with red herring, bringing the straight salted version together with chopped apple, beetroot, onion, pickles and mustard before adding sour cream. Some recipes allow **Vinegar** pickled herring, but there's something between the salt and the sour cream that's satisfying—the pickles should be salt-based too. You can add things to this, but, apart from dill, which is always good with herring, it doesn't need them. There are many of such salads and some, rather than mixed, appear in layered forms. These may have provided the traditional source material for the most spectacularly beautiful of all herring salads, herring under a fur coat, or *shuba* (see second image section).

Layers of chopped salt herring, potato, onion, carrot, beetroot and mayonnaise are (or can be) topped off with chopped egg and dill. It's easy to see how mayonnaise came to take over from sour cream in the Baltic, Russia, Belarus and Ukraine. If you're not a fan of mayonnaise, it would work with sour cream and you could tell your guests it's a kind of ur-*shuba*, but the mayo adds something unctuous to the dish.

Easy to make, *shuba* always impresses and, from first time consumers it almost invariably leads to the question, 'Why a fur coat?' 'Maybe it's all the layers,' you shrug.

'The egg and dill on top... forget the colour, maybe they could look a bit like fur.' It's all unlikely, but there's another, equally improbable answer to hand. As has been explored elsewhere in this encyclopaedia, origin stories linked to herring should always be taken with a lot of salt, but...

In 1918 the merchant Anastas Bogomilov owned a number of bars in Moscow. His customers tended to drink a lot of vodka, get into fights with each other and smash the furniture. So far, so plausible. It was coming up to New Year and as a way of reducing his costs (or possibly introducing a new compensatory income stream) he asked one of his chefs, Aristarkh Prokoptsev to come up with a new recipe which would at least soak up some of the alcohol. With revolutionary fervour, in Aristarkh's hands the layer of salt herring represented the proletariat, the potatoes the peasantry. Who knows what the carrots and onions meant, but he topped it all with beetroot and a provençale sauce, both of which stood for the red flag of socialism. He called his creation *Shovinismu i Upadku—Boikot i Anafema* (boycott and anathematise all chauvinism and decadance). Try saying that after half a bottle of vodka. But Aristarkh had thought of this: the acronym ShUBA means fur coat and it became known simply as shuba.

Revolutionary zeal rarely lasts forever and at some point someone added *herrings under a* as an alternative explanation. The provençale may have been replaced by mayonnaise even before the People's Commissariat of the Food Industry came into being.

Tsarist Russia with its aristocracy in love with all things French had fallen for mayonnaise early. The Soviet Union might have rejected it as bourgeois, but by then the people had already claimed it as a fundamental right. In 1936 Anastas Mikoyan, the People's Commissar for the Food Industry visited the USA to learn about mass production processes and came back with everything he needed to introduce a mayonnaise gloop across the USSR. Stalin had personally authorised production and distribution and in 1939 Mikoyan oversaw publication of *The Book of Tasty and Healthy Food*, which sang its praises. Some say Soviet mayonnaise helped mask the quality of some Soviet foods, but the same might be said of its popularity in the West. The *CCCP Cook Book* (2015) describes a serious up-mayonnaising of Soviet food culture in the 1960s.

INGREDIENTS

4 salt herring fillets, chopped
Some specify fillets preserved in oil, some add oil separately, some don't mention it.

1 onion, finely chopped
White, yellow and red are variously specified; some suggest brief boiling to soften the flavour, but a bit of bite is good.

2 medium potatoes, peeled, boiled and grated or diced small
Ideally a variety between waxy and floury should be used.

2 medium carrots, peeled, boiled and grated or diced small
Some suggest fresh grated (patted dry to remove moisture).

2 beetroots, boiled or baked in foil, peeled and grated

Mayonnaise
Amounts vary between 200 and 350 ml.

2 boiled eggs
Whites and yolks separated, each finely grated.

Dill to garnish

METHOD

Prepare the ingredients before assembly. For a multi-coloured cake effect, use an upside down 7" removable-base cake tin (base removed), working within it, directly on to a serving plate: lift the tin to reveal when set. For the mound effect, just smooth each layer over the edges of the one below.

You can start with a layer of herring, followed by onion, then potato or use half the potato as layer 1, top it with the herring, then onion, then the rest of the potato. At this point introduce a modest lattice of mayonnaise. Add the carrot, then another modest mayonnaise lattice, then the beetroot. Now add a good spread of mayonnaise and top with the grated egg whites, the grated yolks and the dill. Don't press down the layers, but refrigerate for at least 6 hours, preferably overnight. When it's cold, carefully lift the cake tin to reveal it in all its glory. It should be possible to cut slices.

Marxist-Leninists may call for the provençale's return and/or vodka. Many meals would be improved by a toast, 'To ShUBA!'

SMITH, ADAM: THE WEALTH OF NATIONS

Adam Smith was not a bad man—he had his little ways. The dogmas of neoliberalism and 'free' markets are not entirely down to him, but his thoughts on the herring fisheries do not burnish his reputation. Added to Book IV in the 1784 edition of *An Inquiry into the Nature and Causes of the Wealth of Nations*, they are, at best, disingenuous.

His herring paragraphs and figures presented an argument against the 'bounties': government subsidies aimed at encouraging the large, decked herring busses which enabled long voyages, offshore fishing and onboard processing. First Scottish, then Scottish and English, then British kings, queens and governments had been unsuccessfully trying to encourage a home buss fleet for 300 years. The rapid growth of Dutch wealth, empire and naval power had been attributed, by the Dutch themselves, to their buss fishery off the coasts of Britain. The Dutch had employed subsidies, but Smith was against them. If you were going to have subsidies, he advocated a shift towards support for the smaller, undecked boat fishery, which Smith saw suffering on the Firth of the Forth. Unlike today's free-marketeers, Smith thought any government investment should benefit the poor at the very least.

Born in Kirkcaldy, Smith grew up with a herring fishery on his doorstep. In 1778 he was appointed Commissioner of Customs in Edinburgh. He knew about taxes and subsidies. Today's excitable free marketeers still quote his herring buss quip, 'It has, I am afraid, been too common for the vessels to fit out for the sole purpose of catching, not the fish but the bounty.' It is clever. Maybe we can forgive him the pleasure taken in his own witticism, but it did not and does not stand.

THE INVISIBLE HAND

There was an earlier bounty awarded on each exported barrel of salted herring, but in 1750 (see **Pamphleteers**) a bounty was introduced on the buss tonnage to encourage the necessary boat building. Smith saw subsidy as support for businesses which simply aren't profitable enough. Take it away and a merchant's 'own interest would soon oblige him to employ his stock in another way.' Elsewhere in Book IV, Smith explains how, acting in his own interest (the pursuit of the greatest profit), each individual makes the choices which are best for the nation. He similarly argues, in intending to 'advance the interest of the society' rather than his own, the individual usually doesn't.

Back to the herrings: 'the effect of the bounties… can only be to force the trade of a country into a channel much less advantageous than that in which it would naturally run of its own accord.' In *The Theory of Moral Sentiments* (1759) Smith had already noted the mysterious way in which the rich, 'are led by an invisible hand to make nearly the same distribution of the necessaries of life, which would have been made, had the earth been divided into equal portions among all its inhabitants.' Viewed from the twenty first century such naivety may seem staggering, but it was still early days for capitalism.

SMITH AND THE ARGUMENTS BEHIND THE BOUNTIES

The arguments of herring buss advocates were well-rehearsed and generally available, but Smith does not really engage. Nor does he tackle the obvious point that small, undecked boats were limited by weather, distance and capacity from a full exploitation of the extent of the herring resource, which should have been more accessible to Britain than to the Dutch.

He dismisses, as cost inefficient, the argument that fishermen trained in handling larger vessels provided a pool of skilled seamen, facilitating the development of a maritime empire, a line taken directly from the Dutch. Smith, whilst wanting global trade, criticised the upkeep costs of colonialism, but he does not take the opportunity, at this point, to clarify his thinking.

Smith's analysis restricts any understanding of buss economics to activity in Scottish waters, which seems willful. The whole idea of the buss fishery was predicated on the exploitation of Britain's entire eastern seaboard and much of its western one. On busses he argues, 'the mode of fishing… seems not so well adapted to the situation of Scotland,' which is arrant nonsense. Small boats were effective, even necessary, for some inshore fishing, but he cannot have been blind to the Dutch *Groote Visserye's* hugely prized success off Scottish coasts since the early fifteenth century.

Even more problematic is his lack of engagement with quality control. The bounties deliberately introduced leverage. In order to receive them, the busses had to adopt appropriate curing procedures. It is clear, from a letter Smith wrote to William Eden in 1780, he was fully aware of the problem: 'Dutch cured Herrings' are so 'vastly superior to British cured you can scarcely imagine the difference.' The quality of British salt herring was a barrier to trade. Dutch protectionism banned the import of any foreign salted herring and Britain banned the Dutch product. In his letter Smith argues, if the ban were lifted, competition would rapidly improve the quality of British curing. It is interesting to note, he does not ever say why his 'invisible hand' had made no headway over the previous 300 years. It is also interesting to note that first Scottish, then English herring curing only began to improve from the second half of the eighteenth century onwards.

COOKING THE BOOKS

Smith's sins of omission go further. Jenkins, in *The Herring and the Herring Fisheries* (1927), accuses Smith of 'deliberate manipulation of statistics.' For the purposes of making claims for the bounties, buss owners only submitted the returns from their first fishing voyage of the year—which would be in Scottish waters. The buss fishery was predicated on two or three voyages a year, each lasting up to two months or more. Smith bases his statistical bounties-to-catch barrel count exclusively on the submitted returns, ie on the first voyage alone. An easy mistake, perhaps, but a disappointing one if you're a tax inspector.

Jenkins suggests the years (1771–81), chosen by Smith for statistical analysis, aligns suspiciously with a series of unusually low catches. Both boat and buss fisheries might have suffered from the American War of Independence, which disrupted Scotland's lucrative herring trade with the slave plantations of the Caribbean. The period also fell in the middle of the greatest 60-year Bohuslän herring boom ever (see **Swedish Fisheries**). The Swedes were exporting to the Caribbean directly as well as to Britain's provisioning fleet in the Shannon. It is hard to assess the impact of the White Herring Fishery Act of 1778, which, at the prompting of a Glasgow MP, put back the authorised starting date for the British buss fleet from June to October, cutting out all the East Coast herring seasons from Shetland to Scarborough... On all these factors, however, Smith is silent.

His other arguments are that 'the herring buss bounty seems too large and is proportioned to the burden of the ship, not to her diligence or success.' Two years after his new *Wealth of Nations* edition, influenced by its arguments for boat fishery subsidy, the government extended bounties accordingly. It was a win, but maybe not one at the heart of Smith's economic philosophy. The man can be forgiven for not imagining the growth of the British—and particularly the Scottish—herring industry, but whether the bounties were too large or not, they did a job in building the momentum from which it became possible. As the fishery—along with the reputation of the Scotch cure—grew, they were reduced and then abolished.

The busses themselves played a part in this growth, although, even in the eighteenth century, they were being superseded by the luggers, which combined bounty-qualifying tonnages, reliable access to offshore shoals and rapid returns-to-port for onshore curing. Scotland became a leader in the development of its traditional small boats through half-decking, full-decking and considerable increases in size (see **Herring Boats**).

SMOKEHOUSE TALE

It was 2021 and I'd managed to trace only two smokers in the United Kingdom still producing red herring. Both of them were in Lowestoft. There was Will Buckenham at The Old Smokehouse in Raglan Street, founded in 1760 and—predating the kipper—the oldest working smokery in the country. And there was Gerry Skews at Waveney Valley Smokehouse, a new operation using modern stainless-steel ovens, but in an old traditional building. I visited both and tasted Gerry's reds, which were excellent. It was June and Will had long since run out.

For reds he would only smoke November's inshore catch. They were always ready by the end of January and gone by Easter. He gives ten weeks as the smoking period for reds, but it will have been intermittent. Hung on their speats, they will have been left up, waiting on the firing for the next batch of kippers and bloaters. His kippers and bloaters were wonderful, but when I phoned up, planning a trip to taste his reds the following February, due to COVID it had not been worth making any that year. By the following year the pandemic had driven him out of business. Moore's

Smokehouse in Peel on the Isle of Man, which opened in 1882, also closed recently. The old smokehouses are disappearing. Robson's in Craster and Fortune's in Whitby still smoke their kippers the old way, walls coated with over a hundred years of tar. There are others, but it is an endangered tradition.

WILL BUCKENHAM'S TALE, JUNE 2021

Me dad was here before I was here. He'd probably been here thirty, thirty-five years himself. He passed away about fifteen or twenty year ago and I've been here ever since. So probably, me dad and meself have been doing it the best part of fifty years between us. I picked up everything what I needed to know off him, while he was going, 'cause he'd done smoking all his life, while I've only done it part of my life.

Raglan Street

To start with, me dad used to work at a smokehouse up in Clapham Road and he'd probably done twenty five, thirty years up there as a smoker. His boss, who was in Norwich, she kept saying she was going to close it down and everything was uncertain. Me dad got offered this smokehouse, which is in Raglan Street, which had been empty for about two or three years, by Mr Donny Cole, who'd bought it off Reggie Reynolds. The Reynoldses had been here for years and years and years, probably going back to the First World War. But, anyway, me dad come in here and rented it off the Coles for probably the best part of eighteen years. And Donny Cole asked me dad to buy it, so me dad said to me, if you were going to run it when he'd go, he'd buy it, which is exactly what he done. And when he passed away he left it to me from then, so that's how I become to get it. But the Reynoldses were here before we were all here and a lot of people still know it, even today as Reynolds' Smokehouse. It hain't been Reynolds' for the best past of fifty years, but people don't forget.

Red Herring

We still do the red herrin', but to make a red herrin', you can't just use any herrin' you want. That's got to be an October, November herring. October is when the fishin' used to start in Lowestoft. We used to probably have a hundred ships or a hundred boats go out to catch herrin' and that was the peak time. We used to make red herrin' out of them herrin', which was a full herrin' and a local herrin'. And they were the best ones. It's like an apple. You get keepin' apples and you get non-keepin' apples, well the red herrin' were the keepers and you could make them into red herrin', because it takes a long time to make a red herrin'.

So we do buy the herrin' from October, November and they takes ten weeks to smoke, but what you've got to do first of all is salt them, heavily salt them. That's where the word come in, *rousin'* the herrin', because they used to put them in big vats, years ago, and they used to go in there with a big shovel and turn them over and add more salt to them and after seventy two hours they used to get them all out, put them in the smokehouse and start smokin' them: smoke them for about ten weeks before they were ready. They'd go in as a silver fish and come out as like a golden colour, so that's the smoke got into them and then they're preserved. You can keep them.

The old story was that Reggie Reynolds had some red herrin' and he got called up to war an' he left them in a coal bunker out in the garden here and he come back in five years, after the war had finished, and he went to the coal bunker, he got them out of the coal bunker and he ate them. Whether that's a true story or not, I do not know, but that was one of the stories of the red herrin'.

Tenterhooks

Of course, a lot of people think red herring's not a real thing. Same as you hear of people *bein' on tenterhooks*. Well, we use tenterhooks. It's what we hang our kippers on. That's what they are called: tenterhooks. Yeah. Yeah. It's an actual word. It's like they say, *Oh, it's a red herrin'*. Well, *red herrin'* is a red herrin' and a *tenterhook* is a tenterhook. Yeah. Kippers hang on balks. They're long balks and they've got all little hooks in them and you hang your kippers on them, which are your tenterhooks. Bloaters we put on a wooden speat an' haddocks go on a metal rod, which is a double and they go acrosst or otherwise they'd fall off. I've never ever bought any tenterhooks, because we've still got one or two here what we're still usin' if we need to replace 'em. I do believe you used to order 'em from Scotland. But, yeah, the tenterhook is a real thing and so is a red herrin'.

Supplies & Sizes

You can still buy the herrin' for as much as what we can sell. You can still buy what you want, in the right situation, as long as they're there. Even going back fifty, sixty, seventy years ago, they used to have good years and bad years. Sometimes we have bad years here where you don't get hardly any and then another year there'll be as much as you want. I've even seen boats comin' in now with probably thirty, forty, fifty, a hundred stone on 'em. Then you'd see another boat come in with about five stone on 'em. You just can't tell what you're going to get when you put your nets over.

You can't rely on just local fish anymore, because we haven't got no big vessels goin' in and out of Lowestoft. So, if you just relied on the longshore, you'd probably have cod and plaice and a couple of other bits and pieces and that'd be all you had. That's the reason why the fish merchants do bring stuff in from Grimsby… Hull… They bring it from everywhere by lorry to keep us going anyway. If it wasn't for them doing it, then obviously we wouldn't have the variety of fish and you wouldn't be able to get a livin' and if you can't get a livin' you can't be here. The kippers we make, the herrin' we buy now come from Norway, 'cause the Norwegians have got a big fishin' fleet still and they can supply everybody with the herrin' they want and they have nice big ones and they can make really, really good kippers.

We do kippers, we do bloaters. In the right season, like in October, November we do cut the small herrin' and we do bloater the small herrin', because you can't beat them, but, 'cause of the size of them, some people say, 'Oh I could eat twelve o' them!' Yeah, but they can't eat twelve of the Norwegian ones, because they're a lot, lot bigger. On the small herrin' they could do, but they couldn't eat twelve of the big ones.

Scottish Girls

The small herrin' were the local herrin'. They'd start the season about the 10th, 11th of October, every year, and the fishing fleet used to go out and catch just, literally, herrin' for the market here. The Scottish girls come down and put them in barrels, along the beach somewhere, used to put them in big barrels and salt them all down and they'd send them all to wherever they sent them to. The Scottish girls used to follow the herrin' down the coast from Scotland all the way down and round the country, wherever the herrin' were next, each place.

Declining Markets

A lot of the people who buy them are just locals. A lot of our trade do come from Norwich. A lot of people come from Norwich down to Lowestoft to get good quality smoked fish, kippers, red herrin' when we've got 'em, because they know that's better than what they can get in the city. And we get a lot of people from Felixtowe, places like that. I've noticed over the years, you do a few less red herrin' each year, because you only want to be sellin' them for, say, six months after you've got 'em done. Sales of red herrin' and kippers and bloaters have all dropped down over the years, because there's too many takeaway shops, MacDonalds, too many convenience foods and people just don't want the inconvenience of having to cook it.

Goin' back over the years, there was roughly two hundred and eighty of these smokehouses in Lowestoft. There was virtually one on every street corner. That's the volume of herrin' what was comin' in at the time. I ain't gonna say they was all used all the time, 'cause obviously if you were followin' the fish down, if you come from Scotland and you got smokers down, you'd probably just use all the herring were here and then you'd move somewhere else. But, yeah, there was two hundred and eighty of these. And, yeah, there's now probably about, what? Proper ones, like what we call original, probably about two.

Nowadays, they bring in what we call as hot smoked, which we can't do. That cooks the fish at the same time. We can't do that. We're still traditionally the cold smoke. We still end up with a product what you've got to cook at the end. Yeah. Yeah. Still a lot better, really.

Brining & Smoking

Everything you do you have to use a brine. You can't smoke anything without a brine. So when you buy your herrin' in, you cut 'em to be kippers, which obviously, you stand and cut 'em all and open them up, scrape all the bone, wash 'em all through, then they go in a salt brine for about fifteen to twenty minutes. You then take them out of there and they hang in the smokehouse for about, say, three or four hours and then you can light a fire up on them.

A traditional kipper fire is five pods, like a pyramid, and you put five pods down. You can be a mile long, as long as you do your fives all the way down: one, one, one in the middle, one, one, one in the middle… You could keep going for a mile long: dunt matter how long it is. The five fires is what you need for a traditional kipper fire.

The same as bloaters. We brine them for about four or five hours, just in salt, and then speat them up—what we call speats. We do them as the whole fish and the speat just go through the gills. Then you put them in the smokehouse and they stay for about four or five hours before you light the fires. It just gives them the chance to drip dry a little bit, get some of the water off. If not, if you try to light them up too early, the water what's drippin' off everything will put the fires out. So you've got to let them drain a little bit, otherwise your fires'll keep going out. I've had that problem before.

A kipper is done overnight. I'll just light a fire about half past four and some days—or some mornin's—you come back and there's still a little bit of red ember left. So they smoke from half past four to, probably, seven o'clock, you know, constantly smokin'. An' that does it. A bloater'll take exactly the same time. You can put them in beside the kippers or underneath the kippers or above the kippers and they will smoke in the same time as it does to do a kipper.

The little sprat, when we smoke the sprats in the wintertime, they take two nights to smoke. Although they're tiny, the smoke don't go into them in one night, you have to give them two nights. You'd think, being a smaller fish, they'd be done in a matter of hours. No. They take us two nights. 'Cause they're like a miniature, if you like, of red herring. They'll come out a nice an' strong flavour and they're really good, but we only do them in about November time.

Salt & Smoke

The salt, that is where the problem is, because, years ago people never had fridges, people never had freezers, so salt was like a preservative and you needed that to keep anything, where, nowadays you don't need to salt, because you can buy 'em, take 'em home an' freeze 'em. An' that's why you don't need the salt and obviously people don't want the salt in their own bodies like they used to anyway.

Salt, in our way, is not a preservative, not for kippers an' that. It's just a thing we have to do so we can smoke 'em. Yeah. Yeah. 'Cause if you heavily salt, like a red herrin', that's preserved. That's preserved. But with a kipper you only want so much salt in 'em, so you don't need to freeze 'em. Because if you put a kipper or a bloater into a freezer, that do gain 1% more salt by freezin' it. Yeah. I don't know how a freezer can do that, but that's what a freezer can do.

Years ago there'd have been two smokers here. You'd have had a day smoker and a nighttime smoker, because when you'd got a lot of the stuff in the house, you'd need to bring 'em down: bring the bottom layers all down and then bring all the top ones down and then re-lay another small fire, just to finish them top ones off, because the smoke'd be gettin' a bit weaker as it go through the fish. Yeah. So, then you'd need two smokers, but now we just do it with one smoker, 'cause you ain't got to go right to the very top like we used to. Yeah. There's less demand, less herrin' so therefore you haven't got to do that.

Kippers by Post

I can remember we used to have what we call as a swing bridge down here and there used to be a restaurant and a place on the corner, used to be called Fane's. They used to be able to send kippers away from there. And when we were workin' up at Harry Groom's smokehouse, which was in Clapham Road, we used to send a hundred stone of kippers down there in a day and they'd be boxed in pairs and sent away. That's how many tourists we had here in them days. And they'd send them back to their relations all over the country. And then Fane's 'd be phonin' up in the afternoon, 'Have you got any more kippers?' 'cause they'd run out. That's the quantities that you'd be able to do then. But not now.

We only serve to the general public, now. Years ago, you used to have a good postal service and they would guarantee the next day delivery and that people would get the product the next day, which was no problem. But if you try to put kippers through the post today, somebody could get 'em tomorrow, they could get them next Wednesday, next Thursday. You just cannot guarantee on the postal service what we've got today to what you could goin' back probably sixty or seventy years ago, when it was guaranteed.

I do believe Yarmouth kept their guarantee, kept their postal goin' for quite a long time, up to two or three year ago, but they took Lowestoft's away many, many years ago. It's all right sending something away and they get it first thing tomorrow mornin'. Fine. But you get a warm night or a hot night and that fish is layin' in a sortin' office somewhere, that ain't goin' to get there as good.

How to Eat Reds

The way me dad always told me, what you do with them is you simmer 'em in water, plain water for about six minutes. That just helps take some of the salt out and put some of the moisture back into 'em. And then you tip the water off and you put the red herrin' on to your plate and have it with a little bit of English mustard and that kills the salt. And you can't beat 'em for the flavour. I've got one or two friends who come in an' they tell me they slice theirs up and eat 'em as they are. They just cut the skin off and eat the flesh. Yeah.

SOVEREIGNTY OF THE SEAS

Maritime sovereignty was not always the top priority of earthly powers and potentates. Consistent enforcement required a standing navy and the longer the coastline, the more that cost. Scotland has a huge coastline and had very little money; the Dutch at half the size and with a relatively small coast were, from the Scottish perspective, fabulously wealthy. This rankled with the Scottish kings, and all the more so because the Dutch put their economic miracle down to the herring shoals God had provided specifically for them off Scotland (and England). When, in 1603, Scotland's James VI was crowned James I of England, Stuart obsession with maritime sovereignty increased in proportion to their additional seashores. When, in 1634, James' son Charles commissioned the building of a flagship he was thinking about herring and he named it *Sovereign of the Seas*.

It is not that maritime sovereignty had not been a concern before the Stuarts, but, in emergencies, ships could be requisitioned from merchants and fishermen. Imports generally required ports, where goods could be taxed. Strangers who wished to fish in one's waters could pay a fee and one's nation would be told, 'These are our friends.' Should a stranger not choose to be a friend, one could rely upon the natural xenophobia of one's own fishermen. Fish had to be cured, nets had to be dried and mended, provisions had to be purchased, vast quantities of beer had to be drunk: money was made and there was always the danger of this trumping xenophobia, but strangers had to come ashore, where they were vulnerable.

The problem came with the Dutch early fifteenth-century invention of the herring buss (see **Herring Boats**), a factory ship which did not need to come ashore; and which was considerably bigger than the boats of one's xenophobic subjects. It is true that the busses were vulnerable to piracy, but this had led to convoys accompanied by the kind of men-of-war the Scots had not been able to afford and which even the English did not possess in any number.

CANNON SHOTS & CROW'S NEST KENNINGS

How far did early concepts of maritime sovereignty extend? In the early seventeenth century the Dutch were advocates of *the cannon shot rule*—the distance from which a shore-mounted cannon might stand a reasonable chance of hitting something other than water. At the time this was only about a mile, but cannons improved and out of this came the three mile limit to territorial waters. The Stuarts favoured *a land's kenning*—fourteen landlubber's miles or twelve nautical ones (the twelve-mile limit), based on the distance from which, up in the crow's nest at the top of the main mast, a sailor (on a fair day and with good eyesight) might see land.

Standing in an open fishing boat with your eye 5 feet above sea level the horizon is only 2.738 miles away. A crow's nest would have to be 105 feet above the deck for the sailor to make out a horizon at 12 nautical miles and a ship would need a keel length between 78 and 84 feet to support such a mast. Only the very largest medieval cogs would have been able to ken 12 nauticals. With cliffs or coastal hills, you could achieve some fairly satisfactory kenning, but good luck without them. Taking refraction, visibility degradation, weather and atmospherics into account, 12 nautical miles was always a best-case scenario, but with a 127 foot keel *Sovereign of the Seas* was going to give you a good shot. In the event of any dispute between crow's nests it would also have more cannons than any ship in the Dutch navy.

RELATIONS WITH THE DUTCH

England had been comparatively relaxed about the Dutch busses. For much of the sixteenth century, The Netherlands were still part of the Holy Roman Empire. Henry VIII blew hot and cold with Emperor Charles V, but in one of the warmer phases he may even have granted Dutch herring fishers free access to English waters (they claimed he had, anyway). With the Dutch Revolt of the 1560s, a new Protestant nation emerged. Even more convinced of its God-given, herring shoal-funded destiny, it could have become a bone of contention, but Elizabeth I was more interested in its potential as an ally against Catholic Spain and France.

On its own Scotland had lacked the heft to deal either with the Holy Roman Empire or the new Dutch state. In 1532, James V had improbably declared war. Largely forgotten these days, it lasted nine years. There is a story of Dutch fishermen's heads being sent home pickled in their own brine, but although his licensed privateers seized a few busses, it probably was not as many as other privateers had and at the cost of reciprocal losses. James VI & I saw his new 'united' kingdom as heft at last.

JURISPRUDENCE

The Dutch played a long game. King James I shouted at their ambassadors, but England's weakened navy offered him few other options. His fleet could be counted in tens, while the Dutch busses were counted in hundreds, never mind their navy.

A cat was thrown among the pigeons when the Dutch commissioned one of their renowned jurists, Hugo Grotius, to write and publish *Mare Liberum* (The Free Sea, 1609). Technically it had nothing to do with herrings. The Portuguese had complained about a Dutch East Indiaman seizing one of their vessels in what they considered to be Portuguese East Indian waters. Grotius challenged the very concept of waters that were 'Portuguese'. The sea, he said, was more like the air than it was like the land:

> The air belongs to this class of things for two reasons. First it is not susceptible of occupation; and second its common use is destined for all men. For the same reasons the sea is common to all, because it is so limitless that it cannot become a possession of any one, and because it is adapted for the use of all, whether we consider it from the point of view of navigation or of fisheries.

Grotius later claimed he had only been talking about the freedom to seize other nations' ships on the 'high seas'—although his high seas began only a mile offshore. James understandably read *Mare Liberum* as an attack on his herring rights and commissioned top English lawyer John Selden to pen a counterblast, *Mare Clausum* (The Closed Sea). He could have asked Scottish jurist William Welwod, who had already written the first book on maritime law, *The Sea-Law of Scotland* (1590). Welwod wrote a response to Grotius, anyway, updating and expanding the earlier work with *An Abridgement of All Sea-Laws* (1613). From a fishing perspective, his arguments are by far the most interesting:

> If the uses of the Seas may bee in any respect forbidden and stayed, it should be chiefly for the fishing, as by which the fishes may be said to bee exhaust and wasted; which, daily experience these twenty yeares past and more, hath declared to be ever true: for whereas aforetime the white fishes daily abounded even into all the shoares on the Easterne coast of Scotland; now forsooth by the neere and daily approaching of the busse Fishers the sholes of fishes are broken, and so farre scattered away from our shores and coasts, that no fish now can be found

worthy of any paines and travels; to the impoverishing of all the sort of our home-fishers, and to the great damage of all the Nation.

It still resonates: maritime sovereignty should first and foremost protect the livelihoods of those who fish from a sovereign's coastline. James wanted grandiloquence, and Selden dug up the historical precedent of England's Edgar I, who had claimed to be *King of the Seas* (he may have only been claiming lordship over various islands, but words is words). Selden also claimed the precedent of King Canute sitting on his throne on the beach and addressing the waves:

Thou, O sea, art under my dominion, like the land on which I sit; nor is there anyone who dares resist my commands. I therefore enjoin thee not to come upon my land, nor to presume to wet the feet or garments of thy lord.

Canute had intended a demonstration of the limits to earthly power, but, for Selden, sovereignty had clearly been asserted. James liked *Mare Clausum*, but he was a cautious man and chose not to aggravate a difficult situation. He did not publish it.

ENTER CHARLES I

The English navy stood at a mere thirty ships in 1625, when Charles was crowned King of England, Scotland, Ireland and France—choosing to ignore the fact that Calais, the very last bit of English France, had been lost in 1558. Meanwhile, the Dutch navy and the Dunkirk privateers weren't even respecting the canon shot rule, thinking nothing of chasing each other into English ports, even marching across English soil.

Charles was not a cautious man. As King of France he laid claim to its land's kenning too. He'd happily ensure peaceable traffic through the English Channel for all nations' merchantmen. As long as they lowered their flags respectfully, he'd neither seize nor sink them. The wily Cardinal Richelieu, in charge of the French navy, simply told it not to raise its flags in the first place.

AN ASSOCIATION FOR THE FISHING

Charles had a vision of a united British herring fishery, just like the Dutch one. It would be An Association for the Fishing, a joint stock company as part of which English adventurers could fish in Scottish waters, Scottish in English and everybody else would have to pay. He wrote to the Scottish parliament:

> This is a worke of so great good to both my kingdomes that I have thought good by these few lynes of my owne hand seriouslie to recommend it unto yow. The furthering or hindering of whiche will ather oblige me or disoblige me more then anie one business that hes happened in my tyme.

The Scottish parliament helpfully drew a map of the waters they would specifically like to reserve for Scottish boats: all the firths and The Minch on top of the fourteen miles out, for the purpose of calculating which, the Outer Hebrides and Orkneys were to be considered as part of the mainland. The Shetlands had their own fourteen miles, but the English would be welcome to the herrings off Fair Isle.

Charles pulled the kind of rank only divine right grants you, but, when it came to it, neither the English nor the Scots invested in anywhere remotely close to the 200 British busses of Charles' plans—and such English adventurers as there were proved incompetent fishermen. Given time they might have learnt, but most of the handful of busses built or bought were seized either by the Dutch or by the Dunkirk privateers.

SOVEREIGN OF THE SEAS

Charles' naval shipbuilding programme was also generating a few problems. His new flagship, still under construction, had been magnificently imagined: Selden writ large. The decorative design had been provided by the poet, playwright and set designer Thomas Heywood, working with court artist Anthony van Dyke. Conceived in black and gold it sported elaborate carvings and inspirational mottos. Heywood himself was inspired to write an account of its construction:

> What Artist tooke in hand this ship to frame?
> Or Who can guesse from whence these tall Okes came?
> Unlesse from the ful grown Dodonean grove,
> A Wildernesse sole sacred unto Jove.
> What Eye such brave Materials hath beheld?
> Or by what Axes were these Timbers feld?

This is where things get a bit personal between me and Charles I. The tall oaks did not come from any Dodonean Grove. Mostly they came from Chopwell Wood, to the South West of Newcastle upon Tyne and just behind our house as I write. It has never recovered from the loss of every single mature and healthy oak. But let us put that to one side.

With the timber still seasoning, in 1635 Charles at last published Selden's *Mare Clausum*. It was of a piece with *Sovereign of the Seas*, which he knew was going to be a corker. The black paint was cheap enough, but the gilding came to £6,691. Its 102 cannons came to £26,442, each inscribed (at an extra £3 a pop) with *Carolus Edgari sceptrum stabilivit aquarum* (Charles established Edgar's sceptre of the waters). Twelve of them later had to be removed because they affected the ship's stability, but never mind: King Edgar himself rode its beak-head on a horse, trampling the heads of all seven kings of the Anglo-Saxon heptarchy.

A contemporary picture of it carries a Latin poem by Henry Jacob and its English translation by Thomas Cary (some suggest a variant spelling for the poet Thomas Carew, but Carew was quite a good poet):

> Triton's auspicious Sound usher Thy raigne
> O're the curl'd billows, Royal SOVERAINE,
> Monarchal ship, whose Fabrick doth outpride
> The Pharos, Collosse, Memphique Pyramide...

The total cost of *Sovereign of the Seas* was £65,586. Naval building was funded through Ship Money, an occasional tax levied on coastal towns for the naval protection offered their fishermen, merchants and harbour investments. A flagship, however, needs a fleet and on top of *Sovereign of the Seas*, Ship Money had to pay for all of these other necessary new ships. Charles extended the taxation to his inland towns. The Dutch had long done the same, but, there, the population believed the whole nation benefited from the herring fishery profits. Heywood wrote, optimistically:

> Seeing his Majesty is at this infinite charge, both for the honour of this Nation, and the security of his Kingdome, it should bee a great spur and incouragement to all his faithful and loving Subjects to bee liberall and willing Contributaries towards the Ship-money.

In England it wasn't and they weren't. Nor did it help that the expanding navy wasn't instilling fear in other navies. And then there was the question of that Spanish fleet parked off the Isle of Wight. Charles had signed a secret treaty with Spain as an ally against the Dutch and the French, but he could not tell his people, 'The Spanish are our friends', as he was suspected of being a closet Papist.

He sent ships north under the Earl of Northumberland and a number of Dutch fishermen did pay for one of his personally signed licences. The amount secured, set against the expedition's costs, was glossed over, but the following season the Dutch navy came north in numbers. The English tactical retreat seemed of a piece with its other humiliations.

England's taxpayers were not happy. In 1649 Charles lay his head on an oak block which might have come from anywhere except Chopwell Wood, where there was nothing left of sufficient size. *Sovereign of the Seas*, meanwhile, did not see action until the Battle of the Kentish Knock (1652). It was briefly renamed *Commonwealth*, then just *Sovereign*. The Dutch, when they saw it, were genuinely impressed. They called her *Den Gulden Duvel*, the Golden Devil.

SURSTRÖMMING

Surströmming is fermented herring—*strömming* is the word for the smaller **Baltic Herring**; *sur* means sour. A Swedish delicacy from the Gulf of Bothnia, it is salted enough to discourage dangerous bacteria and the decomposition of the protein, but not quite enough to prevent fermentation and the good bacteria, which make it sour. It is a food to be eaten outdoors and in good company. A bucket of water is advisable.

Once upon a time the whole process will have been done in the barrel, but these days it is started off in barrels and then canned. Fermentation continues in the can, which consequently swells visibly as the noxious gases expand. Hydrogen sulphide, with its smell of rotten eggs, is joined by propionic and butyric acid, both of which also carry strong perfumes considered by some to be anti-social.

By tradition and necessity the cans are opened outside and under water (the bucket). This allows the gases to escape without spraying your face or clothing. If you choose to take it into the kitchen or dining room after opening, it has the capacity to penetrate every room of a reasonable-sized house with sulphurous intimations of mortality. Different brands can vary in strength, but some aficionados like to wait for the swelling cans to approach spherical, before pronouncing it ready, although this can risk liquification.

You can reduce both smell and strength by washing the fish once it is out of the can, but this is frowned upon. At their moderately advanced stage of decomposition, filleting the herrings is easy, but you can also buy it ready filleted. You take a fillet and lay it on a piece of buttered Swedish flatbread (*tunnbröd*) together with slices of raw onion and boiled potato. If you like, you can take another slice of buttered flatbread and make it into a sandwich. It is at this point that the good company comes in. Ideally, each mouthful should be washed down with ice cold schnapps or aquavit. Everybody then breaks into song. After the song, another mouthful and repeat. Fermented herring may be an acquired taste: the flavour is strong but far from unpleasant; the texture may be a little slimy, but it slips down a treat. There is more than an element of celebratory ritual in it all. 'Death, where is thy sting-a-ling-a-ling?' Together, you have faced it. Together, you have swallowed your fear and you are all still alive. You sing because it is good to be alive and singing together.

AN ORIGIN STORY

In *North Atlantic Seafood* (1979), Alan Davidson recounts a suspiciously precise origin story given to him by Dr Alander of Göteborg, who had been told it by a fishery inspector in the Gulf of Bothnia. Some inhabitants of sixteenth-century Gävle set sail every spring in search of herring, which they salted at sea. The good ship *Haxe*, their boat, accommodated wives and children as well as goats, empty barrels and a store of salt. Having fished all summer, they would return and sell their catch at Älvekarleby. One year they caught more than their supply of salt could properly preserve: some of the herring began to ferment. Unable to sell it to their sensible Swedish customers, luckily they came across some guileless forest people—Finns—to whom, confident they would never see them again, they sold the semi-salted stuff. Next year, they set sail with ample salt. They returned with their perfectly preserved herrings, only to find the forest people waiting for them and turning their noses up at what was on offer. 'Give us the same as last year,' they demanded. Traditional Swedish attitudes to the Finns are much the same as those informing English jokes about the Irish.

The barrels are opened each year around August 21st. Another fishery official told Davidson of the time when, as a young man on the island of Ulvön, he witnessed 200 barrels being opened. Birds began to drop dead from the sky and all tugmasters in the surrounding seas immediately changed course for the island's harbour.

Fermenting Fish

Fish fermentation has a long history. Norwegians do it with trout, producing the slightly milder *rakørret*. *Liquamen* and *garum*, the fermented fish sauces of the Romans, will have come with a broadly similar smell. Fermented **Dried Herring** is popular in the Phillipines, whilst *Fesikh*—salted, fermented and dried grey mullet—is popular at Egypt's *Sham Ennessim* festival (see **Mediterranean Food**). There are apparently no rock salt deposits in Sweden and it is obviously harder to get it from the low saline waters of the Gulf of Bothnia.

Some twenty-first century cultures have lost a tolerance for strong smelling foods.

SVETOVIDOV THE SYTEMETIST

The only borders herrings have ever recognised are those of food and habitat, but the development of an internationalist vision in herring studies took a while. Even Bloch, in his late eighteenth century dismantling of **Grand Migration** theory, split his great work into German fish (3 vols) and foreign fish (9 vols). No prizes for guessing where herring appears. Herring internationalism reached its height in the towering figure of the Soviet systematist Anatoli Svetovidov.

His comprehensive *Clupeidae* (1952) represents just one book in the monumental series *Fauna of the USSR*. He got the job because the Zoological Institute of the Academy of Sciences had liked his work on *Gadiformes* (cod, pollack, saithe, etc). Soviet science was a juggernaut and A.N. Svetovidov its humble servant. It is possible to argue that the internationalism of Soviet fish sciences came out of a sense of borders as flexible as those of the herring, but having been given the subject, Svetovidov was driven by the scientific need to examine the whole picture:

> As in my work on the Gadiformes, here too I could not confine myself to forms encountered in the waters of the USSR ... The geographical distribution and evolutionary history of the entire herring family is thus covered in a

more extensive manner in order to present an accurate picture… I consider it well worthwhile to acquaint other ichthyologists engaged in the detailed study of herrings in the USSR with the whole family. As there has been no comprehensive study of the Clupeidae, such workers often lack knowledge of the herring family in toto.

Never was a truer word said.

When considering the **Atlantic Herring**, Svetovidov shares Hodgson's sensitivity to the idea of herring races, preferring populations and local forms (see **Racial Theory**). The development of characteristics is seen in a broader evolutionary pattern which encompasses both genetics and individual environmental adaptations. He draws on a host of sources, only listing essential works in his bibliography of one hundred and five Russian texts and ninety-three in other languages. He adopts the Atlantic herring classification system proposed by Le Gall in 1935, which, looking at the European forms, unites seven basic types into three groups: the Atlantic or oceanic herring, including spring Atlanto-Scandian and winter Scottish spawners; the coastal herring, which includes the autumn and winter spawners of the English Channel, the winter and spring spawners of the southern entrance to the Irish Sea and the autumn spawners of the North Sea (Bank herrings); and the herrings of semi-saline waters, including Norwegian/Swedish fjord, Zuider Zee and Ems/Jade/Morle estuary varieties, along with the Baltic herring as a distinct sub-species within the group.

He knew the herring's tendency to variation and, as with the Baltic herring, he saw the Pacific herring, for example, as a subspecies. Suitably humble before the Zoological Institute, he is forceful in his arguments with colleagues:

After the present work was completed and had gone to print, I became acquainted with the article of Ponomareva (1951) that is cited in the description of Cl. Harengus harengus and Cl. Harengus pallasii. In her article, L.A.

Ponomareva regards low-vertebral-count herrings and high-vertebral-count herrings as two distinct species—Cl. harengus and Cl. pallasii… However, all her arguments in favour of this classification are hampered by limited authority on this matter and insufficient acquaintance with the literature.

Herring **Taxonomy** is still bedevilled by Ponomareva's ill-informed classifications.

SWEDISH FISHERIES

All the nations of the Baltic engage with the herring. Estonia may have the strangest herring song (**When the Herring Lived on Dry Land**), but Sweden has the largest fishery. Its northern reach gives it access to all the low-salinity tolerant **Baltic Herring** variants, its southern and western reach to the **Atlantic Herring** populations. It could, quite reasonably, claim the historic Scania fishery, which was substantially based on its shores, but at the time those particular shores were Danish.

Due to its vast hinterland and the popularity of herring in so much of it, the Baltic has been a net importer of the fish since Scania's decline, but that has not prevented overfishing. Between Gotland and Stockholm the Baltic reaches a depth of 459 m, but generally it is shallow, averaging only 55 m. On the one hand this is good: herrings tend not to go down further than 200 m, anyway, and less energy is required by the more concentrated span of their nightly rises to the surface. On the other hand, shallow waters concentrate the effects of pollution and of climate change. Add to this the reported tendency of the **Russian Fisheries** not to play ball with EU conservation measures and the difficulties can be easily imagined.

Putting aside **Surströmming** and **Reduction Plants**, in terms of herring history, Sweden's main fisheries contribution has been focused on the herring periods of the Bohuslän fishery on its Skagerrak coastline. Herring shoals may come and go, but here they can come in huge volumes and last for up to sixty years before disappearing for sixty or more. Reliable evidence for these periods goes back as far as the sixteenth century.

UNDERSTANDING THE BOHUSLÄN PERIODS

The most recent high volume period was 1877–1906 and writing at the very beginning of it, the Swedish scientist Axel V. Ljungman proposed that the arrivals and disappearances were related to the 111 year sunspot cycle. With gaps between the beginnings of the four documented periods of 104, 87 and 130 years, maybe a rabbit should have gone off somewhere, but the inherent principle of astronomical influence was taken forward by Otto Petterson and Gustaf Ekman, who explored the predictability of resulting variations in salinity and temperature associated with the phenomenon of internal waves. The problem with this was that these waves were vertical oscillations of water and did not fully account for what was necessarily experienced as a horizontal arrival.

After the herrings went away in 1906, Bohuslän fishermen started to go further afield, becoming regulars on the **Icelandic Fisheries** during their herring era. A small Bohuslän period began in 1963 and, noticing that it had seemed to alternate with herring abundance along the west coast of Norway, Norwegian scientist Devold argued the periods involved a spring spawner shift from there. By digging up the pits where the carcasses of the late eighteenth-century Bohuslän herrings had been dumped (conveniently preserved in anoxic conditions), the Swedish scientist Höglund (1972) discovered that they were from the mixed Southern North Sea populations. The minor 1963 period only lasted until 1965: if people had only known, from this they might better have foreseen the North Sea population collapse of the 1970s.

The late 1990s saw further investigations into the coincidence of Bohuslän herring periods with cold winters over Western Europe. The Dutch herring academic Ad Corten argues that the movements are associated with 'negative phases' of the North Atlantic Oscillation ('a multi-annual variation in the mean atmospheric pressure distribution,' if you were wondering). These produce strong easterly winds during the autumn, driving surface water out from the Skagerrak and consequently encouraging a sub-surface counter current. Juvenile herrings feeding off the coast of Jutland on zooplankton (in particular *Calanus finmarchicus*) are still not strong enough to resist the current. If the zooplankton also drifts in that direction, recovering spents would presumably follow it too. Once off the Bohuslän coast, a particular herring recruitment returns year after year, even though, as it comprises stronger and stronger swimmers, this represents an active selection. *Calanus finmarchicus* only drifts, so subsequent recruitments drift with it.

SAY NO TO INDIRECT CONSUMPTION!

Sara Hornburg's 'Follow the herring—A case study on the interplay between management and markets for marine resource utilization' (2023) pictures a 'heated public debate' on the direction of its fishery effort. In 2009 Individual Transferable Quotas were introduced and, as elsewhere, resulted in a transfer towards fewer, larger vessels. 'The share of landings directly destined for feed (aka reduction fisheries) has increased from around 50 to 77% of volume from the total pelagic sector between 2013 and 2022.' This is happening against the increasing recognition (see **Medicine and Health**) that eating the herring itself, rather than via fishmeal fed livestock is better for the national diet and for the health of the planet.

Eat more herring!

TAXONOMY

Taxonomy is from Ancient Greek: *nomos*, law or custom; *taxis*, order or arrangement. Law and order would be inappropriate (in the hands of taxonomists there would be too many miscarriages of justice): the word means 'a custom of systematic arrangement.' These days the word can classify just about anything, but it was coined for natural history, a dream of precise statements as to where, in the grand scheme, each lifeform sits. The word emerged in the early nineteenth century, but the system of naming and grouping began with Carl Linnaeus' *Systema Naturae* (1758). From taxonomy's earliest days, herrings have been uncooperative.

HOW IT WORKS
Of Empires, Kingdoms & Phyla

Life was divided into two *Empires* (aka *Domains*, *Realms* or *Superkingdoms*) plus the Viruses (intracellular parasites squatting in the cells of others). To be in an Empire, you must be a property-owning cellular lifeform. Empire One was the *Prokaryota*, including the *Kingdoms* of *Bacteria* and *Archaea*. *Archaea* can live in extreme environments and were thought to be bacteria but deserving of their own kingdom. These days the former kingdom of *Archaea* is recognised as another empire. The *Eukaryota* (the kingdoms of *Plantae*, *Fungi* and *Animalia*) is now Empire Three.

Logically, dukedoms or counties might have come in for the next level down, but in 1866 Ernst Haeckel, zoologist, eugenicist and all-round promoter of scientific racism, came up with *Phylum*, metaphorically derived from the Greek, *phylon*, race or stock. The one we are interested in is the *Chordata*. At some stage in their lives, all chordates have a cartilage notochord, which, in vertebrates, develops into the spinal chord. They have pharyngeal slits (which in fish become gills), a tail behind the anus and a groove in the pharynx (which in some fish helps with filter feeding).

Of Clades, Classes & Orders

Amongst the chordates, there is the *Clade* or natural group, *Euteleostomi* (bony vertebrates). Clades can be recognised at any old level below kingdom. There are not really enough levels in taxonomy to cover the complexity of life and/or evolution, so while each kosher level can be a clade, they are also there for the in-betweenies. In systematic approaches to taxonomy, *Cladistics* has, by and large, won out over both *Phenetics* (don't ask) and evolutionary *Darwinian Classification*, but this only happened in the second half of the twentieth century, so there is much overlapping terminology.

The euteleostomi are also referred to as *Osteichthyes* (bony fish), but pickier taxonomists pointed out that it had to include the *Tetrapods* (we, for example, are tetrapods, but are not generally regarded as fish). 400 million years ago, the tetrapods emerged from a clade within the *Class* (or alternatively clade) of euteleostomi: *Sarcopterygii* (lobe-finned fish), some of which emerged from the waters, their lobe fins becoming limbs. Tetrapod means four-footed but is used to mean four-limbed (with a special dispensation for snakes). Some went back into the water, some started to fly, but all of them ceased to be fish.

Twenty million years earlier, however, the euteleostomi had already produced another cla(ss)(de), the ray-finned fish or *Actinopterygii* (from the Latin, *actino* or 'having rays'). Predating the lobe option, for fins they developed skin membranes supported by spines. This was the point at which the only later to be interconnected destinies of the herring and mankind separated. From the actinopterygii, the *Neopterygii* (better movers) and from them the *Teleostei* (more effective jaws). Hundreds of millions of years later, the teleosts became primary suppliers to mankind's hooks, **Nets** and **(Herring) Boats**.

Teleosts begat *Otocephala* (swim bladders linked to the inner ear), which begat the *Order* of *Clupeiformes* (swim bladder connected by pneumatic duct to the gut, enabling replenishment with air via the mouth and its expulsion via the anus—see **Farting**).

Suborder & Family

Among the clupeiformes there are two *Suborders* and seven *Families*. The *Denticipitoidi* is a suborder with only one family, the *Denticipitidae*, with only one *Child* or *Species*, the denticle herring, which lives in the rivers of Benin, Nigeria and Cameroon. The six remaining families belong to the suborder *Clupeoidei*. These are the *Engraulidae* (140 species of anchovy, of which we tend to eat only nine); *Spratelloididae* (no sprats, but 10 species of round herrings); *Pristigasteridae* (longfin herrings, once numbered among the *Clupeidae*, but now not); *Chirocentridae* (two species of wolf herring); *Dussumieriidae* (round herrings which aren't *Spratelloididae*)... and, sixth of the *Clupeoidei* (seventh of the clupeiformes) the *Clupeidae*: herrings (other than the above), sprats, some sardines or pilchards, shads, hilsa... and menhaden. All but the menhaden inspire culinary devotion.

Of Genus & Species

'Clupeiform' derives from *Clupea*, which Linnaeus had used as a genus for the herring, because it was Latin for pilchard or sardine (the prime fish of its kind to be recognised with a name in the Classical world). Taxonomically, the sardines of this genus are not *Clupea* but *Sardina*. After Linnaeus came up with *Clupea harengus* for the Atlantic herring, his followers proposed *Clupea pilchardus* for the European pilchard, but in 1792, on the shores of the Mediterranean, Julius Walbaum (there's always one) came up with *Sardina pilchardus* and that is what stuck. Outside taxonomy, sardines can be *Sardinella*, *Sardinops*, *Dussumieria* (round herrings, see above) or *Escualosa*. What they are never, is *Clupea*.

Of Species & Below

Notwithstanding their differences, taxonomists allocate all of commercially-fished herrings of the broader North Atlantic region, including the Western and Central Baltic, to the species *Clupea harengus*. It has one subspecies, the Baltic herring named by Linnaeus *Clupea harengus membras*. In taxonomy, genus and species combine to give you a binomial. A subspecies gets a *Genus species subspecies* trinomial. Plants can have as many nomials as you like, but the animal kingdom is only allowed three.

As a species, the Atlantic herring can be larger or smaller; autumn, winter, spring and summer spawning. Think of the difference between the large Craster kipper (mostly Norwegian spring spawners these days) and the dinky little Manx kipper. Both are straight *Clupea harengus*. As we have seen, in his metaphorically dodgy **Racial Theory**, Friedrich Heincke enumerated fourteen distinct races of Atlantic herring, including the White Sea herring, which is now a subspecies of the Pacific herring. In 1931

RIGBY'S ENCYCLOPAEDIA OF THE HERRING

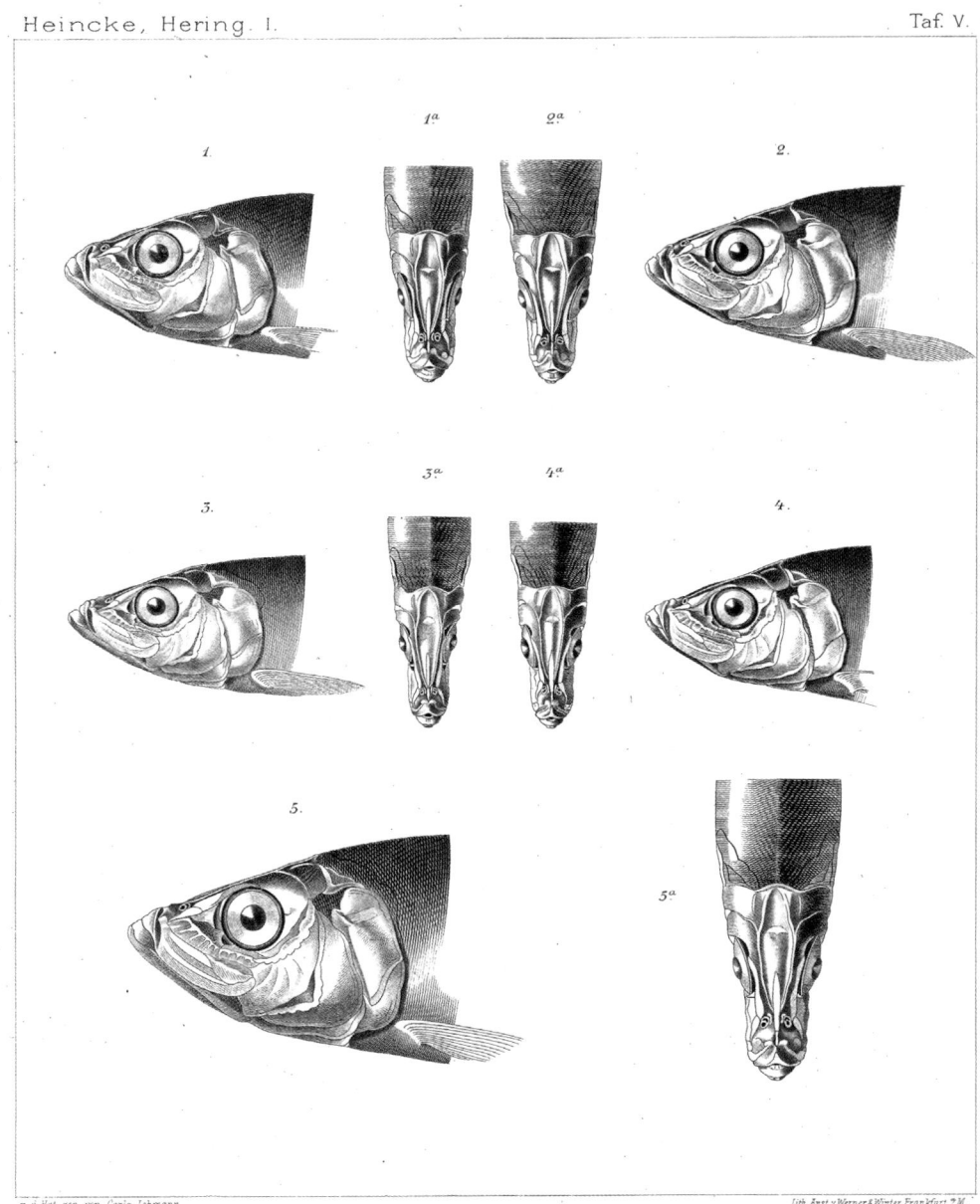

Herrin's Heids, a Heincke selection of Atlantic (species) and Baltic (subspecies): 1 Atlantic herring from Bergen; 2 Spring spawning Atlantic herring from Rügen; 3 Baltic herring from Stockholm; 4 Baltic herring from Memel; 5 Giant Baltic herring from Stockholm. (Author's collection.)

Werner Schnakenbeck gave them trinomial subspecies status, but too many marine scientists were already baulking at racial theory's baggage and it did not catch on, even when 'race' was swapped for 'population'.

Herrings adapt genetically to water temperature and salinity at spawning and early juvenile stages (see **Atlantic Herring: A Natural History**). What is species adaptation, however, and what is species? When is a subspecies merely a population? When does it become a species?

As noted elsewhere, in a period of Arctic warming two million years ago, our hero the Atlantic herring swam over the top of the Russo-Siberian landmass and became the Pacific herring (**Svetovidov** still turning in his grave, but *Clupea pallasii*), differentiated from the Atlantic by a lower average vertebral count. There are populations with lower average vertebral counts among those classified as Atlantic. As said before, difference is the herring's constant. Recently, geneticists have discovered greater difference between Spring and Autumn spawners than between Pacific and Atlantic. Mitsuhiro Nakaya *et al.* have even discovered significant 'Difference in Body Proportions between Hatchery-Reared and Wild Pacific Herring' (2013).

And those White Sea herrings? In the early Holocene (10,000 to 11,000 years ago) some Pacific herrings swam back West and became the subspecies, Chosa herring (*C pallasii suworowi*) and White Sea herring (*C pallasii marisalbi*). In the World Register of Marine Species (WoRMS) these have now been synonymised under *C pallasii Valenciennes*. This refers to an initial identification by Achille Valenciennes in 1847. The Atlantic and Baltic herrings are similarly synonymised as *C harengus Linnaeus*. But the White, Pechora and Kara Seas are within the eastern range of the Atlantic herring and... Hanna M Laakkonen *et al.* report 'Introgressive hybridization between the Atlantic and Pacific herrings in the north of Europe' (2014). Mitochondrial analysis reveals evidence of miscegenation. In 'Comparative biology and population mixing among local, coastal and offshore Atlantic herring in the North Sea, Skagerrak,

Kattegat and Western Baltic', Florian Berg *et al*. (2017) suggest, on the basis of 428,773 herrings collected between 1970 and 2015, they all interbreed all of the time (Heincke's turn to turn in his grave).

Of Demes, Metapopulations, ESUs & More

Taxonomy hasn't yet collapsed under the weight of its contradictions, but new terms have proliferated since the late 1930s. A *deme* was an alternative to population but is now a local population. There is a *metapopulation*, which, according to Robert L Wilbur *et al*. in 'Is it a Deme, a Stock or a Subspecies' (1998), is 'an aggregation of patchily distributed local populations that are interconnected between the local populations.' As they work their way through the various definitions, under Species, Wilbur and his chums say of Darwinian thinking:

> This typological or morphological concept of a species may have reached its peak when some taxonomists even tried to decipher species based on percentages of shared and unique morphological characteristics... The morphological species concept began to fall apart when systematists realized that it did not work well for some species that demonstrated considerable polymorphic diversity or when two species shared extremely similar morphologies.

Species like the herring, some might say. Perhaps explaining WoRMS' synonymisations, they note, *Reduced attention to subspecies* is underway due to modern genetic techniques and they advance their own preference for the *Evolutionary Significant Unit* (ESU), but the proliferation of synonyms for population groupings continues apace. Other terms may apply: the *Biological Species Concept* (BSC), the *Phylogenetic Species Concept* (PSC) and the *Distinct Population Segment* (DPS) are also all out there.

Why does this matter? Well, **Quotas** are set within broad sea areas on the taxonomic binomials. They are predicated on legally binding acts in which language is important, however problematic. Logic suggests that *Clupea harengus Linnaeus* and *Clupea pallasii*

Valenciennes should be synonymised, but conservation demands the protection of herring diversity: an increased attention, not just to notional subspecies, but to the distinctiveness of all the different populations. The herring's diversity, enabled by genes linked to its immune system, may well be integral to its wider abundance. Smaller populations could entirely disappear in the reduced attention of the taxonomically-determined quota.

TWO CONTEMPORARY ARTISTS

Trying to find out who I had interviewed on a 2005 minidisc I had simply labelled, *Achiltibuie* (see **Appearances**), I was pointed in the direction of Anne Macleod, whose husband, Ali 'Beag' Macleod, had only recently died. It hadn't been him, but as well as identifying the voice as that of Jim Muir, she pointed me in the direction of Ali's cousin Will Maclean and his work, *The Ring Net*. In conversations on a possible herring project with my good friend, the Scottish artist Keith McIntyre (see **Atlantic Herring** and the first image section), he too talked about Will Maclean. It was not just that I loved the work I saw, it felt as if the herrings were calling.

I had been pointed to Penelope Payne by another friend, the curator Matthew Jarratt who was organising a sculpture festival at Cheeseburn in Northumberland and was showing her work, *The Weight of Salt*. I loved it. I first met her in a post-COVID-lockdown meeting at The Old Low Light in North Shields, which was developing an exhibition about **Herring Lasses**. It was a day of almost blinding sunshine. The meeting was outside so we could all be socially distanced and it was a joy just to be seeing people again. We were both happy to help the Old Low Light in any manner we could and we also agreed to meet up and talk.

Herrings can seem a bit of a niche field: it is always good to encounter fellow enthusiasts.

WILL MACLEAN

Between 1973 and 1978 Scottish artist Will Maclean developed *The Ring Net*, a detailed documentation of a herring fishing method, largely conducted by paired boats (see first and second image sections and **Ring Net Struggle**). Moving between visual art, graphics, boat plans and photography, for its innovation alone it could have been included in **Documentary**, but it forms part of a life's work that resists such a neat **Taxonomy**. Ring nets, which originated in Loch Fyne in the 1830s spread extensively on the West Coast of Scotland, on to the East Coast and into international practice. The method came to an end with the wide scale adoption of purse seining, pelagic trawling and the herring population collapses of the 1970s. Maclean's *The Ring Net* was developed alongside, but separately from Angus Martin's *The Ring Net Fishermen* (1981), the first of several books he has written on the Scottish West Coast herring fishing.

INTERVIEW WITH WILL MACLEAN

My father was harbourmaster in Inverness and he was from Coigach and my mother was from Skye and, although we lived in Inverness, we were in a kind of West Coast bubble and my father was a native Gaelic speaker. I always knew ring netting from the earliest days of my childhood, because my grandparents lived in Kyleakin and my uncle and all my cousins worked on the ring net boats there. And as a child, I used to go and sit in the fo'c'sles. At the weekends, if there was a local football match, say in Glenelg, the men would take the boats down and we could all pile on the boats and go down there or over to Kyle at the weekend. And it was just so magical.

Later on, if any of the men wanted to take a holiday or were off sick or anything, when I was a student on holiday, they would ask me to come and take their place. And I would work the cork rope and just generally get to know it. And then for a while, I actually got a proper job there as the cook on the *Misty Isle*. The whole community in Kyleakin, in the fifties and sixties revolved around the ring net boats, so I just grew up with it. I was teaching in a school, an art teacher, and I was complaining to Richard Demarco, the gallery owner I used to show with, that I really needed a project to get my teeth into. At that time, he was chair of the Scottish International Education Trust, set up by Sean Connery and a number of other wealthy people to fund projects related to Scottish culture. So I got funding to make a visual record of the ring netting, because that was what I knew about.

It was '73. I had no concept that ring netting by the late seventies would have disappeared. I didn't go into it thinking, 'Ah, I've got to do this before it changes' or anything. It was just a continuation of the culture that I knew. My mother said, 'There's a man from Campbeltown: he knows about the fishing.' That was Angus Martin. So we teamed up. I said, 'Well, I'll do the exhibition.' And he said, 'Well, I'll do the book.'

I was thinking about Joseph Banks and Captain Cook and the voyages where the artist was a recorder. I wanted to record things that people would not necessarily record unless they'd go into it at that depth. 'When they went to the toilet, what did they do?' They had a drum, an oil drum with a tyre around the front of it, and they sat on that. 'How did they locate the herring in the early days?' They used a piano wire with a weight on it and they unrolled it and they dragged it. And the old men knew by the strikes on the piano wire what fish were there and how many fish were there. That level of detail fascinated me.

Angus was the same. Angus had these amazing conversations with the men. I soon discovered that you didn't get much unless you could offer them part of the information. 'How many corks were on the leader?' or how many this and that: then they would respond. If you sat down and said, 'Tell me about the fishing,' they wouldn't know what to say. But if you got into it and said, 'Why do you never turn against the sun? Why do you watch a gannet?' Then the information would come out.

Angus had been a ring netter. His family were well known and respected. The old men talked to him endlessly. You'd be recording and halfway through the conversation, they would start to talk about other families and then they would say, 'Hope that thing's not switched on…' And I respected the fact that it was a conversation that we'd had in private. Of course, they've all gone to the Fiddlers' Green now, anyway. Angus treble-referenced everything he did and everything he sent me. He said one of the big compliments that he had for his book was that none of the fishermen could find fault in it. The fisherman that did go to see the exhibition, they were puzzled initially that it should be important enough to be in an art gallery, but they were proud of it and proud of me for doing it.

Particularly what fascinated me was this thing they referred to as **Appearances**. Prior to the advent of the echo sounder, which was quite crude really, they still relied on the old Appearance methods: banging the anchor to watch the herring, the reaction of the phosphorus. I was amazed. I'd go out and stand with the old boys on the bow and they would chap the anchor and I would just see this flash like a light bulb under the water. And they'd say, 'Oh no, that's mackerel,' because the ball disappeared like a star. But when they saw something that was like a fat bulb going off in a flash gun, *Boof!* they'd shout back, 'They're here!'

It took me months and months, because you were looking at the surface of the water. You had to learn to look underneath the surface and when the sea was coming over, you were bouncing up and down and it was just an amazing thing to have the privilege to have been part of that experience, like watching the gannet going down or watching a whale breaching or watching for oil on the surface of the water. That went with the development of echo sounding and radar and all the rest of it. They would just come round and if the herring was on it, they used to call it a spot, *spot mhor*—it was more a black mark, really—and they'd say, 'That's where they are!' and they'd back round them and ring them.

It was three or four years Angus and I worked together, back and forth. He collected a phenomenal amount of information. And then he would send me rough drawings of whatever I was interested in. I was back to school teaching by then and I used to get the kids busy, then I'd go and draw a tractor… I would write to Angus and say, 'how did they make the buoys in the old days?' And he would write back and say, 'well, there were certain farms that bred dogs for their bladders. And these farms would sell the bladders to the fishermen and then it went on to canvas and then it went on to plastic.' He'd spend hours talking to the old boys and he would ask them about this and that and then, if I said to him, 'Do you have any information on the flambeau?' (the lights they held up at night) he would go through his archives or he would maybe go and speak to them again and say, 'How did the flambeaus work?'

If I did a set of drawings of winches, I would start with a McBain winch, then Angus would send a photograph of an earlier winch and I'd write to the manufacturers and they'd send drawings, so I could build a sheet up: this was the development of the ring net winch. And it was the same with the brailing—for lifting the herring. I wanted to have a notion of the technical development. I didn't think I was doing a documentary because I didn't know about documentaries and I didn't feel that I had any kind of knowledge or skill in that direction, which is interesting. I just wanted to make the art side of it. Whereas Angus, coming out of a different culture, was much more aware of the history and the relationships with the families.

If I was drawing a thing like the little mizzen sail they put up to keep the head to the wind, I could draw it, but then if I wanted to add to it by saying when the sail was hoisted and what the sail was made of and when it was used, it was something I did, just to inform the drawing, really. The text never came first. The drawing always came first. I wasn't in any way precious about it. I just wanted to have a thing that had as much information about it as I could put into it. I'd write to the space I'd created. It's all drawing after all. Text is just a different kind of mark-making. You can read it, but in my mind it was a series of marks that enhanced the composition.

Two things intrigued me. One was Letraset, because it was amazing: you got proper letters! And I had an airbrush and I used wax resists and that whole thing… The Rotring pen was another, but I gave up on Rotring because it was so fiddly in there. I went back to mapping pens. I still use a mapping pen, the old nib. The Rotring is very mechanical. It just gives you one line, but a mapping pen gives you fat lines and thin lines, different qualities: such a simple tool and it's just so magical to use.

We did four years in art school. Two of them were graphic design. So I wasn't entirely naive about the notions and structures of graphic design. I loved the whole notion of it. Artists like Eric Ravilious and Bawden, I just love them. I never tire of Ravilious—*Sickbay in Dundee* with the aircraft outside the window, it's amazing!

The exhibition wasn't done in any order. There was a section on *Appearances*, a section on *Developments of Boat Hulls*, the *Development of the Decks*—the Loch Fyne skiffs were open, then part-decked and then fully-decked… And now I'll talk about the *Development of the Net*. I just hopped from one thing to another. As to the order of the sequences, the exhibition toured and it depended on the curator.

There was no notion, going through an art school in the sixties, something like *The Ring Net* could have been considered as part of the visual arts. But, as I said earlier, I didn't think I was doing documentary either. The only thing was this loose notion of Banks and Cook and the early drawings that came back of strange fish and plants and things like that—extraordinary, wonderful stuff. That was the only kind of role model that I had in mind, really.

Beyond The Ring Net

Now held at Scotland's National Gallery of Contemporary Art, *The Ring Net* includes over 250 photographs, nearly seventy drawings and well over thirty prints and tracings. Some of the images can be seen in its online collection. Herrings and herring boats weave in and out of Maclean's work over the forty and more years since it was first exhibited (see first image section).

> Having invested all those years in the discipline of the boats and the fish, it became an archive in my mind. It's imprinted on my brain. It gives you a kind of freedom. I often think of the fisherman on Skye. He'd have been fishing all week and yet, on the Saturday he'd go down and stand in the wheelhouse. I suppose that's where he could think clearly.

PENELOPE PAYNE

The Weight of Salt, on display at Cheeseburn, had really struck me. Fifteen bricks of salt, each wrapped in differently-stitched, thick blue cotton, the salt leaching through the material, it was beautiful and also evocative of the herring lasses' story. When I interviewed her at her studio in Cullercoats, just north of Tynemouth, she had just completed her extraordinary *Horizons* performance in Cullercoats Bay (see second image section for both works). She was working on a fishwives piece, *Scold Vixen Harpy Shrew* (see first image section).

INTERVIEW WITH PENELOPE PAYNE

I saw one of the Cullercoats paintings by the American artist Winslow Homer and, soon after, a photograph of one of the herring girls that he used to paint there, Maggie Jefferson, most commonly known by her later married name, Maggie Storey. It was the detail of their clothing that really caught my imagination. They have these very, very particular, black or blue skirts with stitched concentric circles of pleating around them, all the way down, and I thought, that's amazing, that's so much effort. Some women had more, some less, but the Winslow Homer paintings picked up these details. He paid so much attention to these women and really respected them as beautiful, strong, independent people. To him they were heroic.

I made a video piece with a pleated panel, which I took down to the water every day and dipped it into the water, into the salt water of the sea. It was just a recording of how the salt gathered on the skirts after each immersion and how the passage of time changes materials. I just love the thought of salt: antiseptic and a corrosive; we cover our food in it, but it can be so destructive to our health. It's like this Yin and Yang thing. The women's skirts with all the different pleats expressed some kind of individuality within this collective of the fishing community. Salt, though, was really painful for the women, working with very sharp knives, very quickly, cutting fingers and working in salt. The two ideas came together, salt blocks wrapped in these skirts that were stitched individually. And then the salt started to do its thing, to bloom out of the material, get caught in all the stitching, so this individuality I was considering with these women, suddenly appeared by itself and it was just an extraordinary moment. First of all nothing happened and suddenly I realised that the surface of the fabric was just a tiny bit glittery and then I could just make out these tiny little shapes as the salt crystals were growing out and growing out. And it was beautiful, it was like this passage of time, development and history and it was a really important piece to me.

I'm a bit obsessed with the skirts. For me they represent women. We use the image to represent women on every toilet door. I was taking these beautiful, pleated skirts that these fisherwomen used and I was thinking about their individuality again. And I thought about Cullercoats as place. It's quite a special bay. It's this horseshoe shaped bay with these two stone piers either side and a big cliff behind you, so it's quite sheltered.

I was thinking about all these different things and I just started drawing the horizon line between the piers and thinking about the place and thinking about it as a place people worked. And I started drawing and I started drawing the skirts and I started drawing them back into the landscape and I was drawing along the horizon line and all these ideas started to formulate, started to crystalise and it was about how these skirts, how the story of female labour is still stuck. That we can't move beyond this idea that women have these designated roles. I was drawing these skirts, I started blocking the horizon line with them, so it was this clarity of idea in the end, that these skirts were blocking these horizons for these women, that their stories couldn't move any further forward.

I made a skirt into a banner. I made one originally and it took about three metres of fabric. I pleated it, folded it and I held the pleats down using herring bone stitch. It has no relevance to the women. They didn't use herring bone stitch particularly, but I loved the story of it and it's a beautiful stitch to sew. It's very lyrical, because it flows backwards and forwards and it's lovely, so anyway, I stitched this banner and had it in the studio. I loved it and it took ages to make and I had plasters round my fingers from the sewing and I thought, 'Oh my God! I'm connecting with these women and the clooties on the fingers of these poor women!' My needles were hurting my fingers so much, I had calluses and I thought, 'Oh, this is amazing!' I loved the process of it. A lot of my work is about piece work and time that things take to make. And then I was thinking, 'What if there were many banners?'

Then tar came into it. Tar is obviously used throughout the fishing industry because it's a sealant and you need it for the hulls of your boat and they use it on rope and lots of things and it's lovely and I started using the tar on the back of the banner to seal in the stitching, but it was also sealing in stories, sealing in histories somehow.

We were full on COVID at this time and everything was proving difficult and funding was proving difficult, but I got invited to take part in this exhibition at Middlesbrough Institute of Modern Art and they showed five of the banners, which I'd got other women to make. There were two of mine and three by other people and it was this collective making that really started to pull the whole piece together.

I asked my mum first, I said, 'Would you make a banner? I'll give you a length of material and some cotton and some needles and some pins, I'll show you how to do it but I want you to make it yourself and I want you to put your own personality on this very prescribed set of materials…' So I asked a couple more people if they'd make them and they were like, 'Yeah. All right. OK.' I started sending the word out, inviting people to make the banners and there was a lovely ripple effect. And it's quite an expensive thing to do, so I was very aware of, 'Oh my God, it's going to cost me huge amounts of money,' but people all over the country started doing these banners, London, Bristol, Scotland and I thought, 'OK, no, this is great!' And then they all came back and it was wonderful I was thinking literally of all my friends and I thought I can bribe that person to come and do it and maybe persuade that person and oh, I don't know, maybe I could get 25 people.

I picked a date, said, 'I'm going to do it then. It's going to happen. Whatever the weather is going to be is going to be, whoever turns up is going to turn up.' I started asking people and going down to the beach, 'Would you fancy doing it?' And I asked a couple of swimmers and suddenly, I had loads of people saying, 'Can we do it? It sounds amazing.' So eventually, on the beach on a February morning, I had sixty-odd women walking out in a procession across the bay and holding up these banners at sunrise, blocking the horizon and it was just the most incredible, emotive, stunning thing that I've ever been involved with.

BEYOND HORIZONS

Featuring the banners and a film of the performance, an exhibition of *Horizons* was premiered in an old North Shields smokehouse, the walls of which, years after it had closed, still smelt powerfully of kippers. After an artist residency in Siglufjörður (see **Icelandic Fisheries**) Penny was invited to show it at Djúpavík in an old **Reduction Plant**. *Scold Vixen Harpy Shrew* (see **Herring Lasses** and first image section) was first shown at Middlesbrough Institute of Modern Art (MIMA).

ULLAPOOL & THE BRITISH FISHERIES SOCIETY

Lochbay on Skye, Pultneytown by Wick, Tobermory on Mull, Ullapool on the north shore of Loch Broom: a dream of herring towns, dreams of the future. Pultneytown was the success story, but Ullapool the purest expression of the British Fisheries Society plan for the economic development of the Highlands. If herrings had been only a little bit more reliable, it just might have worked…

A CONTEXT

Population, then as now, was understood as key to development. The failure of Darien, Scotland's own bid for empire, and two Jacobite rebellions, had left the nation out of pocket. Lairds couldn't afford traditional responsibilities towards their people and, with the Clearances, from the mid-eighteenth century, they essentially adopted the English model of enclosure. Their own road to the sunny economic uplands, forced their poor downhill towards the urban centres of the lowlands, to the coast and beyond. Emigration—sometimes with 'assisted passages'—was, for many, less choice than second brutal eviction. A number of Scotland's innovative bankers had moved to London, where, together with other self-exiled members of their nation's good and great, they became concerned at how the Highlands and Islands might be regenerated if depopulation continued at such alarming levels.

The British Fisheries Society was a joint stock company, its shareholders driven as much by charity as hope for riches. It had grown out of a House of Commons committee. While making recommendations across the whole of the fishing industry, its overwhelming concern was with Scotland and its lack of infrastructure. The development of herring fishing in the north of Scotland seemed a miracle solution: enhancement of the national wealth, livings for the evicted (and ambitious incomers), a salve perhaps for the consciences of the evicting classes.

Overwhelmingly involving London-based Scots, the Society's distance from the settlements it established was a problem from the start. Coigach, where Ullapool came to be built, was one of the estates forfeited after the '45 Rebellion. In the 1780s the Jacobite exiles were returning, keen to modernise and rebuild but short on investment. The Society did not have much trouble buying the land from Lord MacLeod, but fine judgements had to be made in selecting sites for all the settlements.

Sustainability demanded land for the settlers as well as a harbour and curing stations. The Society knew about herring unreliability and wrote it into the plan: allocated plots were designed to be of a size and quality to supplement fishing, but only just. Too small and/or the soil too poor, settlers would starve; too large, too fertile and they might not bother with the fishing at all.

Philanthropy has its own fine judgements. A Society board member, the Duke of Argyll had been a vociferous advocate for a settlement on his own land in Mull. Having secured the investment, he had to ask himself, 'Are the evicted poor the kind of people I want for Tobermory? Are fishermen?' Instead, he set about attracting that better class of settler, who might deliver him a successful trading port.

On reflection, Lochbay (now Stein) was judged to have been too generous with its plots of land: the settlers largely stuck to cultivation. Ullapool was founded in 1788. A report for the Commission for the Annexed Estates in 1755 had already recommended a settlement there: 'as the herring fishing succeeds so well here, it is probable that numbers of sea-fairing people would resort to it.'

BUILDING ULLAPOOL

The town is often described as having been designed by Thomas Telford, but the original plan for its buildings and gardens was drawn up by David Aitken, the surveyor involved in selecting the site. Initial building designs—a house for himself, curing and net mending sheds, a smoking house, tradesmen's shops, a salt and cask store and ten houses for skilled settlers—were developed by Robert Melville, who claimed experience in the fishery trade and successfully proposed that he himself should become the Society's agent. Roderick Morrison, a partner in a fishing station on Tanera, northwest of Ullapool, proposed a pier, a warehouse and an inn.

The Society's architect Robert Mylne amended the proposals and building work began, but there were difficulties with Melville, who was temperamental and lacked the engineering instinct: the pier, for example, ended up larger than planned and in the wrong place Another survey was commissioned, this time from the young Scottish engineer Thomas Telford, then working for Sir William Pulteney, who had become a director of the Society. Telford became the Surveyor of Buildings and designed the church, but essentially improved, rather than changed the plan. He did develop the ones for Lochbay and Pulteneytown, however.

THE SETTLERS

Those intent on the modernisation of the Scottish Highlands often complained about the Highlander's character. Crofting mentalities were shaped around sustainable self-reliance with the bad harvest backstop of landowner charity. In Ullapool, the Society tried to keep to its intentions but had difficulties attracting settlers. Quite reasonably suspicious as to what its true intentions were, many crofters still preferred the wild risks and uncertainties of emigration.

In 1788 the Society was told, 'a colony of experienced Fishers are collected to commence operations.' Melville himself had decked boats, but the settlers only had small, open boats. Virtually the whole of Ullapool would turn out when the herring came into the loch, but no one followed the fishing beyond its shores. They made no use of the curing station further west on Ristol, built to support more adventurous voyages. Melville seems to have deployed his larger vessels for storing and packing the catch, while the smaller boats did the fishing. This unsatisfactory state of affairs only lasted until 1798, when the large shoals stopped coming. It was constantly expected they would return, but they did not. Fishing fleets from further afield were catching the herring before they entered Loch Broom, but there were probably changes in the drift of the plankton on which they fed.

A modest revival from 1812 to 1819 was countered by the closure of Ullapool's customs house in 1813. Tax on the necessary curing salt brought regulations that were difficult to negotiate without a registered building. Ullapool fishermen could catch the herring but were barely able to do more with it than supply their own needs. When the herring returned to the West of Scotland in numbers after 1832, the boats and nets of the Ullapool men were too small to benefit much.

THE FISHERIES SOCIETY FAREWELL

The herring's at best intermittent goodwill was problem enough, but there was a series of crop failures from 1817 and the original fine judgement in allocating the plots of land suddenly proved too fine. Ullapool was starving and the settlers petitioned the Society for help. It sent supplies of oatmeal, seed oats and potatoes, but on the East Coast, Pulteneytown was proving to be a success. Unsurprisingly, the Society's focus began to drift away from its failing western settlements. Having already sold Tobermory and the uncompleted Lochbay, it finally sold Ullapool in 1849.

Ullapool survived. If it never really developed its own fishing industry, it played host to the fishing fleets of others in the nineteenth and twentieth centuries, including

Eastern Europe's **Klondyking** factory ships between the 1970s and 1990s. The herring may not always have appreciated the town, but it has more than proved itself as a useful ferry port, a cultural centre and a base for tourism. Telford's church is now the excellent Ullapool Museum and the town has reinvented itself. More on its story can be found in Jean Dunlop's *The British Fisheries Society 1786–1893*, the later date referring to the Society's final demise.

VINEGAR

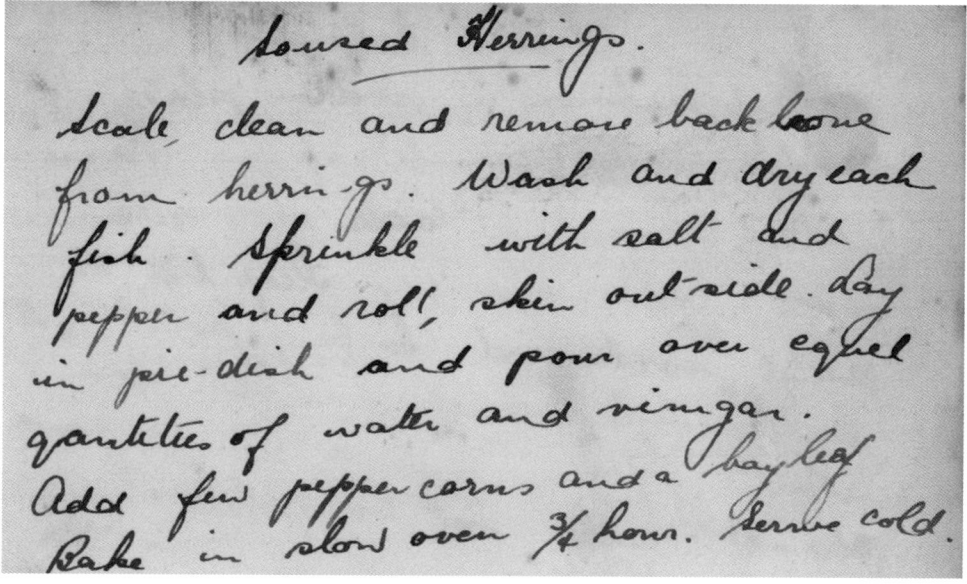

Soused herring, from my great grandmother's recipe book.

Growing up, we sometimes had kippers for breakfast, but if it was herrings for tea, they were either fried in oatmeal or soused. The soused recipe is in the handwritten book my great grandmother started and her daughter, Nanny, continued—favourite verses from the first page, recipes (upside down) from the back, meeting, surrounding, even pasted over the poems in the middle.

Recipes for soused or baked herrings abound and the family one has nothing to recommend it, apart from as a basic template. A few more spices could be added, some replace the vinegar with cider, which works well; and why not throw in some sliced apple? Soused for many means spiced, vinegar-pickled, raw fillets—what I think of as marinated. My parents had friends who went to Norway and brought back jars of neatly chunked, vinegar-pickled raw herring. It was fantastic and I've never tasted the like of it since, even in Norway, but there's no competing with memory. Marinated herrings need to be lightly salted—or you can start with some salt herring (if you think it's too salty, soak it for an hour or so). Apart from that lost Norwegian ideal, there are three classics: Bismarcks, rollmops and glassmaker's herring.

BRATHERING

Before we get to the vinegar-marinated salt herrings, there's a German halfway house between baked-soused and them. Brathering is fresh herring fried in flour or breadcrumbs and, counter-intuitively, then marinated—*vorsprung durch technik*, as they say. The herrings can be filleted or just beheaded, cleaned and trimmed. They're fried in butter or oil and left to cool while you make a marinade, half & half vinegar and water or vinegar and vegetable stock (red or white wine vinegar—both are suggested). Add salt, sliced onion, bay leaves, cloves, mustard seeds, peppercorns, bring to the boil then let it cool and pour it over the herrings. You then leave it in the fridge for three days for the marinade to soak in. It is usually served with potatoes—boiled or fried.

BISMARCKS

Vinegar pickled, Bismarcks are trimmed into single fillets and then, usually, cut into shorter lengths. In homage to their origin story, they are still sold in small barrels as well as in jars. At some point in the mid-nineteenth century, Johann Wiechmann of Stralsund had a win on the lottery and with his wife Karolina set up a grocery business. She was a pickle queen and began to produce pickled herring. Filled with love for the Prussian Minister President, Johann sent Otto von Bismarck a barrel of his wife's best, and he liked it. With the unification of Germany in 1871, Bismarck became Chancellor. Wiechmann's excitement knew no bounds and he sent Bismarck another barrel with a suggestion, it might take his name. It was so good, Otto agreed.

In a twist of fate, Bismarckhering became generic for this style of marinated herring and the Wiechmann's recipe fell into disuse, but in 1997 Stralsund reclaimed it, relaunching what is held to be the original Wiechmann delicacy.

ROLLMOPS

As the name (from the German *rollmopse*) suggests rollmops are salted herring fillets rolled around sliced onion, gherkin and/or other pickled vegetables. Some suggest spreading wholegrain mustard on the fillets first. Once you've rolled the salt herring fillets, use a cocktail stick to hold each one together and put them in the jar with your marinade.

GLASSMAKER'S

Glassmaker's, glassmaster's or glassblower's herring (from the Swedish *Glasmastarsill*) involves soaked, salted herring fillets cut into chunks again and a distilled white or a white wine vinegar (1:1 with water), but with a broader selection of sliced vegetables, herbs and spices: sliced carrot, red onion and leek, bay leaves, dill, sliced fresh horseradish, white and black peppercorns, allspice berries, cloves, sliced fresh ginger and mustard seeds. Why glassmaker's? The general suggestion is that it is because the glass jar is part of the essential attraction. You sit round the table, all looking through the beautifully clear glass—and with a beautifully clear marinade, the beautiful fillets and their accompaniments do look beautiful—and you dream collectively of how good it is going to taste.

MAKING YOUR OWN

I have often been disappointed by commercial marinated herring. Usually it is a tad too sweet for me, sometimes the spicing—particularly when canned—leaves a chemical taste. The answer is obvious: make your own. Use less sugar, use more; use less vinegar, use more. Think about the flavours you would like to have bouncing off each other. It might take a few goes to tweak things to your palate but just do one jar at a time. Each attempt will be perfectly edible.

The first thing to say is that, though fish in cold waters tend to be less susceptible to parasitic worms, if you're salting your own fresh herring, it should be frozen for twenty-four hours first to kill off any nematodes. If you buy salted whole herrings or fillets, this should already have happened. Requirements to pre-freeze have virtually eliminated *Anisakiasis*, which can cause stomach pain, nausea, vomiting. (Cooking, of course, also kills off nematodes, which can be found in any fish.)

The vinegar can be distilled white, white wine, cider, sherry or whatever, but it should be clear and should form at least 50% of the marinade. The water can be replaced by or mixed with dry white wine or cider. Half the spices and vegetables are often briefly boiled in the marinade to bring the flavours together. Drain, keep and use the flavoured marinade and throw away that half of the spices and vegetables. Hugh Fearnley-Whittingstall, chef and TV personality, has a great marinated herring recipe, which uses cider vinegar, cider and, in a stroke of sheer genius, orange zest. Orange zest and herring is one of those combinations that may have been brought down to Earth by the angels as evidence of God's love.

Salt the freshly defrosted herrings overnight, fillet them, cut them into large chunks and put them in a marinade, the contents of which can include: white vinegar, dry white wine, water (proportionally 3:1:1), thinly sliced onions, maybe some chopped carrot, a little salt, some lemon juice, a selection of spices and herbs—see those listed above, but don't feel restricted.

AND BREAD

The simplicity of bread with herrings is always going to be a winner, but special mention should go to two beautiful serving traditions. The Swedish *Smörgåsbord/*

Danish *smørrebrød* will always beckon. It comes with fresh fried, salted or smoked herring too, but marinated herring with some of the pickling vegetables and spices, laid on thickly buttered dark rye bread… is a many-splendoured thing. The North German *fischbrötchen* or fish roll is also a wonderful showcase for rollmops, Bismarcks or brathering.

WHEN HERRINGS LIVED ON DRY LAND

From Estonia, 'The Herring Lived on Dry Land' wins the prize for the strangest herring song. Hearing of my interest in herrings, German music journalist Henning Bolte told my wife about it. In Estonian the song is called *Heeringas Elas Kuival Maal* or, as often as not, just *Heeringas* (The Herring). It is like one of Rudyard Kipling's *Just So Stories—How the Camel Got His Hump* or *The Crab Who Played With the Sea*. Herring is popular in Estonia and the song is well-known.

Strictly speaking, the herring of the song, which is more like a cat, may have become a giant **Baltic herring**, the normally small subspecies which has adapted to the less salty, even brackish waters of the North East Baltic and the Gulf of Bothnia. This would seem unduly harsh, though, as its love of salt is the problem. I had the outline of the story from Henning, but not the lyrics or the tune. In 2022, I went with my wife to a European jazz conference in Sofia. At the dinner, I sat next to the great Estonian guitarist Jaak Sooäär…

'There's this Estonian folk song,' I said, 'about the herring…'

'Oh, yes!' he said and immediately started to sing it.

'Is it a traditional song?' I asked.

'Yes, but it's not a really old one.' The really old ones are referred to as *runic songs* and have a particular verse structure, nothing like that of *The Herring Lived on Dry Land*, which, he said, was probably from the nineteenth century. 'I don't know all the verses,' Jaak apologised, 'but give me your number and I'll send them to you.' And he sent a link to the lyrics in Estonian.

With the help of Google Translate and a video of Estonian school children singing it to a shadow puppet performance, here is an English version, which will go with the tune, although, please note, the boat in the original song does not have a name. In my translation I have called it the *Queen of Balts* because it rhymes with salt. Estonian is a Finnic language: they are not Balts. The Balts settled in Lithuania and I am imagining the boat was a Lithuanian vessel involved in the pre-saline-seas salt trade. It is called poetic license. Search for *Heeringas* online and you'll find the tune.

THE HERRING LIVED ON DRY LAND

Back in the time when time began
The herring lived upon dry land:
Just like the cat, the story goes,
It did not like to wet its toes.

A good ship called the Queen of Balts
Set sail, her hold all full of salt
And salt back then was not so cheap,
The price it fetched would make you weep!

So down in the hold a herring sat
A-catching mice and catching rats,
A herring that was o so sweet
And liked some salt upon his meat.

He chewed the salt out of the sack
And licked his lips and went right back
And he didn't see as he licked his lips
The hole he'd chewed in the side of the ship.

The ship went down with her sacks of salt
And it was all that herring's fault
And Neptune raged and shook his head,
'O Herring! Now, you've made your bed!

'The Queen of Balts, once bold and free,
Is at the bottom of the Baltic Sea.
So for your crime, you'll have to pay:
You'll have to be wet, now, all your days!

'And nets will come and you'll be caught
And packed up tight in barrels of salt!'
And that's the reason, since that time
The Seven Seas have been made of brine.

WITCHES

In the Highlands and Islands of Scotland witches could be tricky but they had their uses. Say you were a fisherman, becalmed in the north of Lewis and wanting to return to the south of Harris: you could buy wind from a witch, who might give it to you in the form of knots. The first, *Thìg gu fòill* (Come gently) would give you a light breeze to get you going, but it is a long voyage and the second, *Teann na's fhearr* (Come better) would give you the kind of stiff wind you could work with. This encyclopaedia is full of useful knowledge, but maybe none more valuable than the advice, however curious you might feel, have nothing to do with that third knot, *Cruaidh-chàs* (hardship). I'll leave it there.

Winds were the speciality of witches. The reason we smash the bottom of the shell after eating a boiled egg is to prevent one of them using it as a boat. Out at sea in it, they could cause all kinds of havoc stirring up winds: herring fleets have foundered. The truth is, though, it did not have to be an eggshell. Any dish, pot or basket would do. There were ways of dealing with the problem, however. You might have realised your own wife was a witch and you would see her out on the water with her friends, each in their own eggshells. All you had to say was *God speed!* They would all drown. For more on this, I'd recommend *Witchcraft & Second Sight in the Highlands & Islands of Scotland* (1903) by John Gregorson Campbell.

Things started to get unpleasant around 1400, when a hysteria about witches spread across Europe. The last Scottish execution for witchcraft was in 1727, the last European one was in Switzerland in 1782, the most well-known from the latter period resulted from the Salem witch trials of 1692/93 in Massachusetts. James VI & I was a noted enthusiast both for herrings and the persecution of witches. Thomas Nashe in *Lenten Stuffe* (1599) notes 'the confession of the six hundred Scotish witches executed in Scotland at Bartelmewtide was twelvemoneth, that in Yarmouth road they were all together in a plumpe on Christmasse eve was two yere when the great floud was, & there stird up such ternados & furicanos of tempests.'

They seem to have been annoyed that the herrings had gone down to East Anglia. Given their predilection for herrings, it is perhaps not too much of a surprise to find our fish at the heart of the penultimate witch trial in England.

AMY DUNY & ROSE CULLENDER

In March 1662, at Bury St Edmunds Assizes two Lowestoft women, Amy Duny and Rose Cullender were accused of witchcraft. The suspicions of their neighbours had been longstanding, but came to a head when Duny was refused herrings by Samuel Pacy's wife, whose daughter then fell ill:

> Amy Duny came to this Deponents House to buy some Herrings, but being denied she went away discontented, and presently returned again, and was denied, and likwise the third time and was denied as at first; and at her last going away, she went away grumbling; but what she said was not perfectly understood. But at the very same instant of time, the said Child was taken with most violent fits, feeling most extream pain in her Stomach, like the pricking of Pins, and Shrecking out in a most dreadful manner like unto a Whelp, and not like unto a sensible Creature.

The other main family in the proceedings suffered after similarly denying herrings to Cullender:

> Edmund Durent… Sworn and Examined, said, That he also lived in the said, Town of Leystoff, and that the said Rose Cullender, about the latter end of November last, came into this Deponents House to buy some Herrings of his Wife, but being denied by her, the said Rose returned in a discontented manner; and upon the first of December after, his Daughter Ann Durent was very sorely Afflicted in her Stomach, and felt great pain, like the pricking of Pins, and then fell into swooning fitts, and after the Recovery from her Fitts, she declared, That she had seen the Apparition of the said Rose, who threatned to Torment her. In this manner she continued from the first of December, until this present time of Tryal; having likewise vomited up divers Pins (produced here in Court.) This Maid was present in Court, but could not speak to declare her knowledge, but fell into most violent fits when she was brought before Rose Cullender.

Young girls all over Lowestoft were vomiting up pins, lath nails and even a Two-penny Nail with a very broad head. When Deborah and Elizabeth Pacy were sent to stay with their aunt in Yarmouth, the crooked pins and nails were carried to them in the mouths of a succession of Amy Duny's diabolical familiars, who were disguised as bees and flies.

Sir Thomas Browne, the most famous physician of his time, was called as a medical witness. He had views on the subject, which he had already expressed in his bestseller, *Religio Medici* (1643): 'I have ever believed, and do now know, that there are Witches: they that doubt of these, do not onely deny them, but Spirits; and are obliquely and upon consequence a sort not of Infidels, but Atheists.'

As a physician, he had no difficulty with evidence that a number of teats were discovered on the lower belly and in the private parts of Cullender. Having said that, despite having had twelve children he was not an expert on female anatomy. 'I could be content,' he wrote, 'that we might procreate like trees, without conjunction, or that there were any way to perpetuate the world without this triviall and vulgar way of coition.' On pins and nails, however, he was an expert and told the court:

> That in Denmark there had been lately a great Discovery of Witches, who used the very same way of Afflicting Persons, by conveying Pins into them, and crooked as these Pins were, with Needles and Nails.

It is hard to think what further proof the court might have needed, but the evidence was completed by one further fishy tale:

> Ann Sandeswel... Deposed.... That her Brother being a Fisherman, and using to go into the Northern Seas, she desired him to send her a Firkin of Fish, which he did accordingly; and she having notice that the said Firkin was brought into Leystoff-Road, she desired a Boatman to bring it ashore with the other Goods they were to bring; and she going down to meet the Boat-man to receive her Fish, desired the said Amy to go along with her to help her home with it; Amy

Replyed, She would go when she had it. And thereupon this Deponent went to the Shoar without her, and demanded of the Boatman the Firkin, they told her, That they could not keep it in the Boat from falling into the Sea, and they thought it was gone to the Devil, for they never saw the like before. And being demanded by this Deponent, whether any other Goods in the Boat were likewise lost as well as hers? They answered, Not any.

The girls, who between their fits and swoonings had been unable to give much in the way of coherent evidence during the trial, miraculously recovered upon Duny and Cullender's conviction and the old women were hanged a few days later.

The account drawn on here was published twenty years later in the public fervour surrounding England's last witch trial. In this published form it was, itself, influential in creating the hysterical narratives which supported the Salem trials.

X FORMERLY KNOWN AS THE DIFFICULT LETTER

X BRAND

X was going to be for *X, Crux or Kruis Brand*, the sign of the cross burnt on to all barrels of herring caught after September 14th. Why? Because it is the Day of the Exaltation of the Cross, Triumph of the Cross, Holy Cross Day, even Holy Rood Day, commemorating the dedication of Jerusalem's Church of the Holy Sepulchre in 335 CE. Emperor Constantine's mother, St Helena had found the True Cross a few years earlier and it had been split three ways between Rome, Constantinople and Jerusalem.

Things got complicated in the seventh century, when the Jerusalem section was temporarily lost in the Sassanian conquest. A rival Feast of the Cross tried to muscle its way in, celebrated on May 3rd, but Rome scotched that in 629 by arranging the September 14th celebration for the return of the Jerusalem bit. The Nestorian or Syriac Church celebrates the original finding of the True Cross, which was apparently on September 13th, but what do Nestorians know of the herring?

The true significance of the date was established by the **Dutch Fisheries**, marking the categorical end of the herring spawning season in the Scottish grounds where they began their Grand Fishery. After that point, having discharged most of their fat content along with their **Roes**, they become less economically desirable spents (until they have the chance to feed up again). The Cross brand on the barrel inevitably leant one way or the other—like the mark of an illiterate on any document: X. Maybe, when you are asked to put an X in any box, the combination of illiteracy and faith is simply assumed. I have speculated on whether there could be a connection with *Brand X* washing powder, which in the television adverts was never as good as Daz when I was growing up in the 1950s/60s. I never found a smoking gun, however.

X RAY

A friend thought the whole X Brand thing was spurious and sent me a link to an article about *X-ray* technology calculating the weight of herrings vacuum-sucked past a camera's eye, but I've now already said all I would want to say about that.

XYLOPHONE RAG

In memory of another friend, the percussionist Bruce Arthur, who died in 2002, I considered inventing a fictional *Xylophone Rag*, because he loved them. I would have called it *Herrings on Holiday* and attributed it to Bruce's hero George Hamilton Green Jnr (*Dotty Dimples*, *Fluffy Ruffles* and many more). I worked for twenty years with trombonist and composer Rick Taylor, who would have written it. He wrote the music for *Rigby's Red Herrings* back in the late 1990s, the BBC radio series out of which this encyclopaedia grew, but he died in 2019.

X FORMERLY KNOWN AS TWITTER

I was a latecomer to Twitter and only started using it to publicise new blogging entries at herripedia.com. I once persuaded a follower to try a bloater, so, clearly, the potential to become a social media influencer was there, even though my followers and those I have followed have tended not to be counted in their millions. My feed was full of posts by marine scientists, historians, archaeologists, fishermen and women, fishmongers, cookery writers, chefs, herring lovers, kipper and bloater enthusiasts and general devotees of random knowledge. It was a kind of modern idyll, but nothing lasts forever. X let loose the dogs of war, although it was still a while before their snarls invaded my space.

There have been many beautiful herring tweets over the years. The one I would like to celebrate here, a perfect example of everything I have enjoyed on the platform, was a thread posted on X in May 2024 by marine historian Poul Holm of Trinity College Dublin's Centre for Environmental Humanities (which seems to share his herring love). In eight tweets it opened up on a Historical Plankton Index for the North Sea. What can you say? Wow!

If you're not saying, 'Wow!' stick with me, because you should be. More zooplankton means more herrings; warm seas mean less phytoplankton means less zooplankton. We're talking about an enabled calculation of variations in the amount of plankton in the North Sea from 800 CE to the present (HPI) on the basis of the Atlantic Multidecadal Variability (AMV)—as outlined in a 2017 paper by Jianglin Wang and others, establishing historical changes in Sea Surface Temperature (SST). Historians have traditionally been sceptical about phenomenological causes for historical events, but this enables a correlation between sea temperatures and the narrative of herring fisheries.

X: POUL HOLM'S THREAD

#1 So what does the historical plankton index mean? Bad news unfortunately for today, very positive news for the early modern times... In academic detail:

#2 800–870: Strongly positive (HPI_AMV median: 3.19). North Sea fisheries at the time largely restricted to riverine environments (Barrett et al., 2004; Hoffmann, 1996). Viking Age archaeology does indicate that this may have been a time of increased cod fishing (Star et al., 2017)

#3 871–1290: Negative (HPI_AMV median: -0.22), with particularly low levels 1291–1300 and 1331–1340. Archaeologists have identified increased nearshore herring fisheries in the North Sea from around 1050 and increased offshore demersal fisheries in the 13th century (Barrett, 2019).

#4 1351–1450: Slightly Negative (HPI_AMV median: -0.08). Decline of plankton production was a potential additional environmental challenge, but may not have had much impact on fisheries relative to the likelihood of the industry contracting anyway because of the Black Death.

#5 1451–1920: Positive (HPI_AMV median: 2.20). The North Sea fisheries experienced sustained growth for almost half a millennium (Holm et al., 2019).

#6 In the first three centuries, 1451–1750, the Flemish and Dutch herring fisheries dominated landings. It should be noted that the HPI_AMV median reached a high of 3.50 in the half century 1451–1500 when the Flemish North Sea fishery took off.

#7 The expansion of commercial fisheries will likely have benefitted from strong marine productivity in the decades of 1591–1610, 1631–1650, 1691–1710, 1721–1730 and 1741–1760.

#8 1921–2010: Negative to strongly negative (HPI median: –0.72). The 20th century was a period of dramatically increased fishing power and repeated crashes of fish stocks, eventually leading to management intervention. Negative plankton production will have exacerbated problems.

THE ARTICLE

The thread draws on a paper by Cordula Scherer, Francis Ludlow, Al Matthews, Patrick Hayes and Holm (all of the Trinity College Centre) and Riina Klais (of the Estonian Marine Institute), 'A Historical Plankton Index: Zooplankton abundance in the North Sea since 800 CE'. Sea Surface Temperatures can vary from year to year, decade to decade, but there have also been broader periods, such as the Medieval Warm Period which lasted from the mid ninth to the mid thirteenth century and the Little Ice Age which lasted approximately from 1300 to 1850. Two historical plankton indices were developed in the research. As well as the AMV, there is one derived from the work of the UK Met Office's Hadley Centre, which enables SST reconstructions going back to 1870. The key element of the research was testing the indices' plankton abundance projections against catch records from the Dutch herring fishery in the seventeenth century.

As someone who took his Maths O Level a year early so he could give it up, I drew confidence from the statement that the researchers had detrended the data by fitting and then subtracting a 'cubic spline'. To test catches least affected by war (the Dutch fishery only went into decline after the 2nd Anglo-Dutch War) they chose to focus on a period, from 1600 to 1664. They also eliminated The Netherland's southern ports, as bearing the brunt of the herring piracy exercised by Dunkirk's privateers, and focused on Enkhuizen, Delfshaven and Schiedam.

The bottom line is that the Historical Plankton Index works. The levels of as much as 20% of historical catches can be accounted for by projected plankton levels. It becomes a major, previously unrecognised factor in herring history. With reducing

North Sea plankton abundance since 1920, its coincidence with the overfishing enabled through new fishery technologies and markets leads to greater insight into the population collapses of the 1970s. As there is a time lag of a couple of years between reduced plankton biomass and reduced herring biomass, perhaps even more importantly, as today's sea temperatures rise, it enables a predictive tool in marine conservation (see **Quotas**).

Wow.

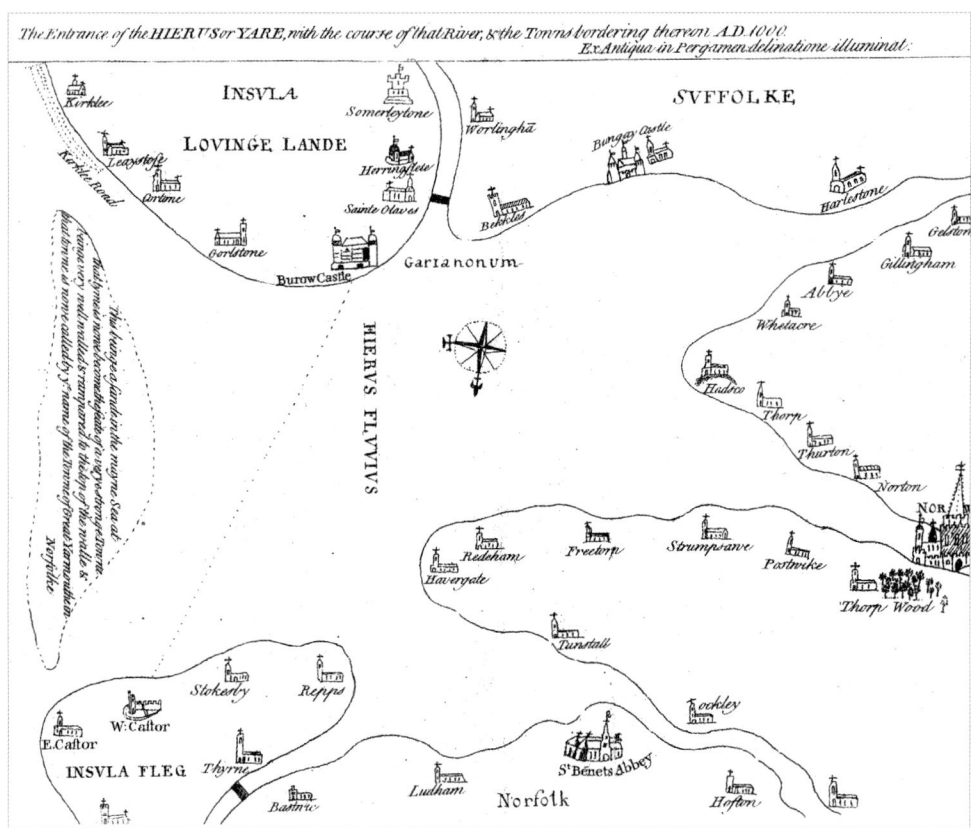

Map of the Mouth of the Yare, AD 1000 from John Ives' *Remarks upon the Garianonum of the Romans*, 1774 or 1803 edition (taken from A.M. Samuel's *The Herring*, 1918). The text in the outlined sandbank reads, 'This beinge a sande in the mayne sea at that tyme is nowe become the seate of a very stronge towne beinge very well walled & rampared to the top of the walle & that towne is nowe called by ye name of the Towne of Great Yarmouthe in Norfolke.'

YARMOUTH'S GREATNESS

The East Anglian coast is better known for crumbling into the sea than emerging from it. The thirteenth and fourteenth centuries were notably problematic for Dunwich and seven of its churches are now below water. Those with a sensitive ear can still sometimes hear their bells pealing. In contrast, by the thirteenth century Yarmouth was just getting started. Barely even a sandbank by 1 CE, by 495 it was big enough for Cerdic the Saxon to beach his boats upon.

Some say he was not a Saxon, some that he landed on the coast of Hampshire. It would have been more convenient for his founding of the House of Wessex and thus the line of England's kings and queens, but Hampshire is not famed for its herrings and in *The History of Great Yarmouth* (1619) Henry Manship confidently states he landed on the sandbank which became known as *Cerdick Shore* and, later, Yarmouth. He spent twenty years fighting all-comers in the sandbank's neighbourhood before sailing West to fulfill England's destiny.

Manship does not mention it, but Cerdic was directly descended from Woden, who has, ever since, been quietly providing the unimpeachable guarantee of royal legitimacy to all who have followed. More importantly, traditional histories suggest England's herring fisheries began on Cerdick Shore, not long after his landing. In his *Lenten Stuffe* (1599) Thomas Nashe dates Yarmouth's miraculous discovery of the smokehouse principle to the papacy of Vigilius, which ran from 537 to 555 (see **Red Herring Joke**), but he had read Manship's papers and may have just checked to see who had been Pope a few decades after Cerdic.

Sticking with traditional historians, Henry Swinden's *The History and Antiquities of the Ancient Burgh of Great Yarmouth in the County of Norfolk* (1772) has a St Bennet's Church erected on the sandbank in 647 with 'a godly man placed in it to pray for the health and success of the fishermen that came to fish at Yarmouth in the herring season.' By 670 the Abbey at Barking had secured a herring silver tax on the fisheries. It is important to place against this what contemporary historians such as James Barrett are saying, about how low Anglo-Saxon marine fish consumption was before the Fish Event Horizon (roughly 950 to 1050). Where there's *herring silver,*, there has to be a silver darlings fishery. It speaks of a herring fair that was established relatively early on.

Yarmouth became famous for reds, rather than silver or white herring, but as to when herrings were first smoked in England, all we can say for certain is that it will have been at some point between the papacy of Vigilius and the fifteenth century, when red herrings get their first literary mentions in England and France (see **Life of St Herring**).

A combination of emerging out of the North Sea and smoked herring is probably enough for any town to develop a rarified sense of its own identity, but its fishermen probably belonged to Gorleston at the time of the Conquest; it wasn't granted a charter until 1208; and it only became Great in 1272 to distinguish it from Little Yarmouth (now Southtown). Yet the sense of its identity was remarkable: there is not just Manship's history, but *Nashe's Lenten Stuffe's* fantasia for the town, Henry Swinden's *History and Antiquities*, Charles Palmer's annotated republication of Manship in 1854, his Volume Two *Continuation of Manship's History* (1856) and then his three volume *Perlustration of Great Yarmouth, with Gorleston and Southtown* (1872, 1874 & 1875).

What is beautiful about these histories is the place they give to the town's officers and bailiffs. Manship is as attentive to their memory as he is to Yarmouth's dealings with kings and queens. Swinden gives a complete list from 1260 to 1771. There were forces at play which might explain the intensity of this historical self-projection. They are central to Manship's account and they are all to do with herring: he lists them as 'the four cardinal winds' which 'continually set forth boisterous blasts, and storms of suits, troubles, costs, expenses, and molestations.'

THE WEST WIND

Manship starts with the North and goes clockwise, but for the sake of historical narrative I am starting with the West, by which he means the Barons of the Cinque Ports. You might think their fleet would have appeared from the South, but even their easternmost limb (Margate) is to the west of Yarmouth and, more importantly, 'western men they be by us commonly called.'

The *Domesday Book* records salt pans at Gorleston, which is a giveaway for an existing herring industry. Under the Normans, control over the herring fair lay with the Cinque Ports, originally Sandwich, Dover, Hythe, New Romney and Hastings. These each established further *limbs* around the coasts of Kent, Sussex and even Essex. The Cinque Ports claimed their control preceded the Conquest and that they had been largely responsible for the herring fair's development. Yarmouth's fishermen and fish merchants do not seem ever to have gone along with this view, but the Barons' boys would turn up each year from Michaelmas (September 29th) to Martinmas (November 11th).

Yarmouth played a long game and wrote the strategy into its coat of arms and motto. The Cinque Ports' coat of arms had the front half of the royal three lions to the left and the sterns of three ships to the right. Yarmouth had the same half lions but with the back halves of three herrings, as if to say, 'this is where the money is coming from.' Its strapline was *Rex et Nostra Jura* (The King and Our Rights): conspicuous loyalty to the Crown went hand in hand with a constant whinge. The Cinque Ports had to supply naval vessels to the king on an as-needed basis. Yarmouth was able to offer more on top every time a king's calculations indicated a need beyond that upon which he could already depend.

In 1297, Yarmouth's capacity to supply was constrained by the Cinque Ports sinking twenty of their ships off Sluys, where Edward I had gathered a supposedly united fleet to fight the French. By way of a return match, in 1316 Yarmouth sank several Cinque ships and was fined £1,000, but the town simply delayed payment until their ships were needed again and the fine was never enforced. Gradually Yarmouth took away more and more of the Cinque Ports' privileges until their role at the Herring Fair came largely down to attending a ceremonial feast.

SOUTH & NORTH WINDS

Lothingland or Lovingland (*South Wind*), a manorial estate stretching from the southern bank of the Yare to beyond Lowestoft, complained early about the Cinque Ports/Yarmouth deal on the principle that any privileges should be split between both banks on a 50/50 basis. It did not like its herring fishermen having to pay taxes to sail out from a shared river mouth. Yarmouth's boys may once have been Gorleston (South bank) boys, but, as they secured more and more of the Cinque Ports' perks and privileges, sharing wasn't on their minds.

Maybe England's kings and queens felt they had enough trouble dealing with just two parties, but Lothingland never really got anywhere. As Yarmouth's economy grew, Gorleston's declined, but Lowestoft, just 10 miles down the road, 'ever since the 46th year of Edward III (1358) till this present, have troubled this Township, touching the extent of its liberties by sea to the southward.' Lowestoft did not get far either, and it still rankles.

There were also jurisdictional arguments between Yarmouth and Caister (*North Wind*). First it was the Bardolfs, then the Fastolfs, then the Pastons. It seems mostly to have been about grazing rights. Sir John Fastolf followed his triumph at the **Battle of the Herrings** (see also the **Red Herring Joke**) by commissioning the building of Caister Castle in 1432. When he died childless, his lawyer John Paston announced the entire estate had been verbally bequeathed to him. Not everybody believed this, but lawyers are lawyers and having one in charge may have contributed to the Caister/Yarmouth settlement which separated their lands with both a ditch and a cross.

THE EAST WIND

One cause of Yarmouth's belligerence is made painfully clear in Manship. The town arose out of the sea and the sea gave it herrings and trade, but it also brought storms, further drifting sands and no end of expense. When an entrance to the harbour became blocked, the cost of clearing it or cutting a new one was high. The bailiffs on each occasion naturally get their special credit, but Manship is also proud of the way his townsfolk set to with the work required. Even so, petitions for capital support from the royal purse were regularly required and were generally successful. Each petition will have used up credit and, everyone knows, one way or another the generosity of kings always comes with a price tag.

Between the lines of Manship's history is a sense of outrage at the suggestion that Great Yarmouth was anything other than entirely justified in its privileges. Where were all these people when we were digging new cuts, when we were building new quays, when we were begging at the king's table? We fought and paid for everything we have!

MORE WINDS

All four winds were mitigated by the herrings, but English herring consumption never recovered from The Reformation. It is not hard to imagine this as a fifth wind filling the sails of the town's autobiographical motivation. The Dutch might have had a laugh about herrings, but they also recognised a centrality for it in their nation's economy. Look at Enkhuizen's coat of arms: recognising the herring as the **King of Fishes**. The quality of Yarmouth's red herrings was celebrated across Europe. Why can't we get a bit of respect here?

It may be stretching things a bit to link such thoughts to Yarmouth coming out for the Parliamentarians in the English Civil War. It could have been Charles I's aggressive Ship Money increases, as it was for many other towns. It could simply have been down to Lowestoft coming out for the King. It is worth noting, the Crown had complained in 1629 about the quality of the 24 herring pies Yarmouth had sent that year (see **Past(r)y**): the cold pies of cooling monarchism.

Royalist privateers provided a sixth wind. It will have come as no surprise to find a Lowestoft man, Thomas Allin, at the heart of the trouble. Allin, merchant, shipowner, pirate, virtually wiped out Great Yarmouth's herring fleet and claimed to have captured thousands of men in the process. From 1645 some convoy protection was provided from Parliament and the town built its own man of war. With the Restoration, it was, of course, Allin, baronet, admiral, who received the nation's grateful thanks. Yarmouth's MP Miles Corbet, who had hosted his fellow regicides in Yarmouth for the meeting at which Charles I's execution was agreed, received the one-way ticket to Tyburn.

EAT MORE HERRINGS

Yarmouth had always produced plain salted or white herrings too. Yet along with the rest of Britain, its efforts in this direction received less acclaim. The Victorian Age could be seen as that of the town's triumph. Joined in its herring season by the Scottish curers and their **Herring Lasses**, its sandy beach a magnet for the new tourism, its railway connections opening up markets for its new mild-cured bloaters and kippers, things just got better and better... until, after World War I, they no longer did (see **British Fisheries**, **Herring Boats**, **Herring Industry Board**, **Quotas**, **Reduction Plants** and **X** for some of the reasons).

Postcards from holidaymakers kept the smiles going: 'Just a line from Yarmouth' with its speated line of bloaters and its jokey 'Quite Fresh' play on both herrings and weather. Postcards of herring girls and barrels abounded, but no port seems to have adopted the Herring Industry Board's 'Eat More Herrings' slogan with greater enthusiasm than Yarmouth. Carnival floats of drifters carried the message on sails, a painted sign covered a whole wall (see second image section), but did anybody listen?

Maybe 'Staycation' Britain and herring port holidays will bring a revival in the fortunes of bloaters and kippers, although, at time of writing, there no longer appears to be a smokehouse in Yarmouth producing either. What there is, is the excellent Time & Tide Museum, continuing to tell the town's stories and, in particular, its herring history. And on the quay there is *Lydia Eva* YH89, at 95 foot (29 m) the last surviving steam drifter built in 1930, manned by volunteers who keep its engine bright as a button and will happily talk to you about every inch of her.

Go to Yarmouth! It's Great and it's great!

Z IS FOR ZENO'S PARADOX

Without the help of freeze frame technology, in his Paradox of the Arrow, the fifth-century BCE philosopher Zeno pointed out that, at any given instant in an arrow's flight it is motionless. Time is composed of instants and therefore the arrow is always motionless. In his Paradox of Achilles and the Tortoise, the former chases the latter, but before he can reach it, he must reach halfway. However slowly, the tortoise continues to move forward and Achilles still must get halfway between halfway and where the tortoise is now. Distance being infinitely divisible he never gets to more than a new halfway point and therefore never overtakes. I must have been about fourteen when I first heard of Zeno: a philosopher in your corner for the constant struggle with PE teachers.

He wrote a book of forty paradoxes, but it was lost and only six survive. One of those which did not was Zeno's Paradox of the Herring Encyclopaedia. It has three parts. The first rule says, in researching any single entry, by the time you are halfway through you will have doubled the amount of research required to complete it. The second rule says research into any one entry will require the rewriting of two other previous entries. The third rule says, by the time you are halfway through writing the encyclopaedia, you will have doubled the number of necessary entries, all of which will be subject to the first two rules. A herring encyclopaedia is never finished. Just as Zeno foresaw the freeze frame, he imagined the internet too.

This encyclopaedia began in the world of **Herringism**. The internet had recently become a magic source of niche secondhand books. Now there are vast collections of digitised rare books, many of them downloadable. You want to find the original Latin text for Alexander **Neckam**'s thirteenth-century poem on the herring? You can download the whole of *De Laudibus Divinae Sapientae*. Search on *halec* (medieval Latin for herring): bingo! The trouble is, every time you go online to check some minor detail you find another beautiful new avenue to explore. You're like a pig in clover, but...

It is not just digitisation. The internet has become a sea of papers on the herring. Every day I am emailed about at least one academic paper which, 'from your reading history,' I should be interested in—there is a tendency to repeat notifications, but at least half the time they are right. There was a time historians turned their noses up at the herring. I get details of papers by historians, archaeologists, marine scientists, geneticists and everything in between. We are living through a golden age of herring research. Our hero swims between trade, global warming, DNA sequencing, conservation, art, literature, curing and cookery and his adventures, never richer or more relevant, never seem to stop. Halfway is never more than a tiny fraction of itself. Completion is an illusion.

ZUIDERZEE

There is a Dutch folksong with a chorus, 'Der haring is het Zilver van der Zuiderzee' (the herring is the silver of the Zuiderzee). In the full pomp of *Die Groote Visserye*, the Dutch authorities would not even allow the inshore herrings of their own coastline to be used for the all-important salt herring trade. They were decreed fit only for smoking (as if the smokehouse represented a bottom rung of culinary options). They began to change their minds after the Second Anglo-Dutch War, when their grand buss fishery started its slide into decline. But then, this now-prized unique herring of the Zuiderzee disappeared altogether in 1932 when the Dutch completed construction of the *Afsluitdijk*, the dike which closes off the former bay from the North Sea.

At Fécamp's herring festival in 2024, I met René Godvliet, who was hot-smoking herring—not *bokking* or **Buckling**, but an artisinal tradition they refer to as just 'smoked herring'. He lives behind the Afsluitdijk, just a few miles out of Enkhuizen on the shores of the *IJsselmeer* and knows Nanne Kalma who wrote the song. Was the irony deliberate? 'Yes,' he grinned, rolling himself a cigarette.

The Dutch are at ease with irony as well as herrings. 'Don't listen to him,' his colleagues called out, 'he speaks Fisher Latin.' Fish people tell tall tales, they explained. You shouldn't ever believe a word they say.

After World War II, for a few years there were still sightings of Zuiderzee refugees… in the Thames estuary… off the coast of Suffolk…

Even as far north as Northumberland…

ACKNOWLEDGEMENTS

The development of this encyclopaedia has occupied me for over twenty-five years. There are many people to thank, some of whom may have long forgotten the ways in which they contributed. What is worse is that I may have forgotten their part in it too, so big thanks to those first. I would also like to thank all of those mentioned in the preface, *Y is for Why?*, and throughout the text.

Professor Brian Vickers will have forgotten me, but at Cambridge in 1972 he taught me sixteenth- and seventeenth-century English literature. He encouraged me to look at Thomas Nashe, maybe sensing a greater potential kinship than had been evident with Sir Philip Sidney or Edmund Spenser. *Nashes Lenten Stuffe* stuck with me, opening my imagination to the herring's possibilities.

Sue Roberts commissioned and produced Rigby's Red Herrings for BBC Radio 4; my then agent Andrew Hewson pushed me towards a genuinely alphabetical encyclopaedia. The first public manifestations came in poems and performance pieces with my late friend and collaborator, the trombonist and composer Rick 'Big Boy' Taylor, who would happily set more-or-less anything I wrote to music.

Anita Elefsen of the Herring Era Museum in Siglufjörður, Piers Crocker and then Erik Hennum-Bergsagel of the Norwegian Canning Museum/Iddis in Stavanger, Benjamin Loesel of the Fisheries Museum in Fécamp, Siobhan Beatson of Ullapool Museum, Linda Fitzpatrick of the Scottish Fisheries Museum and Tor Scott of the Scottish National Gallery of Modern Art have all been particularly helpful, but I would also like to thank Timespan in Helmsdale, Eyemouth Museum, the Old Low Light in North Shields, Time & Tide in Great Yarmouth, the Pomor Museum in Vardø, the Norway Fisheries Museum in Bergen, Ålesund's Fisheries Museum and Sunnmøre Museum for their contributions to my understandings. There are, I know, so many beautiful herring-related museums and collections with herring-related content: I only wish I had been able to visit them all.

Many have tolerated my interest in the herring, but some have actively encouraged it, so big thanks, in particular to Steve Hinton, Virginia Alison, Jonathan White, David Little and his brother the late Alastair Little, Simon Tepper, Guy Cook, Jerry Podmore, Mike Hogan, John Gordon, Martin Kisch, Morag MacInnes, John McGill, Leila Burrell-Davis, Clare Birks, Christopher Holden, Katrina Porteous, Fiona Cooper, Fred D'Aguiar, Ian Duhig, Bill Herbert, Val Scully and Claire Malcolm. Over the years I worked with Amber Films/Side Gallery, in and outside the collective I learned much about working with the non-linear, interconnecting archive narratives of its film and photography collection and for that I would particularly like to thank the late Murray Martin, Richard Grassick, Peter Scott, Kerry Lowes, Dean Chapman, Ellin Hare, Peter Roberts, Sirkka-Liisa Konttinen, Pat McCarthy, Richard Cross, Martyn Dade-Robertson, Marian Dörk and Alex Butterworth. Thank you to Charles Bell and Jim McMaster for help chasing various rabbits down their respective holes.

My progress with the herrings has been the subject of enjoyable conversations over several years with all at Lindsay Brothers, fishmongers of Newcastle's Grainger Market. When they have been able to get a box or two of them from North Shields fish market, I think they have almost been as happy as me. I would also like to thank Alistair Blair and the Fish Society for all the frozen herrings when they have not been at Shields, especially for the artisinal Dutch maatjes fillets.

Thanks to Sam Llewellyn (*The Marine Quarterly*) and Nathan Hill (*Fish*) for commissioning herring pieces. A planned Larking with the Herring project never happened, but the artist Keith McIntyre has contributed in so many ways, not least by introducing me to fellow Scottish artist Will Maclean, who, as well as his work, has introduced me to enough beautiful secondhand book possibilities for another encyclopaedia. Matthew Jarrett introduced me to Penelope Payne. Keith's, Will's and Penny's works have immeasurably improved the encyclopaedia, as have the photographs of Martin Figura and the late Nick Hedges, both of whom I got to know through my work with Amber/Side. I would like to thank the late Jim Muir of

ACKNOWLEDGEMENTS

Polbain, historians the late James Campbell, Carsten Jahnke, Poul Holm and George Muirhead, archaeologist Anton Larsson, fish smoker Will Buckenham and Shetland fiddle player Chris Stout for their generosity, correspondents P. Nahon (for pointing me in the directions of Proverbs and *Life of St Herring*) and Odd Jakob Haaland (for the vintage *Skippers* label), as well as traditional musicians Karen Tweed, Chris Wood, Sandra Kerr and Rob Harbron, who have all helped in different ways. Huge thanks are due to Ingrid O'Mahoney and Isis Olivier for translation help that was way beyond what could ever have been expected. There are simply too many individuals on social media, who have helped and encouraged this work, but huge thanks to all of them.

I would like to thank my friend, the writer Michael Chaplin for introducing my work to Hurst Publishers and all at Hurst, especially Michael Dwyer, for being so open to it and for making the process of creating this book such an enjoyable collaboration. Lastly but not least, thank you to my family who have put up with all this for so long. My daughter Annie and her husband Wayne, my son Sam and his wife Sarah have all contributed to the ways in which the encyclopaedia has grown; grandchildren Nina, Cora and Martha have, throughout their entire lives, gone along with so many conversations they knew were somehow leading towards a little-known fact about the herring. My wife Ros may have, just occasionally and entirely justifiably, rolled her eyes or, for a moment, allowed her attention to drift, but she has uncomplainingly eaten a lot of herring dishes and none of the work would have been possible without her.

ILLUSTRATIONS

IN THE BODY OF THE TEXT

Title page. The racially measured herring, *Natural History of the Herring* (1898), Friedrich Heincke. Author's collection.

Page 42. Willem Beuckel, lithograph by Hilmar Johannes Backer (1821), copied from a stained glass window in Biervliet Church. In the collection of the Rijksmuseum, Amsterdam. Public Domain. https://commons.wikimedia.org/wiki/File:Willem_Beuckel_lithograph_1821.jpg

44. Yallop's Yarmouth Bloaters (Just a line), postcard, early twentieth century. Author's collection.

50. Herring-Boats in Wick Harbour, largest fishing station in the world, *The Penny Illustrated Paper*, November 5th, 1881. Author's collection.

59. Yarmouth Illustrated - The Herring, *The Graphic*, August 25th 1883. Author's collection.

71. *Tyne Brand Herrings* (front cover), published by Tyne Brand Products with acknowledgements to *Picture Post*, photograph by Felix H. Man (Hans Bauman), 1950s. Advertorial publication by Tyne Brand, closed 1976.

72. From *Tyne Brand Herrings*, 'Each machine, operated by two girls', photograph by Felix H. Man (Hans Bauman), inside pages. Advertorial publication by Tyne Brand, closed 1976.

73. From *Tyne Brand Herrings*, 'Full speed ahead', inside pages, photograph by Felix H. Man (Hans Bauman), inside pages. Advertorial publication by Tyne Brand, closed 1976.

74. *Tyne Brand Herrings* (back cover). Advertorial publication by Tyne Brand, closed 1976.

81. Herring Fishing, from *Historia de Gentibus Septentrionalibus* (History of the Northern Peoples, 1555) Olaus Magnus. Alamy.

95. Still from *Drifters* (1929), John Grierson. Alamy.

154. Hareng saur production, from *General Treatise upon Fisheries and History of the Fish they provide, both for the subsistence of Men and for several other Uses relating to Arts and Commerce* by Henri-Louis Duhamel du Monceau (1769), image taken from *The Herring* (1918), A.M. Samuel. Author's collection.

159. Advertisement for the libretto of Coquelin Cadet's recital of *Le Hareng Saur* by French poet Charles Cros, accompanied on the piano by Ernest Cabaner, designed by Pierre-Désiré Lamy, c. 1875–1880. Public Domain. https://commons.wikimedia.org/wiki/File:Charles_Cros_-_Le_Hareng_Saur.jpg

189. Herring lasses, photographic feature, *The Sphere*, 1913. Author's collection.

223. Make the most of Herring Week (The King of Fish), poster published by Herring Industry Board, c. 1940s/1950s. Author's photograph.

250. The figure of a Glyster pipe and Syringe, *The workes of that famous chirugion Ambrose Parey* (1649). Wellcome Collection, Public Domain.

263. Thomas Nashe, from *The Trimming of Thomas Nashe, Gentleman* (1597). Public Domain. https://commons.wikimedia.org/wiki/File:Thomas_Nashe_in_chains_-_Lichfield,_Trimming_of_Thomas_Nashe_(1597).jpg

ILLUSTRATIONS

268. Title page of *De Harengo*, Paul Neucrantz (1654). From the British Library Collection, 1257.d.17.

274. *Drift Netting*. By kind permission of the Scottish Fisheries Museum.

276. *Ring Netting*. By kind permission of the Scottish Fisheries Museum.

278. *Purse Seine Netting*. By kind permission of the Scottish Fisheries Museum.

279. *Mid Water or Pelagic Trawling*. By kind permission of the Scottish Fisheries Museum.

304. *Beer Street* (1751), William Hogarth, nineteenth century reproduction. Author's collection.

318. Prophetic herrings from *The Divination of Reasonable Creatures* (1632), Johann Faulhaber. From the British Library Collection, C.29.f.1.

331. *Extent of Variation in the Position of the Dorsal Fin, Pelvic Fins and Anal, as well as of Body Length, excluding Tail Fin, in the herring, Natural History of the Herring* (1898), Friedrich Heincke. Author's collection.

338. Herbert Beerbohm Tree as Falstaff in *The Merry Wives of Windsor*, 1889. Alamy.

341. Sir John Oldcastle, hanged and burned in 1417, from *Hollinshed's Chronicles* (1577). Public Domain. https://commons.wikimedia.org/wiki/File:Oldcastleburning.jpg

353. *Herring Cooking* (from *The Ring-Net*), Will Maclean. National Galleries of Scotland. Purchased 1980.

406. Herring Heads from *Natural History of the Herring* (1898), Friedrich Heincke. Author's Collection.

423. *Soused Herrings* from the recipe book of Annie Ewens née Partridge. Author's collection.

438. *Map of the Mouth of the Yare*, AD 1000, from *Remarks upon the Garianonum of the Romans* (1774/1803), taken from *The Herring* (1918), A.M. Samuel. Author's collection.

IMAGE SECTION 1

1. *Rudder Requiem*, Will Maclean. Courtesy of the artist.

2. *In the memory of gannets*, Will Maclean. Courtesy of the artist.

3. *Gannet Fishing* (from *The Ring Net*), Will Maclean. National Galleries of Scotland. Purchased 1980.

4. *Ma heid's fair fu' o' fish* (2019), Keith McIntyre. Courtesy of the artist.

5. *The Herring Kiss* (2019), Keith McIntyre. Courtesy of the artist.

6. Pacific herring spawning, Vancouver Island. Rolf Hicker Photography/Alamy.

7. Herring shoal in a cave, Scotland, José Benito Ruiz. Alamy.

8. Arthur Beech's basket making tools. Author's photograph.

9. *Making herring barrels* (1909). Alamy.

ILLUSTRATIONS

10. Trinidadian red herring stir fry-stuffed dumplings on stir fry. Author's photograph.

11. Jeanie Wilson and Annie Linton (1843), David Octavius Hill and Robert Adamson. Alamy.

12. *Dutch East Indiaman Passing Herring Busses* (late seventeenth century), Bonaventure Peeters, in the collection of the National Maritime Museum. Alamy.

13. *Praise of Pickled Herring* (1647), Joseph de Bray, in the collection of the Old Master's Gallery, Dresden. Alamy.

14. *Two Smoked Herrings* [Hareng Saur] *on Yellow Paper* (1889), Vincent van Gogh, privately owned. Alamy.

15. *Two Skeletons Fighting over a Smoked Herring* [Hareng Saur] (1891), James Ensor. Royal Museums of Fine Arts of Belgium, inv. 11156, photo: J. Geleyns.

16. *The Fight between Carnival and Lent* (1559), Pieter Breughel the Elder, in the collection of the Museum of Art History, Vienna. Alamy.

17. Herrings €4 kg, Fécamp Herring Festival, November 2024. Author's photograph.

18. Grilled herrings by night, Fécamp Herring Festival, November 2024. Author's photograph.

19. Gansey knitted by Mary Muir Murray of Cellardyke, twentieth century. Courtesy of Scottish Fisheries Museum.

20. Gansey knitted by Margaret Shirran Lowrie of Aberdeen, 1949. Courtesy of Scottish Fisheries Museum.

21. *Nordlandsbåt* (1998), Stig Tobiassen. Author's collection.

22. The *Adenia* (LK193) built in 2019, moored at Lerwick harbour, Alan Morris. Alamy.

23. William Campbell, Lossiemouth (1909). Courtesy of Scottish Fisheries Museum.

24. Richard Padwick with his model of the zulu *Muirneag* (SY486). Author's photograph.

25. The zulu *Cellandine* (BF737) and a fifie (BK234) entering Great Yarmouth harbour. Courtesy of Scottish Fisheries Museum.

26. *Skye Fisherman, in memoriam* (1989), Will Maclean. Courtesy of the artist.

27. Mike Smylie's smokehouse. Courtesy of Mike Smylie.

28. A selection of herringist works. Author's photograph.

29. The artist Penelope Payne with *Scold Vixen Harpy Shrew*, MIMA, 2022. Courtesy of the artist.

30. *Packing Herrings*, postcard, early twentieth century. Author's collection.

31. *Scotch Girls Gipping Herring, Yarmouth,* postcard, early twentieth century. Author's collection.

32. Boat house, Herring Era Museum, Siglufjörður, Iceland, 2019. Author's photograph.

33. Edward, Prince of Wales, based on a photograph taken in 1913, Norwegian sardine can label. Courtesy of MUST/Norwegian Canning Museum.

34. *Fish-Pyramide Sardines*, Norwegian sardine can label. Courtesy of MUST/Norwegian Canning Museum.

35. Crown Prince of Ethiopia, Norwegian sardine can label. Courtesy of MUST/Norwegian Canning Museum.

36. Cocktail, sardine can label. Courtesy of MUST/Norwegian Canning Museum.

37. Wilwin Brand, Norwegian brisling [sprat] can label. Courtesy of MUST/Norwegian Canning Museum.

38. Norrig Kippered Herrings, can label. Courtesy of MUST/Norwegian Canning Museum.

39. Herring Book covers, Herring Industry Board recipe booklets, 1935–38. Author's collection

40. Chopped herring. Author's photograph.

IMAGE SECTION 2

41. Hanging kippers, I. Marshall's smokehouse, North Shields (1979), Nick Hedges. Courtesy of the photographer.

42. I. Marshall's smokehouse, exterior, North Shields (1979), Nick Hedges. Courtesy of the photographer.

43. The Smokehouses, North Shields (2025), Charles Bell. Courtesy of the photographer.

44. Operation Archery (the Måløy Raid). Alamy.

45. *Renga, Ringa* or golden herring, on sale in a Cairo market for the Egyptian Spring festival, *Sham Ennessim*, Amr Sayed. Alamy.

46. *Renga*, a Greek dish. Author's photograph.

47. *Monkey Business* (1931), Marx Brothers film poster. Public Domain. https://commons.wikimedia.org/wiki/File:MonkeyBusinessMarxBros.jpg

48. *King Oscar–Out to Conquer the World*, poster. Courtesy of MUST/Norwegian Canning Museum.

49. Nineteenth century sardine can opener. Author's collection.

50. Laurence Olivier eating scrambled eggs, Pullman car of the Brighton Belle, March 1970. Alamy.

51. Herring scales, from the North Sea in 1914, Norway Fisheries Museum, Bergen. Author's photograph.

52. Herring pasties. Author's photograph.

53. Herring pie. Author's photograph.

54. *The Merry Drinker* (c. 1625) Hendrick ter Brugghen, oil on canvas. Collection Centraal Museum, Utrecht, purchased with the support of the Rembrandt Association, 1955; photo Ernst Moritz

55. *Whipping the Herring out of Town—A Scene of Cork* (c. 1800) Nathaniel Grogan.

Collection Crawford Art Gallery, Cork.

56. Election of the Herring Queen, Fécamp Herring Festival, November 2024. Author's photograph.

57. The racially measured herring (full page), from *Natural History of the Herring* (1898), Friedrich Heincke. Author's collection.

58. Red herring, H.S. Fishing Company, Great Yarmouth, Martin Figura. Courtesy of the photographer.

59. Mike Kelly, smoker, H.S. Fishing Company, Great Yarmouth, Martin Figura. Courtesy of the photographer.

60. Former herring reduction plant, Djúpavík, Iceland, Penelope Payne. Courtesy of the photographer.

61. Former herring oil holder, Djúpavík, Iceland, Penelope Payne. Courtesy of the photographer.

62. Female and male roes. Author's photograph.

63. Crispy fried soft roes. Author's photograph.

64. Mixed roe puffs. Author's photograph.

65. Atlas Small Sild, Formerly Known as Sardines, Norwegian label. Courtesy of MUST/Norwegian Canning Museum.

66. Skippers (Norwegian Brisling), Angus Watson & Co. label. Author's collection.

67. Shuba or herring under a fur coat. Author's photograph.

68. Will Buckenham in the yard of The Old Smokehouse, Raglan Street, Lowestoft, 2021. Author's photograph.

69. Inside Will Buckenham's smokehouse, Raglan Street, Lowestoft, 2021. Author's photograph.

70. Will Buckenham speating bloaters, The Old Smokehouse, Raglan Street, Lowestoft, 2021.

71. *The Flambeau* (1973–1978, from *The Ring-Net*), Will Maclean. National Galleries of Scotland. Purchased 1980.

72. *Herring Chute* (1973–1978, from *The Ring-Net*), Will Maclean. National Galleries of Scotland. Purchased 1980.

73. *The Weight of Salt*, Cheeseburn Sculpture Festival (2021), Penelope Payne. Courtesy of the artist.

74. *Horizons*, Cullercoats Bay, February 2022, Penelope Payne. Courtesy of the artist.

75. Zuiderzee herring, *Natural History of the Herring* (1898), Friedrich Heincke. Author's Collection.

76. Closing the Afsluitdijk (1932). Alamy.

77. *Eat More Herrings*, Great Yarmouth. Alamy.